The Enjoyment of Theatre

FIFTH EDITION

Kenneth M. Cameron

Patti P. Gillespie

Allyn and Bacon

BOSTON • LONDON • TORONTO • SYDNEY • TOKYO • SINGAPORE

Senior Editor: Karon Bowers
Vice President: Paul A. Smith
Marketing Manager: Jackie Aaron
Editorial Production Service: Chestnut Hill Enterprises, Inc.
Text Design: Carol Somberg/Omegatype Typography, Inc.
Manufacturing Buyer: Megan Cochran
Cover Administrator: Linda Knowles

Internet: www.abacon.com

Between the time Website information is gathered and published, some sites may have closed. Also, the transcription of URLs can result in typographical errors. The publisher would appreciate notification where these occur so that they may be corrected in subsequent editions.

Library of Congress Cataloging-in-Publication Data

Cameron, Kenneth M., 1931–
    The enjoyment of theatre / Kenneth M. Cameron, Patti P.
Gillespie. — 5th ed.
      p.   cm.
    Includes index.
    ISBN 0-205-29590-8
    1. Theater.   I. Gillespie, Patti P.   II. Title.
PN2037.C27   1999
792–dc21   99-35230
                                                CIP

Printed in the United States of America
10 9 8 7 6 5 4 3 2 1   RRD-VA   04 03 02 01 00 99

Contents

C H A P T E R   **7**

The Actor   115

C H A P T E R   **8**

The Director   145

C H A P T E R   **9**

The Design Team: Scenery, Lighting, and Costumes   185

Preface

The Enjoyment of Theatre goes into its fifth edition in a world much changed from that of its first in 1980. As the twenty-first century begins, the computer, the Internet, and the end of the Cold War have urged us into new surroundings, even while the art of the theatre and its relation to life have kept the roots in a distant past. The problems of creating a new edition, therefore, mean balancing the new and the old, trying to preserve what is essential and significant while also accepting what is innovative without being merely faddish—no small job in our world of hype and "push" information.

Users of previous editions will recognize that the book is both old and new merely by flipping its pages. New elements include

- A new feature, "Links to More." Using the model of hypertext, we have tried to suggest interesting, we hope exciting, sources of information and inspiration beyond this book. Some are serious, some frivolous, but all are capable of pulling students closer to the theatre. We have included books, films, plays, and internet sites. Not all will interest every student; rather, what we hope is that every student will find something in at least one. "Links to More" is *not* a bibliography. We tried a bibliography in an earlier edition and found it did little for the students who used the book. Rather, "Links" is a montage of deliberately different experiences. Some of the items are new, some old; some are profound, some superficial. Different chapters' "Links" have different proportions of intellectual glitz and grit. All, we hope, will lead users on to more.
- "Thinking about Theatre" was a new feature in the last edition, but about all that remains is the name. Reconceived in response to users' comments, this feature is now more challenging. Each entry includes a quotation from a famous theatre person that becomes a springboard to thought, sometimes in the form of exercises, sometimes as discussion. We believe it will now grab the introductory student at the appropriate level of sophistication and mind.
- New, too, are sections on the American musical and on gay theatre. The first will, we hope, satisfy those users who have wanted more about musical theatre; we have included here materials on composers and lyricists, principal titles, and the evolution of the musical after the beginning of the twentieth century. The section on gay theatre extends our established materials on political theatres since 1960.

- We have, as well, updated information in all chapters, from the average price of Broadway tickets to the effects on theatre of the 1998 governmental change in Nigeria.

On the other hand, we have kept the structure of the fourth edition, which, we have been told, works for both teachers and students. We have also maintained the theatre of the staged play as the foundation of our considerations of aesthetics and theatre making. We have, as well, kept those features that were new with the fourth edition:

- Study aids: introductory *objectives* and end-of-chapter *key terms,* now expanded to meet user recommendations
- "Current Issues": think pieces at chapter ends that cause students to relate some aspect of the chapter to a tough reality in the world

As in earlier editions, we have selected and captioned our illustrations with care. We continue to believe that one of the most important things the introductory theatre course can teach is *how to see.* We hope that teachers will cause the students to *see* the illustrations, not merely to glance at them. We believe that the illustrations can be used for discussions that will encourage better seeing and better understanding of the visual nature of theatre.

Our two color sections in this edition focus on two such visual aspects of theatre—"Masks and Faces," the actor's expressive self, and "Designs and Environments," the designers' art. They are sometimes related specifically to the text, but we hope that students will be asked to go beyond the text in answering provocative questions about each of them.

Such questions can be found in the instructor's manual. Some teachers have told us, to our surprise, that they were unaware that *The Enjoyment of Theatre* had its own instructor's manual. The manual contains sample test questions (but no answers), discussion questions, questions to stimulate use of the illustrations, and other features. It is available from the publisher through the sales representative or by calling Allyn and Bacon at 1-800-852-8024, or on the World Wide Web at www.abacon.com.

The following reviewers of this edition made many insightful comments: Anne Fliotsos, University of Missouri; G. Arnold Johnson, Lon Morris College; Peter Lach, University of the Pacific; Thomas Ruddick, Edison Community College; and Frederick Schwentker, University of Texas at Austin.

Finally, we repeat, as in previous editions, that *The Enjoyment of Theatre* can be used in several ways, depending on the nature of the introductory course being offered. Teachers can omit sections for use in a one-quarter course or supplement the book for a year-long course. We believe that *The Enjoyment of Theatre* continues to be comprehensive and flexible enough for both approaches. Different teachers will choose to begin at different chapters—some with the arts of theatre makers, some with history, some with aesthetics; the book need not dictate the structure of the course. It will, we hope, support the content of the course, no matter how it is put together.

We want to thank Cheryl Black, Norman Hart, Jessica Kaahwa, and Simeon Shoge for their help.

I

Theatre and Its Audience: Theatre Theory and Criticism

Theatre: Performing Art

OBJECTIVES

When you have completed this chapter, you should be able to:

- Discuss, using specific examples, similarities and differences between: art/life; performance/life; dramatic character/real person; dramatic character/actor; performing art/visual art; performing art/sport (or game)

- List and explain traits that theatre shares with other kinds of performance

- List and explain traits of theatre itself

- Explain in what sense theatre is a system of relationships (rather than a thing)

- Explain how theatre resembles and yet differs from film and television

The enjoyment of theatre depends on an understanding of theatre. What is theatre? And—just as important—what isn't it? Theatre has been called "a mirror of life," "the home of the Now," "the richest of the performing arts." It is all these things and more. We can perhaps build an understanding of theatre if we examine its relationship with some of those things with which it has been compared. To do so, we will consider theatre's relationship with life, with performance, and with art.

LIFE AND THEATRE

Theatre has often been used as a *metaphor for life.* The most famous example is probably Shakespeare's "All the world's a stage, /And all the men and women merely players," but there are many other such metaphors: for example, "This world is a comedy to those that think, a tragedy to those that feel." Indeed, throughout the Middle Ages, scholars and poets so regularly compared life to theatre that the world and the theatre were tied together in the expression *theatre mundi*—theatre of the world.

We need to remember, however, that a metaphor is a special kind of comparison, one that implies, but does not use, the words *like* or *as.* We know that the

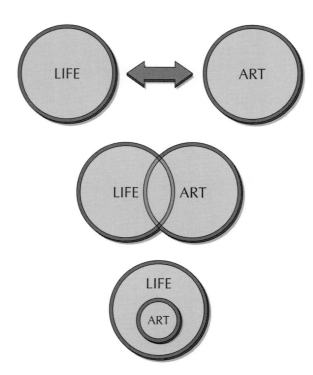

FIGURE 1.1   Life and Art.
The relationships between life and art are varied and complex: art can be viewed as existing within art (bottom); as distinct from it (top); or as overlapping and sharing many traits (middle).

real sense of these quotations is that the world is *like* a stage, and its people are *like* the actors upon it; that the world is *like* a comedy or *like* a tragedy.

A moment's reflection on life and theatre reveals why the comparison is so apt. Life, *like* the theatre, moves forward through time. Just as life seems to have a past, present, and future, plays have a beginning, middle, and end, and in plays, as in life, these stages are defined through time. Life, again *like* the theatre, exists in space; that is, men and women in life take up space and move through space, like actors on a stage. Life, *like* the theatre, has men and women doing and saying things: While some people act and speak, others listen and watch. Those who act and speak in life are *like* actors in the theatre, while those who listen and watch in life are *like* audiences in the theatre. And the lives of real people that we know often don't seem very different from the actions or stories that we see when we go to a play.

Despite such similarities, however, life and theatre are different in many ways, only a few of which need be suggested now: Most lives last for years; most theatre lasts a few hours. Life often seems diffuse, confused, and inexplicable; theatre appears concentrated, orderly, and meaningful. Life may be dangerous, but theatre is safe in a special way. Although theatre may bring us up close to a human activity (like a murder) that is terrifyingly *like* life in its immediacy, we as audience are separated from it and so can watch it in relative safety, experience it without physical danger.

PERFORMANCE AND THEATRE

To *perform* means both to *do* and to *render* or *enact.* A performance, then, can be a *doing* and an *enactment.* To do implies a doer and a thing done; to enact implies a doer, a thing done, and, perhaps, someone to watch it.

Life as Performance

For the reasons just discussed, among others, some people have found it helpful to think of life itself as a performance that is made up of many smaller performances. In order to gain insights into real life, such people have found it helpful to study life's performances *as if* they were a sort of theatre. To highlight the comparison between life and performance, they have used the vocabulary of theatre. In other words, they have sought to understand life by studying parts of life *as if* it were a theatrical performance.

"Performances" in life vary widely. It is possible, for example, to consider a street fight between two angry drivers as a "performance" in which there are "actors" (the fighters), "an audience" (the crowd that gathers around them to watch), and "a stage" or "theatre" (the street). Their "play" (fight) is even based on conflict, as are many plays presented in the theatre.

FIGURE 1.2   Athletics as Performance.
Competition like this one between teams in lumbering skills is different from theatrical
performance, yet both share the presence of audience; they differ in such things as
impersonation vs. competition and rules vs. scripts.

It is also possible to view a church service as a performance, with the priests
considered as "actors," the liturgy a kind of "play text," the congregation "the audience," and the church building itself divided into a "stage" (the altar) and an
"auditorium" (seating for the congregation). (So similar are various religious rituals to theatre that many, but by no means all, scholars think that theatre originated in the religious rituals of an earlier people.)

It is also possible to consider a football game as a performance where players ("actors") oppose one another on the field ("stage") in front of fans ("audience").

Indeed, if we think about a typical day in our own lives, we may come to the
conclusion that almost everything we do—driving to work, attending a class,
watching a parade, eating dinner—can be treated as some sort of performance,
something very much *like* a theatre event.

The metaphor of performance, using the language of theatre, has been so
helpful in studying and thinking about life that a scholarly field called *performance studies* has recently developed. This field strives to understand life (and
concurrently to understand performance) better, using performance as a
metaphor. Performance studies therefore examine many phenomena that are not
theatre, although, as we have seen, such "performances" bear many resemblances
to theatre.

Theatre as Performance

If asked to think about it, we know that it is possible to separate theatre from an argument on a street corner or a religious ritual or a football game. Unlike people at the argument, for example, people at the theatre have decided to go to a special place to become, willingly, an audience for a planned event; they have not stumbled on a theatre accidentally to oversee some unplanned conflict. Unlike people at the church service, people at a theatre do not participate in the event for the purpose of worshiping, nor do they usually interact openly with actors and members of the theatrical audience as they do with priests and other celebrants at a religious service. Unlike people at a football game, theatre audiences do not expect to separate actors into two groups and cheer for one of them because of the way they score points. Games depend on competition rather than enactment; games are governed by rules and time limits rather than by stories.

Despite such differences, however, theatre shares with all these events that we have called *performances,* traits like

- Movement through time
- Doers ("performers")
- Watchers ("audiences")
- A place of performance ("stage" or "theatre")

These performances differ, however, in three major ways:

- Their *purposes* (the reasons for which they were done)
- Their *organizing principles* (the reason they begin and end and seem all to be a part of the same event)
- Their *self-awareness* (the degree to which the people involved know that they are "performing" and why)

For example, a football game intends to attract spectators. A church service, on the other hand, anticipates that people will participate in the activity, not merely watch it unfold, and it is held together not by rules but by a liturgy. The street fight is not undertaken in order for people to watch; it is not self-aware in that sense.

Theatre can be separated from all these performances, then, in terms of its purpose, its organizing principle, and the degree of its self-awareness. We will soon return to these issues.

ART AND THEATRE

In addition to being a kind of performance, theatre is also a kind of *art.* Artists and scholars have struggled for centuries to define art satisfactorily. We need not de-

FIGURE 1.3   Sculpture as Art. Sculptures like this one have content and intention and exist, like theatre, in three-dimensional space; they differ in clear ways, however.

tail these attempts, except to note that most have agreed that art is distinguishable from real life by an artist's intention to create or craft something that will evoke a certain kind of response—an *aesthetic response*—from its audience. Again, the exact nature of an aesthetic response has been endlessly debated, but for our purposes it is enough to say that an aesthetic response includes an appreciation of beauty and some understanding that goes beyond the merely intellectual or the merely entertaining.

Viewed another way, we may speak of art as an activity that makes its product for its own ends: art does not need to have any immediate, practical use in the world. For example, sign painting is an application of some of the techniques of the *art* called painting. But sign painting is an activity intended to be immediately useful in the world—to make signs, probably for purposes of advertising (although a painted sign may also be beautiful). The art we call painting, on the other hand, has no immediate, practical use in the world (although a fine painting is often very expensive and much sought after); rather, an artist paints in order to arouse a special sort of response in the person viewing the work.

Thus, art is self-aware. That is, artists know in a general way what they are trying to do, and they possess a preparation and a discipline that allows them, within limits, to accomplish what they attempt. Artists also intend their art to uplift their audiences rather than to have some immediate, practical use in the world.

We recognize, using such a broad definition, that art can unfold in many different ways—as poetry, novel, storytelling, architecture, music, and dance, to name only the most obvious. All of these arts share some general traits: the artist is self-aware and intends to produce art, something that will evoke an aesthetic response.

But arts differ in several ways:

- Their relationship with time and space. Some arts unfold through time; that is, music or novels require time to move from their beginnings to their end. Other arts exist in space; that is, a building or a piece of sculpture occupies space and does not move from a beginning to an end over time; it is best seen by walking around it, looking at it from several sides.

- Their principles of organization. Some arts are organized by stories; that is, lifelike characters seem to be thinking and talking and doing things very much like what we do in real life. Other arts do not use stories but instead are organized by patterned sounds (music) or patterned colors (painting).

- Their idea of audiences. Novels and paintings, for example, assume they will be enjoyed by solitary individuals; opera and dance, on the other hand, assume that groups of people will assemble to enjoy them. The ways by which arts reach their audience also differ.

- Their mode of presentation. Some arts, like novels, are transmitted by the printed page; others, like film, rely on mechanically produced images; still others, like opera, dance, and theatre, require live performers in the presence of a live audience.

Theatre as Art

Theatre resembles other arts in being self-aware and in intending to evoke an aesthetic response rather than to produce an immediately useful item.

Theatre differs from other arts in its particular relationship to time and space, its principles of organization, its anticipated audience, and its mode of presentation. We can summarize its distinguishing traits as follows:

- Theatre requires both time and space; that is, the actions of theatre unfold through time and must be watched through time, but the actors and scenery also occupy space. Theatre is therefore both a time art and

---

THINKING ABOUT LIFE AND THEATRE

"All the world's a stage,
And all the men and women merely players:
They have their exits and their entrances;
And one man in his time plays many parts, . . . "

—William Shakespeare, *As You Like It,* II, vii.

Make a list of the many "roles" that a typical college student "plays" in life. What "roles" will likely be added and which dropped?

---

a space art. Drama, by which we mean the written text rather than the performed play, is a time art but not a space art. When read, drama, like a novel, unfolds over time, but it does not, like theatre with its actors and scenery, take up physical space.

- Theatre is organized around *action,* characters "living" in virtual worlds ("stories").

- Theatre's audience requires groups of people, not individuals.

- Theatre presents its stories by means of live actors in the physical presence of their audiences. Arts that require live performers in the presence of live audiences are called *performing arts,* so theatre is one of the performing arts.

Taking Stock

To sum up, then, theatre is distinguishable from life although it is *like* life. It is a kind of *performance* similar to (but not identical with) other kinds of performances. Theatre is also an *art,* resembling all arts in some ways but differing from other kinds in important ways.

The ways in which theatre differs from other kinds of arts and other kinds of performances require more discussion.

THEATRE AS PERFORMING ART

Now that we have positioned theatre within a context of life, performance, and art, we can turn to consider theatre itself in greater detail. We will examine its traits (those characteristics that set it apart from other activities), its appeals (ways by which its traits cause it to appeal to audiences), and its internal connectedness (ways in which its traits cohere to form a system).

The Traits of Theatre

- *Theatre uses live actors.* An actor is a performer who impersonates, that is, a performer who uses the pronoun "I" and means somebody other than him- or herself. Thus, actors differ from streetfighters, priests, and football players, who neither intend to perform nor pretend to be someone other than themselves. Actors differ even from jugglers and music-video stars; although these people intend to perform, they do not say "I" and mean someone other than themselves.

A *live* actor in the sense used here is not the opposite of a dead actor but is rather *an actor who is in the physical presence of the audience.* Thus, theatre actors differ not only from other kinds of performers but also from other kinds of actors. *Theatre* actors differ from actors in film or television, for example, because in those media the picture or image of the actor (rather than the actual actor) is offered to the audience.

Theatre actors must *both impersonate and be physically present,* for it is these two traits that separate them from various other performers, on the one hand, and from actors in other media, on the other.

- *Theatre depends on action (which we can think of for now as stories and characters) to organize and bind the theatrical event.* We can think of stories as little worlds created for artistic purposes, worlds that resemble (but are distinct from) the actual world in which we live. We have called the worlds used in stories *virtual worlds,* an expression that recalls the invented worlds of the computer's virtual reality. Part of the reason that theatre's virtual worlds resemble our own real world so convincingly is that these virtual worlds are inhabited by *characters.* Characters might be thought of as virtual people, because characters are artistic creations intended to resemble people. Well-created characters are often so compelling, so lifelike that we can feel as if we know them personally. We may even begin to talk of them *as if* they were real people. But characters are not real people; they are created by a playwright for the play, just as the virtual world is created.

    Like theatre, novels and films almost always depend on stories and characterization for their form. Dance, especially classical ballet, will often use stories and characterization as well as patterns of movement to achieve its form. Sporting events, on the other hand, use rules, time limits, and competition instead of stories to control the game; and music uses tonal and rhythmic patterns through time to shape the composition.

FIGURE 1.4   Theatre's Audience.
Like other kinds of public performance, theatre brings people together only for
the event; when it is over, they disperse, never to come together again in exactly
the same way.

- *Theatre depends on live actors presenting these characters and their virtual
  world to an audience that is physically present.* In this way, theatre
  differs from the worlds and characters of computer games or films,
  where *pictures* of people and places are offered. The actual, physical
  presentation of actors in a real space also sets theatre apart from
  narratives like the short story or novel because, in theatre, stories are
  not *told* but are actually *presented* in front of the audience. In theatre,
  therefore, "people" seem always to be doing and saying things *as if* they
  were real people participating in real life; these "people" are in fact live
  actors portraying characters in a virtual world.

- *Theatre gathers its audience into a defined space at a certain time and
  allows the reactions of the audience to affect the performance.* As the word
  gathers suggests, audience here refers to a group of people rather than
  to a single person, and this group of people has chosen to come together
  at a specific time and place in order to watch a performance. Because
  the audience is in the physical presence of the actors, its responses
  may change the performance itself. For example, when the audience
  applauds or laughs, the actors know that they must pause before going
  on with their lines or the audience will miss something important. If an

audience becomes restless, the actors must decide how to adjust their performance to regain the attention and interest of the audience.

Inasmuch as theatre gathers its audience into a defined space, it resembles activities like football and film more than activities like television or reading a novel. Inasmuch as theatre expects the behavior of an audience to affect the performance, it is much more like opera or storytelling than it is like football, film, television, or a novel.

- *The theatre uses a real performance space, usually with artificial (that is, made-for-the-purpose) settings.* Film can take us anywhere and show us images of actual places, even on a vast scale (the Grand Canyon, outer space). Because film shows *images* of places rather than real places, it can range far in its presentation of objects and spaces. Theatre, on the other hand, must use a defined performance space that is physically in the presence of the audience and limited by existing architecture. It can give us representations, replicas, of actual places (e.g., outer space), but it can give them only on a scale appropriate to its own scale and to the actors working in or in front of the scene.

  Many kinds of activities easily shown on film (horse races, car crashes) are difficult or impossible to show on stage. Film and television can show not only races and crashes, they can also show selective close-ups that direct our attention and heighten our enjoyment of the events: speeding hooves, snorting nostrils, exploding gas tanks, collapsing fenders. Theatre has no close-up, no medium shot.

  Because of the nature of its space, when theatre tries to stage a large event like a horse race (as is it did in the late nineteenth century), it has to compromise. By putting horses on treadmills (on which they could run while staying in place) and placing a painted cloth moving on rollers behind them, stage designers made horses seem to race. But common sense told the audience that there had to be treadmills and moving scenery.

  Nonetheless, theatre audiences love such scenes, even though they know they are seeing an obvious trick; they seem to appreciate the skill required to make the illusion. Indeed, it is one of theatre's paradoxes that the very restrictions of theatre's real space seem to increase the audience's enjoyment of difficult scenes produced there.

The Appeals of Theatre

Because theatre has this special relationship among actors, action, audiences, and space/time, it appeals to audiences in four ways that set it apart from other sorts of performances, arts, and performing arts.

1. *Theatre is immediate.* Theatre has a compelling sense of Now, the present, that comes from its unique combining of art and performance: it

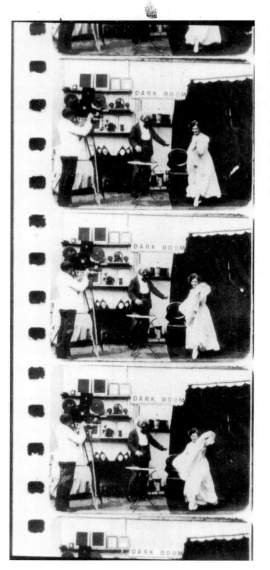

FIGURE 1.5 Film.
Film, like theatre, often uses actors and scripts; unlike theatre, it gives its audiences projected images, not actual people, and it can be shown over and over again in the same way. *The Animated Picture Studio,* 1903, *from the collection of Kemp R. Niver and J. P. Niver in the Motion Picture, Broadcasting and Recorded Sound Division of the Library of Congress.*

happens in real time and only in real time. It is an art that *shows* rather than *tells* about an event, and because of the physical presence of the actor, theatre presents an immediate portrayal of human behavior. We as an audience are actually in the theatre with those very living human beings who embody the stories we came to see. Only the theatre offers this powerful combination of actor, action, and audience to bring us the Now.

2. *Theatre is ephemeral.* The same interaction that gives theatre its power of immediacy also makes theatre ephemeral—fleeting, nonrecoverable. In theatre, the actors show us events; the events happen and are gone, even as a moment in life exists and is gone, never to be recaptured. Although film, television, and video performances exist physically on film stock or as electronic impulses and so can be recovered exactly as they were made, a theatrical performance exists only in space and time and so cannot be recovered. When theatre is recorded on film or video, it ceases to be theatre and becomes either an imperfect record of an event or a film in its own right.

True, actors can repeat a play several nights in a row, but actors are human beings, not machines, and so each evening their performance will differ, the more so because audiences will affect their performances, and audiences will also change each night.

A theatrical performance, then, is not like a performance on television, film, or video. It does not leave a physical record. Exact copies cannot be made of it. It cannot be played over and over. Because both its actors and audiences are human, their interaction is fleeting, and so theatre is ephemeral, nonrecoverable. When the moment in theatre is gone, it is *entirely* gone.

3. *Theatre proceeds at its own pace through time.* We cannot play a performance over, nor can we play it backward, nor can we fast-forward it to see how it will come out. We cannot put a theatrical performance aside for a while and pick it up later. If we don't like a performance, we cannot turn a dial and get another station or hit a button and change channels. If we don't understand a moment in the theatre, we cannot stop and go back to it, hoping to grasp its significance the second or third time through. In other words, as members of a theatre audience we do not control the way the theatrical performance unfolds as we can control the pace at which we watch a videotape or read a poem or novel. For better or worse, the theatre performance proceeds at its own pace and must be followed at that pace.

4. *Theatre intensifies characters and action, presenting a virtual world more concentrated and intense than the real world.* Because everything on stage has been selected and placed there by someone for a purpose, everything on stage is important—it has meaning for the audience. Thus, everything on stage gains a significance that it may lack in real life. For example, it is not unusual for theatre audiences to applaud an on-stage scene when an actor cooks a meal or uses a washing machine. Obviously, cooking or using a washing machine is not very interesting in real life; but on a stage, these simple actions can provoke excitement because theatre transforms them from ordinary to meaningful activities.

The real art of the theatre lies, then, not in copying life, but in presenting heightened visions of life within the special conditions of artistic performance: actors, action, audience, flowing time, and real space. These special conditions give theatre its special qualities: its immediacy, nonrecoverability, pacing, and intensity.

The System of Theatre

Theatre cannot be defined simply; the reason is that theatre is not a thing (an object) but *a system of relationships*—among actor, action, audience, time, and space. Changing even one of the elements of this relationship changes the whole. To understand this "systemness" of theatre, we can explore how it differs from opera and film.

In distinguishing one art from another, we often look first at obvious, somewhat mechanical differences. We might be tempted to think that theatre and opera or theatre and film are separated only by rather mechanical differences—for example, that theatre is only opera without music, or film is only theatre recorded on strips of acetate. Although it is true that such mechanical differences have significance, they alone are not sufficient to explain differences among the arts. We must look instead at other changes that are introduced because of these mechanical changes.

When one important element of a system changes, the system itself changes. A change in the mode of presentation of an art, for example, causes a number of other important changes. We might think that a film is not very different from a piece of theatre except in its mode of presentation. We might even assume that the *fact* of film alone defines the difference between movies and theatre; that is, film is a series of moving images on acetate whereas theatre is live actors in real space in front of real audiences.

But this obvious difference causes other differences. For example, the *art* of film depends on camera work, editing, and juxtaposing images. Such things are impossible in the theatre. The *fact* of film has thus caused these other changes. As a result, the very structure of a film script—the way the action moves forward— is vastly different from that of a play because film gives its information differently and so communicates with its audiences differently.

Theatre's Relationship with Other Arts

Theatre contains within it many of the other arts. For example, scenery and costumes use techniques of the painter and sculptor. Photographs, videotape, and film are sometimes used to establish time and place or to comment on the action. Within plays, there are often dances and songs. In fact, so regularly does theatre incorporate other arts that it has been called the richest of the performing arts.

Theatre often merges with other arts. It is not always clear whether a particular piece of theatre with music is a musical or an opera. *Sweeney Todd* and *Porgy and Bess,* for example, are regularly performed by both theatre companies and opera companies. Songs like "The Impossible Dream" that were first embedded within plays later became famous simply as songs, having lost all association with the original play in which they appeared. Certain kinds of music and dance blend qualities that we associate with theatre, blends that we try to capture in phrases like *theatre dance* and *theatre music.*

FIGURE 1.6 Dance.
Using many of theatre's artists and arts, dance is nonetheless different, an art of movement with its own nonverbal language. *Scheherazade, produced by the Department of Theatre, Speech and Dance at the University of South Carolina. Photo by Athena Starr.*

Theatre often uses other arts to its own purposes and, in turn, is often used by them for their purposes. It is, for example, possible to have the same story at the center of several different arts, but the story may change radically, because of differences among the arts and differences in their reasons for using the story. For example, Shakespeare's *Romeo and Juliet* has been a staged play, a ballet, an opera, several films, and *West Side Story,* a Broadway musical. All are significantly different, even though the Shakespearean text is the basis for much of the films, opera, ballet, and musical. In each case, the artists made choices that selected from Shakespeare's story. For their adaptation, they chose those elements that could be best communicated through their own art. For the opera, the composer selected those moments and events best communicated through music; for dance, the choreographer selected the moments and events best communicated through movement, and so on.

Moreover, each art focuses its audience's attention in a different way. The production of Shakespeare's play may lead us to watch and listen to the actor speak the poetic lines of Shakespeare, but the opera may lead us to listen to the music instead of watching the singer or even following the story, and the dance may ask us to watch movement only, almost ignoring story and character (which may then become little more than a pretext for the movement). The ways by which an art communicates to its audiences helps define the art, differentiating it from other arts.

Each art, by selecting and focusing the audience's attention, may make a completely different point through the very process of selection and focus. To take a single example, when *The Singular Life of Albert Nobbs* was changed from a short story to a play, the basic (true) story and characters remained the same: For much of her life, a young woman disguised herself as a man, Albert Nobbs, in order to get a job, make money, and be independent—at a time when women rarely were able to do any of these things. The novel (written by a man) treated the story as an extraordinary example of the human imagination and resilience, a tale of one person's bizarre life. The play (written by a woman) added a male narrator, rearranged a very few scenes, and caused the visual elements in the play to comment on the

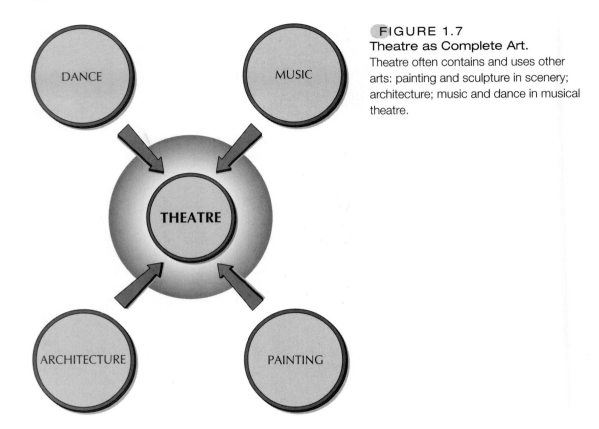

FIGURE 1.7
Theatre as Complete Art.
Theatre often contains and uses other arts: painting and sculpture in scenery; architecture; music and dance in musical theatre.

story itself so that the play became a feminist exploration of women's condition within a patriarchal culture.

Taking Stock

There is no simple definition of theatre, just as there is no simple definition of performance or of art. The problem of defining theatre is complicated still further because theatre, like other human activities and other human-made definitions, overlaps other arts.

The only purpose of defining a word is to call to mind those recurring clusters of traits to which it seems to refer, traits that set its referent apart from some other, often closely related, ideas or activities. The point is not to define theatre rigidly or to put theatre into a box separate from everything else. The point rather is to try and understand the nature of the art called theatre—how it resembles similar activities without being identical to them and how it differs from many activities while retaining many similarities with them.

Theatre.
A Funny Thing Happened on the Way to the Forum, at Western Michigan University.
Directed by D. Terry Williams. Mary Whalen photo.

We have said so far that

- Theatre closely resembles life and various performances within life; it resembles fights, rituals, games, and spectator sports.

- Theatre resembles other arts, especially other performing arts like opera and dance.

- Yet theatre has some traits that set it apart from life, and from other performances and other arts.

- The art of theatre often contains other arts within it; it often merges with other arts; and it often uses and is used by other arts in provocative ways.

- Yet theatre remains unique, with special traits that allow it to appeal to audiences in special ways.

- Theatre has a power of its own.

Defining theatre may seem like an abstract issue. But the very matter of definition is one of today's major intellectual controversies, indicative of changing views in the 1990s and in the early 2000s.

LINKS to more about theatre

Luigi Pirandello, *Six Characters in Search of an Author.* Appearance and reality, the theatre and life.

Suzanne Langer, *Feeling and Form,* 1953. Aesthetics for a linear world.

Richard Schechner, *Performance Theory,* 1988. For the postmodern world.

The Truman Show, 1998. Appearance and reality, life and TV.

< **www.onelist.com** > Click on "theatre students" for a listserv "only for theatre students from all over the world to share and discuss experiences"; requires subscription—instructions on site. Actual listserv is *elseneur@wxs.nl,* but we couldn't access it directly. Try.

CURRENT ISSUES

We have defined theatre as a kind of art. Our position is that art exists and that theatre is one of its foremost expressions. Some people disagree strongly.

Several thinkers now propose that there is no such thing as art, at least not as we have usually thought of it (and as we have talked of it here).

Some argue that in a throwaway culture such as ours, we must have throwaway art. They cry out, "No more masterpieces!" "No permanent paintings or plays!" Once fixed, they say, art becomes dead, ceases to cause any effect, and therefore ceases to be. What is important about painting, they explain, is the act of painting, not the color on canvas that gets hung on a wall; what is important about theatre is the action, not the words that attempt to record it.

Others suggest that art no longer exists because our culture has become too "massified" (a reference to our mass culture) and too democratized to permit it. In a culture that calls Madonna an artist and talks about the art of the television sitcom, they say, the word *art* has lost all claim to meaning. A word no longer capable of differentiating experiences as different as a Mozart opera and a rock concert, of distinguishing between art and entertainment, is a word without further use in the world. Art as a word, in this view, has lost meaning because the kinds of things or activities to which it once referred have lost meaning; therefore, neither the word nor the thing usefully exists in today's world.

If, then, there is no such thing as "art," what place is there for activities that lack practical products (painting, rather than sign-painting)? Are Mozart and

Madonna really the same? Or are we all artists, equally endowed, equally entitled to newspaper space, public attention, grants, applause?

KEY TERMS

Check your understanding against this list. Brief definitions are in the Glossary; page references there will direct you to appropriate pages. (Persons are page-referenced in the Index.)

actor	impersonate
aesthetic response	performance
art	performing art
drama	performance studies
ephemeral art	theatre

Theatre: Art, Audience, and Society

OBJECTIVES:

When you have completed this chapter, you should be able to:

- Describe how theatre is social

- Identify major traits of theatre audiences

- Explain how relationships between theatre audiences and their spaces can encourage or discourage a sense of groupness

- Explain the meaning and implications of "the ephemeral audience"

- Describe theatre audiences in the United States today

- Describe at least one antidote for the unprepared and the unwilling audience

Theatre, as we have seen, is one of the performing arts that bears special resemblances to life and to performances within life. Theatre is also probably the most social of all arts, and its audiences are social in ways different from audiences for many other activities. We will first consider how theatre audiences are social and then consider how the art itself is social.

SOCIAL AUDIENCE

People choose to go to the theatre for many reasons. It is part of theatre's richness that it appeals to people in many different ways simultaneously. Part of theatre's appeal is social: It's a good place to meet people and be with friends. Part of its appeal is sensual, for theatre pleases the senses through the talent of its actors, the spectacle of its visual display (scenery, costumes, lighting), and the beauty of its language and music. It appeals too by engaging the imagination with its stories and characters, which offer us experiences that we have never had—and may never have—but which we recognize as possible for us: exotic yet familiar, good and evil, funny and sad. And theatre appeals intellectually because the issues raised by its plays are the human issues that we confront daily and that our forebears confronted in their time.

Some traits of theatre audiences differ with time and place. Theatre audiences today tend to be from the mainstream of middle-class society: young, affluent, and gender-mixed. Patterns of class, age, and gender were not always as they are now, however. For example, during the early nineteenth century, working-class audiences attended theatre in far greater numbers than today. Young working men often sat in the upper balconies and were notorious for their raucous behavior. They interrupted plays, drowning out bad performances with stomping and boos when they were displeased and, when they were pleased, cheering their favorite actors until the play came to a standstill. During the seventeenth century, by contrast, aristocrats dominated theatre audiences, and they insisted on plays that displayed "propriety" and so reflected an idealized view of upper-class behavior.

THINKING ABOUT THEATRE AUDIENCES

In 1964, Marshall McLuhan, a scholar of media, explained that *"Hot media . . . are low in participation, and cool media are high in participation or completion by the audience."* Assume that McLuhan is correct. Prepare a computer graphic (or a sketch) that shows where dance, film, opera, radio, television, and theatre fall along a continuum between hot and cool media.

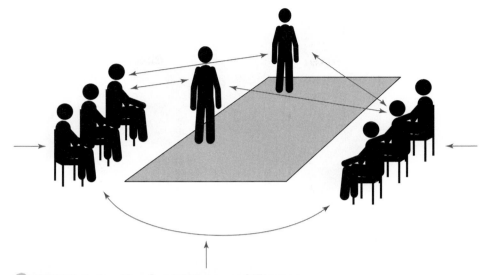

FIGURE 2.1 The Social Nature of Theatre.
Audience members affect each other, and actors affect them and are affected by them; all also relate to the outer society of which they are a part.

Although some traits of theatre audiences change with time and place, some seem embedded in the nature of the art itself, and it is to these traits that we now turn.

We have already identified three ways in which theatre audiences are social.

- They are groups of people rather than individuals.
- They come together at a special place and a special time to watch a performance.
- They affect the way actors perform, and so they affect performances.

But each of these traits is more complex than is at first apparent. It is to the complexity of these three traits that we now turn.

Audiences Are Groups

An audience needs a sense of itself as a group, as a social unit. That is to say, theatregoers enter into a relationship not only with the staged performance but also with one another, and their responses as an audience will depend not only on the performance itself but also on the response of other members of the group. For this reason, achieving the proper relationship among members of the audience is very

FIGURE 2.2   Groupness of Audience.
Members of an audience, if the event and the space are right, share the experience
as a group.

important. Although there are no hard-and-fast rules that will assure an audience's sense of itself as a group, some factors clearly affect its development.

Audience Size

Part of the audience's sense of *groupness comes from its numbers.* For example, a theatregoer's laughter is buoyed up, expanded, made more joyous by other laughter, or the individual's solemn understanding of a serious play is made richer because other people are responding in the same way. This sense of groupness is so important to the enjoyment of theatre that other media often try to reproduce it by artificial means. For example, television uses a "laugh track" to encourage its often solitary viewers to join in the group's laughter.

Determining a good size for any audience depends in part on the nature of the medium. An "audience" of a good size for a novel or short story, for example, is one person, but an audience of one for a football game would be most unsatisfactory; a game's best audience may be forty thousand people or more. A television show's audience is more complex. It may be one person watching alone at home, but the same show may have people watching it at the same time throughout the country so that its total "audience" is in the millions.

None of these groups is a good *theatre* audience: One person is too small and forty thousand too large to comprise a good audience; and a theatre audience requires, as we have seen, that people be brought together at a special time and place.

Finally, it is not possible to say exactly how many people are needed for a theatre audience to achieve a sense of groupness, but it is possible to say with certainty that some groups are too small and others too large to encourage a good performance. Probably the most accurate statement that can be made about the best size for a theatre audience is that it must be of some size that fits well within a defined space.

Audience Space

The size of the space determines, in part, the size of a good audience. A hundred people in a very large theatre will feel uncomfortable, but the same people in a small theatre will happily enjoy the play. A thousand people in an average space on a hot day are too many people, though in a larger space or an air-conditioned space one thousand people may be just the right number to make a good audience. A good audience space for theatre, then, is one small enough to define an audience but not so small as to confine it.

Audience Arrangement

The arrangements of seats interact with size and space to affect the sense of groupness of the audience. People sitting in the middle of an audience are usually more comfortable than those on the sides, because those on the sides are at the edge of (and so sometimes feel outside of) the group. Conversely, people sitting in the midst of large empty spaces often feel uncomfortable, again because they feel themselves alone—outside of a group.

To help shape the space in ways that make audiences feel comfortable and part of a group, some theatres use screens or lights to block off parts of an auditorium that are not needed to seat members of an audience. Theatres may also sell tickets in ways that increase the sense of groupness. For a small audience in a large house, for example, the management may decide to sell no tickets in the balcony or may sell tickets only in front of the stage, toward the center of the audience area. By selling only these tickets, the theatre can define a space within a large auditorium and so help an audience member feel a part of a definite group.

Audience Permission

The audience forms a sense of itself as a group, as a social unit, not only because its numbers sit comfortably in a proper-sized space but also because theatre gives audience members permission to respond in safety. Permission is the unspoken agreement ("the contract") between performers and audience and among members of the audience that it is all right to laugh at the staged events or to be solemnly moved by them. This permission is an extension of the very nature of theatre art: Theatre as art tells its audience that what is being embodied on stage by actors is not really life and that it is permissible to respond to it in unusual ways (laughing out loud at a character who is crying, for example). Permission is thus a social phenomenon, and theatregoing a social as well as an artistic experience.

FIGURE 2.3
Groupness and Behavior.
Dress, age, time of day, and other factors affect how an audience responds; different audiences develop different codes. *Photo by Neil Fleitell.*

Audience and Self-Image

Theatre audiences, as a part of developing a sense of groupness, develop a self-image. This self-image influences behavior, including dress. For example, because the theatre audience is a social group, theatre is a public art and requires behavior established by custom as appropriate to its public setting. Theatregoers do not expect to carry beer and hotdogs into a performance, although they feel comfortable eating and drinking when attending a baseball game. Similarly, theatregoers do not expect to wear pajamas to the theatre, although they freely wear them at home watching television. For another example, some theatres—or some special nights at a theatre—strive for formality, with men expected to appear in black ties and women in formal wear. Other theatres or evenings in a theatre seek informality and comfort, with jeans and sportswear dominating. The two groups usually expect different experiences from their night out at the theatre, and they will behave accordingly.

Impeding "Groupness"

A major force in theatre tugs against the idea of groupness, and that force is money. The economics of theatre demands that the audience be big enough to pay the investors, the actors, the rent on the building, the author's royalties, the heat and light, the maintenance of the space, and so on, and a desire for profit demands that the audience be bigger still. Thus, although the *art* of theatre may suggest that the best-sized audience for a particular space is two hundred, the *business* of theatre may demand an audience of three thousand.

Some people argue that business in theatre is a false force and should be denied, but ignoring it in today's theatre is simply not possible. And perhaps it should not be ignored. After all, actors and playwrights and maintenance personnel have a right to make a living just as much as bankers and teachers and secretaries. Some compromise between the needs of theatre's art and its business is probably inevitable.

The compromise, however, must be a careful one, for when the sense of suitable group behavior breaks down, people attending a play may behave as individuals rather than as an audience. Then they may respond oddly to the onstage action, laughing at the wrong places or talking during the action. Or if their numbers are too large, what should be an audience can become a mob that may actually compete with the actors for attention. Such a theatre situation is sometimes found in primary or secondary schools that use gymnasia (instead of theatres) for performances; in such circumstances the students may become uncontrollable and become a mob rather than an audience. In past times, some theatre mobs occasionally rioted, causing loss of life.

Theatre artists, then, want to encourage each of their audiences to develop a strong sense of itself as a group for two reasons: First, when a theatre audience has a strong sense of itself as a social entity, the theatrical event is more successful; second, when a theatre audience lacks that sense, its commitment to suitable behavior may also break down.

Audiences Are Ephemeral

Although the theatre audience is a social group, it is a group for only a short time. Just as the theatrical performance is *now,* so too is its audience. For all their sharing and their common experience, the people in a theatre audience will probably never come together as a group again. They are drawn together for one theatrical event, at a certain time and in a certain place, and then they are gone, as ephemeral as the art of theatre itself.

But people who enjoy the theatre will choose to go to the theatre again and again, becoming a part of other audiences, entering into contracts with other performers, laughing and crying at other plays, and then, again, leaving that sense of groupness to enter everyday life until the next time.

Audiences Affect Performances

No one can say for certain how any theatre audience will respond during a play; no one can say for certain how an individual within an audience will respond at any given moment. Performances differ, audiences differ, and individuals in an

FIGURE 2.4   Expectation and Groupness.
Even outdoors and with the performers in full view before the performance, an audience builds its identity and its expectations. Kampala, Uganda. *Photo courtesy of Jessica Kaahwa.*

audience differ. Individuals' attitudes toward a performance, for example, may vary from extreme involvement (identification) to extreme objectivity—or anywhere in between these extremes. Thus any observations about audience response are generalizations to which there will always be exceptions. What follows are common types of responses.

Applause

Clapping hands are what we most often associate with a good performance in the theatre, for in theatre as in athletics and speech-making applause signals approval. Actors customarily *take their bows* so long as the applause continues, but actors who *milk* the audience for applause (trying to make the audience extend its applause) are considered in bad form. In past times if audiences continued their applause beyond what was expected, actors might repeat a part of the performance (*take an encore*), just as concert singers do today. In some instances, an audience rises to applaud—this *standing ovation* signals special favor and is prized by actors.

Applause most often comes at the end of a play, but it occasionally will erupt during a scene.

Laughter

Laughter has been called the actor's reward in comedy, the actor's torment in serious drama. This seeming contradiction is because audiences seem to laugh for two widely different reasons: because they are truly amused and because they are uneasy. *The laughter of amusement* may range from enormous belly laughs at farcical action (pratfalls, a pie in the face) to low chuckles of appreciation that reflect approval of a sympathetic character or clever speech. Such laughter is anticipated by actors because it comes from the play (its plot, character, language, etc.) or from the performance (an actor's gesture, an intentionally comic costume, etc.). *The laughter of unease,* on the other hand, springs not from amusement but from stress. It is the stage equivalent of the "nervous laughter" familiar in real life. The laughter of unease comes from an audience that is rejecting, for some reason, the experience of the performed play. Such laughter is unexpected by the actors and uncalled for by the performance. It can be shattering for an actor, who may find an audience laughing uproariously at a deeply serious moment.

Tears

People do not cry in the theatre as openly or as often as they have in other ages, perhaps because we live in an age that discourages public weeping. (Public laughter is still approved.) Instead of tears, today's audiences may respond with a lump in the throat or suppressed sniffles. In any case, such emotions are outward signs of "empathy," the "believing with" an emotional moment. It is notable that tears usually do not flow for deeply serious actions; they more often appear for small, sentimental events like the death of a pet.

FIGURE 2.5 Ephemeral Audience.
The theatre audience is a merely temporary group, bound only by the performance, as in this crowd waiting to enter a New York theatre.

Silence

"You could hear a pin drop." Although we associate applause with the theatre, silence is often the clearest sign of a very successful performance. At the end of a well-performed tragedy, for example, silence is often the audience's response, as if applause were too frivolous for the moment. Normally in a group of people, some few will be making small noises: shifting positions, coughing, rattling a program. To find a thousand people who do not make a single sound is rare, and it comes only when a performance has them in a very tight grip. Silence suggests the rapt attention that comes when a body is being *held still.*

Such silence cannot be preserved for an entire evening, and so release points are built into the performance (just as the pauses between movements of a symphony offer a time to cough or change position).

Responses of Dissatisfaction

Audiences have several ways (some of them unconscious) of showing that they are not captured by a performance. *Noise*—coughing, shuffling feet, whispering, rattling programs—signals unease or boredom. All the sounds that are suppressed when an audience is attentive burst forth when that attention wanes. Although each individual believes that he or she is being quiet, the cumulative effect of several hundred people beginning to shift in their seats or cough is loud—and horribly revealing.

In other ages, audiences consciously set about to show disapproval in the theatre by issuing catcalls, booing, calling out to the actors, or even throwing objects on stage. Today such deliberate expressions of disapproval are quite rare, but occasionally a dissatisfied patron may get up and walk out of the theatre.

Responses of dissatisfaction often come because of a bad performance, but they may also come about because of a bad audience. In fact, because actor and audience are in such a close relationship in the theatre, they do affect one another, and so bad performances and bad audiences are often related. Some of the reasons for "bad performances" will be treated in the coming chapters. Reasons for "bad audiences" can be briefly suggested here.

Audiences are likeliest to be dissatisfied if they are unprepared or unwilling.

The Unprepared Audience. The unprepared audience is one that does not understand the nature of theatre and so does not know the customs of theatrical performance or audiences. Such audiences are usually new, or fairly new, to the theatre. Members of an unprepared audience may confuse theatre with real life, as when an audience member in one of America's theatres of the western frontier during the nineteenth century ran on the stage to prevent Othello from strangling Desdemona. They may be embarrassed by the intensity of theatrical performance (caused by the physical presence of the actors) and thus laugh nervously at love scenes or scenes of suffering. They may be so used to talking during television pro-

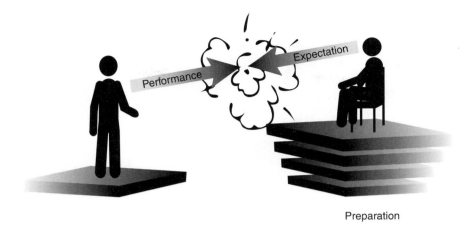

Preparation

FIGURE 2.6 The Badly Prepared Audience.
Without preparation, audiences risk false expectations and great disappointment when expectations collide with actuality.

grams that they talk openly to their friends during a theatrical performance, not realizing that the actors can hear them and that their behavior is actually affecting the way the actors perform.

The Unwilling Audience. The unwilling audience can be any audience that is alienated from the performance. Some people simply dislike musicals or comedies; if trapped in a performance of either, they will show signs of great unease. Or perhaps they did not know the play or read its review and so did not realize they were going to attend a kind of theatre they disliked. Less obvious, but far more common, are audiences who are shocked or dismayed by elements of performance that they are unaccustomed to or that they disapprove of. These elements run a wide spectrum—nudity, religious subjects, raw language. In some such cases, as with the unprepared audience, there may be an ignorance of the nature of art and the "harmlessness" of theatre. With the unwilling audience, however, the ignorance exists despite considerable theatre experience. The unwilling audience should know better but refuses to. In other cases, personal belief or religious conviction may simply rebel against what is being portrayed on the stage, a situation almost always preventable by a careful reading of reviews and announcements of the show.

We all begin as an unprepared audience. We all have a potential for being an unwilling audience. We grow away from the first with experience and knowledge; we avoid the second with alertness to theatre's essential nature, to the role of audience in performance, and to information about the performance.

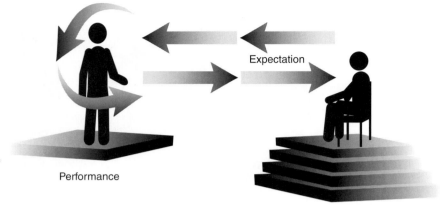

Performance

Preparation

FIGURE 2.7   The Well Prepared Audience.
With proper preparation, audience expectation joins with and augments the actuality of performance.

SOCIAL ART

Thus, theatre is a social art in large part because its audience is a social group that is aware of itself as a social group and that behaves as a social group, if only temporarily. But theatre is a social art for other reasons as well: its own nature, the working methods of its artists, and its relationship with the larger society.

The Nature of the Art

Theatre (unlike music or architecture) presents human actions that depend on characters (artificial human beings) who live in virtual worlds, experiencing conflicts, deciding on actions, and succumbing to powerful emotions. Plays, then, are both human and social, depending as they do on virtual people who live in societies created by a playwright. Theatre (unlike film or television) presents its action by using human actors in front of live audiences, and there is an *interaction* between them; therefore, the mode of performance places human beings in a social situation. Theatre thus provides a connection *both* between the audience and the play *and* between the audience and the performers.

The Working Methods of Theatre's Artists

The work of theatre artists is social in two ways. First, theatre artists (unlike novelists or painters) work together, forming production teams, in order to offer a

LINKS to more about theatre

Peter Brook, *The Empty Space,* 1968. A great director on theatre.

Richard Southern, *Seven Ages of the Theatre,* 1961.

Paul Thom, *For an Audience: A Philosophy of the Performing Arts,* 1993.

< **library.websteruniv.edu** > The Eden-Webster Library on the Internet. Click on "Net resources by subject," then "theater and costume," then "comprehensive lists of sites" for many areas of theatre.

unified vision of the play to the audience. (We will discuss this in greater detail later.) Second, the artists must take the audience immediately into account as they plan their art. For example, playwrights must imagine what real audiences will come to the theatre to see and then write plays that will bring audiences into the theatre and affect them after they get there. Actors must imagine how audiences will respond to moments of performance and then perform in ways that prompt appropriate responses. Designers and directors must figure out ways to guide the responses of audiences through visual cues, so that the play "means" for audiences what they want it to "mean."

The Relationship Between Theatre's Audience and the Society

Theatre is also social because the audience that is present physically in the theatre is a part of a larger society. This fact has implications for both the practice and the study of theatre. In preparing their art for the audience, theatre artists will inevitably reveal their beliefs about that audience and, incidentally, about the society of which it is a part. It is in this way that theatre (probably more than any other art) both expresses the society of which it is a part and responds to society's pressures, changing its own practices to conform to what society seems to want or need. It is mostly for this reason that theatre is considered one of the humanities and that its study is an important part of a humanistic, liberal education.

Taking Stock

In sum, theatre is social because it presents live actors in front of live audiences telling lifelike stories, because its artists work collaboratively, because its audiences are drawn from (and so representative of) the larger society, and because the audiences are themselves social entities that depend on a sense of "groupness."

FIGURE 2.8   The Accidental Audience.
Without the help of arranged space and prepared audience, street performers must work to get and hold an audience.

Audiences' sense of "groupness," depending on a relationship among size, space, and seating arrangement, affects the behavior not only of other audience members but also of the actors.

Audiences for One and All

Something to be prized about today's theatre is its seeming appreciation for diversity and variety. Perhaps a healthy culture is like a healthy environment. Both seem to thrive on—both may even depend on—variety and diversity. Perhaps the healthiest individual is one who can enjoy a variety of quite different activities: games, sports, media, and performing arts. Perhaps the best audience member is one who goes to a movie one night, an opera another, a football game another, one who enjoys staying home to watch TV and going out to the theatre and playing tennis or golf. And perhaps the healthiest society is one that can embrace and support all such activities—and more.

Interestingly, people who go and respond to theatre today also tend to support other arts and entertainments, including sports. Devoted theatregoers are also members of audiences for ballet, baseball, television, and opera. Overlap is significant. In fact, breadth of taste seems to typify theatregoers. Shakespeare and baseball, Beethoven and Molière—audiences are able to love them all.

CURRENT ISSUES

In part because the audience for theatre has been declining through much of this century, some people believe that theatre is in crisis. In addition to declining attendance, they cite as evidence of theatre's decline the downward spiral in the number of new plays opening on Broadway each year and the lower number of people who participate in theatre at the community level.

Theatre, they believe, is at a crossroads and must make a decision about what kind of audience it strives to serve if it is to survive. They agree that the place once filled by theatre is now being filled by movies and television. They see the salvation of theatre in seeking out some new niche within today's mix of arts and entertainments. But the identity of "the proper niche" is passionately disputed.

Some argue that theatre once appealed to mass audiences and that it will survive only if it does so again. Such people argue for the return of an inexpensive, popular theatre aimed at working-class audiences. Such a theatre might be found, they suggest, in a return to the techniques of vaudeville, circus, and magic and to community-based plays that treat concerns of the middle and lower classes in locally recognizable settings.

Others absolutely disagree and argue instead that theatre is now an elite art and that its salvation depends on admitting, and building on, its current strength as an art of primarily the professional and managerial classes. Such people, taking opera as an analogy, urge that theatre stop trying to pander to mass tastes and try instead to build on its small but committed audience. In their view, theatre should offer challenging plays performed in ways that build on the special traditions of the theatre.

FIGURE 2.9   Audience for Today and Tomorrow.
With theatre no longer at the center of the culture, and movies and television dominant, who will be the audience for the theatre? *Photo by Neil Fleitell.*

How does an expensive activity like theatre survive? Who should its audience—its source of income—be? How should it attract and satisfy this audience? Or is the institution itself doomed in a mass culture (because, for example, its audience size is so limited)?

KEY TERMS

Check your understanding against this list. Brief definitions are in the Glossary; page references there will direct you to appropriate pages. (Persons are page-referenced in the Index.)

applause	standing ovation
empathy	to milk an audience
ephemeral	to take a bow
identification	to take an encore

How to Read a Play

OBJECTIVES

When you have completed this chapter, you should be able to:

- List and explain Aristotle's six parts of a play

- Explain the interrelationships among the six parts

- Describe different kinds of plot

- Explain "wholeness of action"

- Distinguish among tragedy, comedy, tragi-comedy, melodrama, and farce

Seeing a play and reading a play are different experiences. They require different tools and different approaches. Seeing a play is the complete theatrical experience.

Reading a play from a book, on the other hand, offers a very incomplete experience. Because of the incompleteness of the written text, some theatre artists talk of the playscript as a "notation" for production, others as "a pretext rather than a text." An analogy with music may help clarify this idea: a written play is

FIGURE 3.1   The Mind's Eye: Environment.
If a stage direction says only, "The Forest of Arden," the reader may start with a mental schematic (top) and fill it in as the play supplies details (left). An actual stage setting (right) may be quite different: *As You Like It* at the University of South Carolina, *directed by Jim Patterson, setting by Dennis C. Maulden, lighting by Ann Courtney, costumes by Rebecca Dosen.*

like musical notes written on a page; the performed play is like the music that comes when a musician transfers the notes into music.

Reading a play means making the effort—and knowing how to make the effort—to understand the play as it will appear in the theatre. This idea is often hard to keep in mind because the written play can be read with pleasure *as if* it were complete and self-sufficient; but it is important to remember that the written play is only one part of an art form—it is not self-sufficient. We must try to learn to read plays *as if* we were seeing them.

Reading a play is also different from reading a newspaper or a novel. The newspaper and novel are complete in themselves; their language fills them out. A play, on the other hand, is only a part—a vital and important part—of a different kind of experience. Because the play is intended for performance, its written text leaves broad areas blank. These blanks the play reader must learn to fill in through clues embedded in the text (such clues are, in fact, clues to performance). For example, in a novel, many paragraphs may be devoted to describing the place where the novel takes place; in plays, such lengthy descriptions are absent, because the place of the play will be shown visually, through scenery, in the theatre. A play *reader* must visualize the place from clues.

Reading a play requires special techniques that can be learned. We will examine the process of play reading in three stages: preliminary work, play analysis, and organizing a coherent response.

PRELIMINARY WORK

Before beginning to read the play, some preliminary work will more than repay the time. The idea here is to get ready to enter a new world: what does the world look like? who are the "people" living in this world?

Title

Reading begins at the beginning—with the title, the first piece of information. The author believed that it said something important about the play; therefore, it is a clue to at least one important part of the play. Titles like *Richard II* and *Cats* are very straightforward; on the other hand, titles like *Half Off* and *Top Girls* are mysterious until well into the play.

Cast of Characters

This list gives vital information on the size and traits of the cast—their names, ages, sexes, and relationships. Introductions are as important in reading a play as they are in entering a room at a party.

Opening Stage Directions

The description of the play's setting (the place where the play takes place) is usually given here as are descriptions of the play's opening moments. In plays that have been produced, these stage directions often reflect the actual Broadway or London production; in other plays, they give the playwright's vision. Reading them, we may be able to visualize (and hear) the play's opening.

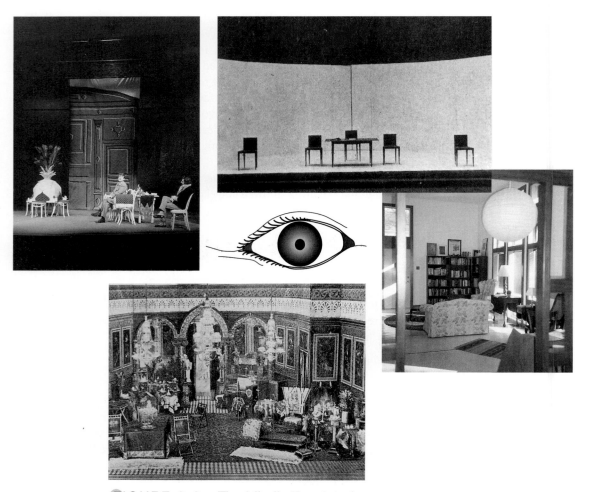

FIGURE 3.2   The Mind's Eye: Interiors.
"A living room," the stage direction may say, or a character may describe a room. The reader must build it mentally from the necessities of staging as he or she reads: doors that work; chairs for two people or five or seventeen; a window an actor can lean out of or jump through or comically be unable to open. Possibilities here include a real room (right), a realistic stage setting of 1893 (below), a setting of fabric and soft sculpture for *The Importance of Being Earnest*, produced at Bowling Green State University (above left), and an almost abstract setting by Emil Pirchan (top).

Time for Questions

The reader should think about the information so far and begin to ask questions. What kind of theatre is being used? What is the historical period of the play? What did buildings, furniture, clothing look like in this period? What is the opening mood—joyful or somber, tense or relaxed? How do characters get on and off the stage? Is the setting indoors or outdoors? Are there doors, and if so, where? Where do the characters enter from? And other like questions.

First Reading

Then, with the beginning as strongly visualized as possible, the reader begins to read the play, underlining and making notes on:

- What happens in the play?

- Who makes things happen and who tries to stop things from happening; also, what is the relative importance of the characters?

- What key words, images, and ideas run through the play (including, what is the relevance of the title)?

Ending

It is important to pause briefly over the ending to determine what the system of rewards and punishments was for the play. Were the rewards serious or playful? Who ended the play better or worse off than they began it?

PLAY ANALYSIS USING THE PARTS OF THE PLAY

After the first reading, the reader is familiar with the play and has a sense of what it is about and of what happens in it, as well as of who its characters are. The next stage aims at an orderly and informed analysis of the play. Such an analysis may finally result in a judgment about the play.

Plays can be analyzed for many different sorts of information. A historian, for example, may read a play in order to discover something about the period in which it was written; a linguist may read it in order to study ways in which language is used or ways in which the use of language has changed over time. Many critical methods are available to help with an analysis of plays, and several will be discussed in the later chapter on criticism.

For now, however, let us agree that a theatre person most often reads a play for information about how it will appear in the theatre. One useful method of extracting this sort of information was first offered by the Greek Aristotle, whose ideas are adapted here for modern use.

Aristotle identified the following six parts of a play:

1. Plot

2. Character

3. Idea

4. Language

5. Music

6. Spectacle

Two important points need to be made here. One, the order of the parts is important because it suggests the precise nature of the relationship among them. Two, the six parts should not be thought of as boxes into which sections of the play are placed; rather, they are parts of a system, a network of interrelationships so connected that a change in any one can have important effects on all others. These relationships are exceedingly complex, but in brief, reading down the list gives a sense of control (the nature of the plot controls the kinds of characters that must appear in it; the kinds of characters control the kinds of ideas possible in the play, etc.). Reading up the list suggests source (music, in the sense of sounds, is the material out of which language is made; ideas are the materials out of which characters are made, etc.).

Although very old, this breakdown is still useful. We can go through almost any play and show how every aspect of the play—every speech, movement, event—relates to these six parts.

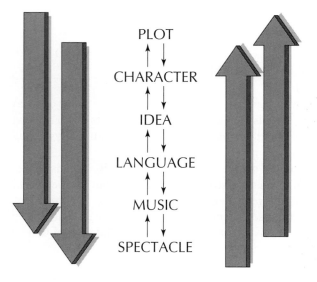

PLOT

CHARACTER

IDEA

LANGUAGE

MUSIC

SPECTACLE

FIGURE 3.3 Parts of a Play.
The six parts of a play comprise a system; change in any one changes all the others. As the arrows show, the relationships are reciprocal: e.g., plot determines the kind of character needed; character is the stuff of which plot is made.

Plot

Plot is the ordering of the incidents in a play. This means that plot is not only *what* happens in the play; it is also the *order* in which things are made to happen and the *reasons* why things are put in that order by the playwright.

Parts of Plot

Plot is itself made up of many parts. Aristotle and later critics have offered names for the most common of these parts.

> Exposition—the giving of information about past events. The greatest amount of exposition often comes at the beginning of the play, when the audiences know least about events and characters. In some plays, however, important exposition is delayed until very late; in a murder mystery, for example, the most important facts about past events ("whodunit") come at the end.

> Point of Attack—the place in the *story* where the playwright begins the *plot.* Greek playwrights tend to begin their plots late in the story and so are said to have a late point of attack; Shakespeare tends to begin his plots toward the beginning of his stories and so is said to use an early point of attack.

> Action—the central chain of events in the play, particularly as those events are the central character's attempt to achieve an important goal. Action and character are tightly bound and are understood through each other, so that an answer to the question "What is the play's action?" always requires the inclusion of character.

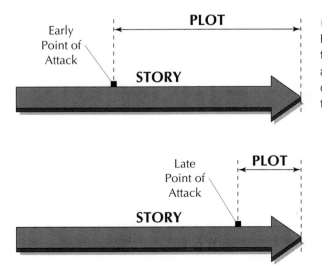

FIGURE 3.4   Plot and Story.
Plot is the arrangement of the incidents, the *way* the story is told. When plot and story begin at about the same point, the play has an early point of attack. When the plot begins late in the story, the play has a late point of attack.

Successful action in most plots has a beginning, a middle, and an end (in terms of logic, not time). That is, *beginning* means that nothing necessary comes before it; *end* means that nothing necessary is still to come. If the action is not a logical whole, the play will not be understandable to its audience as a work of art.

Wholeness is fundamental. It is one of the most important aspects that distinguish art from life, which it imitates.

Unlike a play, a life is not perceivable as a whole, especially while it is being lived. Our lives are diverse and complicated; we carry on several "actions" of which we perceive only dimly (and often incorrectly) the beginnings; the ends are always over life's horizon. People often say they do not understand their lives; they are confused or have lost control or are having an identity crisis. They do not see the whole of their lives.

In a play, on the other hand, wholeness is visible and allows the audience to understand, and so to learn. A dramatic *character* may be confused or out of control or in an identity crisis, but the audience sees the whole of the situation (beginning, middle, and end) and so is not confused. It is important to remember that drama is able to reveal life to us because it is an invention and not real life.

Three other words are often used in describing action:

Suffering—awareness; a passive state of undergoing emotion, of allowing emotion to work on character.

Discovery—the passing from ignorance to knowledge. When characters discover, they usually are led to decide (act). Discovery therefore propels action.

Reversal—any change in the direction of the action, usually occasioned by a discovery that is contrary to a character's expectation.

Complication—the opposing or entangling of the action. Often, at the beginning of the play, the action seems simple—for example, a character desires to accomplish something. This desire becomes complicated by obstacles, particularly by the efforts of other characters to frustrate the action, or even to destroy the central character.

Most plots have many complications. Each complication changes or threatens to change the course of the action because the character must deal with the complication before pursuing the original goal. Complications are either *caused* (by some agency like another character or a god or a force) or *accidental* (the result of something like a storm, a flood, or a chance meeting of characters). Caused complications are usually thought to be better than accidental ones.

Conflict—a hundred years ago, it was common to say that "drama is conflict." Nowadays, we more likely say that conflict is central to many dramas but not all. Conflict between opposed characters may provide an easily un-

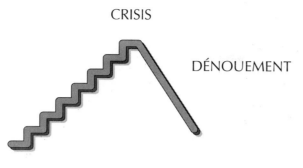

CRISIS

DÉNOUEMENT

COMPLICATION

FIGURE 3.5 Complication, Crisis, Dénouement.
Rising action typically comprises many smaller complications. The turning point (crisis) initiates the falling action (dénouement).

derstandable moral or philosophical opposition (good versus evil), but other conflicts are between a character and a force (like fate, society, gods, which may be personified).

Rising Action—action of increasing complication.

Crisis—derived from the Greek word for decision, crisis means "decisive moment," a turning point in the action. We expect to find rising action from complication to crisis; after the crisis, we anticipate falling action.

Falling Action, Resolution, or Dénouement—"the untying"—the unraveling of complication, the declining action as crisis is passed and complication is resolved.

Kinds of Plot

In one sense, there are as many kinds of plots as there are plays, but some basic patterns tend to repeat and so have been given names. Two in particular may be cited.

1. *Causal plot* (also known as *linear,* or *climactic,* or *antecedent-consequence* plot). The incidents of linear plot can be seen to lie along a line of causality from beginning to end. The word *climactic* is sometimes used because such plots build to a *climax,* the most exciting moment of the plot for the audience. (Note that the term differs from *crisis; climax* refers to an audience's response to plot and not to a part of the plot.)
    Causal plots are of two major types: *single line of development,* with no subordinate lines (for example, Sophocles' *Oedipus the King*) and *multiple lines of development,* consisting of a major line and several subordinate ones, often called "subplots" (for example, Shakespeare's *Hamlet*).

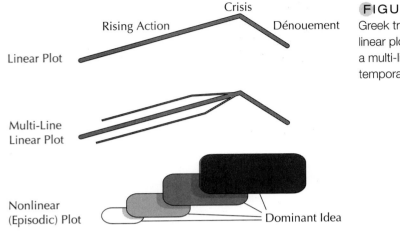

FIGURE 3.6   Kinds of Plot. Greek tragedy typically had a simple linear plot, Shakespearean tragedy a multi-line linear plot. Many contemporary plays have episodic plots.

2. *Episodic plot* (also known as *contextual* or *thematic* plot). The incidents (episodes) of episodic plot do not follow each other because of causality; rather, they are ordered by the exploration of an idea. Social-problem plays and plays by Bertolt Brecht often use this kind of plot, with each scene exploring a new aspect of a social problem or enlarging the study made to that point. An extreme example is a nineteenth-century play (Georg Buechner's *Woyzeck*) for which the author never settled on a final ordering of scenes.

Remember, however, that only the imagination of playwrights limits the way plots are organized. Many nontraditional and experimental arrangements are constantly being tried, and old organizations, like plots of spectacle, language, or character, are occasionally still used.

Character

A dramatic character and a real human being are not the same thing. Dramatic characters are inventions of playwrights. The fact that dramatic characters pursue human goals, speak human words, and embody human responses means only that dramatic characters are part of an artistic creation that is about life, not that it is life itself. Dramatic character is, at best, an imitation of selected aspects of humanity.

In addition to being imitations of people, dramatic characters are also functions within a plot. That is, they were created by the playwright to perform certain tasks within the plot. Each character can be analyzed in every scene for its function, using the play's parts: for example, to further the plot, to reveal information about character, to express ideas, to contribute to spectacle.

Dramatic characters, as imitations and functions, have no existence before the play and no future after the play is over. They are no more than what the playwright has created for the play and for us.

Dramatic characters are performed by actors to create a convincing imitation of real people.

Kinds of Characters

Some kinds of characters repeat often, and so critics and scholars have designated them as follows:

Protagonist—the central figure in the main action.

Confidant(e)—a character in whom the protagonist or another important character confides.

Antagonist—in a play with conflict, the character who opposes the protagonist.

Raisonneur, or *author's character*—one who speaks for the author, directly giving the author's moral or philosophical ideas; usually not the protagonist.

Foil—one who sets off another character by contrast: comic where the other is serious, stupid where intelligent, shrewd where naive.

In many plays, authors divide characters into *sympathetic* and *unsympathetic,* the former created to appeal to audiences, the latter to repel them. The fate of these groups at the end of plays usually embodies the major moral stance of the play and so should be noted.

Sources of Character

Because playwrights cannot describe characters to us directly, we must seek clues about their appearance, motivations, and behaviors. A reader must remain alert for such clues, especially noting places such as these:

- *Stage directions*—although some playwrights do not discuss characters in stage directions.
- *What other characters say*—however, we must understand these other characters in order to know how to interpret what they say.
- *What the characters say about themselves*—with the same problem of interpreting what they say.
- *What the characters do*—their acts.
- *Relationships among characters*—under increasing complications, the real nature of relationships—hate, love, friendship, dependence, forgiveness—shows more clearly.

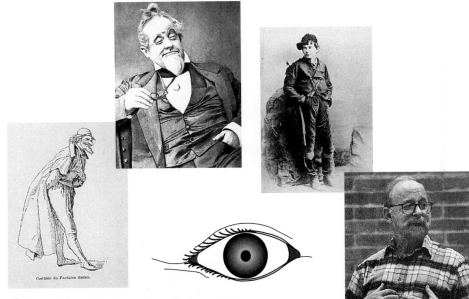

FIGURE 3.7 The Mind's Eye: Character.
The play reader may get only a name or sex and age but must visualize such characters as Pantalone (left), a Southern judge (top), or an Irish farmer (top right). Professional actors like Walt Witcover (right) go far beyond such mental pictures. (See also C-12.) *Photo courtesy of Walt Witcover; top right courtesy of the Department of Rare Books and Special Collections, the University of Rochester.*

- *Most importantly, the plot itself*—for example, decision reveals character; complication forces decision. Characters often change as the plot develops; leading characters often behave and think differently at the end of the play; they have "learned." Accounting for such changes helps one gain understanding of both character and play. Some critics even say that "the play is understood by its ending," a great oversimplification but often a useful notion.

Idea

No play is without meanings. A play does not have to be filled with intellectual speeches to offer meanings, and a careful reader learns how to find and understand them. Even the silliest comedy has meaning because it imitates human action and because it expresses a time and a society; true, the playwright did not set out to teach, but we can extract meaning nonetheless.

Plays seldom offer single, simple meanings. The best offer many meanings, and any attempt to reduce these to "the idea of the play" or "the theme of the play" greatly oversimplifies the work.

Kinds of Meaning

Meanings fall into two major categories: *idea*—meanings contained entirely within the play; and *extrinsic meaning*—those meanings (perhaps wholly unintentional) in the society and the period of which the play is an expression. We are concerned here with idea.

FIGURE 3.8 Idea.
The reader learns to consider how idea will be conveyed in theatrical terms. Here, Heiner Muller's *Quartet,* with Lisa Lias and Steven Angus, directed by Zeljko Djukic, with costumes and makeup design by Natasa Djukic, at the Open Theatre/TUTA. What is the idea of the actors' positions? Their makeup? Their costumes?

Sources of Idea

The play's idea comes in part from its *plot*. We tend to generalize from example, and the playwright, by choosing and ordering events, has created an example (the play). We then may generalize from that example, seeing that (in this playwright's view) certain causes lead to certain (good or bad) events.

In plays organized by conflict, the victor in the conflict embodies the "good" way of behaving, while the loser embodies the "bad." They are rewarded or punished accordingly, through (for example) money, love, promotion, or pardon. For example, comedies often end with the formation of a new society; by discovering who is included and who excluded from this society, a reader can often grasp the major idea of the play by asking questions: Why were these people included and those excluded? What were the traits of each group? The behaviors of each group?

The play's idea comes also from *character*. In a good play, the major ideas are embodied in the character and action of the protagonist. If the character is positive (approved by the author, "good"), then the protagonist embodies a good. These "goods" and "bads"—the defining elements of the play's moral world—are best understood through the system of rewards and punishments in the play. Typically, the protagonist explains his or her own idea near the play's crisis; rewards and punishments usually appear in the play's dénouement.

The play's *language* itself can reveal idea. Important characters' speeches before and after crises are especially revealing, as are important characters' speeches when they are on stage alone or with a confidant(e). The speeches of *raisonneurs*, especially when close to the complications and crises, often reveal idea, as do many speeches during the *dénouement* when the playwright (through the characters) is tying up questions and resolving issues raised by the play.

Language

As we have seen, language through the speeches of characters is an important carrier of meaning in the play.

But language as an act, separate from the meaning of the words, can also reveal idea, as, for example, whenever words or images repeat often in a play. The frequent appearance of the word *death* in a play about love would suggest that the play's idea is probably *not* "Love conquers all." Similarly, repeated images or metaphors carry meaning. One such image in *Hamlet* is of weeds, which support an idea about the protagonist as fighting against an evil, choking, destructive environment.

As an "act" separate from the meaning of the words, language is also one of the most revealing clues to character. The choice of words and the length of sentences can tell the reader something about the circumstances of a character—social class, level of education, complexity of thought, for example. As well, the rhythm of a character's speech may indicate something about mood or lifestyle.

Music

In musical plays, the importance of music to character, mood, and rhythm is clear.

In nonmusical plays, the reader must understand that the language itself embodies music, because it is language intended to be spoken aloud, not read. Oral language inevitably has pitch, rhythm, and so on; that is to say, oral language is musical.

Like language, music reveals clues about plot, character, and idea. For example, regular, slow rhythms create very different moods from sharp, staccato ones. Verse, especially rhymed verse, is usually more formal than prose; in serious plays verse seems to add weight to the action, whereas in comedy it often enhances the wit of a line by accentuating a word or nuance.

Spectacle

In reading, it is especially important to try and visualize the action so that the contribution of spectacle to the performance can be imagined. To be sure, much of the spectacle in today's theatre is the work of designers, whose individual genius cannot be predicted from the page. The cues for their work are there, however, in the same text that the reader uses. The imagination must work to keep spectacle in the mind's eye while reading.

Spectacle, like language, can embody idea, clarify character, and forward plot. A burning cross on stage captures a racial situation that needs no words to describe; two female characters, one dressed in red and the other in pink, predispose us to think of them as differing in their degree of "feminine propriety"; a pistol drawn from a purse may be enough to cause the antagonist to retreat in defeat and the protagonist to prevail, without any words being spoken because in this instance what is seen (the spectacle) is enough to communicate the idea.

Spectacle—which on stage is always working on the sense of sight—is the hardest of the six parts to understand from the text. It is necessary to imagine it as fully as possible, but the imagined spectacle of the reader will probably prove

FIGURE 3.9   Spectacle.
Reading the play cannot bring the full experience of seeing spectacle, but it can prepare the reader and suggest what potential for spectacle exists. Here, a moment from the Beijing opera *Princess Iron Fan. Courtesy of the People's Republic of China.*

quite different from the actual spectacle of performance, although both should probably suggest the same meanings.

ORGANIZING A RESPONSE

The result of a play analysis should be an organized response to the text. An organized response should be *informed* (based on a knowledge of drama and theatre), *orderly* (consistent and well-reasoned), and *defensible* (based on the evidence offered by the text and capable of explanation to somebody else).

Response Based on the Parts of a Play

Analysis should reveal how the parts work together in the play. A response prob-ably should not simply begin with plot and then move to each part in turn, but any response will want to be based on answers to questions based on the parts, ques-tions like

- Is the plot internally consistent? What kind of organization does it display? What is its point of attack? Its crisis? Its major complications?

- Is each character active, interesting, and consistent? Does each have a function throughout?

- Are the play's ideas important, and are they embedded in character and plot?

- Is the language interesting and expressive?

- Does the play's music (including its spoken language) support and enrich character and idea?

- Is the spectacle interesting and appropriate? Does it support rather than overwhelm the other parts of the play?

Response Based on Genres

The word *genre* means simply a *kind* or *type*. In general literature, the word cus-tomarily refers to types like novel, poetry, or drama. Within drama, the word is used to distinguish recurring types (specifically recurring *forms*) of drama—tragedy, comedy, and so on.

Generic criticism is a major branch of dramatic criticism, so much so that whole books have been written about, for example, the nature of tragedy. Our un-derstanding of genres often changes under historical pressure, so that within any one category we can have several kinds—Neoclassical tragedy, Romantic tragedy, heroic tragedy, and so on. Here it is possible to give only the broadest useful defi-nitions of five major genres:

1. Tragedy—a work of the highest seriousness, with a serious protagonist in a serious action with serious consequences. In addition, human decision is usually central to the idea of tragic action.

2. Comedy—a work whose issues are usually social and mundane (rather than spiritual or moral), with a protagonist involved in an action without deeply serious consequences. Usually, as well, human decision is limited, comic characters being comic because they are locked into types or into intense self-interest.

FIGURE 3.10   Genre.

Reading should lead to understanding of the play's genre, whether it is the overstated melodrama of the nineteenth century (left) or the deft comedy of Sheridan's *School for Scandal* (right). *Produced at the University of South Carolina, directed by Jim Patterson, setting by Dennis C. Maulden, lighting by Ed Intemann, costumes by Lisa Martin-Stuart.*

3. Tragicomedy—a work that mixes elements of tragedy and comedy, often by giving otherwise serious plays a happy ending, or vice versa, but often by conferring a degree of seriousness on characters and subjects usually not so treated.

4. Melodrama—a work of apparent seriousness with issues cast in terms of extremes (good and evil), the actual issues being less profound than the language suggests. Endings often show good rewarded and evil punished, in keeping with characters who are aligned according to morality; good (hero, heroine) and evil (villain).

5. Farce—a comic work whose aim is laughter, from a non-English word meaning "to stuff," indicating that farce is stuffed with laughter-produc-

ing elements. The typical protagonist in farce pursues a mundane, often trivial action, and characters often lack decision. Both the characters and the plots of farce have been called *mechanical,* and it is in the working out of its machinery that farce often provokes its best laughter.

Using an analysis based on the parts of a play and its genre, a reader should be able to organize an informed, orderly, and defensible response, either in speech or in writing. Such a response should go beyond personal response to the play (although personal response is important). It should demonstrate an understanding of the play and how it might work in the theatre; it should not be merely a gut reaction. Part of the enjoyment of theatre depends on gut reaction—but only part.

Current issues

The very notion of meaning has become increasingly controversial.

Scholars have long agreed that works of art have no one, simple meaning and that part of what makes them art is that they are able to mean many things at once (just as life means many things at once). It was usually assumed, however, that by careful study of the play, its several meanings could be uncovered. The implication here was, of course, that a play's meaning resides within the play.

Some now argue, however, that meaning exists only in the reader or audience member, that the play itself can have no meaning other than that assigned to it by the person reading or seeing it. The implication here is that meaning exists in (or, more accurately, is constructed by) the human being.

The position raises interesting questions. Can a play mean radically different things to each person who reads it? Are all meanings equally valid, regardless of who constructs them? How are individual meanings harnessed (or are they?) so that the audience, as social entity, experiences the play in ways similar enough to retain the necessary sense of "groupness"? In a mass society, if "my opinion is as good as yours," can a group activity pretend to have any meaning of its own?

LINKS to more about theatre

Louis Catron, *The Director's Vision,* 1989.

Ronald Hayman, *How to Read a Play,* 1977.

James Thomas, *Script Analysis for Actors, Directors, and Designers,* 1992.

KEY TERMS

Check your understanding against this list. Brief definitions are in the Glossary; page references there will direct you to appropriate pages. (Persons are page-referenced in the Index.)

action	exposition
antagonist	foil
causal plot	generic criticism
character	genre
climax	idea
complication	plot
confidant(e)	point of attack
conflict	protagonist
crisis	raisonneur
dénouement	reversal
discovery	spectacle
episodic plot	suffering

How to See a Play

OBJECTIVES:

When you have completed this chapter, you should be able to:

- Describe major differences between reading and seeing a play

- Explain how an experienced audience member can both participate in and observe a performance

- Explain differences between actor and character and between real person and dramatic character

- Explain differences between plot and story

- Explain differences between dramatic and theatrical style and discuss how they may be related

Reading a play and watching a performance are different sorts of activities. The play text comes to us only as words on a page. The performance that we see results from putting together several arts—the written text, the actors, the scenery, costumes, and lighting. Text is repeatable, but performance is not—we watch it moment by moment, responding to many stimuli (sensual, emotional, and intellectual) and unconsciously fusing them into a whole. The written text appeals to our intellect and emotions; performance in the theatre appeals most immediately to our senses and only through them to our intellect and emotions.

Studying a play is therefore different from studying a performance. In studying a play text, we analyze—we take a play apart to see how it *might* work on stage. In studying a performance, we "take it in" through our senses (mostly sight and hearing) and see/hear how it *does* work on stage. In analyzing a play, we can stop and think, or return to a difficult passage and reconsider it. In studying a performance, we watch and hear a moment go by—in real time; later we can only *recall* (not retrieve) that moment.

For such reasons, criticism of performance requires an approach somewhat different from that of play analysis.

Performance criticism can use, cautiously, Aristotle's six parts of a play text, but with the understanding that the nature of theatre radically alters the relationships among these parts. For example, spectacle is primary, because theatre is visual. (Modern theatre especially has endowed spectacle with great meaning—in light's ability to focus attention and create mood, in setting's and costume's ability to give information about time and place, and so on.) In the analysis of a play text, plot, character, idea, and language dominate. But in the analysis of a performance, these four parts (residing mostly in the play) *are submerged within and expressed through music and spectacle, through being spoken by actors and appearing physically on stage.*

An example can clarify this point: character in a play text is revealed only through written words and intellectual constructs called *decisions.* Character in performance, however, is revealed through the work of the actor, for whom the written text (and its six parts) is the basis of the artistic creation but is not the

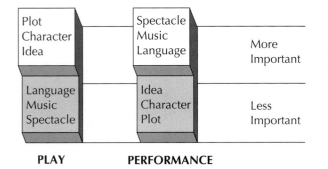

Plot Character Idea	Spectacle Music Language	More Important
Language Music Spectacle	Idea Character Plot	Less Important

PLAY | **PERFORMANCE**

FIGURE 4.1 Parts of Performance. In reading the play, plot, character, and idea claim first attention; in watching a play, spectacle, music, and language dominate.

artistic creation itself. Character in performance depends not only on what the words of the play *say* but also on what the actor *does*—with voice, body, costume, and makeup. To discover character in performance (to understand what the actor is doing with and to the text) means to ask not only the questions asked during play analysis but another set as well, including such questions as these: How does the actor say the words? How does the actor react to the words and actions of others? How does he or she stand? Move? Wear costumes? Create rhythms? Create images?

Performance criticism thus introduces a whole new set of questions to textual analysis: What are the arts of the actor, the scenic designer, the costume designer, and the lighting designer? And how are these arts fused with the written play?

Play analysis examines only the art of the playwright; performance criticism, however, examines the arts of the other theatre makers as well. For this reason, Aristotelian analysis remains a good starting point for thinking about performance, but it is only a starting point; it must be supplemented.

We can consider the techniques of performance criticism in three parts: preliminary work, performance analysis, and organizing a response.

PRELIMINARY WORK

The preliminary work of performance criticism begins before the audience member arrives at the theatre and continues to the opening of the curtain. The preliminary work includes considering

- The art of theatre itself

- The nature of the work itself

- The program distributed to the audience

- The clues offered by the theatre's physical surroundings

The Art of Theatre

Analyzing a performance means in part knowing enough to do so. Knowing the role of each theatre artist, for example, enhances the ability to understand a performance. Understanding the role of the theatre audience in performance—that it can affect performance and so has some responsibility to "work" with actors in creating the event—suggests a need to consider responses as a part of the critique of performance.

Thus, *a knowledge of the art of theatre supports a critique of any single performance.* Attending theatrical performances, taking courses in theatre arts, and reading books about theatre provide this general knowledge. In a lifetime of attending plays and reading about theatre, a person becomes a knowledgeable member of an audience and so is better equipped to engage in performance criticism.

FIGURE 4.2   Expectation. "Preliminary work" may sometimes mean simply responding to advertising or word of mouth. Here, an attention-grabbing advertising flyer for a feminist version of *Peter Pan*.

The Work Itself

An audience member should take the time to learn something about the material to be performed before arriving at the theatre. Some people like to read a play before seeing it; others prefer simply to learn something about it through reviews and advertisements. From whatever source, audience members should arrive at the theatre with a general idea of what they are going to see—because expectations will affect the way a performance is perceived. Just because *Cat on a Hot Tin Roof* has a funny-sounding title does not make this play a comedy, and anyone arriving at the theatre expecting a comedy may be angered or confused by the performance. Taking children to see *Who's Afraid of Virginia Woolf* because it sounds like a children's story will probably result in an unhappy shock.

The Program

An audience member should read the program before the play begins. It almost always indicates the place or places where the action will unfold and introduces the characters who will appear on stage, giving their names and major relationships. Programs often include a synopsis of the play's major action, highlighting the most important moments and thereby suggesting where the audience's attention should focus. Sometimes in the program there will be notes written by the director, designer, or dramaturg. Such notes may be especially helpful, for they sometimes point to the major issues with which the production grapples or explain the director's special point of view in staging this play. (Programs also often offer helpful, if inessential, information, like what good restaurants are close to the theatre and what attractions are coming next to that theatre.)

The Physical Surroundings

An audience member will be repaid for spending a few minutes looking around the theatre and listening to sounds, because theatre artists will often try to establish a proper mood for a play even before it begins. Country and western music in the background probably reveals something important about the production and sets a mood quite different from that established by a Bach concerto or a rap song. Lighting may be used to establish mood, and scenery (where visible) may suggest things like time, place, and social class.

Sometimes oddities (for example, small platforms with scenery or lighting stands) appear in an area normally reserved for audience seating. Such spaces alert an audience member that the performance may spill over from the stage and into the auditorium, a signal that the play may be unusual in other ways as well.

The purpose of the preliminary work is to become prepared for the moment when the performance itself begins. The more prepared for the performance, the better able the audience is to follow the performance as it moves at its own rate through time.

PERFORMANCE ANALYSIS

The goal of performance analysis is to reach greater enjoyment through understanding—not merely a statement like "I really liked that," or "I was bored." Rather, the audience member needs to be able to *explain* the reasons behind such responses. These reasons usually have to do with the selection of the play, the appropriateness and skill of the actors, the suitability of the visual elements, and so on. Much of the rest of this book will deal with ways of understanding and evaluating the several arts involved in performance. The purpose of this section, however, is to offer a way of looking at the contributions of these arts, to serve as an introduction to issues involved in the complex problem of performance analysis.

To analyze a performance, an audience member must do two things at once: *participate in the performance* (entering into the action, empathizing with the characters, and so on); and *watch the performance* ("standing back" from the story and characters in order to observe how the effects are being achieved). This dual view of performance is as rewarding as it is difficult to achieve, but with practice any audience member can learn to participate and observe simultaneously. Again, if carefully used, Aristotle can help us think through this dual view, and the vocabulary in Chapter 3 can, with adaptation, serve us here as well.

Part of learning to maintain a dual view is understanding how the performance appeals through both the play and the specific performance of that play. The play's central values in performance are its story, characters, and ideas, reached through language, music, and spectacle, as expressed in acting, scenery, costumes, lighting, and sound.

Values of the Play

Drama, as imitation of human action, allows audience members to generalize from particular stories, characters, and ideas to more general human truths. Because the stories, characters, and ideas are invented and concentrated for the play, they seem even more important than similar events (unselected and unfocused) seem in real life. Thus, the *concentration* of theatre art accounts for much of its power, but that same concentration complicates the task of performance analysis.

Story

Plays, as imitations of human actions, are compelling because they tell stories. Stories are similar to, but not identical with, Aristotle's *plot.* While experiencing theatre, we cannot analyze plot—we cannot perceive the ordering of the incidents and the reasons for that ordering—we can only follow and respond to the story of the play, to the tale of "what happened."

Stories are made up of incidents that have coherence; that is, the incidents seem to follow one another for a reason. Stories are not only compelling in themselves (we are interested in what happens); they are also compelling because they serve as the framework within which the characters, words, ideas, and values of the play unfold. In a sense, then, we understand the characters, ideas, and values of a performed play through the story that it tells.

Stories in theatre gain much of their interest through their use of *suspense* and *surprise.*

Suspense is the unfolding of events in such a way that audiences want to know what happens next. "And then what happens?" they ask. Suspense requires preparation—curiosity must be created. And suspense must be satisfied—the audience must learn what happens, and what happens must be understandable in terms of what the audience expected might happen. *Suspense, then, requires preparation, connectedness, and resolution.*

Surprise is a happening that is unexpected at the time but quite logical when viewed in retrospect. Therefore, surprises, to work, must be prepared for within the world of the performance; that is, surprises are not the same as mistakes or accidents. For example, if during a love scene on stage a bed collapses, it is a surprise if the bed was supposed to collapse (perhaps for purposes of comedy); if the scenery simply broke down, it is not a surprise but an accident.

FIGURE 4.3   Values of the Play.
Performance is an intensification of events, from which comes much of theatre's power.
Here, Lorraine Hansberry's *To Be Young, Gifted, and Black,* at South Carolina State
University, directed by Frank Mundy.

In the first case, an audience would delight in the added comedy as the actors, through dialogue and action, swiftly incorporated the collapse into the overall story of the play, thus revealing that the collapse was intentional. An audience in the second instance would become uncomfortable as it became clear that the bed broke because of inadequate stage carpentry. If, for example, the bed broke during the scene in Shakespeare's tragedy where Hamlet confronts his mother, the audience's discomfort might lead it to laugh in extreme embarrassment because it would be swiftly apparent that the bed's collapse was not part of the planned performance.

Some surprises come from the merely unexpected—something happens that we simply did not anticipate (the bed collapses). Some surprises come from reversals of the expectation—something happens when we had expected something quite different would happen (we had expected the husband to arrive but the priest arrived instead). Some surprises are a slight twist of an otherwise expected event—something happens that is similar to but not quite the same as what we had expected (we thought the butler committed the murder but discovered that the maid did).

Characters

In performance, characters and story are interrelated, as characters and plot are in a play. We understand each through the other, although they remain independent. But characters in performance, unlike characters in a play, are created by the actors' choices of vocal and physical traits as well as by the words printed on pages of a play. Characters in performance are therefore very complex creations that are based on the characters in the play but are nonetheless different from them.

Audiences respond to characters for different reasons. Often a character is appealing because audiences can identify with it. "I recognize myself in that character," or "I can identify with her" are strong sources of pleasure or suffering in the theatre. We like to see the mirror held up so that we can watch those like ourselves. Some characters are said to have universal appeal (or to be a universal character); the appeal of such characters is that they are recognizably like human beings of many different times and places.

Some characters, although we do not identify with them, appeal to feelings deep within us. Such characters, we say, appeal to us at a subconscious level, through some subconscious reference. For example, the Greek tragedy *Oedipus Rex* has survived for 2000 years and given us a psychological term (the *Oedipus phase* or *complex*) that explains much of its power. One critic said it causes us to "think the unthinkable"—a man who has children by his mother and murders his father.

FIGURE 4.4   Seeing Character.
The Stage Sailor of nineteenth-century drama was a stock type; in a sense, the costume was the character. The same thing might, perhaps, be said for the Dormouse in *Alice in Wonderland,* but not for Alice (right), who appeals to us both as an interesting young girl and as a complex psychological—and, arguably, mythic—creature.

THINKING ABOUT PERFORMANCE

Barbara Stanwyck, an American film and TV actor, remarked, *"My only problem is finding a way to play my fortieth fallen female in a different way from my thirty-ninth."* Explain this quotation in terms of the relationship between character in play and character in performance; between character and actor; between character and genre (see Chapter 3).

All these things are in the play text. In performance, however, they are given a terrible immediacy that gives them life, size, and horror—*this* man and woman, *this* bloodshed, *this* scream.

Still other characters appeal because we recognize others in them, a trait especially clear in the case of historical characters. Seeing an actor portray a character we think we know offers a special treat for audiences, who will often flock to see an actor portray former luminaries in works like *Abe Lincoln in Illinois* or *Picasso at the Lapin Agile.* Here the delight is not only in enjoying the character in the performed play but also in watching to see how closely the actor meets our preconceptions of the real person. To take advantage of this associative response, the performance must depict people with whom the audience has strong ties and must present them in convincing—and perhaps visually recognizable—ways.

It is important to stress that characters in performance, like characters in a play text, are not real people. They are *like* real people. Because in performance we hear and see live actors actually speaking and moving before us, we need to be clear that, although the actors are real, the characters are invented, with no existence outside the performance itself.

Idea

Generally the ideas that are revealed through a performance are given the least thought while we sit in the theatre and watch, but they are often the aspect of the production that we talk most about once we leave the theatre. There is a good reason for this phenomenon. Performance is transitory; theatre is "the home of the Now." When we leave the theatre, the vividness of the acting, the onstage images and sounds fade. We seldom remember sensory stimuli clearly; afterward we can only describe them. We are therefore left with the intellectual content of the play in performance, which is verbally expressible and so may remain fresh and sharp in our minds.

In fact, the ideas within the performance may become more important with the passing of time. If experiencing the immediacy of the performance has moved us, it has become part of our lives, and now we want to know what it means *to us.*

Ideas are embedded in all play texts and performances. Some ideas are more interesting and more important than others, to be sure, but ideas exist in all.

Whereas the ideas of play texts come mostly through the plot and dialogue, however, ideas in performance come most immediately through the specific choices made by the actors and designers (of scenery, costumes, lighting, and properties). For example, images in performance can communicate ideas vividly, even without words (although words of course deepen and extend the ideas). For example, an actor with a shaved head, wearing paramilitary garb quite clearly communicates an ideology even before he speaks. A set that positions a computer so that it looms menacingly above the actors makes a clear (although nonverbal) statement of a power relationship, a statement that the actors' words and performance enhance and modify. It is through such means that specific *performances* of Shakespeare's *Julius Caesar* have offered ideas about Nazi Germany and South American dictatorships, even though the *play's* ideas were about the nature of rule in Republican Rome and, perhaps, Elizabethan England.

Ideas that are not well integrated into the performance are distracting and theatrically unsatisfying. Indeed, to update an old theatrical adage, "If you want to send a message, use a fax." The saying means that ideas are not the end-all or be-all of performance. Ideas are only one important element of judging the importance of a play in performance, even though they tend to dominate later discussions of performance, lingering after the immediate, sensory elements of performance have faded from memory.

Idea in performance succeeds only if other, theatrical, values of the play succeed—because ideas come to audiences through the other elements of specific performance.

Values of the Specific Performance

Story, character, and idea reside mostly in play text; music (what we hear) and spectacle (what we see) reside in performance. Indeed, the word *theatre* literally means *seeing place* and *auditorium* literally means *hearing place.* Therefore, audience members will also want to ask questions about the elements of performance that may be distinct from the play text itself. Three such elements are central to understanding most performances: the *given circumstances* of the performance, its *theatrical conventions,* and its *style.*

Given Circumstances

We may define the given circumstances of a performance as those basic traits that determine the world of the stage: the age, sex, social class, and physical health of the characters; the time and place of the action; the mood established on the stage; and so on.

Usually the written play determines the given circumstances, but not always. For example, the play *Everyman* comes from the English Middle Ages, and so the performance usually proceeds *as if* it were unfolding then and there. But a director may wish to emphasize the timelessness of this action and so perform it

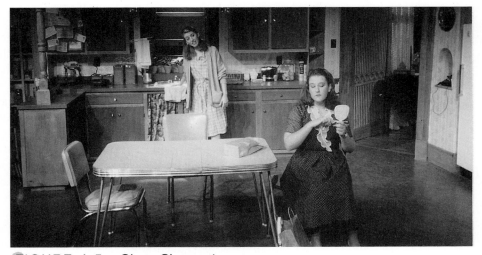

FIGURE 4.5 Given Circumstances.
Period, socioeconomic status, age, even psychology are communicated visually. *Crimes of the Heart, by Beth Henley, at the University of the Pacific. Directed by James R. Taulli. Production design by Peter Lach.*

as if it were taking place in England of the 1990s or in the Western United States during the gold rush. In producing a French comedy of the 1660s, a director might want to do it "authentically," making it as close as possible to what the original production might have been. Or the director might decide that the fun within the play is more important than the circumstances of its original production and so select materials based on their brightness and color, even using techniques of cartoons or caricatures as guiding principles. Clearly all such decisions will necessarily affect not only the visual aspects of the production but also the sounds selected as background and the techniques used by the actors.

Whatever the decision about given circumstances, the circumstances for every production must be made clear to the audience through the visual aspects of production (scenery, costumes, lighting, properties), the sounds and music of the production, and the work of the actors. An audience member engaged in performance criticism must determine what the given circumstances of production are and then examine how those circumstances were communicated through the arts of production. Only then can some evaluation of this aspect of production be made, through answering questions like these:

- What seemed to be the source and purpose of the production's given circumstances?

- Were the circumstances clear?

- Were they consistent throughout the production?

Conventions

A *convention* can be thought of as a contract between theatre artists and audiences, an agreement to do things a certain way for the good of all. It is a shortcut between what is meant and what is done. Each of the arts within theatre has conventions. Several examples can clarify.

In today's theatre, it is a convention that months or years can pass between the acts of a play, even though common sense tells us that, in fact, only a few minutes have passed.

A convention in scenic design is the agreement between actors and audience that when a setting depicts a room of a house, a door in that room leads to another room of the house or to the outdoors. Common sense tells us that the door actually leads to an area backstage. Another sort of scenic convention allows a yellow cardboard circle hung aloft to represent the sun.

An acting convention from the eighteenth century was that a hand raised to the forehead, palm out and the eyes cast upward, indicated suffering.

FIGURE 4.6 Convention and Surprise.

It is a convention of the realistic theatre that the audience is not in a theatre. Here, a nineteenth-century drama called *Hearts Are Trumps* played against the convention by putting an audience of actors behind the principal performers and reminding the real audience of their situation. The real audience looked at the audience-in-play and was, presumably, pleasurably startled.

In musicals, characters sing their emotions. This use of music is a convention, because common sense tells us that music neither accompanies our lives nor changes as we shift activities and moods.

Such agreements between artists and audiences serve to enhance performance and so work for the good of both. Audience members trying to understand and evaluate a performance need to watch for the conventions operating in a production:

- Are the conventions clear?

- Are the conventions similar to other, familiar theatrical conventions? To conventions on television? Or are they in some way distinctive?

- Do the conventions seem aimed at promoting the view that the onstage world is quite like real life, or do they aim rather to call attention to the differences of the stage from life?

Style

The word *style* is one of the most useful and yet one of the most confusing that is applied to any art. Part of the confusion comes from the word's being used in so many ways in daily life: clothes are "stylish"; there is "New Orleans style" jazz, different from "Chicago style"; there are kosher-style dill pickles; many performers are said to have their own personal "style."

In art, including theatre art, the word *style* is used to describe a recurring cluster of traits that seem to set one type off from another type of the same art—two styles of painting, for example, or two styles of music. Dramas (written texts) have style, and so do performances. It is therefore possible to speak both of dramatic style and theatrical style.

Generally, a play written in a particular style will also be performed in that style; therefore, the dramatic and theatrical style are often the same. But in some instances (for reasons which we will return to later), theatre artists may decide that the performance should be in a style different from that of the written play.

Styles tend to change over time. For example, seventeenth-century plays and productions displayed something we now call a Neoclassical style, while early nineteenth-century plays and productions generally showed what we call a Romantic style. Contemporary theatre is marked by its tendency to use many different styles among its productions, but, for a single production, there is usually a single style.

Style can be analyzed by considering ways in which various elements are expressed and combined. Different cooking styles emphasize different sorts of foods and different spices. Different styles within visual arts differ in their preference for certain ways of manipulating mass, line, color, and texture. Different styles within literary arts tend to prefer certain kinds of language, characters, and plots over others. The ways in which individual elements are manipulated are related to style.

Although it is not possible to study style in detail here, some of its major areas of difference can be profitably suggested. Let us examine three: abstraction, detail, and material. And let us remember that describing a style requires statements about all three.

Abstraction. Abstraction is *removal from observable reality.* An artist may choose any point along a continuum from quite abstract to wholly lifelike. For example, a painting that is simply a splash of red interrupted by dots of black is quite abstract, whereas a near-photographic portrait of Marilyn Monroe is quite lifelike.

Similarly, a theatre artist can either *reproduce observable reality,* or render parts of reality as *generalized but understandable shapes,* or *abandon reality* almost entirely. For example, scenic designers might choose to reconstruct a room onstage, making it as much like a real room as possible; or they might make all walls transparent and use furniture specially made of steel; or they might choose to show only an open space with platforms and geometric shapes. Lighting designers might, through color and angle, suggest real sunlight, or they might choose to flood the acting area with blue light.

FIGURE 4.7   Style: Abstraction.
These costumes are abstracted from reality by covering the faces and limbs with metal cylinders, hiding detail, making straight lines where the bodies had curves, evoking machines. *From Huntley Carter, The New Spirit in the European Theatre, 1914–1924.*

Costume designers might use real clothes taken from a thrift shop, or they might construct a covering of metal and cardboard in such a way as to disguise the shape of the human body.

Decisions about the level of abstraction are choices about style and are themselves often closely related to the selection and use of detail.

Detail. At issue here is both the *amount* of detail and the *kind* of detail. Again, an artist can choose anything along a continuum from no detail to overwhelming detail, and along various continua of kinds of detail: natural/artificial, expensive/cheap, urban/rural, and so on. For example, the abstract painting could be a splash of solid red with a single black dot, or it could be highly textured layers of many shades of red with numerous black dots of varying textures. The portrait of Marilyn Monroe might show her dressed in a solid fabric or in a highly patterned one, wearing no jewelry or bedecked in brooches and rings.

Similarly, theatre artists can make choices about amounts and kinds of details. An actor, for example, can move often, crossing the stage, sitting and standing, gesturing nervously (much detail); or she may remain quite still, using no gestures,

FIGURE 4.8   Style.

The same Greek tragedy, *Prometheus,* was the basis for both productions, yet the performances were clearly very different. The visual differences are matters of style, although it is clear that matters of idea, character, even of the theatre itself are also involved. *Top, directed by Richard Scammon, photo courtesy of Indiana University and Vera Scammon Broughton; bottom, at the University of Maryland, directed by Edith P. Catto, photo by Edith P. Catto.*

and speak in a monotone (little detail). A scenic designer may fill a room with furniture and bric-a-brac (much detail) or leave the same room utterly unadorned except for a single chair stage center (little detail). The costume designer may choose a rich silk dress covered with dollar signs sewn in brilliants (much detail) or a plain black leotard (little detail).

Again, all such decisions are matters of style, and they often interact with the materials selected for rendering the details.

Material.   Choosing materials means making decisions about such things as mass, line, color, and texture. Different materials produce different effects. An oil painting differs from a charcoal sketch; a building in stone differs from one in brick.

In theatre, too, certain kinds of materials predispose audiences in certain ways. For example, a setting built entirely of aluminum tubing calls on an audience's association with science or industry, perhaps, and invites a sense of detachment, coldness, cleanliness. Such a setting is different from an otherwise identical setting made of bare wood, which an audience might associate with an earlier time and so derive a sense of tradition, comfort, and warmth. Similarly, costumes made of burlap will "say" something to an audience quite different from otherwise identical costumes made of satin or wool or cotton, each of which encourages its own set of associations for an audience.

In examining visual elements in production, performance critics must therefore ask questions like these:

- Are the colors pastel or saturated?

- Are the textures smooth and shiny or rough and pocked?

- Are lines curved or jagged?

- Are masses large and unbroken or broken up?

Although more difficult, similar kinds of questions, applied to actors, can lead to an understanding of their style in a performance.

- Are the actors *seeming to be* real people involved (unknowingly) in a real situation, or are they clearly aware of themselves as performers (perhaps they address the audience directly from time to time)?

- Are the actors using many small details of voice and movement, or are they relatively still, both vocally and physically?

- What materials of voice and body have the actors selected for the performance (soft or loud voices, erect or slouching posture, and so on)?

Again, all such questions are questions relating to style. An audience member functioning as a performance critic will want to notice the choices made with respect to level of abstraction, the amount and kind of details, and the choice of materials. And he or she will want to evaluate the appropriateness and consistency of the choices.

LINKS to more about theatre

James H. Clay and Daniel Krempel, *The Theatrical Image*, 1967. How to see in images.

Jill Dolan, *The Feminist Spectator as Critic*, 1988. The title says it all.

Kenneth Tynan, *Curtains*, 1961. Reviews by a man who loved theatre.

ORGANIZING A RESPONSE

The result of critiquing a performance should be an organized response to the performance itself. Because most performances are based on plays, a piece of performance criticism will most often need to address two related questions:

- What are the major values of the play?

- How are these values revealed or transformed through performance?

As with a play analysis, performance criticism should be *informed* (based on knowledge of theatre), *orderly* (consistent and well reasoned), and *defensible* (based on evidence offered by the performance itself and capable of explanation to someone else).

Good performance criticism often *synthesizes* the values of play and performance; that is, the critic does not usually begin with a discussion of story, characters, and idea and then move to a discussion of given circumstances, convention, and style. Rather, the critic tries to communicate how the performance (the work of the actors, director, and designers) reveals the story, characters, ideas, and values of the play. In the course of the discussion, many of the questions given earlier in this chapter will be answered for the particular production.

Some other guiding questions might be the following:

- Are the *given circumstances* of the production clear? How do they relate to the given circumstances of the play itself? How are these given circumstances made clear?

- What are the *conventions* of the production? Do they seem to work with those of the play? How or how not?

- What is the *style* of the production, and how is that style achieved? Is it the same style as that of the written play (if that question is answerable)? Are the various theatrical arts in the same style?

- Is the *story* clear? How do the several elements of production enhance its suspense and surprises?

- Are all *characters* clear? Are they interesting? How has each actor made the character clear? Interesting? How have the several elements of design contributed to these goals?

- Are the *ideas* clear? Compelling? What elements of production have worked to further these goals?

- Did the *audience* seem attentive and appreciative, and how did the audience responses fit with my own?

CURRENT ISSUES

The acknowledged power of performance has raised questions about its responsibility for its effects on the public. Can theatre or television or music video or song lyrics really cause social problems, or are such fears grounded in a misunderstanding of the nature of art? Today, heated debates over arts' role in the supposed

FIGURE 4.9 Negative Theatrical Images. The "Jim Crow" laws that were the reaction against Reconstruction in the American South took their name from the performer shown here—a white man in blackface portraying a "comic negro." The laws comprised virtually an American form of apartheid. How complicit was the actor? The American theatre?

breakdown of contemporary society are underway. The debates have centered around the (as yet unknown) answers to questions like the following:

What effects, if any, does violence on television have on children? Are pornographic images of women harmful to all women? Does it matter that black males in movies and on TV are more often shown as poor and criminal than as affluent and successful? Does the rarity of Hispanic-American characters in the media carry a hidden message to the public that such people are unimportant? Do the cruelty and vulgarity celebrated by some rap music undermine civility, a trait perhaps required by a society where people must co-exist?

Even if the answers to such questions were agreed upon—and they certainly are not—it is unclear what, if anything, should be done. Should each person be allowed to decide what he or she wants to watch and hear, or should the government adopt policies controlling certain kinds of performance? Should one set of principles govern responsible adults and another children? Should one set of principles govern performances to which one chooses to go (e.g., film and theatre) and another the performances that might be encountered accidentally in one's own home (e.g., TV and the Internet)?

Such issues are especially difficult to resolve in our society because of the constitutional protections afforded speech. This debate over the social responsibility of arts and artists is a classic confrontation between two cherished American rights. In the current debate, society's right to control possibly dangerous words and images (legally construed as speech) is pitted against an individual's freedom to use or receive words and images so long as they cannot be proved to pose a clear and present danger (yelling "fire" in a crowded theatre being the legal standard most often used to illustrate "clear and immediate danger").

KEY TERMS

Check your understanding against this list. Brief definitions are in the Glossary; page references there will direct you to appropriate pages. (Persons are page-referenced in the Index.)

abstraction	story
auditorium	style
conventions of drama	surprise
conventions of theatre	suspense
given circumstances	theatre (building)
(of performance)	

II

Today's Theatre and Its Makers: Theatre Practice

Making Theatre Today: The Context

OBJECTIVES:

When you have completed this chapter, you should be able to:

- Identify the principal theatre configurations and stage shapes

- Differentiate among the main producing structures in the United States, with an understanding of the strengths of each

- Explain several types of theatre funding

Before studying the people who make theatre happen, we need to examine the contexts in which they work in the United States. In what kinds of spaces can they make their plays? Are some arrangements of actors and audiences better than others for certain sorts of plays? What kinds of producing arrangements are available, and what are their strengths and weaknesses? Finally, how can theatre productions be financed, and what are some implications of the different funding sources?

THEATRE SPACES

Given the diversity of theatres around the country, it should not be surprising that they choose different sorts of physical spaces in which to work. With various elaborations, three basic theatre spaces now dominate: proscenium, thrust, and arena stages. In addition to these three, a few less common arrangements can be named and briefly described.

Proscenium Stages

The most popular theatre shape in Western Europe and the United States since the seventeenth century, proscenium theatres are marked by a proscenium arch that separates the stage and the auditorium.

The stage behind the proscenium arch is typically equipped with a rigging system, which allows scenic pieces to be "flown" (lifted out of sight above the stage floor), and a trap system, which allows objects and people to sink below the stage floor or to rise from it. Some are equipped with wagons or "slip stages" that allow scenery to be moved into place from the *wings,* the spaces on each side of the stage. In most proscenium theatres, there is an area that extends a few feet in front of the arch, an area called the *apron* or forestage.

The auditorium is arranged so that almost all seats face the stage. Ground-level seats are *orchestra* seats. Above them are *balconies* (also called *galleries*), which may curve around at least part of the side wall. Older proscenium houses have small, separate balconies, called *boxes,* usually on the side walls of the theatre near the stage. These boxes were at one time the most prized seats in the theatre, but they are now usually avoided because of their bad angle for viewing the stage (bad *sight lines*).

Thrust Stages

Some plays, especially those of Shakespeare and his contemporaries, were not written for production in a proscenium theatre. For this reason, several theatre companies, especially those whose repertory stresses plays from the past, have sought a variation of the theatre used in Shakespeare's day. Such groups have built theatres with thrust (also called Elizabethan, or Shakespearean, or three-quarter-round) stages.

In such theatres, there is no arch separating the actors from the audience. Instead, audience members are placed on three sides of the action, usually on a raked (slanted) floor to improve sight lines, and in balconies. Actors enter the playing area from the back or through *vomitories* (passages that run through and under the audience and open near the stage itself). Because in this theatre elaborate stage machinery cannot be concealed behind a proscenium arch, and because, too, of the close physical relationship between the actors and the audiences, thrust

Alley Stage

Proscenium Stage

Thrust Stage

Arena Stage
(Theatre in the Round)

FIGURE 5.1 Basic Theatre Spaces.
Actor-audience relationships in four configurations: alley (audience on two sides of the actor); proscenium (audience on one side); thrust (audience on three sides); and arena (audience surrounding actor).

stages tend to rely on acting, costumes, and properties rather than complex scenic effects. Indeed, in such theatres, without a front curtain and proscenium arch to mask them, all scene changes and all actors' entrances must be made in full view of the audience.

Of the many thrust theatres, perhaps the best known are those at the Festival Theatre in Stratford, Ontario, Canada, and at the Guthrie Theatre in Minneapolis, Minnesota, both of whose repertories stress revivals of masterpieces from the past.

Arena Stages

The audience in the arena theatre surrounds the playing area, hence its other name: *theatre in the round.* Many people prize the closeness of actors and audiences in arena staging, an intimacy especially well suited to many plays in the modern repertory.

With neither a proscenium arch nor a back wall to mask movements, all property and scenic shifts and all actors' entrances must be done either in blackout or in full view of the audience. Perhaps for this reason, arena stages tend to avoid elaborate scenic effects in favor of close attention to the details of costumes, properties, and acting.

Although less common than either proscenium or thrust stages, arena stages exist throughout the country, most notably at the Arena Stage, Washington, D.C., and the original Alley Theatre, Houston, Texas.

Other Configurations

Sometimes from choice and sometimes from necessity, acting companies may take their performances to audiences instead of having audiences come to them. For such performances, a wide assortment of spatial arrangements must be found or created.

The booth stage has long been a popular solution. Here, actors erect a curtain before which they play, either on a raised platform or in a cleared area. The result is very much like the thrust stage, with the curtain serving both as a place from which to make entrances and as a background against which to perform. Because it meets the basic needs of performance and can be quickly erected and dismantled, the booth stage has long been the favorite of traveling companies.

Alley stages place the audience on two sides, with the actors performing between them, and often with scenic units at each end. In some countries, such arrangements are found in regular theatres; in the United States, however, they are used mostly by actors who find it necessary to perform in school gymnasiums.

Finally, only the imagination limits the space in which actors perform for audiences. In the United States, we have records of theatre taking place in streets, parks, factories, and even elevators—again, an index of the great diversity of our theatre.

PRODUCING SITUATIONS IN THE UNITED STATES

Its center is still New York City, but American theatre now touches most cities throughout the country. Although its diversity makes classification difficult, we can divide American theatre first into *professional* and *amateur* (each with several subcategories). Because some theatres resist these categories, we have a third group: *theatres for special audiences.*

Professional Theatre

Broadway

Say the word *theatre* to an American, and he or she will probably think immediately of New York's Broadway. The word, in fact, has several different meanings. *Broadway* is, first of all, the name of a street in New York that runs the length of Manhattan. But the word *Broadway* also designates the whole area around Times Square (Broadway and several streets adjacent to it), where most of New York's commercial theatres are located. The word was once used in various union contracts to specify a certain kind of theatre in which only union members could work, and then only for a certain fee or salary. And the word *Broadway* refers to a whole complex of qualities that people associate with the glamorous, glittering world of the legitimate theatre: elaborate settings, rich costumes, distinguished stars, polished performances, and sophisticated musicals and plays.

Although New Yorkers attend the Broadway theatre in large numbers, tourists also make up a sizable part of its audiences. From across the country, people flock into its theatres as part of "seeing New York." They expect to see plays written by the best-known playwrights, performed by the best actors, and designed by the best artists available, for which they are willing to pay—in the late 1990s—about $45 for an *average* ticket. At such prices, Broadway audiences comprise mostly the affluent: a social group that tends to be middle-class or above, white, mature, and somewhat conservative in taste and politics. In 1998, NPR reported theatregoers had an average family income of $91,000.

Broadway is best known for its musicals, where spectacle, rather than idea, is prized. The remaining repertory consists of occasional serious

FIGURE 5.2 Broadway.
"Broadway" is an area of New York City that includes side streets like this one, where the marquees of three theatres can be seen in one block.

dramas, comedies, mysteries, biographies, and one-person shows. Because of the high costs of producing on Broadway, its theatres seldom offer untried plays; they feature instead revivals of successful plays from past Broadway seasons or recently written plays transferred from successful runs elsewhere, most often London, Off-Broadway, or the regional theatres.

Broadway's reputation today rests in large part on the high quality of its productions. Because many theatre professionals believe that they have not established themselves until they have succeeded on Broadway, Broadway sets the standards of American acting, directing, and design. Broadway artists command among the highest salaries paid in the American theatre, and unions protect them by establishing minimum salaries and controlling working conditions. The major theatrical organizations are the Dramatists Guild (for writers), the Actors Equity Association (for performers), the Society of Stage Directors and Choreographers, United Scenic Artists (for designers), and IATSE (for technicians).

Much of Broadway's appeal, and also many of its problems, stem from money. Its costs of producing continue to climb, for several reasons. As real-estate prices in Manhattan soar, so do the costs of renting theatre space. Personnel costs rise with the demands of the unions. Costs of the goods and services needed to open a show—lumber for scenery, fabrics for costumes, advertising in newspapers and on television—have become almost prohibitive; and then, there is the money needed to keep the show running once it has opened. Costs are now so high that even a fairly modest show must run months (rather than weeks) in order to recapture its original investment, a situation that has made the *long run* a regular feature of the Broadway theatre.

Huge costs have encouraged a "hit-or-flop" syndrome—a Broadway with no place for the modest success: a hit can make *big* money (*Godspell*, 20,000 percent profit); a flop can lose more than a million dollars. "You can make a killing in the theatre, but you can't make a living."

Another result of high costs has been to limit the potential audience for Broadway shows and to increase the power of certain New York reviewers. As

THINKING ABOUT TODAY'S THEATRE

The American actress Tallulah Bankhead (1903–1968) complained that *"it's one of the tragic ironies of the theatre that only one man in it can count on steady work—the night watchman."* From the library or the Internet, discover how many members now belong to the actor's union, Actor's Equity. Then, by consulting the arts and entertainment section of the *New York Times,* find the number of productions currently playing in New York. Based on several familiar plays, estimate an average number of roles in an average play. Calculate how many actors are now working in New York. Evaluate Bankhead's quotation in light of your findings.

ticket prices rise, the number of people able (or willing) to afford the Broadway theatre declines, as does the willingness of audiences to risk a disappointing evening. Audiences therefore look to a reviewer to steer them toward shows they will like and away from shows they will not like. In so doing, audiences invest certain New York reviewers with enormous power. And this audience affects the repertory in other ways as well, for producers actively seek productions to appeal to its tastes. Thus, the cycle of depending on tried-and-true plays, composers, and artists is reinforced. Simultaneously, opportunities for original plays, untested actors, and unknown directors are further constricted.

Broadway has tried to solve some of its money problems. For example, two low-priced ticket sources, the Times Square TKTS booth and the Lower Manhattan Theatre Center, sell tickets at half price on the day of performance for shows not sold to capacity. The computerization of ticket sales allows out-of-towners to compete with New Yorkers for good seats, and credit card payments by phone eliminate the need to write for tickets or to stand in lines to purchase them. The Theatre Development Fund, established in 1967, supports commercial productions of special artistic merit; and New York City offers incentives for the construction of new theatre buildings. The success of these efforts to make Broadway more accessible cannot yet be gauged.

FIGURE 5.3   Building Theatre Audiences.
At one end of Times Square, the TKTS booth sells lower-priced tickets to New York theatres.

Although detractors of Broadway have long deplored the grip that big business seems to have on it and have predicted its death many times, Broadway continues to be the model of much theatre in the United States. A testament to its authority in theatrical matters is that many other theatres, both amateur and professional, strive to imitate it.

The Road

Many communities regularly import recent Broadway hits by booking the touring theatrical companies (*road shows*) that each year criss-cross the country. Although such road shows originate in New York, they seldom employ the original Broadway cast; but they do use professionals. Because road companies travel with complete sets and costumes, they are usually able to offer polished performances of recent hits to audiences outside the major cities, who would otherwise be unable to see them. Business is best for big-name musicals, good for plays with well-known stars, risky for everything else, although certain kinds of shows that may never see Broadway—for example, family-values or gospel plays for black audiences—have found a niche on the road.

Dinner Theatres

Throughout the United States, dinner theatres offer successful Broadway plays of past seasons as the mainstay of their repertories. The quality of such companies varies widely. Some use union personnel, and their quality tends to be higher than those that rely on non-professionals.

Restrictions of space and budget cause almost all dinner theatres to simplify the scenery and costumes of the originals in favor of smaller casts, smaller orchestras, and fewer sets, but, like Broadway, most seek to entertain rather than to elevate or instruct their audiences. In addition to the play itself, they add the sociability of drinks and dinner, so that an evening in the theatre is a festive occasion, not unlike going out for dinner before seeing a show on Broadway.

Off-Broadway

The name *Off-Broadway* derives from the location of its theatres, which lie outside the Times Square theatre district. In addition to location, Off-Broadway houses were once contractually defined by their limited capacity (no more than 299 seats) and by their lower-than-Broadway salaries (as negotiated with the major unions).

Originally (in the 1950s), the goals of Off-Broadway differed from those of Broadway. Off-Broadway sought to serve as a showcase for new talents: Untried artists could work; established artists could experiment with new techniques; new plays could find production. Off-Broadway artists hoped to remain aloof from both threats of censorship and the problems of high-risk commercialism.

Although Off-Broadway continues to offer employment to actors, directors, and playwrights (producing three or more shows for every one of Broadway's by the mid-1980s), its production costs have risen and, with them, its need to succeed at the box office. As risk has become less practical, Off-Broadway has become a

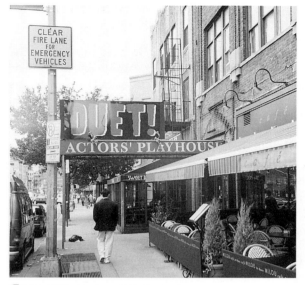

FIGURE 5.4 Off-Broadway.
"Off-Broadway" is now spread over much of New York City, but the historical Off-Broadway started in Greenwich Village, where this theatre still operates.

rather less expensive version of Broadway, for which it now serves regularly as a try-out space. Shows that succeed Off-Broadway may move to Broadway, often with the same casts, directors, and designers, but with much larger budgets.

Even though Off-Broadway and Broadway overlap in several respects, the lower ticket prices Off-Broadway attract a more diverse audience and thus allow a somewhat more varied repertory. In addition to small musicals and comedies, Off-Broadway produces some serious works, even those that are potentially controversial. For about half of what it costs to see Broadway shows, Off-Broadway audiences can choose among revivals from the classical repertory, recent successes, and original plays. Some of the productions are very good; some are not. But modest risk-taking is part of attending the Off-Broadway theatre and, for those who support it, remains a major part of its attraction.

Off-Off-Broadway

As Off-Broadway moved closer to Broadway—in practice, if not in location—some artists felt the need for an alternative theatre where authors, directors, and actors could work closely together to produce plays in an artistic, rather than a commercial, environment. Thus, Off-Off-Broadway grew up in the late 1950s as a place dedicated to the process of creating art and exploring the possibilities of the theatre. It did not want to become a tryout space for Broadway or to succumb to Broadway's or Off-Broadway's commercialism.

Productions feature imaginative, but seldom elaborate, sets and costumes. Although the casts and designers in such spaces are not necessarily union members and are seldom paid even their expenses, they continue to work, exploring the limits of a vision that is often socially, politically, or artistically alien to current American values. Lower ticket prices encourage attendance by people priced out of the Broadway theatre, and the excitement caused by unknown plays and artists draws adventurous patrons to coffeehouses, lofts, cellars, churches, and small theatres tucked away all over Manhattan and even some of the other New York City boroughs, where they watch artists perform plays that stimulate them.

Although sometimes amateurish and often controversial, the offerings of Off-Off-Broadway provide a genuine alternative to the commercialism of both Broadway and Off-Broadway. Off-Off-Broadway remains the focus of what is left of experimental and political theatre in America.

Regional Theatres

The vitality of regional professional theatres is one of the most heartening developments in the American theatre. In more than fifty major cities throughout the United States and Canada, more than sixty professional theatres bring art to their audiences. Unlike the Broadway theatre, these groups are usually organized as not-for-profit enterprises and so in theory can be more adventurous with play selection, production style, and personnel decisions. They contribute to theatre throughout America by diversifying and enriching its repertory, developing new audiences, training and revitalizing theatrical artists, and providing employment opportunities. Perhaps for these reasons, regional theatres have been called "the conscience of the American theatre."

Regional theatres offer five major benefits:

1. *A forum where new plays and classics can coexist and provide an alternative to the comedies and musicals that are now the mainstays of Broadway.* Some, like the Arena Stage of Washington, D.C., have earned reputations through the excellence of their classical revivals. Others, like the Actors Theatre of Louisville, have been especially successful in sponsoring new plays. Such theatres have reversed the tradition of plays' beginning in New York and then trickling down slowly to the rest of the country. Much new drama now appears first around the country. The best of it moves beyond its local area and throughout the country, often ending in New York.

2. *A source of new audiences for live theatre.* The art of theatre suffers without knowledgeable audiences, because theatre artists become complacent, accepting the ordinary or the mediocre rather than demanding the excellent. With the growth of regional professional companies, audiences across the country have come to appreciate live theatre as an art form and a cultural resource.

3. *A training ground and an energizing center for theatrical artists.* Colleges and universities begin the training of many young artists; the professional regional companies serve to introduce young artists to the profession, allowing them to work intensively with experienced artists. Today, many of our best talents in acting, directing, and designing begin their careers at one of these regional companies—and some elect to stay there throughout their careers.

4. *An important opportunity for the seasoned professional.* Commercial theatre can dull an artist's creativity and vitality because its repertory is restricted and because its productions, when successful, can run for months or years, a numbing experience for an artist. Moreover, the commercial theatre seldom offers those roles from the classical repertory that stretch the actor's craft. For these reasons, the best actors are often anxious to spend time with a resident theatre, where they can play a wide variety of

roles from many of history's best plays. The exchanges between the regional and the New York theatres seem to be raising the standards of the whole profession.

5. *More jobs.* In New York City, job opportunities are dismal. There are at least five times as many professionals as there are jobs. Regional theatres offer an alternative to New York. For several years, more professional actors have been working outside than inside New York; and designers, few of whom get more than *one* show per season in New York, are now shuttling back and forth across the country, providing scenery, lighting, and costumes for professional productions.

The network of regional professional companies is large and growing. Both in quantity and quality, they are a major force in the American theatre. They may be, when taken together, what so many critics and scholars have long sought: America's National Theatre.

FIGURE 5.5   Regional Theatre.
Professional theatres in many cities now offer much of the country's most exciting work. Here, Edward Albee's *Three Tall Women* at Syracuse Stage. *Directed by James Peck, with Darrie Lawrence, Maeve McGuire, and Judith Lightfoot Clarke. Photo by Douglas Wonders.*

Amateur Theatre

Amateur theatre is theatre performed and produced by people who do not earn their living in the theatre. The two major kinds of amateur theatres in the United States are educational theatres and community theatres.

Educational Theatres

Theatre existed in American colleges and universities even before there were professional theatres here. Theatre and drama were at first extracurricular, performed at special events like commencements. They were later included within the curriculum of departments like classics or English. Drama and theatre became college subjects in their own right only early in the twentieth century, when George Pierce Baker (1866–1935) instituted classes in playwriting (and later play production) at Radcliffe College (1903), Harvard (1913), and Yale (1925). By 1914, Carnegie Institute of Technology was offering the first theatre degree. Shortly after World War II, most colleges and universities organized departments of drama (often in combination with speech) and offered, in addition to coursework, both undergraduate and graduate degrees.

Although differing in principal emphases, the functions of educational theatres now closely parallel those of the regional professional companies: training future artists, developing new audiences, expanding the theatrical repertory, and providing jobs.

Obviously, the major goal of academic programs is the education and training of students. With the demise of the resident stock companies, training in acting, directing, playwriting, design, and technical production has been largely assumed by the academic institutions. Although many persons complain of the limitations placed on such training because of the basically conservative, even stultifying, atmosphere of many academic organizations, the fact remains that most training for the profession now takes place in this world. Although each program is unique, the general pattern of instruction involves some combination of formal classroom work and public performances of selected plays.

The number of educational theatre programs alone is sufficient to render their influence strong. Whereas the United States now boasts more than sixty professional regional companies, it supports more than two thousand theatre programs in colleges and universities. In small cities without resident professional companies, theatre productions at the college are the best for miles around, and in smaller towns, such productions may be the only opportunity to view a live performance. College and university theatres introduce thousands of students at all levels of education to a variety of plays. For many students, these are the first brush with live theatre.

Happily, because education is a primary goal, such theatres usually display a strong commitment to a wide range of plays and production styles. Alongside standard musicals, comedies, and domestic dramas, collegiate seasons are likely to include significant works from the past and experimental works for the future.

FIGURE 5.6   Educational Theatre.
More than two thousand college-level programs bring live theatre and theatre education to the United States. Here, *Flyin' West* by Pearl Cleage *at Western Michigan University, directed by James Daniels. Mary Whalen photo.*

Consequently, audiences for university theatre productions often enjoy more variety than in community or dinner theatres.

Too, the number of people required to maintain theatre in an academic setting has given the employment potential of the profession a healthy boost. At the college and university level alone, more than ten thousand productions are mounted each year and more than four thousand teachers are employed. When the growing number of high school drama classes, elementary programs in creative drama, and producing groups devoted to children's theatre are considered, it becomes clear that the academic complex is a major source of jobs. Indeed, educational theatre, considered at all levels, is probably the largest employer of theatre artists and scholars in the United States.

Community Theatres

Community theatres exist throughout the country. Cities with one or two regional professional companies may have a dozen community theatres. In towns with neither professional nor educational theatre (except, perhaps, the annual high school play), a community group may produce plays in a school, a church,

FIGURE 5.7   Community Theatre. Amateur theatres within local communities provide both art and recreation. This, the Elden Street Players, is one of more than thirty-five community theatres in the Washington, D.C. area. *Jo May and Herbert Rothenberg in The Night of the Iguana. Photo by Richard Downer.*

or a civic auditorium, providing entertainment and recreation for both participants and audiences.

Community theatres vary enormously. Some pay none of their participants, drawing directors, actors, and office personnel from volunteers in the community; others pay a skeleton staff—a technical director, box-office manager, and an artistic director—who work for a governing board of community volunteers. Almost no community theatres pay their actors or stage crew except under very special circumstances.

In communities without professional companies, community theatres fill the important role of introducing new audiences to the theatre and of keeping live theatre a part of the cultural life of a community. Where professional companies do exist, community theatres serve important recreational needs of people for whom participation in theatre is a greater pleasure than sitting in an audience. In their constant search for volunteers to help with production, such theatres regularly introduce many new people—especially young people—to the world of the theatre. Community theatres are, in fact, the first theatre experience for many people who later enter the profession. Finally, the relatively modest ticket prices of most community theatres bring into their theatres many who might not at first pay the price of a regional professional company. Some of these newcomers will become lifelong supporters, not only of their local community theatre but also of the regional professional companies and, when in New York, of its commercial theatres.

Theatres for Special Audiences

Some theatres cannot be categorized according to our earlier scheme, for they have both professional and amateur companies. Such theatres define themselves not by their financial structure but by the specific audiences that they aim to serve.

Children's Theatre

Among the most long-lasting of such groups are the children's theatres. Whether an established professional company, a university program, or an amateur group composed of community volunteers, whether using adult or child actors, a children's theatre aims to produce plays with special appeal to young audiences in order to instill in such audiences a love of the theatre.

The repertory usually consists of plays specially written for youth, using stories and issues of interest to that age group. Their range is great—from imaginative retellings of popular fairy stories, myths, and legends to treatments of contemporary social problems like drugs and divorce. Production styles vary, but most avoid narrow realism. With relatively modest ticket prices (adults often get in at reduced rates when accompanied by a child) and an unusually high commitment to their audiences, children's theatres introduce many young people to the art of the theatre and, from this large group, recruit some as lifelong supporters of all kinds of theatre.

Political Theatres

In another kind of theatre for special audiences, the goals are openly political: black theatre, Chicano theatre, feminist (or women's) theatre, and gay theatre. These groups note (correctly) that theatre through the ages has been controlled by middle- or upper-class white males. Although their individual aims vary, political theatre groups share common assumptions:

- That the interests of middle-class white males are not their own.

- That group awareness can be heightened by art. They seek, therefore, a theatre that can display their group's experiences and explore its problems.

These theatres serve their audiences in very different ways. Some favor intense political statements; others avoid polemical works altogether. Many urge a continued separation of their theatres from those of the mainstream; others work to integrate their own art and artists into the commercial theatre as quickly as possible. Some of the theatres produce works with high production values and traditional dramatic texts; others disregard accepted production values and work largely through improvisation. Some seek modest social change; others advocate revolution. Some have budgets of hundreds of thousands of dollars; others have no budget at all. Some charge audiences to attend; others perform in the streets and parks—wherever people congregate—and charge nothing.

Whatever their techniques, these theatres for special audiences strive to offer an alternative to the traditional theatre, which they believe has either demeaned them or ignored them.

THEATRE FUNDING

From its beginnings, American theatre has been organized as a profit-making business: Businesspeople invest money in a theatre company or a production and hope to recover their investment, with interest, from box-office receipts. This same pattern persists today on Broadway and Off-Broadway, though now the stakes are higher and the sale of film, television, and video rights joins the box office as a likely source of revenue. Broadway funding saw a new development in the late 1990s when a major entertainment corporation (Disney) brought a film-proven property (*The Lion King*) to Broadway at a reported cost of $20 million.

⊕FIGURE 5.8
New Funding Patterns.
On New York's 42nd Street, the Disney Corporation's lighted sign symbolizes the entry of this major entertainment conglomerate into Broadway.

Educational theatres are subsidized. Although the out-of-pocket costs of their productions must often be defrayed by the sale of tickets and program advertisements, the salaries of the faculty (who usually direct, design, manage, and mount the productions) are almost always paid by the university. Because the students who act and crew the productions are seldom paid, the majority of the labor costs associated with producing plays is charged to the university, not to the production. This substantial subsidy allows such theatres to be somewhat adventurous in their selection of plays.

With an occasional exception, government funding for theatre in this country has been conspicuously absent. Thus, one closely watched development was the establishment in 1965 of the National Endowment for the Arts (NEA), whose purpose was to encourage the development of the arts throughout the country. It did so in two major ways: by establishing state arts councils as coordinating and funding units and by subsidizing some existing performance groups. To receive grants, theatres had to be organized as not-for-profit theatres, a radical departure from the Broadway model.

The NEA continues to be controversial. Not all citizens agree that government should fund art when urgent social problems remain unsolved and unfunded. Not all citizens agree that taxpayers should pay for art that some find offensive. The latter issue led to a threatened cutoff of the NEA's funding in 1990 and 1995. Both issues promise to be debated for some time yet.

The precedent set by the NEA may help account for a relatively new phenomenon: Cities and counties, through their parks and recreation departments, are supporting theatre as a form of recreation, for citizens who seek an alternative to well-established programs in sports and crafts. Through both advice and money, recreation departments strive to improve the work of local community theatres, which they view as an important resource for the participants and their audiences.

Some people are encouraged that new patterns of funding may be emerging in the United States, patterns that will make it possible to produce theatre freed from the hit-or-flop syndrome, from the drudgery of the long run, and from an unemployment rate of more than 90 percent among Actors Equity members.

CURRENT ISSUES

Until recently, the word "professional" was a praise word in American theatre contexts. In many cases, it still is. Some university programs are still called "professional training" or "pre-professional" ones, and many people still use "professional" to mean trained, competent, and experienced. By contrast, "amateur" has connotations for many people of lower quality, lack of sophistication, zeal instead of skill. Yet, amateur theatres—college and university, community, political—far outnumber the professional, and in some cases their different goals are bringing professionalism into question.

Professionalism has not always been essential to the theatre. As theatre history shows (see Chapters 11–13), much of the first two thousand years of theatre was done by amateurs. Yet, since about Shakespeare's time, a line has been drawn between those who make their livings and devote their lives to the theatre, and those who engage in it out of love. Despite hardships, the professionals have built a body of lore and tradition that has set them apart and elevated them, and the amateurs have mostly copied them and admired them.

Now, however, social changes may have altered the importance of professionalism in theatre. People with agendas as different as those of children's theatre and political theatre are questioning such aspects of professionalism as "talent" and training. Talent, they contend, is a false idea, one that destroys participation in some kinds of theatre (e.g., children's). To look for and encourage "talent" in a child, they say—that is, to ape the values of professionalism—is to cause a child or beginner to falsify, to suppress his or her real wants, to head toward the insincere smile and the pert manner of the TV commercial. Or, the po-

LINKS to more about theatre

Marvin Carlson, *Places of Performance: The Semiotics of Theatre Architecture,* 1989.

Margo Jones, *Theatre-in-the-Round,* 1951. Seminal work.

42nd Street. The Myth of Showbiz—instant stardom, your name in lights, true love—or, Theatre As It Never Was.

< **www1.playbill.com** > Showbiz website. Theatre Central is reachable from here, or directly at < www.theatre-central.com >. Not exactly rocket science, but hit "Sites" and mess around.

litical theatre person contends, professionalism causes performers to use standards other than the political—again, to falsify in the name of a skill or of a well-written speech or a well-shaped scene. The professional, they say, is so habituated to gloss (even to glitz) that he or she cannot be serious, cannot be committed more to idea than to craft.

From yet another point of view, proponents of participatory theatre say that the purposes of professionalism are irrelevant to the situation of most people. Ours is an age of participation, they say, of democratic group activities; it is not how well people do things, but what they put in and what they get back that matter. Competence and experience are meaningless in such a context.

Yet again, some contemporary audiences show unease with extreme polish or obvious skill. Carefully crafted speech has given way to inarticulateness, in some cases; at the extreme, people want to watch real people and not actors at all. Only the real, they appear to be saying, is authentic. Professionalism is the opposite of authenticity. (But would they ever say this about professional sports?)

What, then, is the place of professionalism? Is "professional" a synonym for artificial? Or for elitist? Is the study and perfection of a craft like acting the enemy of authenticity? Is the ability to do something well, through long training and practice, itself a symptom of untrustworthiness? Or, to look again at the example of sports, what is it about the theatre that would make its professionalism suspect while professionalism in sports is almost worshipped?

Contrarily, what should people who want to participate rather than enter professional theatre do? Should they actually avoid training? Should they consciously avoid the example of the professionals? Or should they call themselves something other than amateurs and leave that word for people who take their standards from the professionals but cannot devote their lives to—or make a living from—the theatre?

KEY TERMS

Check your understanding against this list. Brief definitions are in the Glossary; page references there will direct you to appropriate pages. (Persons are page-referenced in the Index.)

alley stage	Off-Broadway
apron	Off-Off-Broadway
arena stage	orchestra
balcony	proscenium (arch and theatre)
booth stage	regional theatre
box	road show
Broadway	sight lines
educational theatre	thrust stage
forestage	vomitory
gallery	wings

chapter 6

The Playwright

OBJECTIVES

When you have completed this chapter, you should be able to:

- Understand the implications of the words *playwright* and *playwriting*

- Differentiate dramatic dialogue from ordinary language

- List and discuss conditions that seem to encourage playwriting

- Explain the playwright's relationships with dramatic and theatrical conventions, with audiences, and with the rehearsal process

THE NATURE OF PLAYWRIGHTS AND PLAYWRITING

We must not misunderstand the nature of a playwright's craft. Playwrights create replicas of human action—not records of it (novels) or responses to it (poems). The complexity of playwriting is suggested by the very language that we use to describe it—play*wright* and play*writing*. Plays are both *made* and *written*.

Playwright

Wright means *maker*. Just as a wheelwright is a maker of wheels and a cartwright is a maker of carts, a playwright is a maker of plays. Because playwrights use words on paper to set down their creations, they seem to be merely "writing." They are in fact, however, creating and organizing actions, using human-like beings (characters) to do so; they are creating replicas of human actions and then setting forth these replicas in language (writing). It is partly accident that what a playwright does looks like what a novelist or poet does—setting down words on paper. If playwrights had a different set of symbols to work with (like a musician's notes or a choreographer's notations) the differences between playwrights and other writers would be clearer.

Playwriting

Although we refer to a play*wright,* we also talk of play*writing* and so acknowledge the importance of *writing* to what a playwright does. Playwrights set forth their replicas of human action in large part by inventing "language" for dramatic "characters" to speak to one another; that is, play*wrights write* dialogue that actors (pretending to be characters) will speak to one another. Dramatic dialogue, therefore, is not like ordinary language; it must forward plot, reveal character, and express idea. The fact that playwrights write words for actors to say and for audiences to hear means that their language must be more active, more intense, and more selective than either everyday speech or other kinds of fictional speech (novels). Playwrights also "write" nonwords: silences, gestures, rhythms, visual images.

Drama and Literature

This dual nature of play*wright* and play*writing* gives a clue to a quality of drama and dramatists that is sometimes misunderstood. Drama is not *primarily* literature, and dramatists are not *primarily* literary artists, although both can be studied (and indeed in colleges and universities often are studied) *as if* they were. There is a dimension of literary art in drama, of course, but there are other essential dimensions as well. Many highly respected novelists and poets are quite incapable of writing for the stage (great romantic poets like Wordsworth and Shelley are examples); such people were fine literary artists, but they were not good theatrical artists. Conversely, the language of many highly regarded playwrights, when analyzed as literature, seems alternately feeble or overblown (Eugene O'Neill comes to mind at once), but when actors speak the lines in the theatre, the effect is powerful and lasting; such playwrights are fine theatrical artists, but they are not good literary artists. Only the rare person is both literary artist and theatre artist in equal measure, Shakespeare being the premiere example.

We can see, then, that playwrights are only in part literary artists. Playwrights are similar in some superficial ways to other literary artists but distinct from them in the playwright's need to respond to the special requirements of the theatre—its conventions, its audiences, and its demand that living actors enact what is created.

CREATING PLAYWRIGHTS

Why someone becomes a playwright instead of a novelist or poet, a secretary or a salesperson, is something of a mystery.

From the Theatre

Playwrights frequently come from within the theatre; they are "people of the theatre," who are "theatre-wise." For example, the Roman actor Plautus was a playwright who wrote plays for himself and his actors, and the French actor Molière was a playwright who created vehicles for himself and his troupe. Shakespeare, only a minor actor, wrote many of his most famous roles for other actors in his company, actors whose special strengths and weaknesses he understood and exploited. Such people of the theatre most often work within the dominant theatrical styles of their day, and they probably dominate the theatrical mainstreams.

From Other Fields

Playwrights may start out as something else—not as actors or directors, but as something from outside the theatre altogether, like journalists or stock-checkers. These are not people of the theatre; they are not theatre-wise. Indeed, these people, ignorant of the current conventions of the theatre, may write in new and refreshing ways and so exert a strong appeal to those bored with current practices. (Or they may write naively and unappealingly.) Their good plays benefit from the newcomer's gift of ignorance: that is, newcomers may not follow (because they do not know) the plays of the mainstream theatre in form, style, length, subject matter, or language. Plays by such newcomers may rarely find commercial production, but they are often welcomed in the avant garde, where they are considered experimental. Then, if their appeal lasts, they may form the basis of a new kind of theatre. Indeed, much of the vitality of *new* movements in theatre of any age comes from the entry of people from entirely outside the theatre who write a play or plays that are unwittingly innovative.

FIGURE 6.1   The Playwright and the Play.
Molière, both playwright and actor, was the greatest of French comic dramatists. Right, his *Miser* at the University of the Pacific, *directed by James R. Taulli, designed by Peter Lach.*

Inviting Conditions

Although what draws people to theatre and to playwriting remains a mystery, several conditions seem to encourage playwriting.

Other Playwrights

It is not an accident that new playwrights often appear in groups. Whether they are the University Wits of the Elizabethan period or the Off-Off-Broadway playwrights of the early 1960s, they are drawn to playwriting by the same theatrical conditions at the same time—in the case of the University Wits, the explosion of theatrical interest in Oxford and London; in the case of the Off-Off Broadway playwrights, the explosion of theatrical excitement in New York City. Their very number, in turn, increases the excitement, which in turn attracts more new playwrights, so that working playwrights tend to produce other working playwrights.

A Vital Theatre

A dying or dead theatre rarely attracts new playwrights; a vital one does—and paradoxically, a vital commercial theatre attracts new playwrights both to itself and to its avant-garde opposite. A theatre's ability to attract new playwrights, then, is one measure of its own health.

FIGURE 6.2 The Playwright and the Play. Henrik Ibsen, the "father of modern drama," and a scene from his *Rosmersholm,* with the great Eleonora Duse.

Good Social and Economic Treatment

Playwrights need a theatre that offers them a decent living and an acceptable place in society. It is sometimes argued, for example, that the English theatre did not attract would-be playwrights in the eighteenth century because the licensing laws made the craft financially unattractive, and many turned to the novel instead. In the United States today, it is said that playwrights can "make a killing but not a living" in the theatre, meaning that one playwright may occasionally hit it really big, earning money to live on for a lifetime, but that most playwrights cannot find enough productions to support themselves. They often turn instead to movies and television. When, on the other hand, a theatre offers large financial rewards, as the American theatre did from the 1920s to the 1950s, many new writers are drawn to it.

TRAINING PLAYWRIGHTS

Unlike actors, directors, and designers, playwrights do not, as a rule, go through structured periods of formal training. To be sure, there are playwriting programs in American universities, but their record of producing playwrights who write plays of recognized quality is not comparable with the impressive records in acting, directing, and design. Courses in playwriting often familiarize theatre students with the problems of the playwright and give an enriching new slant on the other areas of theatre work; advanced degrees in playwriting are frequently combined with scholarly work in such a way that playwriting becomes an adjunct of critical study. Playwriting as an academic discipline, however, suffers from the same problems as creative writing in general, and when it seems to produce results it is because the same factors are at work: teachers who are themselves artists and who teach as much by example as by precept; constant encouragement of creativity itself, so that the student is surrounded by other writers and playwrights; and strong professional links with agents, producers, and publishers, so that entry into the mainstream is greatly eased.

To be sure, certain techniques of playwriting can be taught and learned. When a theatrical style remains in vogue for a long period, playwrights can be "taught" the hallmarks of that style, meaning really that they can be taught how to imitate the plays that have already succeeded in that style. Thus, in the realistic theatre, would-be playwrights could be taught to put exposition into the mouths of characters who had a reason for explaining things; they could be taught to prepare for the third-act resolution by planting information in Act I; they could be taught that taxi drivers and duchesses do not speak in the same way; and so on. Insofar, then, as playwriting is a craft, such teaching was and still can be effective. Its limitations lie in the difference between the craft and the art of writing for the theatre and between the imitation of an existing style and the innovation of a new one (the newcomer's "gift of ignorance"). At some point in every age, however, the relevance of an existing theatrical style ends, because styles that have dominated for a long time become increasingly drained of their potential for saying something new.

When imitation of an existing style is not the main object, the teaching of playwriting is far less certain and much less successful. Here is where the gifted newcomer, without experience in the theatre, may suddenly appear to take plays and playwriting in wholly new directions. For a time, critics may cry out that the new works are "not really plays," audiences may be enraged, and teachers of playwriting may be mystified—and lessonless. (The young Tennessee Williams was not thought very good when he tried studying playwriting in a university.)

FROM PAGE TO STAGE: PROFESSIONAL ISSUES

Writing the Play

Plays begin as a great variety of things: a story overheard, a chance remark, a note jotted down on a slip of paper. Plays may set out to retell a legend or myth; they may treat a bit of history or a slice of daily life; they may be adapted from a novel or a ballad; they may be an imagined, onstage symbol or gesture.

And from such beginnings, different playwrights take widely different tracks.

The success of the playwright depends, in large part, on how well he or she copes with the peculiar demands of plays (as distinct from forms of writing like poems or novels). For, whatever else a playwright must do, he or she must take into account the nature of the theatre and the role of its audiences in performance.

Conventions

Playwrights always have to strike a balance between their own imaginations and the realities of the theatres in which they work. Plays must, among other things, provide a framework for other theatrical arts, especially acting and design, and so plays are circumscribed by both theatrical and dramatic conventions. These matters, and the technical means of accomplishing them, are things that playwriting courses can teach or the playwright can learn in the theatre itself as apprentice, actor, etc.

In the modern realistic theatre, for example, playwrights have had to strike a balance between their own impulse to expand meaning and the stage's impulse to limit meaning to the same role that it plays in real life. For earlier playwrights, language was a primary means of theatrical communication, and early realistic plays about upper-class life could be heavily verbal because the people that the plays were about were (or so it was believed) articulate and literate. However, as the theatre focused more on inarticulate protagonists in a democratized theatre, verbalism became a less useful tool, and playwrights found themselves trying to find a compromise between their own impulse to "say" things and their characters' inability to do so.

Other times have required playwrights to strike different sorts of balances. The Greek theatre, for example, limited the playwright to only three actors and

FIGURE 6.3 The Playwright and the Play. Athol Fugard, South African playwright, actor, and director, in his own play *The Captain's Tiger. Photo by Neil Fleitell, courtesy of Mr. Fleitell and Athol Fugard.*

thus affected the number and flow of characters within plays; Shakespeare's theatre used men to portray women's roles, a practice that surely affected the nature of female characters in drama. Playwrights in seventeenth-century France were expected to use language and portray morality appropriate to aristocrats; playwrights of the early nineteenth century were expected to permit pyrotechnic displays of acting and to incorporate incredible feats of spectacle. Whatever the age, no playwright escapes the compromise required between the creative impulse and the conditions of the theatre.

Audiences

"The drama's laws/The drama's patrons give," wrote Samuel Johnson in the eighteenth century. He meant, of course, that audiences—by their attendance and their responses—decide what traits plays ought to have and which plays are good or bad. Audiences, rather than critics or theorists, establish the "laws" of drama.

The remark illustrates the uneasy relationship between the playwright and the audience, for, to the playwright, the audience is a fickle monster that can make the artist either rich and loved or humiliated and poor. Between playwright and audience exists a relationship that is often ambivalent in the extreme.

Audiences do not care for "the laws of drama" so often promoted by critics, theorists, and scholars. Audiences care about their own responses. They are, however, often conservative and cautious. When they go to a theatre, especially a mainstream, commercial theatre, they want to be entertained, to get their money's worth. They seldom want to be lectured at, shocked, offended, frightened, or bored. As a result, they look with enthusiasm on any novelty—so long as it resembles what they are already familiar with.

The audience's desire for something that is new enough to be interesting but familiar enough to be comfortable often leaves playwrights in a quandary. They may be torn between their own wish to innovate and the audiences' insistence that they imitate features of earlier works. And playwrights must find their audience if they are to work as playwrights. What to do?

Getting the Play Produced

In recent years, the number of theatres in which new plays can be produced in the United States and Canada has increased. Many plays now begin their lives in regional theatres; in addition, organizations like the National Playwright's Conference of the O'Neill Theatre Center give first productions to a wide spectrum of scripts, many of which are later produced elsewhere. New York, however, remains

FIGURE 6.4   The Playwrights and the Play.
Co-authors Anne Fliotsos and Bob Johnson and a scene from their musical parody
*Oedipus! The New Musical Comedy. Courtesy of Anne Fliotsos and Bob Johnson.
Photo of Mr. Johnson by Adina Wachman.*

THINKING ABOUT PLAYWRITING

Lorraine Hansberry (1930–1965) wrote to an aspiring playwright whose play she had been asked to read: *"I longed for tightness in the writing . . . every single line MUST count."* And indeed, ordinary speech and dramatic dialogue are very different. Take a tape recorder (or a notebook) to a social gathering. Record three or four minutes of conversation. Listen to it carefully to grasp how it differs from dialogue on television or in film. Then convert this ordinary social speech into dramatic dialogue.

the goal of most playwrights. There are two reasons: money and status. Broadway royalties are far higher than anywhere else, and Broadway production is subject to the best reviewing and is the most prestigious.

Plays are not produced at any of these theatres by accident. Nor are many new plays that attract widespread attention (except at an institution like the O'Neill Center) scripts that come out of nowhere. Most are submitted to regional theatres or Broadway or Off-Broadway producers by agents. Far less often, a play may reach a producer by way of an actor or a director. In any case, the playwright's first high hurdle is finding that first production, whatever the medium used to reach a producing organization.

The new playwright may at first write plays that attract only a small audience, but the playwright will be encouraged if even a small audience is supportive. After a small initial success, the playwright may move toward the mainstream; an audience may be moving toward the playwright at the same time, both being the product of historical change. Sometimes, audiences accept new language, new ideas, and new forms with a speed that is startling.

If the moment is not right, however, the playwright may not find an audience, may not even find production, and then will stop writing or go to television or films.

Working with the Play in Rehearsal

Producers have readers who read scripts and make comments. When a script is accepted for production, it already has an accompanying list of such comments as well as the producer's own views; added to these will be the ideas of the director when one is chosen. Each principal actor will add ideas, and each of these people—producer, director, actors—may have still other ideas that have come from friends, spouses, lovers, and relatives. The playwright having a first play done is tempted to try to please everybody. By the time several plays have been done, however, the playwright may be downright rude about suggestions coming from any source at all. Between these two extremes lies the kernel of the playwright's work during the production period: accepting ideas for changes that are wisely based in the unique circumstances of the production.

Perhaps regrettably, in the modern American theatre the director is assumed to have considerable critical skill and to be an expert in everything from dramatic structure to dialogue. Changes in a script, however, are rarely simple; as the Broadway playwright William Gibson said some years ago, altering a play is like taking bricks out of a wall: for every one that is taken out, half a dozen others have to be put back. At times, the playwright wonders what it was about the play that ever caused people to want to do it, because they have asked for so many changes that nothing seems to be left of the original. Confronted with this situation, the playwright may throw a temper tantrum, go home, or say, as more than one successful playwright has, "Do it as it is!"

Paying the Playwright

A few playwrights do make livings, especially as the number of regional theatres has multiplied, but the hit-or-flop life of Broadway still prevails; the playwright can still make only a killing, rarely a living. Standard Broadway contracts, under the aegis of the Dramatists Guild, give the playwright a percentage of the theatre's weekly gross, a percentage that climbs as the gross climbs past certain plateaus. On a hit, these figures can be impressive—thousands of dollars a week. On a modest success, they can be a thousand a week or less. On a flop, nothing. Considering that few playwrights have a successful play every year, we can easily see that the income from even a hit must be spread over several years, and that after an agent's commission and professional expenses and taxes are taken out,

FIGURE 6.5
Playwright and Payment.
Playwrights are now paid royalties on performances; before the mid-nineteenth century, they received a flat fee or proceeds from a "benefit" performance. Here, a ticket for such a benefit.

the prorated remainder may be less than many businesspeople take home. There is, of course, the significant additional income of film and television sales—and perhaps most importantly, there is the secondary income of amateur and stock production.

Amateur rights are handled mostly by two organizations, the Dramatists Play Service and Samuel French, Incorporated. They collect royalties on productions by amateurs (community, school, and university theatres) for the life of the play's copyright—since the Copyright Law of 1977, the author's life plus fifty years. Although the royalty on a single performance of a play is small, the collective royalty per year on a play that is popular with the nation's several thousand community and college theatres can be large, and even plays that fail on Broadway can become staples of amateur theatre and go on providing income for decades.

Yet, with all this, relatively few people make a living as playwrights. It is a difficult craft that requires special talent, and it is made far more difficult by the conditions under which plays must find production. Many potential playwrights now move to television and film, and there is some question whether—despite grants, theatres, and organizations that encourage new plays—playwrights may continue to decline in number until the theatre itself recovers its vigor.

Establishing a Career

Once established, the American playwright enjoys one or more years of acceptance and then, more often than not, begins to lose the audience. Yesterday's innovator becomes tomorrow's has-been. Rare is the contemporary playwright who is a lifelong success, even a lifelong presence in the theatre; most reach a plateau and then seem to imitate themselves or to decline. One American playwright estimated that an Off-Broadway or Broadway career lasts ten years. Significant exceptions appeared, however, in the 1990s: three playwrights who had had first successes in the 1960s and 1970s (Edward Albee, Terence McNally, and John Guare) were major prizewinners.

LINKS to more about theatre

George S. Kaufman and Moss Hart, *Light Up the Sky.*

Toby Cole and Helen Krich Chinoy, *Playwrights on Playwriting,* 1960.

Robert Nemiroff, *To Be Young, Gifted, and Black,* 1969. Lorraine Hansberry.

FIGURE 6.6
The Playwright and the Critic.
Goethe and Schiller, major German
playwrights of the late eighteenth and
nineteenth centuries. Goethe was also
a critic and theoretician.

WHAT IS GOOD PLAYWRITING?

Good playwriting is playwriting that produces good theatre. Exactly what makes
a play good is the subject of continuing dispute, even among theatre scholars, but
some of the traits of such plays have already been suggested in Chapters 3 and 4.
The questions at the ends of these chapters can offer a beginning glimpse of what
makes for good playwriting.

The great German theorist Goethe suggested another set of questions to help
assess the worth of a play and playwright: 1. What did the author set out to do?
2. Did he or she do it? 3. Was it worth doing? These questions are useful inasmuch
as they remind us that a playwright may exhibit great technical skill (he or she set
out to do something and did it quite well), yet still produce an inconsequential
play (it wasn't worth doing). Great plays, finally, must do more than entertain, although they must do that at a minimum.

CURRENT ISSUES

In our move from the modern to the postmodern world, we seem to be redefining the relationship between individuals and groups.

Some people seem bent on calling into question the value of the individual, including the individual creator. Groups, teams, networks—all are praised for their presumed democracy and polyvocalism. In business, sports, and computerization, the new, preferred way of working is collectively and cooperatively rather than independently: Movies and television programs are created by groups, science and engineering projects are planned and carried out by teams, and even historians now study the past by exploring how certain groups—immigrants, working women, slaves—lived rather than (as before) identifying the role of selected great individuals. The trend is even felt in social settings: People who don't want to join the group, wear the styles of the group, speak the language of the group, join the activities of the group, and are viewed with suspicion.

Fading, it seems, is the rugged individualist, the individual genius, the solitary thinker once prized as the leader of society. Will playwrights, the true individualists of theatre's past several hundred years, disappear? Change their role? Merge into a team effort?

Some find the new trend—both in theatre and out of it—worrying. If groups are to be increasingly prized, they ask, what are the dangers to privacy? How will individual rights be assured when group rights conflict with them? What will happen to the idea of authorship?

KEY TERMS

Check your understanding against this list. Brief definitions are in the Glossary; page references there will direct you to appropriate pages. (Persons are page-referenced in the Index.)

conventions (dramatic, theatrical)
copyright
royalty
wright

chapter 7

The Actor

OBJECTIVES

When you have completed this chapter, you should be able to:

- Explain the paradox of the actor

- Explain the relationship between actor and character and between character and real person

- Explain the goals of rehearsal

- Understand the actor's vocabulary

- Explain how an actor creates a role

- Discuss the possibilities of acting as a profession

THE NATURE OF ACTING

The actor stands at the center of the theatre. The actor is its linchpin, its keystone; without him or her, there is nothing—an empty building, a hollow space. Directors cannot direct or designers design without actors; the playwright can create only works to be read like novels.

The actor alone *can* make theatre without the help of other artists. The plays that the actor invents may not be very good, it is true, and they may even be merely stories told well (as in oral cultures, when the storyteller is an actor-narrator). The actor can make costumes, can build a theatre, and can provide at least crude scenery for it. Out of such an actor-intensive theatre may occasionally grow a sophisticated one, such as the *commedia dell'arte* of Renaissance Italy (see p. 302). More often, however, such an actors' theatre changes in the direction of the theatre that we know, adding playwright, designer, and director. No matter how far this theatre develops, however, it remains the descendant of that primal theatre—actor-centered.

The Actor and the Performer

Acting must not be thought of merely as an ability to entertain—to clown at parties or to tell jokes superbly. The latter are parts of a talent for *performing*—that is, for reaching and delighting an audience without regard to character or theatrical action. As we have already tried to suggest, there is more to acting than this. A good actor is also a good performer; a good performer, however, may not be a very good actor.

Some kinds of theatre or related arts put a higher premium on performing than on acting; circus high-wire work, for example, requires great performers and has no use for actors. Musical comedy, on the other hand, requires both acting and performing, for the ability to "sell" a song requires performing of a high level. Because performers must often play themselves, strong performers who act theatrical roles sometimes overpower the dramatic character so that it is obscured.

The performer plays *to* the audience; the actor plays the character *for* the audience.

The Paradox of the Actor

The French theorist Denis Diderot (1713–1784) used the expression "the paradox of the actor" as the title for an essay on acting in which he tried to capture what seems to be an essential contradiction in the art: *In order to appear natural, the actor must be artificial.*

This contradiction takes several forms, whose language and whose specifics change from age to age; nevertheless, the paradox remains at the center of most thinking about the art.

Natural Versus Artificial

Throughout the history of acting, almost every change in acting for the mainstream theatre has been seen as a move toward the "natural" or the "real." Partly, changes in philosophy are at work: When an age's idea of "what it is to be human" changes, the manner of depicting human beings on the stage changes as well, and the older concept of "real" or "natural" is viewed as outdated and "nonhuman"— that is, artificial.

However, there is a distinction to be made as well between the idea of what humanity *is* and the idea of what humans *might* or *should be.* Certain ages and certain forms of theatre have prized an idea of humanity that was rigidly defined in its behaviors; such an idea of humanity sets up many "proprieties"—rules based on the ideal—that must be observed. On the stage, elegance of diction, grace of movement, and limitation of gesture may become almost moral issues, and we find such extremes of stage propriety as the "rule" that the left hand must never be used for an important gesture.

Such a strictly limited kind of acting will seem highly "artificial" to anybody who believes that the stage must imitate life explicitly. Much of the conflict between Neoclassical and Romantic acting in the early nineteenth century arose from precisely this difference. The "artificial" actor in such a dispute sees the greatest allegiance to the rules of the theatre, based on an ideal and not on a literal concept of "what it is to be human"; the "natural" actor sees the greatest allegiance as being to life—or to an interpretation of life. Neither idea is better than the other, although bitter battles have been fought over their differences.

FIGURE 7.1   The Paradox of the Actor.
Every age has its own idea of what seems "natural," but the actors' paradox is that they must always seek the "natural" through some at least partly artificial process. Here, gestures and postures from a nineteenth-century book on acting.

Artificial acting must not be confused with performing. Artificial acting may seem like performing because of its planned and deliberate gestures, and its sometimes exaggerated vocal effects. Artificial acting, however, focuses on communicating an idea of character in theatrical action; performing focuses on communicating the performer.

Inspiration Versus Technique

Our own age is one whose theatrical heritage is primarily a "natural" one, at least in the realistic theatre. Modern American actors sometimes speak disparagingly of an actor who is "technical," meaning one who builds character out of careful, conscious use of body and voice—meticulously rehearsed inflections, carefully chosen poses and gestures, and so on. Their belief is that "technical" actors work mechanically and so fail to bring imagination and life to their work. The technical actor is seen as "full of tricks." Again, there is a strong belief that "technique" is somehow an enemy of the convincing, the lifelike, the believable.

At the far extreme from the technical actor is the "inspirational" one, whose work, although carefully rehearsed, is not assembled from external behaviors but is created through application of mental and emotional techniques that supposedly work to reach the actor's emotional and mental center and then somehow push outward into onstage movement and vocalization. In theory, the character created by the inspirational actor will be more "real," more "natural" because it does not rise from conscious intellectual work, but from the inner sources that also give rise to music and poetry. To the inspirational actor, her approach is fresh and her creation original.

Inner and Outer

Technical and inspirational acting have their direct counterparts in "outer" and "inner" acting. As one actor put it some years ago, "I like to build my house first—then I start to live in it." She meant that she liked to create the "outer" part of the role; then, comfortable with that—voice, posture, costume, gesture—she could move inward toward emotional intensity and conviction, believably "living in" the shell she had created.

Other actors work from the inside out. All of their early work will be devoted to mental, emotional, and spiritual exploration. Only when that work is completed do they feel that an outer structure can be built. In the cases of both the "inner" and the "outer" actor, truth to the character is being sought, and the difference is really a difference of emphasis and of sequence. The "inner–outer" distinction is not quite the same as the "technical–inspirational" one; the "technical" actor's work begins and ends with externals, whereas the "outer" actor's work finally leads inward, and the "inner" actor's work leads toward externals in a way that the "inspirational" actor's does not. Inspiration supposedly gives rise to externals through a nonintellectual leap, and, as Diderot suggested, those externals can vary from performance to performance and may supply only an occasional "sublime moment."

◀ C-1.
Mask. Mexico.

▲ C-2. **Mask.** American Indian (Eastern Iroquois), United States.

◀ C-3. **Mask.** India. *Courtesy of Farley Richmond.*

◀ **C-4. Masks, Greek tragedy.** *The Oresteia* at the University of South Carolina. *Directed by Robert Richmond, designs by David Coleman. Jim O'Connor, artistic director.*

C-5. Masks and Mask-like Makeup. ▶ *The Death and Life of Bessie Head,* at the Museum Little Theatre, Gaborone, Botswana. *Courtesy of David Kerr.*

◀ **C-6. Half-Mask, Commedia Dell'Arte.** Interlocken European Commedia Troupe. *Photo by and courtesy of Peter Avery.*

C-7. Modern Mask for Roman ▶
Comedy. Plautus' *Pot of Gold, directed*
by Scott K. Strode, design by Stephen
A. Batzka and masks by James R. Adams
at Manchester College Theatre.

◀ **C-8. Makeup as Mask.** Krishna
in an Indian *Krishnanattam. Courtesy*
of Farley Richmond.

C-9. Makeup as ▶
Mask: Beijing
Opera. A *jing*
actor makes up.
Courtesy of the
People's Republic
of China.

m a s k s and Faces

C-10. Makeup as Mask/Face. ▶
The Scarecrow in
The Wiz at College
of St. Mary-of-the-
Woods. *Directed by
Sharon Ammen.*

◀ **C-11. Makeup as Face.** Steven Angus in Heiner Muller's
Quartet at the Open Theatre/TUTA, *directed by Zeljko Djukic,
costume and makeup design by Natasa Djukic.*

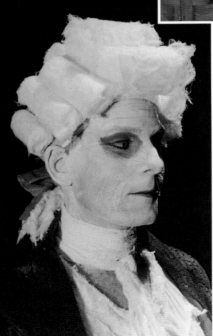

C-12. The Actor's Face. Walt Witcover ▶
as The Mikado in Masterworks Laboratory
Theatre, Inc.'s *Innocent Merriment,
or Gilbert Without Sullivan.*

Being and Pretending

To reach emotional truth, it has been said, the actor must *be* the character; on the contrary, another point of view insists, the actor must always stand aloof from the character and *pretend*. Here is precisely the paradox that Diderot observed. If an actor were really to be the character, how would he or she control onstage behavior? What would keep the actor from becoming inaudible at times? What would keep the actor, as Othello, from actually killing the actor who plays Desdemona? What would cause the actor to modulate the voice, control the tempo of a performance, listen to other actors? And, contrarily, if the actor always pretends, what will he or she be but a lifeless imitation of humanity? How will the actor keep the speeches from sounding like empty nonsense? How will gestures be anything but graceful hand-waving?

Because the actor is at the center of the theatre, this paradox is the paradox of the theatre itself: In order to be convincing, one must lie. The actor both "is" *and* "pretends," exploiting both inner and outer, both technique and inspiration. It is never enough for the *actor* to be satisfied that a sigh or a smile is perfectly truthful; the sigh or smile must also have the carrying power and the communicative value to be perfectly truthful *to the audience*.

The two halves of the paradox of the actor are always in tension. Their relative strengths vary from actor to actor and from age to age. It is only rarely that a really good actor will be found at either extreme.

The Actor and the Character

Understanding Character

It should now be clear that actors neither create real human beings, on the one hand, nor somehow transform themselves and erase their own personalities on the other. Instead they engage in a creative act whose end product is a *construct,* that is, an entity made by human agency for a particular purpose. Both the actor and the audience must be very careful to remember that the creation is a construct and not a full-fleshed, living human being, even though actors and audiences may speak of the construct by its name, just *as if* it were a real person named Hamlet.

THINKING ABOUT ACTING

According to American actor Denzel Washington (1954–present), *"Acting is like investigative reporting. [In both fields] you search out your character."* List the information about character that an actor searches out in the script. In addition to the script, list other tools that an actor can use to investigate character, and describe how each can be helpful.

The construct remains an invention, and one actor's construct may be quite different from another's construct of the same name—Laurence Olivier's from Kevin Kline's Hamlet, for example.

In the literary sense, character is a construct that represents human personality and that expresses itself through *action*. In the sense of the word used by Aristotle, the effectiveness of a character depends on how well it fits into and effects plot. This idea has an important implication for the actor: We define character on the basis of the function within the artistic whole and *not merely on the basis of how well it imitates a human being*. Therefore, a dramatic construct may be a convincing imitation of a human being in its superficial attributes—it may talk like one and may have preferences in clothes and food and entertainment like one— and yet it may be a "bad" character in that it makes no important contribution to the artistic whole and the action. An actor who concentrates on mannerisms of the character and fails to grasp the character's function as contributor to the action will fail and will be guilty of what the Russian actor and theorist Stanislavski called "tendencies."

For the actor, *character* means something like "the imitation of a human being as it expresses itself through the words and the decisions created by the author, *in relation to the other characters in the play and their decisions and words.*" The actor's character exists on the stage (only) and has no life off the stage; the actor's character exists in an artificial time scheme that is quite different from the time scheme of real life. It may be helpful for the actor to figure out where the character is coming from when it walks on the stage, what it has been doing, and so on, but such analysis has to be limited strictly to conclusions relevant to onstage action and onstage time or it will lead to sideshows and tendencies, or even to the creation of a play that the author never wrote (and one that, regrettably for the audience, takes place offstage).

The actor is a person, the character is a construct. In order for the character to *seem* to be a person during the two or three hours of performance, actors use their *consciousness,* their *instruments,* and their *imaginations.*

Constructing Character

Consciousness.   Consciousness refers to matters that are under the conscious control of the actor. Discipline, for example, is essential because actors cannot create character unless they can control themselves and their work. Concentration is crucial, as the expression "the show must go on" suggests. Although a cliché, the expression captures well the actor's tenacious ability to continue when his or her own physical or emotional self is hurt or threatened. Without proper discipline and concentration, no other work of the actor can succeed.

Analyzing text is also important, for actors must be able to break a dramatic text into acting units and understand the complex relationships among parts of the play and its characters. Understanding the play and the character's place in it, however, is not enough. Actors must then discover ways of communicating their under-

FIGURE 7.2   The Actor and the Role.
The greatest of American nineteenth-century actors, Charlotte Cushman sometimes
played male roles, as here: Romeo, to her sister's Juliet. Crossing gender was one way of
competing at the top with male actors.

standing to audiences. In this regard, making good choices is an essential task of an
actor, who must discriminate among possible solutions to each acting problem.
Choices may be as simple as selecting between two qualities of voice for a word or
as complex as identifying a memory among many memories from which an emotion
springs. In today's theatre, actors are aided in this phase of work by directors.

Instrument.   By *instrument* we mean the entire physical self (body and voice) that
the actor uses in playing a character. Whereas the audience does not see or hear the
work of the consciousness or the imagination directly, it always sees and hears the
actor's instrument, for the instrument is the medium through which the others express themselves.

   The instrument is given to the actor at birth; that is, the size and shape of
bones, the delicate tuning of vocal mechanisms, and the size and shape of the body
are given. The instrument can be developed, however, through training.

Imagination.   Imagination is the wellspring of creativity, the mysterious force
that impels all art. Sometimes the imagination works while the conscious mind is
asleep: Imagination opens the door to memory, processes nonrational data, and offers new ideas for performance.

Talent: A Synthesis

Successful actors use consciousness, instrument, and imagination in balance. The
complexity of the process is beyond description. Talent, we may be able to say, is
the ability of the consciousness to inspire in the imagination a set of actions and
sounds that the instrument can express to an audience as theatrical character.

TRAINING ACTORS

Although there are supposedly actors who are "born," and although there have
been young children who were talented actors, it is a fact of theatrical life that all
actors must train long and hard and must refresh that training throughout their
careers. There was a time when would-be actors "came up" as apprentices, moving from small roles in minor companies to larger roles and more important theatres. They learned by imitation and by taking hints from experienced actors.
Nowadays, most professional actors have formal training, either in a college or in
one or more private studios.

   Actor training does not refer to a specific kind of study or to a set period of
time. There are a number of actor-training systems. The most influential in the
United States and Canada are those based on the ideas of Konstantin Stanislavski.

Other systems have very different foundations, such as the psychological theory of transactional analysis or the theory of games and improvisations. Different as these are, they are helpful in varying degrees to different actors. *No one system is best for everybody.* The important thing about these systems is that they organize the work of the actor's consciousness, instrument, and imagination. Without a workable system, the would-be actor makes progress only randomly, repeating mistakes and often making bad habits worse.

Preliminary Training

Most systems require some kind of preliminary training. Many young actors have trouble recognizing this preliminary work as part of acting, although it is essential. (In a college, such work usually comes in the freshman year.) Partly, it is a process of *un*learning mistaken notions and bad habits, and partly it is a process of training mind and body to adapt to the conditions of the theatre instead of the conditions of life (by learning, for example, that behavior that is considered ridiculous in life is sometimes essential in rehearsal and performance).

It is usually thought to be unwise for beginning actors to go directly into the rehearsal and performance of plays or parts of plays—"scene work." Instead they are given preliminary training in the following areas.

Relaxation

Many people who want to learn to act are so tense that they are quite literally unable to act. Physical tension causes sudden, random, or pathological movement (shaking, trembling) and dangerous misuse of the vocal mechanism. Tense actors may think of themselves as *in*tense and not tense; they see themselves as "really into" a role, when the teacher or the audience sees nervous, confusing, and uncontrolled movement.

Relaxation exercises cover a broad range from disciplines as different as modern dance and yoga. All are intended to cause the consciousness to let go of the body, to return it to its natural state of receptiveness and awareness, and to make the body itself supple and loose.

Contact or Awareness

The relaxed body, freed from the tyranny of tension, becomes aware of itself and its environment. The consciousness no longer hurries it along toward some rigid goal; it has time, as it were, to stop and enjoy the scenery (including its own internal scenery). The coming and going of the breath, the comfortable positions of the body in standing, sitting, kneeling, and lying, the sense of the nearness and farness of objects and people—these things and many more can be explored. Sensory awareness is raised, and exercises are given that can be repeated (throughout the actor's life, if necessary) to maintain or renew that awareness.

FIGURE 7.4
Actor Training.
Teacher and students doing a relaxation exercise. Master teacher Walt Witcover, center.

Contact with others can also be taught so that the beginning actor learns to relate to other people, to help them, and to accept the help that they offer. The accepting of such help is, perhaps surprisingly, very difficult for many beginners, probably because not asking for or accepting help is a habit brought in from life. *Taking* and *giving* are the bases of good performance.

Centering

Many disciplines, among them Eastern meditative religions and some schools of modern dance, emphasize exercises that focus on a bodily center—that is, a core of balance and physical alignment, a place from which all movement and energy seem to spring. This idea of a center concerns both the body (balance, weight, and placement) and the voice (breathing and sound making). In yoga, the abdomen below the diaphragm is such a center; in the dance of Martha Graham, the center is slightly above the pelvis.

Centering leads the beginning actor away from the mistaken idea that the physical self is located in the head and the face, that the voice is located in the mouth and the throat, and that the physical relationship to the rest of the world is located, through gravity, in the feet; rather, the actor finds the center somewhere near the crossing point of an X of arms and legs—a center of gravity, a center of balance, a center of diaphragmatic breathing.

Play

Dramas are "plays"; actors are "players." Yet beginners are often anything but playful. A terrible intensity and a terrible seriousness rule the work. To counter this tendency, much of early training is spent reteaching people how to play, in the sense both of teaching them to play games and of teaching them to approach the creative act joyously. Because children often have this sense of playful theatricality in their own pastimes ("Let's pretend"), many theatre games are versions of children's games or of adult "parlor" games that are noncompetitive fun.

Training the Consciousness

Certain areas of the actor's conscious work can be taught through example and through guided participation in production work. These include discipline, concentration, theatrical analysis, observation, and script analysis.

Discipline

Actors are taught to be *prompt, alert,* and *ready to work*—to get enough sleep, to avoid alcohol and drugs when working, and to come in a frame of mind and a set of clothes that will permit maximum work. Actors *prepare:* They do bring the script and a pencil; they have done whatever homework on the play has been requested. Actors are *constructive,* not destructive: They do not make comments about other actors, do not break out of character while another actor is working, and do not indicate in any way that another actor's experiment with a character is wrong or comical or foolish. Actors are *respectful:* They talk to the director about problems, not to other actors or the costume designer or the playwright.

Concentration

The habit of concentration comes from work. In many cases, student actors whose acquaintance with mental work has been limited to the classroom will have difficulty at first with the level of concentration that is needed. Not only the length of time but also the depth of the concentration that is required may seem unreasonable. Yet, it is only through remarkable efforts of concentration that progress is made. An actor who cannot attain such concentration may need to return to exercises in relaxation and contact to find out what is distracting the mind. Where a severe problem continues to exist, there may be a psychological difficulty that a nontheatrical expert will be needed to resolve.

Observation

Observation is a conscious perceiving and recording of sensory data. Observation can be taught through a variety of devices that require attention to detail, such as talking through or writing highly detailed descriptions of objects (a specific chair, a dead fish). It can be encouraged by requiring the keeping of a notebook or diary. The goal is to cause actors to build a "library" on which they can draw in building character.

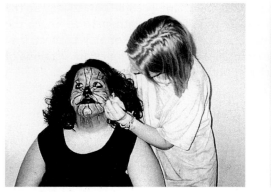 

FIGURE 7.5 The Actor's Face: Makeup.
At some point before performance, actors have to layer the face of the character on their own. Left, the Lion in *The Wiz;* right, an actor in India. *The Wiz courtesy of Sharon Ammen and the College of St. Mary-of-the-Woods; Indian photo courtesy of Farley Richmond.*

Theatrical Analysis

It should be a goal of actors' training to make them aware of their place in the theatre in each production. This does not mean merely that actors must understand their roles; it means that actors must grasp how they relate to the entire complex of the performance, including:

1. *Spatial understanding,* which includes an awareness of each setting in which the actor appears, its shapes and proportions, as well as an understanding of the relationship of the setting to the size and shape of the theatre and its audience. To reach this goal, actors in many theatre training programs are required to study design, lighting, and costume and to work on productions in nonacting jobs.

2. *Research resources,* for which the best preparation is usually a study of the history of the theatre. Knowledge becomes a resource, and formal study in this discipline will include a working knowledge of resources in the field.

3. *Dramatic appreciation,* for which the best preparation is usually a study of dramatic literature and a broad reading in the field. Every actor is expected to know the classics of each period.

Script Analysis

The dramatic script is the foundation of the actor's work. *Imagination* and *instrument* are the means through which the script is embodied. Training in script analysis has three principal goals:

1. *An understanding of the entire drama.* On the first reading, the actor will be making judgments and sorting out impressions. Trained in the theatre, the actor will read the script as a "notation" for a performance: The potential for production will be grasped, at least in general. An awareness of the play's *totality* will take shape. Of particular importance to the actor on first reading will be the *style* of the play, its main *impact* on its audience, and its overall *shape.* Under *style,* the actor will understand the degree of abstraction of the script; the kind of language, whether poetic or mundane; and the historical period. The *impact* will be comic or serious and will be expressed most importantly through language or action, through idea or spectacle. The *shape* will describe the play's gross structure and its overall rhythms, whether it builds slowly or quickly to crises, whether it relaxes gradually from them or drops abruptly. This first contact with the totality of the play will also indicate what demands it will put on its actors—the size of the cast, special requirements of their instruments, the size of the major roles, and the relative degree of intensity of the emotions to be embodied.

2. *An understanding of the place of the character in the whole drama.* The actor is trained to resist one question—*What makes my character stand out?*—and to ask another one instead—*How does my character contribute to the whole?*

Dramatic action means change; when a character is offstage, changes are taking place, and when the character returns, those changes must be noted. The actor balances two lines of development: the character's and the play's.

3. *An understanding of the details that make up the character.* A deeper understanding of the play and the character's part in it emerges from repeated readings, as does a detailed sense of just what the character is. The actor may keep a notebook in which ideas about the character are written down, as well as all those things in the script that indicate the nature of the character. These include those things discussed under "Character" in "How to Read a Play," especially action and decision, with character traits as they appear in the stage directions, the character's own speeches, and the speeches of others. All must be evaluated in terms of the production and should be discussed with the director and the other actors. For example, one character says to another that she shows "facial contortions" and her voice goes up "two octaves." The actor playing the character described must know whether these things are true (that is, whether the other character's description is accurate) and then work out when and where to use these traits.

It is essential for actors, as for all theatre makers, to look at the play in terms of its theatricality, that is, of those things discussed in Chapters 3 and 4. Such a breakdown gives them a grasp of the play's entirety and of its theatrical potential. It should not, however, dictate character. Grasping a play's idea, for example, must never suggest to the actor the reason for the character's existence, nor should the actor worry about how to "play the idea," or, worse yet, how to *be* the idea. The actor who says something like "In this play, I represent goodness" simply has not done the proper homework. Except in pure allegory, characters do not represent abstract ideas; they represent persons (who may embody or apply certain ideas).

In the same way, script analysis should help the actor to avoid moral value judgments. Characters in a play are not "good" or "bad" *to themselves.* Few real persons say, "I am a villain." The actor does not, then, play a villain; the actor plays the representation of a person whose actions may be judged, after the fact, as villainous—by others.

Put most simply, training in script analysis is training *to read.* It is training to understand what is *on the page*—not what might have been put on the page but was not, and not what the actor might prefer to find on the page. Script analysis deals with a very limited amount of information and tries to squeeze every drop from it; it neither invents nor guesses. Most of all, it requires that the actor read *every* word and understand it in clear detail; from that clarity and that detail will come an understanding of the script that can be returned to again and again when acting problems arise.

Training the Instrument

"Stage movement" and "voice production for the stage" sound like (and are) titles of academic courses. They suggest that the subject matter can be learned and that then, like familiarity with Shakespeare's plays or a knowledge of the calculus, they can be forgotten or assimilated. In actuality, the training of the instrument is a lifelong process.

Both body and voice use complicated sets of muscles put into action by the brain, sometimes consciously, sometimes unconsciously and habitually (for example, few of us have to remember to breathe). The actor has to be made aware of the muscles being used, has to improve the condition of the muscles, has to unlearn or relearn or learn a pattern of use of those muscles, has to repeat such patterns so often that they become habits, has to learn precisely what muscular actions will produce what results (sounds or movements), has to learn what combinations of commands and muscular sets will provide new, unusual, and effective sounds or movements. As well, the actor has to learn the "proper" application of certain kinds of voice (singing) and movement (fencing and dancing).

Body and Movement

The actor's body need not be heavily muscled, but it should be flexible, strong, and responsive. The actor does not train as an athlete does (one set of muscles would be developed at the expense of others); instead, the goal is *resistance to fatigue, quick responsiveness,* and *adaptive ability* (that is, the ability to imitate other kinds of posture and movement or to adapt movement to, for example, aged posture and movement or the posture and movement of a body much heavier). The actor also learns the following:

1. *Body language and nonverbal communication.* We all express our emotional states and our basic psychic orientations through *body language.* The actor

FIGURE 7.6
Movement.
Acting sometimes requires vigorous, athletic movement; actors train in fencing, dance, and other disciplines. *She Stoops to Conquer at Trinity University. Bob Brevard photo.*

learns to "move" the physical center to match that of the character. The actor also learns how all of us communicate without words, through such simple gestures as the waving of a hand ("hello" or "come here" or "no thank you") to complex "statements" of posture and gesture that say things completely different from the words that pass our lips. Such training takes two forms: study of the subject (much of it still in the fields of psychology and anthropology) and application to the actor's body.

2. *Rhythmic movement.* Ballroom dancing, simple modern dance, disco dancing, and the like help the actor to move to an external rhythm.

3. *Period movement and use of properties.* Historically accurate, and theatrically effective, use of fans, canes, swords, shawls—the list is endless.

4. *Movement in costume.* Theatrically effective movement and gesture in wigs, capes, hoop-skirts, boots—again, the list is a long one.

5. *Movement onstage.* Traditional interior settings do not have walls that meet at the same angles as rooms, and so stage furniture in such settings is rarely angled as real furniture is. As a result, "crosses" (movements from one point on-stage to another) take unreal routes. On thrust and arena stages, the actor learns to play to all of the audience, to adapt posture and movement so that each section of the audience is treated fairly. Too, there are ways of bending, sitting, and standing that are appropriate to the stage in that they are not awkward or comical, although training in these "correct" ways of doing things is becoming more appropriate to training in period movement.

Voice Production

The human voice is a product of controlled muscular work and chamber resonance (head and chest). Its shaping and control are not simple. Nonetheless, we make sounds and shape them all the time—only to find that our everyday sounds are inadequate for the theatre because they cannot be heard, they cannot be understood, and they are unpleasant. Unlearning and relearning are necessary for most actors.

The human voice is produced when air is forced over the *vocal folds* or *cords,* causing them to vibrate and to set a column of air vibrating, producing sound. This sound induces vibrations in *cavities* in the head and in *bones* in the head and chest. The sound is shaped in the throat and mouth, primarily with the jaws and tongue, and is further shaped into the sounds we call words by initiation of sound; interruption of sound by the interaction of lips, tongue, and teeth; and placement of sound through action of the lower jaw and of the tongue.

LINKS to more about theatre

The Entertainer. The late Laurence Olivier in a film about the theatre.

Toby Cole and Helen Krich Chinoy, *Actors on Acting,* 1949.

Uta Hagen, *Challenge for the Actor,* 1991.

George S. Kaufman, *The Royal Family.* Based on the Barrymores, ham on wry.

< **www.actorsequity.org** > Actors Equity (US) website.

The actor trains the vocal mechanism for maximum control of *every word that is uttered,* as well as for the production of sounds that are not words. He or she also seeks training and does exercises in breath control, relaxation of the vocal apparatus, dexterity, resonance, and such technical matters as dialects and accents.

Training the Imagination

The word *training* may be inaccurate. Actors go through a process in a training atmosphere and are *encouraged* to discover their imaginations. Whether or not the imagination itself can be "trained" remains open to question, and many psychological data suggest that what we have called *imagination* is a capacity of the brain and the mental-emotional self that is always at work but that rarely surfaces. Still, if one can teach the rational brain mathematics, perhaps one can teach the nonrational brain imagination. Most certainly, one can try to encourage the nonrational brain to speak up and make itself heard.

Creative Exercise

In the belief that all people have imaginations and are "creative," teachers devise exercises to free actors from both embarrassment and inhibition. Writing down dreams as a regular part of daily preparation can help many, especially those who insist that they "never dream" or "dream nothing interesting." The very fact of causing themselves to remember and write down dreams leads to an acceptance of the idea of dreaming and hence to a greater willingness to "listen to" their dreams, which demonstrate imaginative elements—images, metaphors, and puns. Dreams are often playful in their structure and their language, and they have both content and form that our rational minds would never think of.

Childhood memory can be turned to good account in the same way. An exercise in memory becomes an exercise in imagination as the actor finds how much detail the mind is capable of holding and of using.

Other exercises in sensitivity or creativity use group participation in building a story or a moment. Each actor in turn builds on the story.

Image Exercises

The creative mind probably works, at least a good deal of the time, in images rather than in words (although many words are themselves images). Image exercises encourage the actor to grasp the mental pictures that the brain offers. For example, simple character creation around pictures, objects, or sounds can be beneficial. An actor is given an object and told to perform a related character for the group: a knife is set out; the actor bends forward, walks with difficulty, the body held to protect its center greedily. From "knife," the actor went to "sharp," sharp in business, a miser, then added the element of "a cutting wind."

FIGURE 7.7 The Trained Imagination.

Truth comes in part from imagination working creatively on the trained instrument and concentration. *Carl Norman in David Rabe's Streamers at the University of South Carolina, directed by Jim Patterson.*

Visualization

Group exercises build a scene, each member contributing details and working to *see* the scene. Such an exercise is useful in touching the actor's sense of creativity, in sharpening concentration and sense of detail, and in preparing for those times in rehearsal and performance when the actor must "see" for the audience:

> HORATIO: But look, the morn in russet mantel clad
> Walks o'er the dew of yon high eastward hill.
>
> *Hamlet*

Sense Memory

Like group storytelling, individual recounting of the "picture" around a memory encourages a sense of detail and of visual memory. As many senses as possible are incorporated. Such memories need not come from childhood; they may come from the day before, even moments before. The purpose is to cause actors to capture a sensory moment in all its fullness and, through both remembering it *and* recounting it, to cause them to be able to create such sensory reality around moments that come not from memory but from the theatre.

Improvisation

No single word and no single tool has been more used and misused in the last several decades than *improvisation.* Improvisation—the creation of quasi-theatrical characters or scenes or plays without the givens of drama—has been used to create theatre (without a playwright), to enlighten an actor about a character (the so-called *étude,* or improvisation based on material in a dramatic script), to structure theatre games, and to teach many aspects of acting. As a tool for training the imagination, it is an application of the techniques already mastered. In a sense, it is the basis of some of the other techniques; having an actor create a character around an image is such a use of improvisation. It can be used to apply the imagination, to stimulate it, or to supply raw materials not within the actor's experience. (That is, an improvisation focused on a frightening event may help the actor who has never experienced fear.)

In order to work, improvisation is kept simple and is carefully focused by the instructor. Improvisations can quickly develop along unwanted lines, especially with actors who want to "tell stories" (create theatrically interesting situations); when that happens, there are often so many processes going on that student actors do not understand what they are doing. For the purposes of the imagination, it may be enough to create, for example, a scene of the sort discussed under "Visualization" and then to have the group improvise their participation in the scene—feeling the air, wading into the water, and setting up a picnic on the beach.

Training in Acting Systems

Ideas originated or articulated by Konstantin Stanislavski, modified by the American Method and subsequent theories, continue to dominate the work of most American actors.

The American Stanislavski System

In this system, the actor is trained to analyze character for:

1. *Given circumstances.* These are the undeniable givens that the actor must accept: age, sex, state of health, social status, educational level, and so on. Often they are contained within the script, either in stage directions or in dialogue; sometimes they must be deduced or even invented. (How old is Hamlet? Was he a good scholar at the university? Is he physically strong or weak?)

2. *Motivation.* Realistic theatre believes in a world of connectedness and cause. All human actions in such a world are caused or motivated. To play a character in such a world, the actor looks for the motivation behind each action.

Some teachers have their students make notebooks for each character with a column in which a motivation can be noted after each line or each gesture. It is important that the student actor understand that, in this system, *all* behavior is motivated—every word, every movement, every inflection. *All action results from choice.*

3. *Objective.* Like motivation, the objective is part of a system of causality. It is the goal toward which an action strives. Motivation leads to action; action tries to lead to objective.

4. *Superobjective.* "Life goal" might be an equivalent of the superobjective if a dramatic character were a real person. The superobjective includes all objectives pursued by a character and excludes all improperly defined objectives. For example, we might say that Hamlet's superobjective is "to set the world right again"; his objective in the first scene with his father's ghost might be "to listen to this creature from Hell and put it to rest" (thus setting the world right by quieting the ghosts in it). In this case, the objective and the superobjective agree. If, however, the superobjective was defined as "to take my father's place in the world," and the objective in the ghost scene was defined as "to listen to the ghost out of love for my father," the two would have to be brought into sympathy. By defining the superobjective, the actor is able to check on the validity of all the character's objectives.

Both the objective and the superobjective must be active. We have expressed them here as infinitives—"to set," "to listen"—but the actor does better to express them in active terms beginning with "I want," so that their strength and vitality are clearly visible.

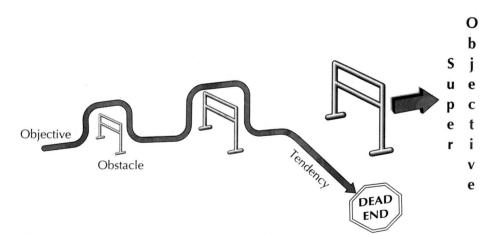

FIGURE 7.8 Objective and Superobjective.

In Stanislavskian terms, every properly defined objective leads along a line toward the superobjective; objectives that deviate from this line are "tendencies" that lead nowhere. Obstacles to achievement of objectives—other characters, events—provide much of the drama.

5. *Through line.* If motivations and objectives are seen as beads, they can be strung on a *through line* that runs consistently through the character's entire presence in the play. The through line (sometimes called the *spine*) may also be seen as the line that runs through all objectives toward the superobjective. The actor learns to recognize that something is wrong when a motivated action does not fit on the through line. Such an action was what Stanislavski called a "tendency." It leads to poor acting because it takes the character away from the pursuit of correct objectives and into vagueness and contradiction, which an audience finds confusing and finally annoying. Much of what we call bad acting is, in fact, the playing of tendencies rather than the playing of a strong through line.

Beyond Stanislavski: Acting in a Postmodern Theatre

Although Stanislavski's system still dominates actor training in the United States, it may be under challenge, especially outside the commercial theatre. Plays different from those associated with modern realism often require quite different approaches by the actor. Today's new plays and new views of theatre—especially those that are highly experimental—may lead to a different sort of training system for the actor as well. What will characterize this new system of acting, if one emerges, is unclear, but some of the following trends may become important in its formation.

Many postmodern plays are not organized by cause and effect; they do not assume a world of causality or connectedness, achieving their unity through ideas, perhaps, or mood or visual images. Actors in such plays might, therefore, be expected to place less emphasis on issues like motivation, superobjective, and through line and more, perhaps, on matters of vocal and physical flexibility, symbolism, and aesthetics.

Many postmodern plays stress multiple levels of reality—several layers of meaning—with irony and parody often important. Actors preparing for such plays may be asked (and indeed *have* been asked by the German theorist Bertolt Brecht) not only to *play* the role but also to *comment* on the role at the same time. Such a request seems to mean that actors must engage the audience in the role while, at the same time, requiring the audience always to recollect that they are watching a role being acted and not a life being lived. One technique for accomplishing this dual focus has been costume manipulation and cross-gender casting: The audience watches a female actor cast in a male role put on and take off her costume (and so her role); in this way, the actor can both play and comment on the role—and at the same time reveal the social construction of gender within a play and a society. Separating the voice and body of the actor is another such technique: The audience hears an actor's pre-recorded voice over loudspeakers while seeing the actor moving and, perhaps, speaking.

Many postmodern plays deny the actor a single role or a stable character, the plays' point often being that human beings themselves lack stable identities. In such plays, actors play multiple roles (including those of animals or inanimate objects) or many characters, and they do so without the changes in costume or

FIGURE 7.9   Acting Beyond Stanislavski.
Caryl Churchill's *Top Girls* opens with a dinner at which women from several countries and historical periods meet in the present. Stanislavskian analysis may not work for a play whose given circumstances are inexplicable. More extreme nonrealistic styles create other challenges that strict Stanislavskian methods do not resolve. *Top Girls, directed by Sharon Ammen at the University of Maryland.*

makeup that have historically suggested such changes. Called *transformations,* such rapidly shifting roles would seem to place a greater premium on vocal and physical dexterity and imagination than on truthful inner work or a strong through line.

Although it is far from certain, it does seem that such requirements, if they come to occupy a major place in the mainstream theatre, may effect major changes in the ways we now think about and train our actors.

AUDITION, REHEARSAL, AND PERFORMANCE

Actor training goes on long after actors begin to take an active part in performance. Most actors continue to work on their instruments throughout their careers, and many return to professional workshops to refresh and sharpen their inner work. After the initial period of actor training, however—college, sometimes graduate school, an independent studio or teacher—the actor begins to look for roles and, having found one, begins the work of building and performing a character. Each step in the process has its special conditions, and for the professional actor these steps will be repeated over and over throughout his or her life.

Audition

Most actors get roles through auditions ("tryouts"). Stars are the exception; sometimes productions are built around them.

Most auditions are done for the director of the production. Usually, the stage manager is there as well, along with someone representing the producer, if there is one. Somebody is there, as well, to read with the actor if a scene with another character is being read. (Usually, the stage manager does this.) At many auditions, actors are expected to bring prepared monologues.

The most important things an actor can show in an audition are basic abilities and the capacity to work creatively with the director and other actors. One of the director's problems in auditions is to try to sort out the creative actors from the "radio actors"—those who have the knack of reading well on sight but who lack the ability to create. Therefore, actors are often asked to improvise as part of auditions and to work with other people. Thus, cleverness in a first reading is not necessarily an advantage for the actor. What may count more is the capacity to work creatively and interpersonally.

Rehearsal

The actor will undoubtedly arrive at the first rehearsal with many questions. One of the functions of rehearsal is to answer those questions and to turn the answers into performance.

Actors often work very slowly in rehearsal. An outsider coming into a rehearsal after, let us say, two weeks of work might well be dismayed by the apparent lack of progress. Actors may still be reading some lines in flat voices, and, except for bursts of excitement, the play may seem dull and lifeless. This situation is, in part, intentional. Many actors "hold back" until they are sure that things are right. They do not want to waste energy on a temporary solution to a character problem. Temporary solutions have a way of becoming permanent: Other actors become accustomed to hearing certain lines delivered in certain ways and to seeing certain movements and gestures; they begin to adapt their own characters to them. The actors begin to commit themselves to a pattern. To avoid this, many find it productive to withhold commitment for a good part of the rehearsal period.

The actor experiments. Some of this experimenting is done away from the rehearsals; homework takes up a lot of the actor's time. Much of it takes place in rehearsals. Again and again, an actor will say, "May I try something?" Or the director will say, "Try it my way." *Try* is the important word—experiment, test. The good actor has to be willing to try things that may seem wrong, absurd, or embarrassing.

FIGURE 7.10
Rehearsal.
Often far from the stage, in a room with the ground plan marked on the floor with tape, actors and directors rehearse, using the plainest of furniture and "dummy" props. *Courtesy of Anne Fliotsos and the University of Missouri, Columbia.*

Most important, the rehearsal period is a time for building with other actors. Actors use the word *give* a lot: "You're not giving me enough to react to," or "Will it help you if I give you more to play against?" Such giving (and taking) symbolizes the group creation of most performance.

At some point during rehearsals, the creative and lucky actor may have a "breakthrough." This is the moment when the character snaps into focus. Motivations and actions that have been talked about and worked on for weeks may suddenly become clear and coherent. The breakthrough may be partly a psychological trick, but its reality for the actor is very important: The creative imagination has made the necessary connections and has given usable instructions to the instrument. The character is formed.

The rehearsal period, then, is not merely a time of learning lines and repeating movement. It is a time of creative problem-solving, one in which the solving of one problem often results in the discovery of a new one. It is a time that requires give and take, patience, physical stamina, and determination. It frays nerves and wearies bodies. The intensity of the work may cause personal problems. Nonetheless, many professional actors love rehearsal more than performance because of its creativity.

Performance

Society has an overblown image of "opening night" that makes the first performance unnaturally stressful. The fantasy of instant stardom, rave reviews, the actor's name in lights, and standing ovations makes performances still more stressful.

Few actors, in fact, achieve stardom or standing ovations, and it is a sad mistake for any actor to think that such things are the only reward for performing.

Performance causes emotional and physical changes in the actor that are associated with stress. Some change, of course, is helpful; it gets the actor "up" so that energy is at a peak, ready for the concentrated expenditure that rehearsal has made possible. Too much stress, however, cripples the actor. "Stage fright" and psychosomatic voice loss are very real problems for some. Ideally, good training and effective rehearsal will have turned the actor away from the root cause of stress (dependence on outside approval of the performance); where this does not happen, the actor may have to return to relaxation work or find outside therapeutic help.

Opening nights raise energy levels because of stress and excitement. As a result, second nights are often dispirited and dull. The wise actor expects this pattern. Again, preparation is a help—complete understanding of the role and the total performance, creative rehearsal work, open lines between consciousness and imagination. Before the second and subsequent performances, the prepared actor reviews all character work, goes over notes, reaffirms motivations and objectives. The good actor does not say, "Well, we got through the opening; the rest will take care of itself."

FIGURE 7.11 Performance.
Shakin' the Mess Outta Misery at Western Michigan University, directed by Von H. Washington. *Mary Whalen photo.*

Once in performance in an extended run, actors continue to be aware of a three-pronged responsibility: to themselves, to the other actors, and to the audience. Those responsibilities cannot end with the reading of the reviews.

In developing his system of acting, Stanislavski was interested both in actor training and in the problems of performance. His work cannot be viewed as merely a study of how the actor prepares; rather, it is also a prescription for the continuing refreshment of the performing actor. His system allows the actor to create what has been called the "illusion of the first time" again and again. Put most simply, this means that the actor is able to capture the freshness and immediacy of the "first time" (both for the character and for the audience) by going back each time to the mental and emotional roots of the truthfulness of the performance. This process is possible only if performance is grounded in truth discovered during rehearsal—or, in some cases, during performance itself.

Continued performance for the trained actor, then, is not merely a matter of repeating rehearsed sounds and gestures night after night; it is a matter of returning to or discovering internally satisfying truths (motivations and objectives) and satisfyingly effective externalizations of them. Such a system may not be perfect, but it is far better than the repeated performance that grows tired and dull with repetition and that leaves the actor disliking both the performance and the audience because of boredom.

Audience response to performance sometimes suggests where a performance is effective or poor, and the actor works at correcting errors as the performance period continues. Thus the creation of a character must seem completed by opening night, and yet it is never truly finished.

THE PERSONALITY OF THE ACTOR

The personality of men and women who act has been a source of fascination for centuries. Actors have long been seen as special sorts of people because of their ability to interpret human psychology and because of their apparent ability to balance both halves of the "paradox of the actor." Too, a number of traditions have come to surround the acting profession, and if they were not always accurate, they came to seem accurate as actors themselves believed in them: "all actors have to be crazy"; "all actors are immoral"; "the theatre attracts misfits and oddballs"; "actors like to show off"; and so on. Such ideas are no better than gossip until they are proved by objective standards, and for every immoral actor and show-off, there is an opposite to disprove the stereotype. Nonetheless, some of these old ideas persist.

Because of a lack of hard data and the persistence of stereotypes, we cannot describe accurately the "personality of the actor." We might note the following, however.

The actor's profession puts him or her outside the mainstream of most lives, because actors work odd hours, work at a very high level of energy and concentration, and live a life of extreme professional and financial peril.

Ruth Ann Phimister

Mr. Finn Became
He Represents M

FIGURE 7.12 *The Professional Actor.* Resumes, professionally made photographs, and photocopied reviews of the actor Ruth Ann Phimister. Such things are part of the professional actor's expenses, along with clothes, travel, continuing training, union dues, and other costs in a competitive, often chancey, profession. *Ms. Phimister's photos by © Elizabeth Lehmann, New York City.*

Part of the actor's reward is applause and other forms of audience approval, and a personality geared toward applause may be an insecure one; yet, to face tryout after tryout, opening after opening, show after show takes stamina and a courage unknown to men and women in secure careers.

The actor's personal relationships are easily threatened by unusual hours, job insecurity, and the need to be able to move geographically on short notice.

Because theirs is a high-stress life, actors are as subject to the allure of drugs and alcohol as the rest of the population, and perhaps more so.

The ability and desire to act, like all creative work, is "different," and the committed actor may be judged an outsider by the rest of society.

Thus, although we cannot draw a profile of a typical actor, we can point out some qualities that frequently occur. What must be clearly understood, however, is that the qualities that make a good actor—creativity, concentration, determination, stamina, access to the imagination, playfulness, the ability to cope with rejection, nonrational thinking, and detailed emotional memory—should be kept separate from qualities that may appear because of the *profession* of acting and its stresses; in other words, the nature of the profession in our society may bring out behavior that is not typical of the art of acting but of our society's use of it. Thus, the "personality of the actor" has to be a composite of those qualities that make up talent and those qualities that appear in response to the environment in which talent is used.

WHAT IS GOOD ACTING?

Understanding the art of the actor depends, first, on the ability to separate the actor from the role. An attractive or well-written role can obscure the actor's lack of imagination; a poorly written role can hide the actor's excellence; an unsympathetic role can make the actor seem unsympathetic. By learning to read and see plays, we learn to distinguish the character from the actor, then to see what kind of material the actor had to cope with. For example:

Good acting has detail and "texture" (variety and human truth), but it is not merely a collection of details; it has what one artist calls a "center," another a "through line"—a common bond tying all details together and making the whole greater than the sum of its parts.

Good acting has the capacity to surprise. Its truth is recognizable, but it goes beyond imitation to revelation.

Good acting, then, has technical proficiency, truth, a through line, and creativity; bad acting calls attention to itself, lacks technical control, dissolves into mere details because of its lack of a through line, and never surprises with its creation.

CURRENT ISSUES

The very power of acting has begun to raise questions about its responsible use in a culturally diverse and democratic society. Underlying these questions seems to be the age-old issue of the degree to which, and the ways in which, life and art interact. If television violence promotes social violence, and misogynistic rap music causes damage to real women (but we do not know yet if they do), then perhaps actors and acting are also implicated in changing the behaviors and attitudes of real people, the argument goes. Although variously posed, several sorts of questions are being asked, not only about professional actors but also about actor training.

Professional actors, like prostitutes (to whom they have been compared, historically), make their living by selling themselves—their voices and bodies—to audiences. The question now being raised is, Should actors sell themselves to just anyone who will buy? For example, should an actor accept a role that pays well, regardless of possible social consequences or the actor's own beliefs about issues raised in the play? Should an actor accept a role that demeans or threatens some cultural group or practice? Should a Caucasian actor play Othello? (They have done so historically.) Conversely, should an African-American actor play Hamlet? (They have not done so historically.) Must roles depicting physically or mentally disadvantaged characters be played only by similarly physically or mentally disadvantaged actors? (The issue here, of course, is partly financial—if a

Caucasian actor plays Othello, an African-American actor is denied a paying job.)

Perhaps the answers to such questions depend on the situation of individual actors. For example, might highly visible, influential actors have a responsibility for monitoring the kinds of roles they play that minor, unknown actors do not have? Does one actor have a moral or ethical obligation to avoid a role that is personally offensive, even knowing that another actor will play it gladly?

Similar questions have also begun to challenge teaching and casting practices within colleges and universities. For example, there is tantalizing, if limited, evidence that the role an actor plays may affect the personality of the actor, at least temporarily. This potentiality has implications for educators: If a character in fact "invades" an actor who plays it, does acting pose a real danger to the developing personality of a youth or young adult? For example, what might be the effect, if any, of having students play violent or psychotic characters? What might be the effect of having young female students play those passive, ditsy, sex-stereotyped roles most often available to them in modern realistic plays? What might be the effect of having African-American or Jewish or Latino or Native American students play roles that either do not depict characters of their own heritage or depict them in unflattering ways? Conversely, might an acting teacher, by careful casting, "improve" the personality of a student actor—for example, casting a shy student in the role of a life-of-the-party? Are there dangers in acting for students with mental instabilities?

FIGURE 7.13 **The Actor and the World.** Ira Aldridge was one of America's great nineteenth-century actors, but his professional life suffered because he was black. Aldridge performed mostly in Europe, a serious actor not content with the stereotypical jobs in comedy and musical theatre in America.

KEY TERMS

Check your understanding against this list. Brief definitions are in the Glossary; page references there will direct you to appropriate pages. (Persons are page-referenced in the Index.)

audition
dialect
given circumstances
  (of characters)
improvisation
instrument
motivation
objective

obstacle
sense memory
superobjective
tendency
through line
transformations

chapter 8

The Director

OBJECTIVES

When you have completed this chapter, you should be able to:

- Describe major tasks of a director, noting which are mostly artistic and which mostly managerial

- Differentiate the worshipful from the heretical director and discuss strengths and weaknesses of both approaches

- Describe the purpose and process of production meetings

- Describe the director's work with actors

- Explain the director's use of space

- Define the art of the director

Thereere have always been theatre people who exercised a strong, central influence on productions, but in the sense that the word is now used, directing is a phenomenon of the nineteenth and twentieth centuries. Despite the relatively late appearance of directors, they are now the dominant figures in theatrical production.

THE NATURE OF DIRECTING

Before the emergence of directors, leading actors mostly interpreted their own roles, decided what they would wear, and decided where to stand and when to move on stage, often without regard to what other actors were doing or wearing. Designers, when there were any, built and painted backgrounds for the actors, intending that the same settings would be used over and over again, for many different plays. Towns or organizations or individual groups decided what plays to produce, and sometimes they would even write the plays to produce. Older performances, then, had a multiplicity of effects, a relatively uncoordinated production.

A Director's Goals

When directors came into being, the responsibility for many tasks formerly done by several people or not done at all were vested in one person—the director. Apparently the previous multiplicity of effects began to seem undesirable, and some closer coordination and unification of effects was sought. Thus, directors came into being to *unify,* to bind all elements of a performance together into a unity— of both interpretation and presentation. *Interpretation* here means not only that the actors and designers all understand the play in the same way but also that they all understand and agree on the nature of the intended audience and the limitations of talent and circumstance under which they will be working together. *Presentation* here means all the elements that the audience will see and hear: the text, actors, scenery, properties, costumes, lighting, and sound all must "fit together," be appropriate for the intended audience, and be developed with due regard for the particular circumstances of the production.

We can deduce something more about directing by recognizing that, in the nineteenth century, when it appeared, illusionistic detail was becoming important in the theatre and industrialism was becoming important in Western society. Inasmuch as the era of the director is the era of the pictorial illusionist and of the industrial manager, we can deduce that, in providing unity, directors are involved in *making pictures and illusion,* and in *organizing and managing.*

To be sure, the degree to which directors unify, make pictures and illusion, and organize and manage depends in part on their situation. For example, in commercial theatres like Broadway's, overall artistic vision may rest with the producer rather than with the director, and many routine details of rehearsal and performance may devolve to a stage manager instead of remaining with the direc-

FIGURE 8.1 Before Directors.
This eighteenth-century theatre ticket by Hogarth shows a scene from *The Beggar's Opera* in a day when directing as we now know it did not exist, and principal actors arranged themselves downstage while lesser figures hung at the edges.

tor. On the other hand, in high schools and small community theatres, more and more tasks fall to the director, so that he or she may personally supervise (or even execute) almost every aspect of a production.

A Director's Responsibilities

In general, however, the following comprise the director's usual responsibilities:

- Selecting or approving the play (including work with a playwright on an original script)
- Interpreting the play
- Approving and coordinating the designs (scenery, costumes, lighting, sound)

- Casting and coaching actors
- Staging (including "blocking," orchestrating voices, setting tempos, and so on)
- Planning and coordinating the production
- Scheduling and conducting the rehearsals
- Serving as liaison among all members of the production team

This list raises several important points. It suggests, correctly, that a director's responsibilities are not only artistic (the first five items on the list) but also managerial (the last three). However, it suggests incorrectly that these responsibilities are discrete and separable. For example, the artistic responsibilities are listed in roughly the order in which the director undertakes them, but in fact they overlap: Some occur simultaneously (coaching actors and staging, for example); others, like interpreting the play, continue throughout the process of production.

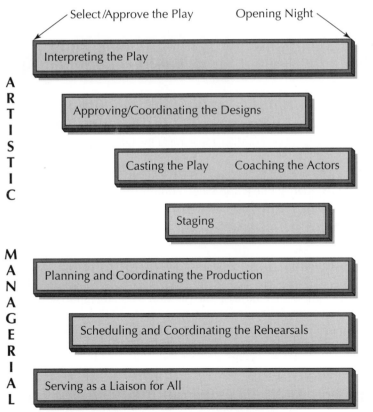

FIGURE 8.2 The Director's Responsibilities. The director is both artist and manager; the work begins at selection or approval of the script and ends sometime after the first performance. He or she works on many tasks, beginning and ending them at different times but usually working on many simultaneously.

Select/Approve the Play   Opening Night

A R T I S T I C

Interpreting the Play

Approving/Coordinating the Designs

Casting the Play   Coaching the Actors

Staging

M A N A G E R I A L

Planning and Coordinating the Production

Scheduling and Coordinating the Rehearsals

Serving as a Liaison for All

The managerial responsibilities are also listed roughly in order, but again there is overlap; for example, a director serves as liaison throughout the production process. Also, the managerial and artistic functions overlap: planning, coordinating, and scheduling take place mostly *before* rehearsals begin, as do selecting plays, coordinating designs, and casting actors. As a part of conducting rehearsals, the director is coaching actors and staging. Perhaps Figure 8.2 can help clarify these relationships.

A Director's Traits

This wide range of responsibilities obviously requires a person of many abilities. Directors need skills in organization in order to plan, coordinate, and schedule. Such skills include an ability to put ideas in order and to combine them with the ideas of other people, as well as the ability to order rehearsals, schedules, and budgets. Directors also need abilities in making decisions, including the clear-headedness to define problems and see the conditions under which they must be solved (including limitations of time, budget, and available talent). Directors need sensitive interpersonal skills to coax performances from actors and to work effectively with all other members of the production team, inspiring each whenever possible, working creatively with them on group solutions to complicated problems, and imposing solutions only when absolutely necessary. Directors must have artistic vision and talent, which, although hard to define, are absolutely essential for successful productions. Finally, directors need both stamina and concentration if they are to exercise their talent and carry out their many responsibilities.

Directors have to be both artists and managers in almost all of their work, and they are unique among professionals precisely because of this unusual combination of traits: on the one hand, the often solitary consciousness of the artist, and on the other, the gregarious organizational intellect of the manager. Within the same person, then, the artist proposes and the manager disposes, sometimes at widely different times and sometimes simultaneously.

A Director's View of Text

What is the director's responsibility to the dramatic text? Is it the director's job to put the play on the stage with utmost fidelity, or is it the director's job to create a theatrical event to which the script is merely a contributing part? Can the director cut lines or scenes, transpose scenes, alter characters? Can the director "improve" the play, or must it be treated as a sacred object?

Directors vary widely in the way they answer such questions. Their views range from veneration of the text to near indifference; the play is seen as a holy object on the one hand, as a merely useful artifact on the other.

The Worshipful Director's Approach

A director who venerates the text might say: "The play is the only permanent art object in performance; it is a work of art in its own right, to be treated with respect and love. Because it has stood the test of time, it has intrinsic value. By examining it, we can know its creator's intentions—what meanings the playwright meant to convey, what experiences the audience was meant to have, what theatrical values were being celebrated. The playwright is a literary artist and a thinker, and the playwright's work is the foundation of theatrical art. It is the director's job to mount the playwright's work as faithfully and correctly as is humanly possible.

"Historical research and literary criticism are useful tools for the director; they illuminate the classic play. Quirky modern interpretations are suspect, however: To show Hamlet as a homosexual in love with Rosencrantz and/or Guildenstern would be absurd and wrong because we know that such a relationship would never have been included in the tragic view that Shakespeare held.

"The director's job is not primarily to create theatre; it is to cause the play to create theatre. The difference is crucial. The director says quite properly, 'I must allow the play to speak for itself and not get in the way.' To do otherwise is to betray the play, and I will not do it *even if the 'betrayal' is great theatre.*"

The worshipful director views a different approach with something like horror; at best, such productions cause regret. Most often, a single word is used by the worshipful director to describe non-worshipful productions: *wrong.* Because they are not faithful to their classic originals, they are *wrong.*

The Heretical Director's Approach

A director who does not venerate the text might say: "*Interpreting the text* means *making a theatrical entity of it for an audience.* Not making *the* theatrical entity of it, and not 'finding its meaning' or 'doing it correctly.' There is no single interpretation of a play that is 'correct.' There are only interpretations that are right for a given set of performers under a given set of conditions for a given audience.

"How, then, can a director judge the rightness of the production? The director does not, any more than a painter judges the rightness of a painting. The director's final criterion is the satisfaction of an overall goal: Is it good theatre?

"It is foolish to think that the director's task is to stage the play according to some other standard. Fidelity to some 'authorized' or time-honored view of the play is not, simply in and of itself, a good thing. It is foolish to say that the director did the play 'wrong' unless what the director did was to make bad or dull theatre. The director has to be faithful to a vision, not to tradition or academic scholarship or propriety; only when that vision fails can the director be said to be wrong.

"Does this mean, then, that the director has no responsibility to the 'meaning' of the play? Yes, in the sense that the director's responsibility is to the meaning of the performance, of which the play is only a part. Are we, then, to have homosexual Hamlets? Yes, if such interpretations are necessary to make the plays into effective theatre and if they are entirely consistent within their productions.

FIGURE 8.3 Worshipful and Heretical Directors.

André Antoine's production of Racine's *Andromaque,* above, was an attempt to recreate the conditions of the original performance, down to candle footlights and an audience on the stage. By contrast, *As You Like It* at the University of South Carolina uses modern dress and a stage and setting unlike Shakespeare's, while body positions and costumes suggest an anti-heroism not necessarily to be found in a worshipful production. *AYLI directed by Jim Patterson, setting by Dennis C. Maulden, lighting by Ann Courtney, costumes by Rebecca Dosen.*

Are we, then, to have productions of classics that are directly opposite to their creators' intentions? Yes, because it is finally impossible to know what somebody else's intentions were and because an intention that was dynamite in 1600 may be as dull as dishwater in 2000; and anyway, theatre people have always altered classics to suit themselves. *Macbeth* was turned into an 'opera' as early as 1670, and *King Lear* had a happy ending in the eighteenth century."

The extremes of the heretical director's views can lead to results that many people find offensive or meaningless; on the other hand, those views can also lead to innovative and truly exciting productions.

A Best Approach

Generally both sorts of directors take a risk: the heretical director takes the chance of being ridiculous, the worshipful director of being vapid. At their best, however, both can create productions that thrill audiences, the one with revelations of familiar material, the other with a brilliant rendition of the strong points of the classic.

THE DIRECTOR AT WORK

Selecting the Play

Directors in community, school, and university theatres most often select the plays they direct; in professional theatre, directors at least approve the scripts (if they are staff directors) or find themselves "matched" to a new play by a producer. Never should a director take on a play he or she does not like. The demands are too great, the depth of involvement too extreme; the dislike would ruin the production.

Directors choose to do plays because the plays excite them; idea and spectacle are probably the most common elements to prompt directorial interest. However, if theatrical elements conflict, directors sometimes find that they have made a bad choice; that is, they may love the idea of the play but may not know how to make the music of the language exciting or how to compensate for a lack of spectacle. As directors gain self-knowledge through experience, they learn what they do well or badly, and they learn to make wise script choices. Most important, perhaps, is the acquired knowledge of learning to study the script in great depth—not to be led astray by enthusiasm for a single element, only to find to one's sorrow later that serious problems were overlooked.

Interpreting the Play

The work of interpretation is an open-ended process, and, like the actor's, it never really finishes; it merely stops. A director who does more than one production of the same play may create quite a different production the second time: The process of interpretation has gone on and has changed as the director and the world have changed.

Finding a Springboard

With the script chosen, the director begins to translate that early enthusiasm into the stuff of performance. To do so, the director needs a "springboard," a taking-off place from which to make a creative leap. The terms *concept* and *directorial image* are also used, but *concept* implies rational thought, and *image* implies picture making, and the director's process at this stage may be neither rational nor pictorial. Certainly, very few directors *begin* their creative work with a reasoned, easily stated idea, and those who are drawn to a script because of (for example) its music or because of the opportunity it gives to display the artistry of an actor will probably not *begin* with images. On the contrary, what many directors begin with is a seemingly random, sometimes conflicting medley of ideas, impressions, and half-formed thoughts whose connections may still be hidden. It is then the director's task—and the exercise of a special talent—to sort all these out and to find their connections and to see which can be given theatrical life and which cannot. Thus, much of the director's early work is not the definition and application of a "concept," but the establishment of a jumping-off place, the sorting out of raw materials from a whirlwind of impressions.

Seldom—perhaps never, except in the most perfunctory sort of work—is the springboard merely "to do the play." A director who sets out merely "to do the play" is like the actor who sets out to learn the lines and not bump into the furniture—going through the motions without ever confronting the real task. This is as true of a classic play as of the most avant-garde script. It might seem that classic

---

THINKING ABOUT DIRECTING

"For a stage set to be original, striking, and authentic, it should first be built in accordance with something seen. . . . If it is an interior, it should be built with its four sides, its four walls, without worrying about the fourth wall, which will later disappear so as to enable the audience to see what is going on."

—André Antoine, French director, 1858–1943

Follow Antoine's procedure and make a ground plan of a familiar room. Next, decide which wall to remove. Do the actors have good entrances and exits? Can they move easily from place to place inside the room? Does any furniture need to be adjusted to aid the actors' movements or the audience's view? Repeat the exercise but remove a different wall. Which arrangement is better? Why?

plays would be an exception because, supposedly, so much is known about them and so many other productions can be drawn on—the director would simply stage the play's established greatness. Such an approach is a guarantee of dullness, at best. A play will not be exciting in performance simply because other audiences have found other productions exciting; it must be made exciting all over again every time it is staged.

Assessing Strengths and Weaknesses

In early readings, the director usually has both positive and negative thoughts about the play and its audience impact. Two lists could be made, one of strengths and one of weaknesses. These two lists *taken together* would show how the director's ideas were forming. It is important to remember that weaknesses as well as strengths are included. Just as artists in any form are inspired by obstacles, so the director is inspired by script problems (as, for example, poets used to find inspiration in the problem of rhyme).

Let us suppose that the director is considering Ibsen's *A Doll's House,* a realistic nineteenth-century play. The play is a classic of its kind and so has established merit; on the other hand, it is also old enough to seem dated to a modern audience in language and some plot devices. Thus, after early readings, the director could list some strengths and weaknesses:

Strengths	*Weaknesses*
Strong subject matter	Creaky structure–melodramatic
Excellent central character	Dated language
Great third-act climax	Some "serious" stuff now "funny"
Good potential for probing Victorian attitudes	Solioquies, set speeches very hard to make convincing today

To the director who is excited by the play and is setting out to do it, these two columns might better be titled "Potentials" and "Challenges." From the realization of the one and the solution of the other will come the director's best work.

Analyzing the Text

No matter what the orientation toward the text, the director must now work to analyze it: take it apart, reduce it to its smallest components, "understand" it. (To *understand* does not mean to "turn the script into a rational description of itself"; it means, rather, to make the director's consciousness capable of staging it.) The job of interpretation has many aspects, which are often explored simultaneously, both before and during rehearsals.

As a beginning, the director will want to ask and answer the kinds of questions suggested in Chapters 3 and 4. But the director's analysis will be much more detailed. Each decision about the play must be measured against an idea of how the anticipated audience will react (with the qualification that every good director knows that mere reaction is not in itself a good thing; the *proper* reaction is what is wanted). In thinking about audience, the director will explore many of the issues raised in Chapter 2, but again in considerably more detail. To see the differences between a director's analysis and the more general analyses offered elsewhere, we can look briefly at five representative areas.

Tone, Mood, and Key.   Funny/serious, cheerful/sad, light/heavy—the possibilities are many and must be identified for each act, each scene, and each line, as well as for the entire play. Neither laughter nor powerful emotion belongs unchangeably to every line of a script. Even when the proper tone is found for the play, the lines alone will not deliver that tone to an audience. Laugh lines must be carefully

FIGURE 8.4   Strengths and Weaknesses.
When *L'Assomoir* was first done at the end of the nineteenth century, its strengths would have included its gritty realism and its social statement; now, a director might see a strength in its roles for women, but weaknesses in a dated social statement and a realism of which many are now weary.

set up and "pointed," with both "business" (small activities performed by actors) and timing; moments that have a wonderful potential for powerful emotion can easily be lost without careful, intense study and work by the director.

Of particular interest in this aspect of interpretation is *mood*—the emotional "feel" that determines tempo and pictorial composition—and *key*—(as in "high key" and "low key"), the degree to which effects are played against each other or against a norm for contrast. High-key scenes may even go to *chiaroscuro* ("light/dark") effects that use the darkest darks and the lightest lights, as in dramatic painting.

The Six Parts.   The director must study the play to find which parts are most important and which can be used most creatively to serve the play. Spectacle (including lighting, costume, the pictures created by the actors' movement, and scenery) and sound (including music, sound effects, and language) are often parts that the director can manipulate and can bring to the play as "extras" that the playwright has not included. Character, idea, and story, on the other hand, are usually integral to the script itself, although subject to considerable interpretation and "bending" by director and actors. Many directors annotate their scripts in great detail for these three parts, some marking every line of dialogue for its contribution to character, idea, or story. Such annotations give the director both an overall sense of the play's thrust and specific instances of that thrust at work.

This area of interpretation is critical. A part misunderstood at this stage can mean a moment lost in performance, or even an important thread through the whole play; to miss a major emphasis can mean a failed production. For example, a play that depends heavily on the beauty and intricacy of its language (sound) will usually suffer if directed to emphasize story or character, with the language overlooked or ignored (a not infrequent problem in productions of Shakespeare's plays); a play of character, if directed for its story, often has incomprehensible spots and long stretches where nothing seems to happen. Thus, the director must not only pick the part or parts that can be given theatrical life, *but must also pick the part or parts that the script gives theatrical life.* This means knowing *which* part(s) is most important; *where* in the play each has its heights and depths; and *how* the director will give theatrical excitement to each.

Action and Progression.   Performance is active and most plays have progressive actions; that is, they occur through time (audience time and their own time), and they must seem to increase in intensity as time passes (as, that is, the audience is led from preparation through complication to crisis and resolution).

There is a trap here for every director, however, in that it is the very nature of audience perception to need greater stimulation as time passes—a familiar enough situation to all of us, who can become bored after a time with something that entertained us at the beginning. Thus, it is part of the director's problem to counter the apparent drop in intensity that occurs as time passes by using every device possible to *increase* intensity, that is, to support theatrically the progressive intensity of the script. When it enjoys a performance, an audience's responses may be compared to a parabola: they start at a low point, rise higher and higher as time passes, and usually fall off after the climax. The director wisely structures the performance to serve this perceptual structure (or another equally satisfying one.) *The director cannot allow a performance to become static,* or it will seem to fall off rather than to remain still.

It is not enough, then, to find the important elements and to know where the script emphasizes them. The director must now find how each element grows in interest as the performance progresses. The word *progression* must be used again and again: What is this character's progression? What is the progression of the story? Is there progression in the spectacle?

If the progression is missed, the audience will become confused or bored. They may say things like "It went downhill," or "It got dull after the first act," or "It went nowhere." Theatre people seeing such a performance often say that "they played the last act first," which is a way of saying that the climactic points or the important parts were so much in the director's mind that the entire play was directed to emphasize them, and the progression was thus destroyed.

The reverse of the question "What is the progression?" is "What can I save for the climax?" In other words, how can the director emphasize the highest point of the performance (usually toward the end, coincident with the story's climax) by contrast or by saving effects for that moment? Preparation and contrast are important; equally important is *saving* something—the final high pitch of emotion, the most exciting tempo, the loveliest visual effect.

Idea. As we have pointed out earlier, idea is the part of theatre that gets the most attention after the audience has left the theatre and the least while it is enjoying the performance. Idea is also an important reason that some directors select a play, many directors being committed to plays because of enthusiasm for their subject or approach. It is therefore important to remind ourselves that idea does not express itself in individual speeches or literal statements that can be neatly extracted from the play. Instead it is woven into the other parts of the play, the texture of the performance, the actors' creation of their roles, and so on.

Idea can become a trap for an unwary director. A director must NOT direct a play so that it is "about the idea." The other parts determine the shape of the production; idea inheres in all of them but must be blatant in none. Even an impassioned "idea" speech at the most thrilling moment of the play must *spring from* action and character and must exist *because of* action and character. If the speech exists only because the playwright or the director wants to "make a statement," the speech will leap out of the performance, and the performance will suffer. Inasmuch as the play's ideas emerge from individual moments and meanings, individual actions and characters, a director carefully directs the moments and meanings, the actions and characters, NOT "the idea." Where meanings excite the director, they become something embedded in the entire performance.

FIGURE 8.5   Idea.
The director's idea can inform all aspects of the performance; here, we would say that we see it in the conflict of social levels of the costumes, in the postures of several of the women, in the book held by one character. But what idea informs the setting? *Our Country's Good at the Western Michigan University, directed by David P. Karsten. Mary Whalen photo.*

Environment.   As the actor determines "given circumstances," the director determines environment: place, time of day, historical period. Much is given in the script, although if it is given only in the stage directions, the director may choose to ignore it. Some directors cross out the stage directions before ever reading them, believing that they were written either for some other director's production (e.g., for Broadway) or for readability for armchair theatregoers. Classic plays often have no stage directions at all.

Questions of tone, mood, and key also influence the director's thinking about environment. There are excellent reasons for putting a murder mystery in a country house on a stormy night, just as there are excellent reasons for putting a brittle comedy in a bright, handsome city apartment. It is not only the rightness of the environment for the characters that the director thinks of (i.e., if they are rich they should have a rich environment, if Russians they should have something Russian, and so on) but the rightness for the indefinable subtleties of mood: the laziness of a warm day, the tension of an electric storm, the depressing gloom of an ancient palace.

Through these early attempts at assessment and analysis, the director develops strong ideas about the production of the play. These will probably change

FIGURE 8.6   Environment.
The director, with the designers, communicates in part through the environment created for the play, while making sure that the environment also provides good acting spaces. Here, *Arthur Miller's All My Sons at South Carolina State University, directed by Frank Mundy.*

some as the director works with the play, but it is the director's springboard and interpretation that shape the whole, guiding the rehearsals and the work of both designers and actors.

Approving and Coordinating the Designs

The director is rarely a designer, but he or she knows the practical needs and the aesthetic values of both play and production. Communicating feelings and ideas about play and production to designers is an important directorial skill, especially when it can be done without insisting on restrictions of budget or personnel.

Communication is best started early. When feasible, meetings between the director and designers begin months before rehearsals; practicality may dictate, however, that they come only weeks or days before casting.

Agreeing on Interpretation.   At early meetings between director and designers, matters of budgets, schedules, and working methods are discussed, but most importantly the director begins to explain his or her interpretation of the play and approach to the production. Based on the director's ideas and images, the designers begin to form their own ideas about the production, which may be somewhat different from the director's. The director weighs all the ideas, accepting some, rejecting or modifying others. Because the goal is for the direction and the designs to work in harmony, unifying the several interpretations is one of the director's first tasks.

Out of these early meetings grows a regular series of *production meetings* attended by the director and designers and perhaps others (the producer, technical director, and stage manager, for example). These regular meetings aim to facilitate communication, to improve efficiency, and to assure artistic coordination.

Agreeing on Presentation.   Having developed a shared interpretation of the play, the director and designers next work together to translate that interpretation into the presentation—the stuff of theatre. Using the results of the director's initial analysis as the starting point, they now collaborate to realize the play's potential physically on the stage.

For example, they will work to provide the actors with a suitable *environment,* deciding how best to convey to the audience a proper sense of place and time. They will come to share a vision of *mood* and decide how best to express it through the visual potency of lighting, set, and costume; they know that inconsistency of mood leads to a severe weakening of the performance. They will work to assure that all elements of the production fit together. The director must be careful at this stage not to be so rigid or so narrow as to cause the designs to make a single statement over and over. In other words, both *unity* and *variety* (or variety within unity) are wanted in the designs. The director also works with the designers to achieve *progression* in the designs just as in the overall production.

ⒻIGURE 8.7   Production Meeting.
Director Sharon Ammen (top right) meets with designers and production staff to create a unified production.

Satisfying the Practical and Aesthetic.   In all of the design areas, both the practical and the aesthetic must be considered. The kind and amount of movement wanted by the director influences costume design; the costume designer's work influences movement (as when, for example, the tight corset of the late nineteenth century or the very broad skirts of the eighteenth century are used). So, too, with colors: Bright pastels may be suitable for a comedy; dull colors and heavy fabrics under gloomy light may match a serious interpretation. Practical considerations influence other decisions: Certain areas will have to be brightly lighted so that the action can be seen; certain actors will have to be in strong colors or outstanding costumes so that they will gain focus. Lighting colors must be carefully coordinated with the colors of sets and costumes so that lights do not wash out or change other colors; the location of lighting instruments has to be coordinated with the location of set pieces and rigging to avoid casting shadows or creating physical interference.

Developing a Ground Plan

The *ground plan* is a "map" of the playing area for a scene, with doors, furniture, walls, and other details indicated to scale. In a realistic interior, the director may almost design the entire acting space simply by setting down directorial needs in detail. The number and location of entrances, the number and location of seating elements, the number and location of objects that will motivate behavior and movement (for example, stoves and refrigerators, fireplaces, closets, and bookcases) are important to the way many directors think about realistic plays and may be determined by such directors even before they meet with their designers. Some directors even give their set designer a ground plan, complete except for minute matters of dimension. Others may remain open until the designer has created a ground plan around a more general statement of needs.

In the nonrealistic play, or sometimes in the realistic play with exterior scenes, directors may have less rigorous requirements. Still, for variety, mood, and emphasis, the director will probably specify differences in level, separation of playing areas, the location of seating elements, and so on. An effect that a director wants to create may require certain things: one director's production of *Macbeth,* for example, had the witches shift magically from a ledge far above the stage to stage level (two sets of actors were used to play the witches); here, obviously, the designer had to provide precisely the levels demanded by the director.

As well, other design elements may be suggested or required by the director; for example, the size and shape of the space where a crowd is used, or where a sense of the isolation of a single figure is wanted, or where a feeling of cramped oppression is sought.

Once ground plans are established, they become the basis for all staging. Drawn to scale, they can be used with scale cutouts of furniture and actors to plan movement and picturization. They are also the basis for the three-dimensional model of each setting that the designer usually provides.

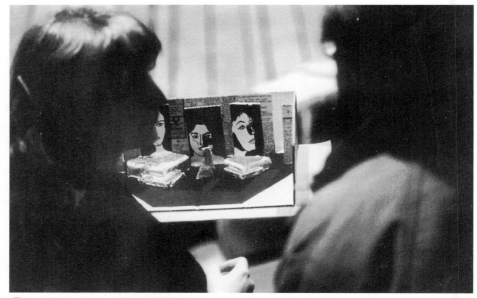

FIGURE 8.8   Three-Dimensional Model.
Director and designer discuss a model of the setting; note that it offers varied stage levels and a nonrealistic setting.

Communicating Decisions

As the production meetings continue and rehearsals near, these and many other matters will have been considered: budget, shifting of scenery, time for costume changes, location of offstage storage space. As decisions are made final, each designer provides the director with a detailed plan in the most appropriate form: color renderings and fabric swatches for costumes; ground plans, scale drawings, renderings, and models for sets; light plots with gel colors for lights. The sound designer (where one exists) may work with an annotated script and lists of sound materials (music, sound effects). These renderings, plans, and other materials represent the culmination of the designers' work with the director: detailed, readable plans for a total production, all in harmony with each other and with the director's interpretation of the text.

Casting and Coaching Actors

Casting

"Style is casting," the late director Alan Schneider said. The remark underlines the enormous importance of casting to the director; its success or failure indelibly stamps the production.

The producer or director puts out a *casting call* and schedules *auditions* or *tryouts*. In New York, much casting is done through agents and private contacts. In university and community theatres, almost the opposite situation holds true, because maximum participation is wanted and closed or private auditions are educationally suspect. In repertory theatres, of course, where the company members are under contract, the director must work rather differently to make the company and the plays mesh, and casting and play selection have a good deal of influence on each other.

The director's conduct of a casting session is a trial of tact, patience, and humanity. Auditions exist for the director, but would-be actors often believe that the sessions exist for them, and directors disabuse them of this error as gently as possible. Both good and bad actors try out, including good actors who are wrong for the play and poor actors who may have a quality that somehow seems right. The director wants to hear and see each one but wants to see and hear only enough of each one to know what each can do. Directors learn to make sound preliminary judgments on the basis of less than a minute's audition. It remains the director's task, however, to be considerate, positive, and polite and to remain open to rethinking these preliminary judgments. The goal is to relax tense actors, to help rid them of nerves that obscure talent by strangling good voices and tensing flexible bodies.

The director or an assistant keeps notes on each aspirant, often in the form of a checklist with headings for physical characteristics, voice, and so on. "Type" may also be indicated—the range of given circumstances that the individual's voice and body would suggest in the realistic theatre. Abilities and outstanding characteristics are noted in enough detail so that the notes themselves will both recall the individual to mind and serve as a basis for later judgment.

In a tryout, the director is looking not for a finished performance but for a display of potential. Script readings, performance of prepared materials, and improvisation and theatre games may be used. Aspirants may be asked to work singly or together or with a stage manager. Some will be called back one or more times because the director feels that they have more potential than was shown the first time or because more information is needed; and, as a final decision nears, the director will want to compare the "finalists" very carefully.

The actual selection of a cast is complicated and, finally, irrational. It is a creative act—the creation of the artistic unit that will bring life to the play. Feelings and hunches are important; so, unfortunately, are personal prejudices. Above all, the director wants to be sure, for replacing an actor after rehearsals have started severely upsets the creative process.

After the director chooses the cast, actors are notified. In university theatres, a cast list is posted. In other situations, the director notifies actors personally or has them notified through agents. Each person who tried out but was not cast should be thanked. If the whole process has been conducted well, there will be inevitable disappointment among those not cast, but no sense of bitterness or injustice.

Once the casting is complete and the designs have been approved, the director is locked into some decisions that are all but irreversible. He or she has decided what the production is to be, settled on designs, assembled a cast, prepared a rehearsal script (including cuts, changes, and notes), and found a dependable assistant or two. The director now begins rehearsals, and time seems suddenly very short. In a few weeks or months, the director must mold the actors and the ideas of production into the performance itself. Throughout rehearsals, the director will continue to analyze and interpret—changing this image, shifting that idea, experimenting, remaining open to fresh insights. In rehearsal, creative actors will bring new ideas, to such a degree that some directors believe they never fully understand a play until it is performed.

Coaching

Most modern directors involve themselves closely in their actors' creation of their roles. The influence of Stanislavski, in particular, has led to a collaboration between actor and director that has developed, in some cases, into a great dependency on the director, a dependency that is sometimes fostered by the teacher–student relationship at universities. Just as there are now playwrights who expect to have their plays "fixed" by the director (a relationship that grew primarily from the Broadway playwright–director collaborations of the twentieth century), so there are actors who expect to have their interpretations "fixed" or even given to them whole by their directors. Particularly in educational and community theatres, great trust is put in the director by the actors, and many interpretations are virtually handed down entire from director to actor.

When the actor and director work in a productive collaboration, however, the director functions as a coach who advises, inspires, and encourages the actor. Significantly, the director works in such a relationship with questions rather than with statements ("Why do you think the character says it just that way?" instead of "What the character means is . . . "). The director will have mastered the actor's vocabulary and, using it, can ask those questions that the actor may not yet be able to phrase. The director is the sounding board and the artistic conscience of the actor—mentor and interpreter, bringing to the actor's work another dimension, another voice, another view of the whole play and all the characters.

FIGURE 8.9   Actor Coaching.
Master teacher and director Walt Witcover working with actors. *Courtesy of Walt Witcover.*

The Director and the Actor.   The director and the actor have had to learn to need each other, for there is no reason to suppose that early directors were warmly welcomed by actors, who, until then, had been independent. There is still much in the relationship to make it difficult for both. The actor is worried about one role, the director about the entire performance; the actor works from a narrow slice through the play, the director from the whole thing; the actor risks everything in front of an audience, the director does not; the actor naturally resents commands, the director sometimes has to give them. Add to these differences the natural indifference or apathy of people brought into a working situation by professional accident rather than affinity, plus the stressful atmosphere of rehearsals, and the relationship can be strained.

Perhaps surprisingly, then, most directors and actors work quite well together. Credit for much of this goes to the director's human skills, although some of it must go to the patience and determination of the actor. The most potent factor may be, in the end, the knowledge that both are engaged in a creative enterprise whose success benefits both.

Actors depend on their director. Therefore, the more precise and sure the director can be, the better. Precision and sureness come from *preparation,* and so the basis of the most productive actor–director relationships is the director's own work in advance of rehearsals.

The Director and the Characters.   Many directors are themselves actors and/or acting teachers. They understand actors' approaches and vocabularies. Only rarely do they try to impose a new system on their actors, and then only if they are director-teachers. Thus, their work on character will be adapted to the system used by the actor playing the role.

Basically, the director does the same character homework as the actor, keeping a notebook, with pages or columns for each character. The director focuses, however, not on the objectives and motivations of a single character (except when working with the actor playing that character) but on shifting patterns of objectives that conflict, part, run parallel, and conflict again. It is not merely that the director maintains an overview of the terrain that the actors travel; it is that the director finds the heart of the play in the coexistence and conflict of character lines.

Too, the director is profoundly concerned with the "outside" of the performance. The director is a master communicator, interested almost obsessively in *things that signal to the audience.* The actor devotes time and energy to the inner reasons for giving signals; the director works on those inner reasons only to help the actor, saving creative energy for the signals themselves.

As the director plans the schedule, attention is given to how each actor will build character. Some actors make great progress early, but one or two may never do so. Still, the director knows that by a certain date, "inner" work must be well under way. By some later date, the director must let go and "sit farther back," working more externally and more comprehensively. The closer the date of the first performance, the less attention the director will be able to give to detailed actor-coaching, which is only one aspect of the modern director's total job.

Staging

"Blocking," "staging," or "traffic direction," as some people wryly call it, is one of the director's inescapable responsibilities. No matter how much the actors and even the director are devoted to inner truth and to characterization, the time must come when the director must shape the actors' moves and timing and must give careful attention to movement, picture making, and rhythm. It is in the very nature of theatre that the visual details of the stage have significance, and the director must make that significance jibe with interpretation.

Significance is the crux of the matter. We live in a world where movement and visual arrangement signify: They give signals. In the realistic theatre, the same things signify that do in life; in the nonrealistic theatre, these things can be kept from signifying or can be made to signify differently only with careful control and effort.

Before the appearance of the director, audiences seemingly found less significance in stage movement, gesture, and picture—or, more accurately, they found a *theatrical* significance in them: The star took center stage, facing front, with other actors flanking and balancing; a hero's movement pattern and posture were heroic; the heroine moved so as to show herself off and to divide or punctuate her speeches. Modern staging, with its meticulous attention to visual symbolism (sometimes called picturization), beauty (composition), and movement was probably not seen before the nineteenth century, except in special cases.

Much of what is taught about directing today is devoted to these matters. By and large, what is taught has been established by tradition and extended by popular theory, little of it having been tested objectively. Much of the theory of pictur-

FIGURE 8.10 Blocking and Business.
Director Anne Fliotsos (left) directs a rehearsal of *The Fantasticks* at the University of Missouri, Columbia.

ization, for example, the supposed "meanings" of various stage areas, derives from the traditional use of the proscenium stage and probably has less relevance to thrust and arena staging. As realistic plays exert less influence on the theatre, and as new theories of theatre evolve, many of these traditional theories of directing will probably fade.

Movement.   As actors are aware of and exploit "body language," so the director is aware of and uses "movement language." Stage movement is often more abundant than real-life movement. In a real situation, people often sit for a very long time to talk, for example, whereas on a stage characters in the same situation will be seen to stand, walk, change chairs, and move a good deal. Partly, this abundance of movement results from the physical distance of the audience—small movements of eyes and facial muscles do not carry the length of a theatre. Partly, it results from the director's need for variety, for punctuation of action and lines, for the symbolic values of movement itself, and for the changing symbolic values of picturization.

Stage movement is based partly on the received wisdom of the movement implied by statements like "Face up to it," "She turned her back on it," "He rose to the occasion." Too, it serves to get characters into positions with which we have similar associations—"at the center of things," "way off in the blue," "out in left field."

The director is concerned with *direction, speed,* and *amount* of movement. Direction reveals both motivation and human interaction; speed shows strength of desire or strength of involvement (impassioned haste, for example, or ambling indifference); amount is perhaps most useful for contrast (a character making a very long movement after several short ones or in contrast with the small moves of several other characters).

Movement also *punctuates* the lines. It introduces speech: The character moves, catches our attention, stops and speaks. It breaks up speech: The character speaks, moves, speaks again, or moves while speaking and breaks the lines with turns or about-faces. (Pacing is frequently used for this reason. In life, we associate pacing with thought, and so a pacing character may seem thoughtful, but the turns are carefully timed by the director to mark changes in the speech itself.)

FIGURE 8.11
Blocking Shorthand.
Directors of traditional proscenium productions sometimes rely on a shorthand of movements: actors "share stage" when they turn about one-quarter toward each other; an actor "takes stage" by making a small movement downstage and out; an actor "counters" by making a small move away and a turn back to balance another actor's movement. These are now rather dated matters.

"Share Stage"

"Take Stage"

"Counter"

Movement *patterns* have a symbolic value much like that of individual movements and can be derived from the same figures of speech: "twisting him around her finger," "winding her in," "going in circles," "following like sheep," "on patrol," and many others suggest patterns for characters or groups. They are used, of course, to underscore a pattern already perceived in the play or the scene.

Visual Symbolism

The exploitation of the stage's potential for displaying pictures is not entirely limited to the proscenium theatre but has its greatest use there. From the late nineteenth century through the middle of the twentieth, the proscenium was seen literally as a picture frame, and the audience sat in locations that allowed it to look through the frame at its contents. With the advent of thrust and round stages, however, this "framing" became impossible, and audiences were located on three or all four sides of the stage, so that each segment of the audience saw quite a different picture. Thus, only certain aspects of picture making have universal application, and of these the most important by far is visual symbolism.

Stage Areas.   On the proscenium stage, there is said to be symbolic value of *stage areas.* These areas are Down Center, Right, and Left (*Down* meaning toward the audience, *Right* meaning to the actor's right and thus the audience's left) and Up Center, Right, and Left. Down Center is unquestionably the most important (or "strongest") area, followed by Down Right and Down Left. Traditional wisdom has it that Down Right is more important than Down Left and that it has a "warmth" that Down Left lacks. The Upper areas are weaker, and Up Left is supposed to be the "coldest." The real value of identifying the stage areas is in creating *variety* and *identification,* variety because it is tedious if the audience has to watch scene after scene played in the same area, and identification because the association of an area with a character or a feeling is an important tool for conveying emotional meaning to the audience. And, unquestionably, the matter of *strength* does have some importance, if only because common sense tells us that

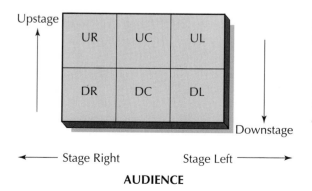

FIGURE 8.12
Proscenium Stage Areas.
"Up" and "down" are away from or toward the front of the stage; "left" and "right" are from the actor's point of view when facing the audience. In other spatial configurations, some other system is used, e.g., a clock face.

the downstage areas are stronger because we can see and hear the actors more clearly there—and, as a result, we want to play our most important (but not all) scenes there.

Stage Relationships. Puns and traditional sayings give us a clue to how another kind of visual symbolism works—and also suggest to us how the mind of the director works as it creates visual images of the sort that communicate to us in dreams. "Caught in the middle," "one up on him," and "odd man out" all suggest strong arrangements of actors. When a director combines them with area identification, for example, they become richer and more complex. The additional use of symbolic properties or set pieces—a fireplace, associated with the idea of home ("hearth and family"), for example—gives still greater force to the picture. Thus, a character who "moves in" on the hearth of a setting while also moving physically between a husband and wife ("coming between them") and sitting in the husband's armchair ("taking his place") has told the audience a complicated story without saying a word.

Sometimes, the playwright's own symbolism creates a rich texture of both picture and movement. Take, for example, this scene from Shakespeare's *Richard II* (Act III, Scene iii):

["King Richard appeareth on the walls" (First Quarto); "Enter on the walls" (First Folio)]:

NORTH: My lord, in the base court he doth attend
            To speak with you; may it please you to come down?

RICHARD: Down, down I come, like glist'ring Phaeton . . . ,
            Wanting the manage of unruly jades.
            Is this the base court? Base court, where kings grow base.
[Richard comes down to stage level; the usurper Bolingbroke kneels to him, as is evident from omitted material]

BOLINGBROKE: Stand all apart,
            And show fair duty to his Majesty.
["He kneels downe." First Quarto.]
            My gracious lord.

RICHARD: Fair cousin, you debase your princely knee
            To make the base earth proud with kissing it . . .
            Up, cousin, up; your heart is up, I know,
            Thus high at least, although your knee be low.

The scene begins with Richard "on high" while his enemies are in the "base court" at stage level. (A base court was a part of a castle, but *base* means "common" or "unworthy," as well as "low" in both the physical and the social sense.) Richard says he will come "down, like glist'ring Phaeton," that is, like the young man who drove the chariot of the sun too near the earth because he could not control the horses that pulled it ("wanting the manage of unruly jades"). But the audience already knows (from earlier reference) that the sun is Richard's emblem, and the director has probably made sure that it is visible on Richard's costume and may even be suggested by the shape of his crown, so the sun is being *debased,* brought down, even as Richard physically moves down to stage level. There, the usurper tells everyone else to "stand apart," that is, to give them room, but the word *stand* may be ironic and the director may use it to make an ironic picture, because they should kneel to the king. Bolingbroke himself does kneel (stage direction, First Quarto), but the gesture is a mockery, as Richard notes, "You debase your princely knee/To make the base earth proud . . . /Up, cousin, up . . . ," reminding the audience that Richard himself was, only moments ago, "up" on the higher level. And Richard goes on: Touching his crown (a traditional bit of business), he says, "Up, cousin, up/Thus high at least. . . ." That is, he will raise himself high enough in the presence of his king (though he should be kneeling) to seize the crown.

Thus, in a quick sequence of moves and gestures, the symbolic flow of the scene is given to the audience. With a scene of this richness and detail, the director need only follow its lead; few modern scenes are this explicitly symbolic, however, and directors usually have to create their own visual symbols to match the interpretation.

Mood. Mood is established most readily with lighting and sound and with the behavior of the characters. However, certain visual effects of character arrangement contribute, as well: horizontals, perhaps, for a quiet, resigned scene; looming verticals and skewed lines for a suspense melodrama. Mood values are subjective and irrational, however, and hard to describe. In reality, what the director remains watchful for are clashes of mood, where movement and visual symbols conflict with other mood establishers.

FIGURE 8.13
Visual Symbols.

Metaphors, conscious or unconscious, are often the basis for staging and movement. Here, for example, "He came between them" (top); "Odd man out" (middle); "She ran circles around him" (bottom).

Focus.   A stage is a visually busy place, with many things to look at; therefore, the audience's eyes must be directed to the important point at each moment. A number of devices achieve *focus: framing* (in a doorway, between other actors, and so on); *isolating* (one character against a crowd, one character on a higher or lower level); *elevating* (standing while others sit, or the reverse, or getting on a higher level); *enlarging* (with costume, properties, or the mass of a piece of furniture);

FIGURE 8.14   Focus.
In the graphic, only two of the seven figures have focus, the seated figure and the closest standing figure. The seated one has the principal emphasis because of the unique position, the added mass of the chair, and the centrality of position (in proscenium staging). In the engraving, the figure in the doorway has focus: he is *isolated, framed* by the doorway, *illuminated* by the moonlight, and *indicated* by the arms and eyes of the others.

illuminating (in a pool of light or with a brighter costume); and *indicating* (putting the focal character at the intersection of "pointers"—pointing arms, swords, eyes, and so on).

Focus is largely a mechanical matter, but it is an important one that affects both movement and picture making.

Visual Aesthetics

Most stage pictures are rather well *composed,* or good to look at, but directors are often careful to study the production with an eye to improving the aesthetic quality of the scenes. What is *not* wanted is easier to say than what is: straight lines, lines parallel to the stage front, evenly spaced figures like bottles on a supermarket shelf. *Balance* is sought so that the stage does not seem heavy with characters on one side, light on the other. Composition is, finally, an irrational matter and a highly subjective one; directors who concern themselves with it in depth learn much from the other visual arts, especially traditional painting.

Rhythm

Rhythm is repetition at regular intervals. The elements of rhythm in the theatre are those things that regularly mark the passage of time: scenes, movements, speeches, words. For the director, rhythm includes *tempo* and *timing,* as well as one aspect of *progression.* The director is concerned, then, not only with the interpretation of character and the visual signals of interpretation but also with *the rate(s) at which things happen.*

We have seen that speed of movement is important to movement's meaning. Now we may say that it is also important to intensity and rhythm. We associate quickness with urgency, slowness with relaxation; change in speed is most important of all. We may compare this phenomenon with the beating of a heart: Once the normal heartbeat (base rhythm) is established, any change becomes significant.

The director establishes the base rhythm with the opening scenes of the play and then creates variations on it, and the shortening of the time between moves, between lines, and between entrances and exits becomes a rhythmic acceleration that gives the audience the same feeling of increased intensity as would a quickening of the pulse.

Pace is the professional's term for "tempo," but it is not a matter of mechanical tempo. Much of what is meant by *pace* is, in fact, emotional intensity and energy, and the director who tries to create a feeling of intensity by telling the actors merely to "pick up the pace" or "move it along" will probably succeed only in getting the actors to speak so fast that they cannot be understood. Tempo has to grow naturally out of understanding and rehearsal of a scene, not out of a decision to force things along. Indeed, the scornful dismissal of such an attempt as "forcing the pace" and "pumping it up" suggests how futile it is.

FIGURE 8.15
Composition and Balance.
Composition and balance are partly matters of style. In the graphics, a realist would reject the top and middle, the top for being too balanced, the middle for not being balanced enough. The bottom, he/she would say, achieves sufficient balance, is interesting, and does not look contrived. A non-realist, however, might prefer the middle or the top. In the photograph below, the composition is balanced but over-composed for realism, of which it is an example: The mass of the crowd and the pointing arms are too contrived. In a sense, it is *over*-directed.

Timing is complicated and difficult, something felt rather than thought out. *Comic timing* is the delivery of the laugh-getter—a line or a piece of business—after exactly the right preparation and at just that moment when it will most satisfy the tension created by a pause before it; it also describes the actor's awareness of the timing that has produced previous laughs and of how each builds on those before. The timing of serious plays is rather different and depends far more on the setting of (usually) slow rhythms from which either a quickening tempo will increase tension or a slowing will enhance a feeling of ponderousness or doom. For example, at the end of *Hamlet,* Fortinbras has the following speech (Act V, Scene ii):

Let four captains
Bear Hamlet, like a soldier to the stage;
For he was likely, had he been put on,
To have prov'd most royally; and, for his passage,
The soldier's music and the rights of war
Speak loudly for him.
Take up the bodies: such a sight as this
Becomes the field, but here shows much amiss.
Go, bid th' soldiers shoot.

[A dead march. Exeunt, bearing off the bodies; after which a peal of ordnance is shot off.]

This follows an active scene of dueling, argument, and violence, and a short, less active scene of Hamlet's and Horatio's final words to each other, with the arrivals of ambassadors and Fortinbras. Fortinbras' speech is jumpy and uneven, effective because it *lacks* regular rhythm, but it finally settles down into the firm, regular rhymed couplet, "Take up the bodies . . . " that sets the final rhythm of the play. The rest could be timed on a metronome, taking the base rate (the pulse) from the couplet. *Go* is a long sound, followed (in one director's view) by a pause of two beats. The words that remain have but a single stress among them, on *shoot.* After this one-beat word, there is another pause of as long as three beats (in the major rhythm of which *Go* and *shoot* are major units). Then, the drum ("a dead march") starts its slow beating on the same tempo; a measured number of beats later comes the cannon sound ("a peal of ordnance"); another measured number of beats later, the lights begin to dim or the curtain to close, still on units of the original rhythm.

This control of a scene may seem unnecessarily rigid, and controlled rhythm of this kind works only when it is carefully planned and rehearsed, because there is no such thing as a timing that is "almost rhythmic." The rhythm is either exact or it is nonexistent, and it is in stage effects like the drum and the cannon that the director can most carefully control it. (It was partly because of the desire for control of such effects, in fact, that the director came into being.)

FIGURE 8.16 Timing. Certain dramatic moments must be timed by the director for maximum effect. Here, as the woman pops up behind the screen, left, the taller man must turn the shorter one's head away at precisely the right moment (so that he will not see her). If the moment is not precisely right, the audience will not find it funny. *The School for Scandal, directed by Jim Patterson, at the University of South Carolina; setting by Dennis C. Maulden, lighting by Ed Intemann, costumes by Lisa Martin-Stuart.*

Planning and Coordinating the Production

In a Broadway production, many managerial functions are performed by the producer or the producer's office. In community and school theatres, the director performs most or all of them: *scheduling, budgeting, personnel selection, research,* and some aspects of *public relations* all fall to the director's lot. Scheduling includes the overall flow of production work from inception to performance, including production meetings, rehearsals, and the coordination of design and technical schedules, at least for purposes of information (including costume fittings for actors, clearing of the stage for construction work, and so on). These schedules are kept by the director or the stage manager on some easily read form like an oversized calendar.

Budgets are rarely initiated by a director, who does not hold the purse strings of the theatre, but the director must be able to keep a staff budget and to understand and honor costume, setting, and other budgets. In many college and university theatres, the director functions as producer and has budget control over the design areas (that is, the production money is budgeted as a single figure, which can be carved up as the director wishes).

Personnel selection (not including that of the actors) covers the director's own staff, most particularly the stage manager and assistants. In many situations, it will extend to the choreographer and the music director, with whom the director must work closely; it may include selection or at least approval of designers.

Research is carried out by a director on virtually any aspect of the production. Designers do their own research, to be sure, but such matters as the actors' accents, social mores, manners and mannerisms, the traditions surrounding the staging of a classic, the historical conventions associated with it, critical comments on it, and the work of other actors and directors in other productions of it concern many directors. It is not their aim to steal ideas from other productions; rather, it is their aim to learn from them, to honor traditions, and to build on what has been done before. This is particularly true in the staging of something like the operettas of Gilbert and Sullivan, for example, where audiences are familiar with the work and the traditions of performance are strong. In some theatres, directors have the help of a dramaturg in this task.

Public relations is not usually a directorial responsibility, but as a matter of taste and even of self-protection, the director often wants at least advisory approval of graphic and written material. Staging publicity photos, providing historical material from research, and appearing on interview shows to publicize the production are only a few of the things that a director may do.

Scheduling and Conducting the Rehearsals

Every director has a rehearsal pattern, and every pattern has to be adaptable to the special needs of each cast and each play. In general, however, a structure like the following is used:

First Rehearsal

The cast gathers, a trifle nervous and unsure. Many are strangers to each other. The director plays the role of host—making introductions, breaking the ice, moving these individuals toward cohesion. (Even when the playwright sits in, it is the director who is the "host.") The play will probably be discussed at some length, the director explaining general ideas and the overall direction; the designers may be asked to show and discuss models and sketches. Certain practical matters are got out of the way by the director or the stage manager (the signing of necessary forms, the resolving of individual schedule conflicts, and so on).

Then the play is read, either by the entire cast or by the director or the playwright. Some directors interrupt this first reading often, even on every line, to explain and define; others like to proceed without interruption so that the actors may hear each other. Either way, once the books are open and the lines are read, the rehearsal period is truly under way.

Rehearsal by Units

Rehearsing entire acts is often not the way to do detailed work, and so the acts are further broken down into *French scenes* (between the entrance and exit of a major

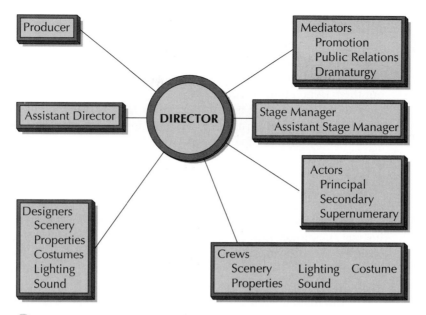

FIGURE 8.17   Director as Liaison.
The director must be at the center of a complex network of people working
toward the success of the production.

character) or *scenes* (between curtains or blackouts), and then further into *beats* or
units (between the initiation and end of an objective). These short elements are
numbered in such a way that, for example, all the appearances of a major character can be called by listing a series of numbers, for example, 12, 13, 15, 17, meaning scenes 2, 3, 5, and 7 of the first act. By scheduling detailed rehearsals this way,
the director often avoids keeping actors waiting. Or this same number system can
be used to call scenes that need extra rehearsal.

   As a very general pattern, it can be said that many directors move from the
general rehearsal of early readings into increasingly detailed rehearsals of smaller
and smaller units, and then into rehearsals of much longer sections when the
units are put back together.

Run-Throughs

A *run-through* is a rehearsal of an entire act or an entire play; it gives the director
(and the actors) insight into the large movements and progressions of the play. After run-throughs, the director will probably return to rehearsal of certain small
units, but, as performance nears, more and more run-throughs are held.

Technical and Dress Rehearsals

As production coordinator, the director cannot forget the integration of lights, costumes, sound, and scenery into the performance. *Technical rehearsals* are devoted to any or all of these elements, normally done with the actors but sometimes without them (when "cue-to-cue" or "dry-run" technical rehearsals are held). In either case, the stage manager usually takes over the management of the script and the cues in preparation for running the show during performance; the director makes the decisions affecting the look and sound of the production and conveys them to the stage manager.

Dress rehearsals incorporate costumes into the other technical elements, and final dress rehearsals are virtually performances in all but their lack of an audience. Nothing is now left to chance: Actors must be in place for every entrance well in advance of their cues; properties must be in place, with none of the rehearsal substitutes now tolerated; costumes must seem as natural to the actors as their own clothes (achieved by giving them, weeks earlier, rehearsal costumes of cheap materials); every scene shift and light cue must be smooth, timed as the director wants it.

And then, for the director, it is over. To be sure, polishing rehearsals may be called even after opening night, or full rehearsals if the play is a new one that has gone into *previews* (full performances with audiences in advance of the official opening) and needs fixing; but, as a rule, when the play opens, it belongs to the actors and the stage manager, and the director is a vestige of another era in its life. The director may continue to check the production regularly, even for months or years if it is a Broadway success, but in effect, after opening night, the director is a fifth wheel. Until the next play, of course.

More than one director has compared directing to being a parent, the child being the production. The director rears it from birth to maturity and then pushes it out into the world. It is a paradox of the craft—as it is, perhaps, of parenting—that the proof of one's success is the loss of one's function.

Serving as Liaison Among All Members of the Production Team

Throughout the work of the production, the director is the person who ensures that all members of the production team are pulling in the same direction, working together to assure a successful production. He or she makes sure that the actors know what the designers are doing, and vice versa. The director makes certain that actors go promptly when the costumers call them for fittings, and that the designers provide needed drawings to technical staff, and on and on. He or she mediates disagreements and serves as final arbiter on differences of opinion. In short, the director is that crucial person who bridges the gap between the theatre's potential and the audience's enjoyment; the director is the person who is most responsible for realizing that potential.

LINKS to more about theatre

In the Bleak Midwinter, directed by and starring Kenneth Branagh. A comic look at the director's craft.

Ellen Donkin and Susan Clement, *Upstaging Big Daddy,* 1993. Directing meets feminism.

Charles Marowitz, *Prospero's Staff,* 1986.

Michael Frayne, Noises Off. Great theatrical farce.

< **www.ssdcl.com** > Site of the Society of Stage Directors and Choreographers.

TRAINING DIRECTORS

There is no one pathway that leads to becoming a director. Many of today's directors began as actors, choreographers, stage managers, or even designers. Some of today's directors have come from fields entirely outside theatre; others have pursued graduate work in theatre, specifically as directors. Probably today's directors in the professional and commercial theatres have somewhat more varied backgrounds than those within the educational theatre, most of whom have a graduate degree in theatre. Most professional directors (but not most academic directors) belong to the Society of Stage Directors and Choreographers.

Directors of whatever background and formal training, however, are expected to have a body of knowledge and skills that will help them to fulfill their myriad functions as directors. Directors must be familiar with a range of plays. They must have a sophisticated understanding of how to interpret plays and a knowledge of the theoretical principles that underpin them. They should be acquainted with the fundamental principles and working vocabularies of the other artists of the theatre—actors, designers, stage managers. They need to know theatrical practices of the past, especially with regard to stage space, acting, and design. They need acquaintance with the basic principles and language of several related fields, especially dance, painting, music, psychology, and history. They need to know at least rudimentary techniques for scheduling, accounting, and communicating. They must know how to find out whatever they need to know for each production; that is, they need basic research skills.

In short, the director, in addition to suitable personal traits, must have a solid, well-rounded education. For this reason, theatre accrediting programs do not recognize undergraduate majors or degrees in directing, only graduate ones. For persons who want to pursue graduate work in directing, there are two usual pathways: a Master of Fine Arts (MFA) degree in directing or a Ph.D. in theatre's history, criticism, or literature, with supervised opportunities in directing.

Because of the complexity of the director's responsibilities, it is difficult to know exactly how to train someone to be a director. Directing, like any artistic practice, has changed since its beginnings. Directing will doubtless change again in the future, but we cannot say with certainty in what directions. We can note that a few theatres now function without directors, most notably theatres organized around cooperative or communal practices. We can also note, by contrast, that a few theatres now function with directors who exert complete control over all aspects of production, taking over responsibilities usually assumed by actors and designers. In the absence of a clear direction for the future, the director's training must remain wide-ranging and flexible.

Given the complexity of the task and the training needed, directors might be presumed to be in short supply. In fact, however, the market for directors, both in educational and professional venues, is glutted. Unemployment rates are at least as high for directors as for actors. Perhaps this situation is less surprising when we remember that for every one director there are many actors, designers, and technicians required: It takes a rather large pyramid of people to support the one directing figure at its top.

WHAT IS GOOD DIRECTING?

To understand directing, we must be able to assess what the director has brought to the play and what the play presented to the director as strengths and weaknesses. Our evaluation of the direction will then depend on answers to questions like:

- How well did the director analyze and interpret the script?

- How well did the director solve the problems presented?

It is important to separate the *production* being studied from the *play* being studied. The production is not necessarily bad because it fails to stage the "playwright's intentions"; nor is it necessarily good because it either stages the "playwright's intentions" precisely or turns them upside down. As we have seen, different kinds of directors take different approaches; we must try to understand the approach and then evaluate it for what it is.

Good directing is seen in an internally consistent, exciting production. It deals with the play's problems and exploits the play's strengths in the terms of the director's approach.

Good directing shows most of all in the work of the actors. If the actors are good and are working in a theatrically compelling whole, the director has laid a good foundation. If the actors have not been unified, if they seem to hang in space when not speaking, if they perform mechanically, if they lack motivation at any point, if they do not perform with each other, they have been poorly directed.

Good directing has technical polish—smooth cues, precise timing, and a perfect blending of all elements—that radiates "authority," the artists' confidence in their work.

Good directing creates compelling pictures and movement, but only when they expand the work of actors and playwright, never when they contradict—and never when they exist for their own sake.

Good directing gives the performance tempo without giving it mechanical speed; there is no sense of too-fast or too-slow, but the organic tempo of a living entity.

Good directing combines all elements into a whole; there is no sense of good ideas left over or of things unfinished. Everything belongs; everything is carried to its proper full development; nothing is overdone.

The good director, then, understands the play and takes a consistent approach to it, bringing the actors to life in a complete production; the bad director does not fully understand the play, often failing to ask detailed questions; does not coach the actors or coaches them only incompletely, or directs them mechanically in postures and positions and movements dictated by a mechanical notion of visual symbolism and visual beauty; achieves not tempo but clockwork timing; and leaves ideas undeveloped and elements unassimilated.

CURRENT ISSUES

When the worshipful director argues that the text is primary and that the author's intentions matter, he or she assumes that playwrights "own" plays. When the heretical director maintains that the written words are "not a text but a pretext," he or she implies that a playwright does not "own" a play and that a play is simply one tool to be used in creating theatre.

These views echo a larger debate now underway. The worshipful director's is at base one that resembles a view we now call *modern:* the belief that there is meaning that inheres in a work of art, that the meaning can be discovered through systematic ("scientific") investigation, and that the meaning remains more or less stable over time. The position of the heretical director corresponds more closely to a view that we now call *postmodern:* that is, that there are many layers of meanings in any work, that each meaning contains its own opposite, and that no meaning is fixed. Is there truth, or is there merely point of view?

If there is merely point of view, can any individual "own" it? Western society has long said that people own things—not only furniture and land but also intellectual "things" like ideas and works of art. Owners of intellectual "properties" are protected by copyrights and patents; plagiarism is called intellectual "theft." Recent shifts in philosophy and, especially, technology raise questions about the very possibility of individual ownership. The Xerox machine allows anyone to reproduce

Ⓕ**IGURE 8.18   Who Owns the Play?**

The London Merchant was an important eighteenth-century play. As *The London Merchant Person,* it was reinterpreted as a feminist work with very different elements: the male hero was now a woman; the Christian pieties of the original were parodied; the costumes were modernized, but elements like the frames on the hips of the character with her back to us were kept as ironic reminders. This, like all heretical productions, raises the question, Who owns the play? Is *The London Merchant Person* a new play or a version of an old one? What would be the situation if the original author were alive? If the play were under copyright? If a theatre had meant to offer it as an example of an eighteenth-century classic? *Directed by Catherine Schuler. Courtesy of the University of Maryland.*

the writings of many different people and to bind them together in a new order; who "owns" the resulting book? Computer networks make it possible for anyone to receive and change and then pass along altered versions of many ideas and essays; who "owns" them? Genetic discoveries allow us to segregate, alter, and replicate chromosomes and parts of chromosomes, producing improved specimens and even new species; who "owns" them?

Questions of ownership are not abstract. They have direct financial consequences. If a director selects a play and then changes it, making it a comment upon itself or a parody of itself, is the play still the playwright's, or is it now the director's? If the playwright is alive and disapproves of the director's vision, can he or she forbid the production of the play or sue the director for producing a damaged play? If there is a production, who should receive royalty payments? Because makeup, costume, and vocal imitation permit new versions of Elvis Presley, who "owns" the resulting image of Elvis? Who should receive the money when Elvis lookalikes perform? If there is no ownership of intellectual property, what is plagiarism?

KEY TERMS

Check your understanding against this list. Brief definitions are in the Glossary; page references there will direct you to appropriate pages. (Persons are page-referenced in the Index.)

balance
beat
blocking
casting call
composition
dress rehearsal
environment (of the play)
focus
French scene

ground plan
pace
picturization
previews
rhythm
run-through
technical rehearsal

chapter 9

The Design Team: Scenery, Lighting, and Costumes

OBJECTIVES

When you have completed this chapter, you should be able to:

- Explain how mood, abstraction, historical period, and socioeconomic circumstances affect design

- Enumerate the major responsibilities of each designer: scenery, lights, sound, costumes

- List the major responsibilities of a technical director

THE DESIGN TEAM

Sitting in the modern theatre, we sometimes take the presence of scenery so much for granted that it is easy to forget that theatre does not have its roots in either spectacular effects or localizing settings. We have become acculturated to the presence of physical environments that so closely suit the mood and meanings of each play that we may lose sight of the fact that the theatre for a very long period used little more than the theatre space itself as environment, and that for centuries after that it was satisfied with stock settings that could do for many plays: a room in a palace, a garden, a forest. We live in a period of magnificent settings and superb designers; however, stage design has not always been considered fundamental to theatre or its performance.

Much the same thing is true of costume designers, although it seems likely that their art (extended to include the making of masks) is a very, very old one, whereas sound designers are so recent an innovation that most theatregoers over fifty are still surprised to see them listed in the program. Creators of lighting effects may be said to go back to the Renaissance, but it is probably more helpful to think of the art of stage lighting as coming into its own when a controllable means of illumination was invented: gaslight (about 1830).

FIGURE 9.1   Before Design.
For most of the theatre's history, "design" was limited to individual items and sometimes was nonexistent. Here, actors of about 1625 performed in front of an architectural facade in clothes and costumes from several sources.

Actors, directors, and playwrights work with life as their material. Theatre designers, however, work with the environment of human life, and their materials are the materials of our world: light and shadow, fabric and color, wood and canvas, plastic and metal and paint. Because their materials are of this kind, designers are far more dependent on technology than are actors, playwrights, or directors. This dependence explains the role of another theatre professional, the technical director. Advances in technology inevitably change the way in which theatre designers practice their art, and, in the case of both light and sound, technology virtually created the arts. Thus, theatre designers stand in both the world of the artist and the world of the artisan or the mechanic, and they usually must be expert in both.

THE NATURE OF DESIGN

Because the designers derive their materials and their subjects from the real world, their art is the creation of worlds on the stage. These worlds are sometimes imitations of the real world, sometimes not; in either case, they use familiar materials, but often in unfamiliar ways. The scenic and costume designers know that their products will be seen under colored light and so will look different on the stage from the way they look in sunlight; the lighting designer knows that the audience must see the actors, no matter what the demands of mood, color, and emphasis, and that the surfaces being lit are different from the things they imitate; the sound designer may be asked to create sounds that never existed in life or to amplify and distort real sounds to match the needs of an unreal world.

The world that the designers create is the world of the play, which is not at all the same thing as a literal copy of the real world. Each designer goes about his or her task differently in creating that world, but they all share a common goal: to create an environment within which the actors can create convincing life. This goal means that the designers must work as a team and that they must work in concert with the director so that a compatible world is created by all of them.

THINKING ABOUT DESIGN

"To surround a play with foreign bodies of scenery . . . [that] obscure its meaning while they pretend to illustrate it . . . [is] an artistic crime."
—Harley Granville-Barker, director, 1877–1946.

Study the illustrations in Chapters 9 and 16 and evaluate their scenic designs in terms of Granville-Barker's criterion.

This environment begins with the play. Contemporary design is tied inescapably to the dramatic text. The world that it creates has its roots deep within that text—not merely in the stage directions, but in the lives of the characters.

Several factors, all to be found in the play, govern how the designers create their world.

Tone and Mood

Designers pay close attention to the differences between comic and serious drama, but these two categories are simply not enough. Every play is its own category and must be approached through the range of tones that it contains: lightheartedness in several early scenes and great seriousness in a last act; both the romantic quality of a protagonist and the fragility of another major character, both funny gags and the real sadness of a central character's dilemma. And they must express these subtleties in the settings, costumes, lights, and sounds that are required by the scripts.

Level of Abstraction

The designers are faced with a wide spectrum of possibilities, from literal realism to fantasy to almost pure abstraction. At one extreme, for example, could be the setting for an American tragedy, where the decision might be made to create a literal replica of a house in New England down to the last detail of the patterns in the wallpaper. At the other extreme might be one of the "space stage" settings of the 1920s—abstract constructions of stairs, ramps, and levels. In costuming, we might find real clothes, purchased in stores and dyed to look sweaty and dirty; at the other extreme, we might find the costumes of some modern theatres, which use elastic fabric, extensions of limbs, and various kinds of padding to change completely the outline of the human body.

In part, the decision about how abstract the designs will be comes from the designers' and director's interpretation of the script; in part, it comes from a decision about how much the abstraction or literalism of the play itself will be emphasized. In a realistic play, for example, the decision to create literal settings and costumes is not an inevitable one; with equal justification, the designers might decide to create a mere suggestion of a house. In the same way, the designers of a play of Shakespeare's may decide that an abstract setting is inappropriate and may go to quite literal, realistic settings.

Historical Period

The shifting of classical plays from one period to another has become common. Designers are confronted constantly with plays that do not have contemporary settings, costumes, and sound. The look and the "feel" of other periods become important aspects of design.

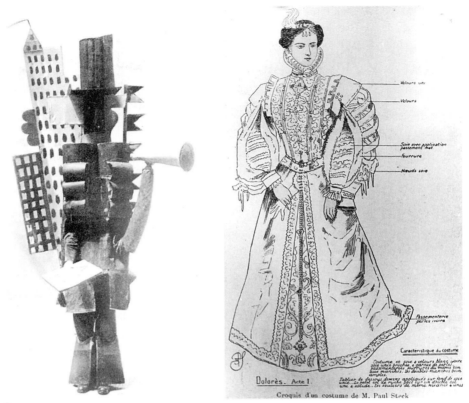

FIGURE 9.2   Production Style: Abstraction.
Designers can copy or ignore surface reality. On the left is an abstract design by Pablo
Picasso, c. 1920; on the right is a designer's sketch for a historical costume based on
real detail. *Picasso design from Huntley Carter, The New Spirit of the European Theatre,
1914–1924.*

FIGURE 9.3   Production Style: Abstraction.
Both sets are interiors. Left, a design by Emil Pirchan that is deliberately nonrealistic and
eliminates almost all detail; right, a realistic design that copies "office" and provides detail.

The lighting designer is also affected by historical period, when, for example, ideas about the direction and quantity of light and the quality of shadow come from paintings and engravings of another period. In setting and costume, some of the implications of historical period are obvious; the kinds of problems that they raise are most often handled by careful research by the designers. Sound, too, may be affected if period music is used or if certain kinds of sounds are called for—footsteps, for example, echoing from the stone walls of an old corridor instead of from modern materials; or the sound of a trumpet flourish; or the sound of *Hamlet's* "peal of ordnance."

Historical period contains a trap for the designers in the perceptions and knowledge of the audience: The designers must consider not only what things looked like in the period but what the audience *thinks* they looked like. What we know of the 1920s, for example, is conditioned by what we have seen in cartoons, old movies, and magazines—but did all women really bob their hair, and did all men really wear knickers and high collars? In the Elizabethan period, did all houses have plaster-and-timber fronts, and did all men wear puffed-out breeches and hose? Did warriors in the tenth century wear plate armor? Or, to reverse the calendar, will all people in the distant future wear tight-fitting clothes of unisex design?

And there is still another trap: contemporary fashion. Audiences are greatly influenced by their own ideas of beauty. As a result, a hairstyle that is supposed to be of 1600 and that was designed in 1930 will often look more like a 1930 hairstyle than a 1600 one; or to take a familiar example from the movies, cowboys' hats in the movies of the 1940s looked far more like 1940s' ideas of what was becoming to men than they ever looked like the actual headgear of westerners of the frontier period.

So designers must think of several things at once when confronted with historical period. It is not enough to go to a book and copy literally what is there.

Geographical Place

Like historical period, geography greatly influences design, unless the decision is made to abandon it altogether (that is, to be abstract instead of literal). The whitewashed houses of the Greek islands are different in color, texture, and scale from the adobes of Mexico or the balconied houses of New Orleans; the traditional clothes of Scotland, Morocco, and Scandinavia are distinct; the light in Alaska and Texas is very different. Sound and light are quite different outdoors from in. Even at considerable levels of abstraction, differences in geography inform some design decisions.

Socioeconomic Circumstances

Wealth and social class influence clothes, furniture, and environment in many places and periods, and, therefore, their imitation on the stage. As with the other

FIGURE 9.4   Production Style: Socioeconomics.

Through the choice of furnishings, properties, and costumes, designers make environments suitable for the circumstances of the characters. At the top, the light colors, floral
patterns, and ample spaces signal a middle or upper-class room. At the bottom, the drab,
patternless walls and costumes together with rough furniture and small window signal
poverty. (Top, from Oliver Sayler, *The Moscow Art Theatre Series of Russian Plays.*
Bottom, from *Le Théâtre.*)

considerations, a decision may be made to ignore such matters, but *a decision must be made.* The matter itself cannot be ignored. And the more realistic the level, the more important these considerations become.

Historical period greatly complicates social and economic matters. As with other historical elements, audiences may have general or inaccurate ideas about what constituted the look of wealth or position or power or poverty in a distant era. What, for example, did a wealthy merchant wear in the seventeenth century that a noble did not? What furniture did the noble own that the merchant did not? What separated serf from artisan in the Middle Ages?

Aesthetic Effect

Put most simply, every designer hopes that the designs will have beauty. That beauty is a variable should be clear—the romantic loveliness of a magic forest cannot be compared with a construction of gleaming metal bars and white plastic plates—but that every designer aims at a goal of aesthetic pleasure seems true. Intentional ugliness may occasionally be aimed at, but even then we are tempted to say that the result is beautiful *because* its ugliness is artfully arrived at.

Composition and balance enter into aesthetic consideration, just as they enter into the considerations of the director. Teamwork is again essential, as setting, costumes, and lights are inevitably seen by the audience as a whole. Thus, unity is also an aesthetic aim, one achieved through a constant sharing of ideas by all the designers.

DESIGNERS AT WORK

Although many of their decisions are reached in concert (at production meetings), the designers do most of their work in solitude or with the technicians who execute their designs—the scene designer with the technical director and builders and painters, the costume designer with cutters and sewers, and so on. At this stage of their work, each specializes and proceeds separately.

The Scene Designer

It is the scene designer's job to create a performing space for the actors and a physical environment for the play's action. The result is the setting, which normally has the added function of supplying the audience with clues about the play's locale.

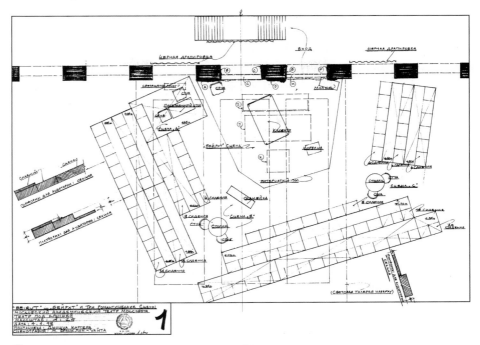

FIGURE 9.5 Designer's Ground Plan.
A scale map of the stage with all structures and levels. Design by M. Franklin-White, USAA, for *Beirut* at the Mossovet Theatre, Moscow, directed by Joshua Karter. (See also color figure C-13.)

Other important questions are:

- The *number of settings* (Can the entire play be played in one set, or must different sets be designed and changed for each scene, or can some sort of *unit set* serve for all scenes?)

- The *shape and size of the stage* (Will the audience surround it or look at it through a proscenium arch? If it is small, how can it be kept from seeming cramped? Will the actors play within the setting or in front of it?)

- The *sight lines* of the theatre (What peculiarities of the theatre's architecture demand that the settings be built in special shapes so that every member of the audience can see?)

- The *means of shifting the scenery* (Is there overhead *rigging* so that scenery can be "flown," or is there an elevator stage or a turntable stage for bringing new settings in mechanically?)

- The *materials from which the scenery will be built* (Is it better to use traditional *flats* of wood and canvas, or will built-up details of wood or plastic be better, or will such special materials as poured polyurethane foam or corrugated cardboard or metal pipe be better?)

- Any *special effects* that make special scenic demands (Are there vast outdoor scenes in a proscenium theatre that require large painted *drops,* or will such unusual events in the play as earthquakes or explosions require special solutions?)

- Any decision to imitate *historical scenery* that creates special requirements (That is, if a seventeenth-century play is to be done with Italianate scenery, what will the effects be?)

- The demands of *budget* and *schedule*

All of these matters may influence the designer before pencil is ever put to paper, although preliminary doodles and sketches may attempt to catch the "feel" of the play long before any practical matters are dealt with. These early impressions will spring from early readings of the play, and they will eventually be incorporated in some form into the *rendering* of the settings that the designer gives the director. Together, they will have worked out the ground plan of each setting, and the ground plan will form the basis of both renderings and three-dimensional models. If the renderings are acceptable, the designer will proceed to elevations and scale drawings of all scenic pieces, and these, with all instructions for building and painting, will go to the production's *technical director.*

**FIGURE 9.6
Behind Design.**
The back sides of the scenery are very different from what the audience sees—mere structure, what one designer called "the tail to the poet's kite."

In addition, the scene designer is normally in charge of the design or selection of all *properties,* the things used by the actors that are not part of the scenery (furniture, flags, hangings, and so on), as well as such "hand props" as swords, cigarette cases, guns, and letters. Where such things must be designed, as in a period play, the designer creates, and the technical staff executes; where they are acquired from outside sources, the designer haunts stores and antique shops and pores over catalogs of all sorts. In plays done with minimal scenery, as in arena staging, the properties take on added importance, and their design and selection must be carried out with the greatest care.

The Technical Director

Broadway productions have large technical staffs, and they contract out such jobs as scene construction and painting. Small community theatres may have only a single technician to do almost everything. In all kinds of theatres, however, a person exists to oversee the execution of designs and to organize and manage the technical production and its relationship with the theatre. This person is the *technical director.*

FIGURE 9.7 Technical Work.
The spaces around a stage are filled with areas for storage and work. Here, part of a scenery shop.

The technical director rules the theatre building around the playing area and behind whatever barrier separates audience from backstage. The job is a tangle of details and responsibilities: he or she knows the theatre building thoroughly and coordinates its maintenance with the building's owner (a university, a foundation, and so on); he or she sees that an ample stock of cables, nails, paint, and a thousand other things are kept on hand; he or she sees to the upkeep of tools, from pencils to table saws; he or she has oversight of backstage scheduling; he or she knows what scenery and properties are in storage and maintains their inventories. In short, the technical director has a huge responsibility, and a day-to-day schedule that can be crushing without the most careful planning (and an even temper).

In university theatres, the technical director usually attends meetings at which plays are first selected; even at this earliest stage, his or her advice will be needed to determine if a potential play is too demanding for the theatre's physical capabilities. Later, the technical director takes part in all production meetings, advising director and designer on the practicability of ideas and the likelihood of deadlines. Throughout, the technical director is responsible for setting and meeting scenic and property schedules. (Lighting may fall within his or her responsibility, as well; costumes generally do not.) On top of all this, in educational theatre the technical director does a great deal of the actual work of construction and painting, as well as instructing students working on the production.

Many technical directors are capable designers in their own right. When not executing their own designs, however, they must work objectively, remembering Lee Simonson's dictum that "technology is the tail to the poet's kite." It is the technical director who causes the poet's kite to fly—but not to fly away.

The Costume Designer

The costume designer clothes both the character and the actor, creating dress in which the character is "right" and the actor is both physically comfortable and artistically pleased. This double responsibility makes the costumer's a difficult job. It is never enough to sew up something that copies a historically accurate garment; that garment must be made for a character, and it must be made for an actor. The actor must be able to move and speak and should also feel led or pushed by the costume to a closer affinity with the character and the world of the play. Generally, actors want costumes to be becoming to them personally, and costumers need tact in dealing with people who feel that their legs or their noses or their bosoms are not being flattered.

In designing for the character, the costumer must keep firmly in mind the *given circumstances* of the character, such as age, sex, state of health, and social class, as well as the focal importance of the character in key scenes (Should it form part of a crowd or stand out?), and most important of all, those elements of character that would express themselves through clothes. Is the character cheerful or somber? Simple or complex? Showy or timid? Majestic or mousy?

FIGURE 9.8 Costume Design.
Costume designers have to design for both the actor and the character. A design often begins with a pencil sketch (left), moves through a color rendering to which actual swatches of fabric are attached (center), before it becomes a costume fitted to the actor (right). A design for Molière's *School for Wives by Helen Huang, USAA, worn by Mitchell Hébert.*

Other important matters are

- *Silhouette* (the mass and outline of the costume as worn)

- *The costume in motion* (Does it have potential for swirl or billow or drape or curve as it moves? Does it change with movement? Will it encourage, even inspire, the actor to move more dynamically? What aspects of it—fringe, a scarf, coattails, a cape, a shawl—can be added or augmented to enhance motion?)

- *Fabric texture and draping* (Does the play suggest the roughness of burlap and canvas or the smoothness of silk? What is wanted—fabrics that will drape in beautiful folds, like velour, silk, or jersey, or fabrics that will hang straight and heavily?)

- *Fabric pattern* (All-over, small, repeated patterns as opposed to very large designs on the fabric, or none at all?)

- *Enhancement or suppression of body lines* (The pelvic V of the Elizabethan waist, or the pushed-up bosom of the French Empire, the pronounced sexuality of the medieval codpiece, or the body-disguising toga; and, for the individual actor, are there individual characteristics like narrow shoulders, skinny calves, or long necks that must be disguised?)

- Where necessary, *special effects* (such as animal or bird costumes or fantasy creatures)

In addition, the costumer must consult with both scene and lighting designer to make sure that the costumes will look as they are designed to look under stage light and against the settings. Practical considerations like budget and deadlines are, of course, always important.

The costumer's designs are usually presented as color renderings, normally with swatches of the actual materials attached, and with detailed notations indicated for the *costume shop supervisor*. From these, patterns are made, where needed; the costumer selects the fabrics and usually oversees their cutting and the construction of the costumes themselves. Most theatre companies of any size keep a stock of costumes from which some pieces can be "pulled" for certain productions, thus saving time and money. Costume support areas of any size usually include, besides the stock, fitting rooms, cutting tables, sewing machines and sewing spaces, and tubs for washing and dyeing.

The Lighting Designer

When stages were lit by candles, attempts to control the light were very crude and seldom very successful. In those days, the lighting designer's work was largely confined to special effects, such as fire. With the introduction of a controllable light source, however, and with the demand in the nineteenth century for more and more realistic imitations of phenomena like sunrise and moonlight, the designer's task became far more challenging and the creation far richer. Very shortly, the possibilities of stage lighting expanded enormously from simple imitation of natural effects, and lighting became a design element as important and as potent as scenery itself.

The possible uses of theatre light are enormous. Through manipulation of intensity and direction, for example, a designer can change the apparent shape of an onstage object. Through manipulation of intensity and color, the lighting designer can influence the audience's sense of mood and tone. Through manipulation of direction and color, the designer can create a world utterly unlike the one in which the audience lives, with light coming from fantastic angles and falling in colors never seen in nature.

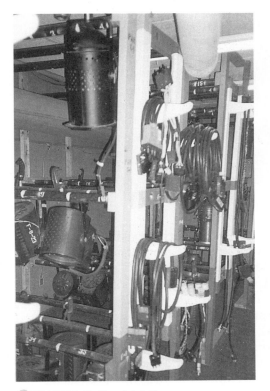

FIGURE 9.9 Lighting.

Lighting instruments in storage; a typical modern theatre may have hundreds, with associated cables, plugs, patch panels, and associated equipment.

Modern equipment has made theatre lighting more flexible than early designers ever dreamed. Small, easily aimed *instruments* (lighting units) and complex electronic controls, often with computerized memories, have made possible a subtlety in stage lighting that was unknown even thirty years ago.

The lighting designer works with three fundamentals: *color, direction,* and *intensity* of light. These are partly interdependent because of the nature of the light source, usually an incandescent filament. *Color* is changed physically by the placement of a transparent colored medium (usually called a *gel*) in the beam of light; this is not usually changed during a performance. *Direction* is a function of the location of the lighting instruments, of which hundreds may be used in a contemporary production. Each instrument is plugged into an electric circuit either individually or with a few others to illuminate the same scene. The location of instruments is rarely changed during performance, and so designers are limited by the number of instruments and the number of electrical circuits available to them. Light *intensity* is controlled by changes in the electrical current supplied to the instrument; this process is called *dimming* and is done by manipulating the levers on *dimmers,* of which several kinds are in use. All have the same goal of changing the amount of light coming from the instrument from zero to full intensity, with the capability of stopping at any point in between.

The lighting designer's plan is called a *light plot.* It shows the location and direction of each instrument, as well as what kind of instrument is to be set at each location—usually either a *floodlight* (soft-edged and wide-beamed) or a *spotlight* (hard-edged and narrow-beamed). The locations chosen are over and around the playing area, so that light falls on the actors and the acting space at an angle, both vertically and horizontally. (Light that falls straight down or comes in parallel to the stage floor gives very unusual effects, although both have their uses.) In addition, such subsidiary instruments as *light borders* or *strip lights* (rows of simple lights without lenses, suspended overhead for general illumination), *footlights* (at floor level along the front of many proscenium stages), and *follow spots* (very powerful spotlights that swivel so that their bright beam can constantly illuminate a moving performer) are sometimes used.

The lighting designer is usually responsible for projected scenery or projected shadows, clouds, and similar effects.

FIGURE 9.10
Technical Rehearsal.
The stage manager and the lighting designer, equipped with headsets to communicate with backstage and the lighting booth, rehearse the technical flow of the entire production. *Courtesy of Anne Fliotsos and the University of Missouri, Columbia.*

The lighting designer has the special responsibility of making everyone else's work accessible to the audience. Light determines what the audience will see. Light creates depth, for one thing, and it can make an actor's eyes seem to sink into deep sockets or vanish in a bland, flat mask. Light gives or takes color, and it can make costume colors glow with vibrancy or fade into dirty gray. Light is selective, and it can show the audience precisely what is to be seen.

In making the other artists' work accessible to the audience, the lighting designer has to consider all three elements: intensity, direction, and color. There are no hard-and-fast rules here; rather, there is need for a manipulation and an experimentation that is like putting colored paint on canvas. Although much of the lighting designer's work is done in production meetings and at the drawing board, much more of it is done in *technical rehearsals,* when, with the director, the designer experiments with colors and intensities and, frequently, makes decisions to change the locations and the plugging of instruments. Because of this experimental work that comes very late in the production period (often only days before opening), the lighting designer's work is crammed into a short time, and he or she works then at great intensity.

The Sound Designer

Sound became a theatre art with good stereo equipment and related amplification, blending, and tuning equipment. To be sure, sound was used in theatres before that time, and as long ago as Shakespeare's Globe, someone had to be responsible for rolling the cannonballs that simulated thunder, but a sound that could be shaped dimensionally and controlled in pure, correct tones was not possible until very recently. To the regret of many, the sound designer's job has been expanded in many theatres to the "miking" of performers, so that today many actors are heard through speakers rather than directly. As good as modern equipment is, it is not yet good enough to imitate in range, vibrancy, and direction the natural voice of the actor. It has proved a benefit, however, to actors who lack sufficient voice to be heard in large theatres.

As equipment becomes still more sophisticated and as expertise increases, the work of the sound designer may become as important and creative as that of the lighting designer. Limited at present to concepts of "sound effects" and "background music," the sound designer may one day be able to wrap the audience in sound as the lighting designer wraps the stage in light, and to play as flexibly with sound as the other plays with light. Rock concerts and sound-and-light shows are already pointing the way.

Training designers

Because theatre designers create environments and use materials of the real world in order to make their art, they must be trained not only as artists but also as artisans. Theatre designers therefore study at least two different sorts of subjects, the artistic and the technical; some designers also need another sort of information, the historical, in order to prepare for their role as theatre designers.

Although some theatre designers (especially in Eastern Europe) customarily design all aspects of a production, most in the United States specialize in one area: scenery, properties, costumes, lighting, or sound. All need certain kinds of basic information. For example, all need proficiency in dramatic analysis. Most need to learn about color, line, mass, composition, balance, and other such basic elements

FIGURE 9.11   Good Design.
A pencil drawing for a production of August Wilson's *Fences,* by Dan Conway, USAA.
(See also color figure C-19.)

of design, and most need to master some basic techniques of drawing and rendering in several media. They require some understanding of visual communication (that is, how people are likely to interpret certain colors, shapes, lines, and proportions). Finally, because every play presents a unique problem in design, all designers need skills in basic research methods that will allow them to pursue the design of any play independently.

Beyond such basic, shared areas of study are others specific to each area, because the technical skills needed by each designer vary considerably. For example, scenic designers and technical directors often study basic construction and (occasionally) carpentry; scene designers will usually take courses in scene painting as well. With the arrival of new metals and plastics came a need for some training in welding and form-making. These designers will also often study engineering in order to discover how the aesthetic requirements of a design can be safely built and safely used. Costume designers usually study basic sewing, pattern-making, drafting, and draping as well as some specialized areas like millinery. Lighting and sound designers take courses in electricity, electronics, and instrumentation. Most designers now are expected to have some proficiency in computers because, for example, most lighting systems are now computerized and many software packages exist to help scenic designers with drafting floor plans, making elevations, and so on. In short, all designers are expected to recognize and exploit the qualities of the materials they use regularly in their work and to develop proficiency in the use of the tools required for working with these materials.

Because of the importance of plays from the past, designers are often trying to capture qualities from another time and place. For this reason, training in scenery, property, and costume design (less often in lighting and sound design) usually includes quite a bit of history. Scenic designers, for example, need to know history of architecture and furniture, among others. Costume designers need to

LINKS to more about theatre

Irene Corey, *The Mask of Reality*, 1968.

Robert Edmond Jones, *The Dramatic Imagination*, 1941. Theory and inspiration by America's exponent of the New Stagecraft.

< **www.siue.edu/COSTUMES/WOW/WOW-INDEX.html** > "Wading on the web! Index of articles by month." A USITT site.

< **www.inch.com/~kteneyck/** > Site of the New York studio of Karen Ten Eyck. Photos, designs, and more. Can be slow to load, depending on your PC, but worth every second.

know the history of fashion, textiles, and accessories (jewelry, wigs, etc.). The history of visual painting often suggests not only the techniques of painters in each age that designers might want to use in order to capture the "look" of the age but also the telling details of design—fabrics, jewelry, upholstery, and so on. Sound designers, especially, often want courses in the history of music.

In other periods, training in design came primarily through an apprentice system where a beginner worked with a more experienced artist until attaining an acceptable level of craft. Now, however, proficiency in design and technical theatre usually comes from pursuing a graduate degree (especially the Master of Fine Arts—MFA) in theatre at a university. After completing their degree, persons wishing to work in major professional theatres as designers must take and pass the rigorous examination of the United Scenic Artists, the union that certifies designers for the profession, and technical directors or technicians wishing such work will need to belong to IATSE.

The job market in design and technical theatre remains strong (unlike that in acting, playwriting, or directing), in part because the need for such people far exceeds the number of them well trained in these fields; university training usually leads to steady work either in the professional or educational theatre.

WHAT IS GOOD DESIGN?

Good design is good art. It is created in terms of the production, however, and it is created within the context of other artists' decisions. Knowing what is the product of a designer and what of a director can often be difficult, however, and, especially in our director-dominated theatre, assessing each designer's work is sometimes challenging.

Good design, above all, serves the actor—giving the actor good spaces in which to act, clothing the actor, illuminating the actor.

Good design serves the production. It does not necessarily serve the "playwright's intentions"; interpretation may have greatly changed this production from those intentions. Obvious changes may have been made—in historical period, geographical location, social class—along with less obvious ones (genre, mood, style); the play may even have become the framework, in this production, for an idea the very opposite of the "intention." In serving the production, good design meshes with other elements and does not call attention to itself.

Good design, where possible, is dynamic, not static: It has the capacity to change as the performance progresses. Such change is clearest in costumes and lighting, less so in scenery, where the number of sets is limited. A set that makes a powerful statement right off the bat and never goes beyond it for the entire performance may be a bad set.

Good design is not redundant. It does not merely "state the theme." It has its own complexity.

FIGURE 9.12 Good Design.
A costume by Martin Thaler, the University of Vermont. *Photo by Robert S. Evans.*

Good design has detail and texture (variety within the whole): Light is not merely a bland wash of light; a costume is not merely a wide stretch of draped and sewn fabric; a setting is not a mere painted surface.

Good design has technical finish. Designers must design within the technical limitations of their theatres, so that everything the audience sees is technically well done. Often, designers oversee the technical work or approve it; nothing second-rate should pass their eyes.

Good design is daring: It tries new technologies, avoids old solutions, and chances failure.

The good designer, then, is one who creates effective works of visual art that serve the actor, that are right for the performance, that are richly textured and dynamic, and that can be perfectly finished by the technical capabilities of the theatre. The bad designer is one who ignores the actor; who creates ugly or uninteresting things; who designs for a predetermined idea of the play, not for this production; who creates statically; who ignores the capabilities of the technical facilities and allows shoddy work to go on the stage.

CURRENT ISSUES

Because we live in a period of magnificent settings and superb designers, we sometimes forget that spectacle (scenery, lighting, etc.) was not always considered fundamental to the art of theatre. In fact, the earliest theatres, as we have said, relied almost solely on actors in community with audiences. Beginning in about the sixteenth century, however, theatre came to be viewed less as a communal activity featuring actors and audiences working together and more as a *thing* produced *by* one group of people *for* another group of people. In other words, art became both *commodified* and *professionalized;* that is, art came to be viewed as some*thing* that was produced (by experts) and consumed (by others), something that could be bought and sold. At about the same time (although not entirely from the same impulses), spectacle came to be considered increasingly important in the production of plays.

Today's commercial theatre has taken commodification and professionalization to new heights (or new lows, depending on one's point of view). Contemporary designers produce ever more spectacular effects, so much so that the play itself is often quite overwhelmed, its words and ideas scarcely visible through the richness of its visual production. And with such visual magnificence has come a niggling worry that, perhaps, in some instances, design is skewing the theatrical experience in ways unhealthy to the art itself, not only because it drives up the already exorbitant costs of production but also because it allows (or even encourages?) the popularity of otherwise inane plays.

This worry is far from resolved. It has caused some theatre artists to call for a return to an actor-centered theatre, one that makes minimal use of modern technologies and the sophisticated designs that those technologies permit. It has caused others to celebrate the development of ever newer technologies so as to give theatre more powerful lures with which to attract audiences. It has caused still others to wonder again about the proper role of design in the theatre—and about the role of art in society. Questions about design have emerged: Should design enhance the text? Supplement text? Replace text? Illustrate or comment on text? Questions about art have arisen: Is theatre art best practiced by communities of ordinary people or by expert professionals? Is an art's worth properly judged by the money that will be paid for it—by its market value? If market value is the proper measure of an art's success, what, if any, is the role of experimentation in art?

Although the answers to such questions are yet unknown, their very existence suggests that the ways in which we think about—and teach—design for our postmodern theatre may be on the brink of a major change.

KEY TERMS

Check your understanding against this list. Brief definitions are in the Glossary; page references there will direct you to appropriate pages. (Persons are page-referenced in the Index.)

dimmer	properties
floodlight	rendering
follow spot	silhouette
gel	spotlight
light plot	strip light

The Mediators

OBJECTIVES

When you have completed this chapter, you should be able to:

- Explain what comprises a good theory

- Discuss the kinds of questions that theorists ask

- Distinguish between a critic and a reviewer

- Discuss what a dramaturg does

- Compare modernism with postmodernism

Mediation surrounds the theatre, preparing the audience for the performance. Mediation informs, educates, and sometimes entertains. Although mediation includes the work of professionals connected with the theatre itself (public relations experts, copywriters, and graphics people, for example), it also includes men and women who may work at several removes from the theatre—who may even, in fact, have no direct connection with the theatre at all.

These people are not theatre artists. Their interest in the theatre is more intellectual or commercial than artistic. Their influence can be great, although it can vary enormously from situation to situation. Their writings can be important evidence of theatrical history. These are people concerned with theory and criticism, dramaturgy, reviewing, and public relations.

THE THEORIST

A theory is an intellectual construct that seeks to define and explain a phenomenon. In the theatre, we have two kinds of theory:

- Dramatic theory, which deals with plays (Aristotle's theory of tragedy, for example)

- Performance theory, which deals with performance, and which has, as yet, no workable, effective example

LINKS to more about theatre

Gayle Austin, *Feminist Theories for Dramatic Criticism,* 1990.

Marvin Carlson, *Theories of Theatre,* 1984.

John Lahr, *The Light Fantastic: Adventures in Theatre,* 1996.

Richard Brinsley Sheridan, The Critic. A playwright has fun with a critic.

All About Eve. George Sanders as an acid-tongued critic (and Marilyn Monroe and Bette Davis, to be sure).

FIGURE 10.1 Mediation: Eighteenth Century.
Eighteenth-century fair theatres advertised themselves through signs, parades, and barkers to attract audiences.

Theorists seek to answer questions like: What is theatre? What is drama? They may seek to answer questions on genre: What is tragedy? What is comedy? They may seek to answer social or political questions: What role has theatre played in the maintenance of the status quo? How is drama implicated in racism?

An ideal theory meets several requirements. It would be

- *Systematic* (reasoned and orderly)

- *Internally consistent* (one part of a theory would not contradict any other part)

- *Sufficient* (the theory would give all the information necessary to understand the phenomenon)

- *Congruent* (the theory would account for all available evidence and contradict none)

Theories are deemed better still when they offer their dense explanations both briefly and clearly (e.g., $e = mc^2$).

Traditional Theories

As a study of the history of theories clearly shows, there are no ideal theories in theatre. Aristotle's is still accepted as the most comprehensive theory of Greek tragedy, and sometimes of other kinds of drama as well. There is no comparable theory of performance, probably because of a failure to agree, as yet, on just what the evidence is, because of the temporary nature of that evidence and because of the bewildering number of cases that must be covered. (Shall we cover theatre dance? Improvisation? Some performance theorists even seek to include phenomena that we have excluded from this book altogether—religious ceremonies, football games, circuses.) Performance theories are further complicated by the need to account for the audience as well as the "play" in any true theory of performance.

Theorists mediate theatre most powerfully through education. Major theories are complex; they form the basis of university-level courses ("Aristotle on Tragedy," "Plato on Drama," "Suzanne Langer's Aesthetic of Drama"). They then filter into the general consciousness through the work of other mediators and artists—not always in a form that the theorists themselves would recognize.

The creation of theory is an activity of major importance. Its goal is self-justifying, and it often has nothing to do with affecting the art of the theatre. At its best, it is a branch of philosophy.

FIGURE 10.2   Mediation: Nineteenth Century.
Posters often showed the most lurid scenes in a melodrama to bring in audiences in a highly competitive theatre. This is the poster for Augustin Daly's *Under the Gaslight,* with the then-new scene of someone tied to a railroad track.

Postmodern Theories

Theories have multiplied in the postmodern period (that is, the period since about 1960, when many previous assumptions about the nature of truth as "scientifically verifiable" and "objective" came under serious attack). Most postmodern theories rest on new assumptions of the world and people's place in it, which the following comparisons may help clarify:

Modernism rests on:	*Postmodernism* rests on:
The industrial age	The information age
Reason, science	Nihilism, meaninglessness
Hierarchy	Participation, dialogue
Autonomous individuals	Socially shaped people
History as progressive	History as nonlinear, discontinuous
Dualities, opposites	Differences, rather than opposites

The very multiplication of theories of drama and performance is itself an expression of postmodernism, where difference and contingency are prized. Among the major current theories, drawn from several disciplines, are the following:

Semiotics, the "study of signs," an attempt to define how audiences make meanings of the performance's auditory and visual details

Deconstruction, the close analysis of text or performance to reveal multiple layers of meanings, meanings often at odds with a conventionally understood meaning and with one another

Feminist theory, an amalgam of film theory and a branch of psychoanalytic theory (Lacanism), with various goals: e.g., to study a historically male theatre vis-à-vis women, to examine gender in performance, to define a feminist aesthetic

THE CRITIC

Criticism is the application of theory, but the line between criticism and theory is not a clear one. Many theorists are also critics, and many critics make theoretical statements; they may not themselves be theorists because their theoretical work is not comprehensive or systematic.

Like theory, criticism has two branches: dramatic criticism and performance criticism.

Dramatic criticism is most practiced in universities. Teaching dramatic literature is sometimes a kind of dramatic criticism. Many scholarly articles are examples of dramatic criticism, although the theories on which they are based may, in fact, not be theories of drama so much as theories of literature (e.g., new criticism, phenomenology, semiotics). The criticism of Shakespeare, for example, is a major academic industry with many theoretical branches.

Specific assumptions often underlie dramatic criticism and explain the critic's analyses. These may be political (Marxist criticism) or social (feminist criticism). The critic may choose to deal only with formal criticism (matters of form, structure, and so on) or only with content criticism (matters of idea, metaphor, and so on), although the two converge.

Because we have no adequate performance theory, we have no adequate performance criticism; nonetheless, we have many performance critics—men and women who are trying at least to describe performances seriously. At this stage, most performance criticism is descriptive and seeks to record the complex impacts of the many discrete moments of performance. Performance specialists are working hard to create theories of performance, but they have the difficulties we have already noted in even talking about performance systematically. (For example, the vocabulary of dramatic criticism is not adequate: the concept of dramatic action

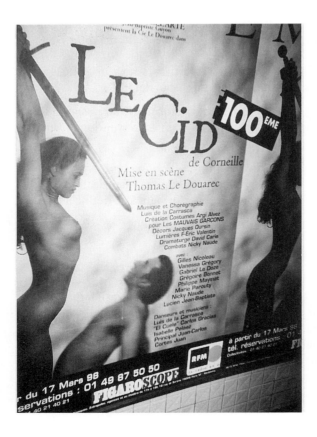

FIGURE 10.3   Mediation: Late Twentieth Century.
Grabbing the attention remains the goal of the theatre poster. Here, a very modern image for Corneille's seventeenth-century classic. *Photo by Michelle Washington.*

does not suffice for the actor-playing-character-in-costume-making-decision at a moment that is only one of thousands of moments. And what is a moment?)

A further difficulty in performance criticism is the intervention of the critic: The act of criticism appears to change what is going on in the performance.

Criticism, whether of drama or performance, is a serious intellectual undertaking. Its need for reflection militates against deadlines and pressure. Probably as a result, most of the best modern critics have had academic connections and have published their work as books. A few critics have been theatre artists.

THE DRAMATURG

Long a recognized figure in European theatres, the dramaturg has only recently appeared in the United States. The dramaturg is a specialist in dramatic literature and dramatic and theatrical history. Dramaturgs now have places on the staffs of some resident theatre companies; their functions include:

- Assisting in the selection of plays

- Reading and evaluating new plays

- Providing historical and literary background to directors, designers, and actors

- Providing program notes

- Assisting directors, sometimes by advising on the production

- Working on plays—adapting, restructuring, translating

A dramaturg is not a theatre artist but may be called on to act as one, particularly as a playwright. The historical and theoretical knowledge needed, however, and the knowledge of dramatic literature, suggest that university-level education is necessary. In fact, some American universities now offer graduate degrees in dramaturgy.

The dramaturg's mediation shows most obviously in program notes but may be present in public relations materials and in aspects of the production itself and the selection of plays.

THE PUBLIC RELATIONS SPECIALIST

Few productions can get along without some sort of advertising, be it only slips of paper photocopied at the local copy center. The directing student doing a one-act at lunchtime will probably be his or her own public relations (PR) person; the New York star will have his or her own PR firm in addition to the producer's PR person and the advertising firm for the production.

THINKING ABOUT MEDIATION

In *The Critic,* a play by Richard Brinsley Sheridan (1751–1816), one character describes another as *"a practitioner in panegyric, or, to speak more plainly, a professor of the art of puffing."*

Write a fifty-word panegyric—that is, a puff piece—for a play, film, or television program. Which mediators routinely write such pieces?

University theatres have somebody who coordinates "front-of-house" activities (all those things that happen on the audience's side of the curtain), including publicity. This will include graphics for posters and programs; paid advertising; and arrangements for radio, television, and newspaper coverage, including photos and interviews. At all levels, publicity people will seek an "angle" or a "hook," something that will catch the attention of the media's gatekeepers: the actor who goes on, even with a broken ankle; the actress whose mother played the same role in the original New York production. With the director and (if such a person exists) the producer, the PR person will create an image or idea for the production that will come out of the director's interpretation; this image or idea will inform color, graphics, and text used in advertising the production (For a play about love, will we emphasize the rose or its thorns? A pink rose or a black one? Will we use the word "love" or the word "passion"?).

The PR person's mediation is crucial in getting an audience into the theatre. It may also be crucial in preparing the audience correctly. Wise audience members remain skeptical of the claims of advertising ("An all-time laugh riot!"), but they learn to be alert to hints that will prepare them for a certain style, genre, and mood, as well as for subject matter in which they are interested.

FIGURE 10.4   Mediation: Late Twentieth Century.
New technology has brought new ways for theatre to inform—and draw—patrons. Here, the National Theatre, London, with a flashing sign that lists current performances on its several stages and can be read easily from across the Thames.

Environment

◀ **C-13. Model.** Designer M. Franklin-White's model for *Beirut,* Moscow. See also the ground plan, Figure 9.5.

C-15. Simplicity of Setting. *A Woman's Worth* at College of St. Mary-of-the-Woods, *design by Deirdre Riegel, directed by Sharon Ammen.*

▼

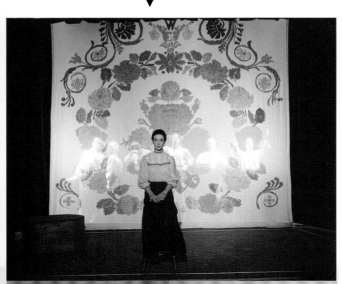

C-14. Painter's ▶ Elevation. A detailed rendering of scenic pieces by the designer, Dan Conway, USAA, for *The Mystery of Irma Vepp* at Syracuse Stage.

d e s i g n s and Environments

C-16. Setting and Costume. ▶
Quilters at the University of
Vermont. *Design by William
Schenk. Costumes by Martin
A. Thaler. Quilt rented from
Western Michigan University.*

C-17. Simplicity of Setting.
A drop for a production in
Kampala, Uganda. *Courtesy
of Jessica Kaahwa.*
▼

C-18. Environmental Theatre. *The London Merchant Person* ▶
at the University of Maryland, on walkways and small stages
surrounded by audience. *Design by Cherie Davis, costumes by
Debbie Serbousek. Directed by Catherine Schuler.*

C-19. Realistic Setting. ▶
Fences at the Cleveland
Playhouse. *Design by Dan
Conway, USAA.* See also
Figure 9.11.

◀ **C-20. Nonrealistic Design
for Children's Opera.** *Little
Red Riding Hood* by Seymour
Barab, *designed by Peter Lach
at University of the Pacific.*

◀ **C-21. Design for Comedy.**
Steve Martin's *Picasso at the
Lapin Agile.* Setting by Michael
Palumbo, lighting by Ann
Courtney, costumes by Arpina
Mackarian, directed by Jim
Patterson at the University of
South Carolina.

d e s i g n s and Environments

◀ **C-22. Design for Tragedy.**
The Oresteia at the University of South Carolina. *Design by David Coleman, directed by Robert Richmond. Jim O'Connor, artistic director.*

C-23. Design for Opera.
The Nightingale at Western Michigan University. *Design by Greg Roehrick, computer graphics by Kevin Abbott, costumes by Gwen Nagle, lighting by Matthew Knewtson. Directed by Janet Stillwell. Mary Whalen photo.*
▼

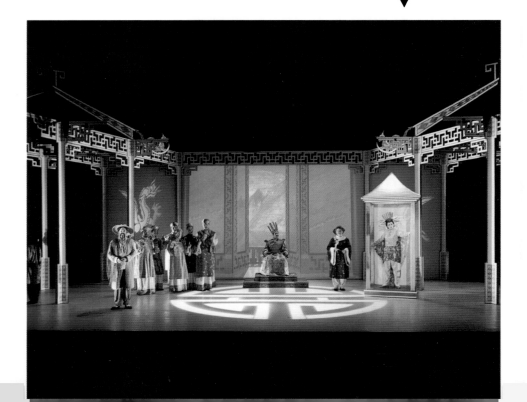

THE REVIEWER

Reviewers are men and women who see plays and then write about them. Their orientation is toward consumer protection; that is, presenting themselves at best as an "ideal audience," they recommend or warn against performances on the basis of a taste shared with their readership.

Reviewers are seldom critics. They do not rely consistently on theory; they rarely pretend to objectivity. They lack the time to reflect on what they have seen, their work usually appearing in a daily or weekly publication. Often, their format is so limited (one minute on radio or television) that little can be said at all.

Reviewers are reviewers of both drama and performance. They do not attempt to tell readers or listeners what performance is or how it works, but they do tell them whether or not the performance is likable within certain limits.

Some reviewers have theatrical backgrounds or education. Some do not. Experienced reviewers have trained themselves to recognize their own responses and to turn them into interesting, often witty prose, one of the functions of reviewing being to entertain.

Reviewers develop degrees of power within their communities, the New York reviewers supposedly having life-or-death power over Broadway productions. Their mediation extends beyond the review itself when quotations from the reviews are included in theatrical advertising. Because of this practice, some reviewers come to write quotable reviews, eager, perhaps, to see their names on

FIGURE 10.5 Mediation: Broadway Overkill.
As signs multiply, individual ones tend to submerge in the general effect.

theatre marquees with those of the actors. When this point is reached, the reviewer, although still a mediator, has crossed over from reviewing into public relations. In this way, a few reviewers become media stars in their own right.

CURRENT ISSUES

Because we live in a transitional period between the older world view called modernism and the newer one called postmodernism, we are witnessing heated arguments about the nature of truth, of people, and of art. As in any transitional period, the views now exist side by side (and alongside them both is yet another view, called by some pre-modernism, which has gained strength recently with the surge of religious fundamentalism in Moslem as well as in Christian cultures). Indeed, many of the most rancorous political issues of our time have been framed very differently by the adherents of each of these world views: Are the issues of abortion to be decided by the church, the scientific community, or each woman, based on individual circumstances? Are racial characteristics marks from God, results of an evolutionary process, less pronounced than differences occurring within racial groups? Indeed, what some people call PC (political correctness) seems to be tied to a shift away from a modern and toward a postmodern sensibility.

FIGURE 10.6   Mediation: The Reviewer.
Reviewers, supposedly the theatre's worst enemies, often are part of its fabric. This theatre is named for a famous newspaper reviewer, and quotations from current reviews are being used to attract patrons.

FIGURE 10.7   Mediation: Myth.
This is Shubert Alley, the heart of "the theatre district," lined with ads and
limos, projecting glamor and glitz.

Unsurprisingly in these circumstances, theatrical performances—especially
in venues outside the commercial mainstream—are participating in these debates.
Whereas the modern director tends to take a worshipful attitude toward the text,
setting about to stage the play's dominant meaning insofar as it can be grasped, the
postmodern director tends to take a more heretical attitude toward the text, seeking to make it comment on itself or "deconstruct" itself or serve as a springboard
for some other vision entirely. For example, a modern director, wanting to stage a
play about man's search for truth, might choose either of two great pre-modern
plays that dramatize the story of Faust—a man who sells his soul to the devil in exchange for knowledge. A modern director would select the text, analyze it, and
stage it in a way calculated best to reveal it. A postmodern director, on the other
hand, might fuse the two texts, add contemporary material, and turn the whole
back on itself, making it an exposé of how patriarchal institutions (the law, the
church, the government) have defined truth in order to oppress women. Part of
the deconstructive point here is, of course, that man's search for truth historically
was made at the expense of women's search. (Deconstructionists argue that any
text contains its own opposites.)

Such "attacks on text" trouble many critics, for in them they see attacks on
what they hold dear. If texts can mean anything at all, what's a critic to do? And
such attacks extend beyond theatre into life itself. If there is no meaning, then
what is the purpose of language: What is its role in life? If there is no stability or
continuity, then how are people to make their way through life? Bad enough,
some said, when the truth of the church and the holy books gave way to the
truths of reason and science, but to deny a stable truth altogether in favor of mere

historic contingencies? Such a change cannot be borne. Bad enough, they said, that the individual person was no longer seen as a special creation of a divine creator and was only an individual with certain natural rights within a social structure, but to suggest that people are not autonomous and free to act is to pose an alternative too hurtful to be allowed.

Although it is not clear what lasting effect, if any, postmodern ideas will have, it is clear that the forms they take in theatre, arts, and society will be interconnected. At this moment in history, that interconnection presents vexing questions: If there are no "correct" meanings, why study literature? If meaning is variable, why is anybody else's interpretation—for example, a critic's or a teacher's—better than your own? If "the past is fiction" (a postmodern saying), why study history? If there is no absolute truth, why bother to be honest?

KEY TERMS

Check your understanding against this list. Brief definitions are in the Glossary; page references there will direct you to appropriate pages. (Persons are page-referenced in the Index.)

criticism (dramatic and performance)	postmodernism
dramaturgy	public relations
feminist theory of theatre	reviewer
front of house	semiotics
modernism	theory (dramatic and performance)

III

The Theatre of Other Times and Places: Theatre History

THE PRESENT AND THE PAST

Because the theatre of the present is not merely a theatre of today's plays and today's techniques but is also a theatre of plays and techniques from many periods, the alert and responsive audience member will be knowledgeable about the theatre's past as well as its present. The prepared audience, for example, studies the past to enrich the present. It studies, too, to understand what the forces of change are and how they work and to learn that audiences and artists of every age have been much like us, subject to the same pressures, glad of the same pleasures.

It is tempting, perhaps, to think of a theatre of the past as filled with people who were somehow different from us—more polite or stuffier or older or stupider or less sophisticated—but as a study of the theatre's history will show, they were

LINKS to more about theatre

Bamber Gascoigne, *World Theatre: An Illustrated History,* 1968.

Alois Nagler, *A Source Book in Theatrical History,* 1952 (and later).

< **www.win.net/~kudzu/history.html** > "Theatre history sites on the www"—rich in many areas. You can access the home pages of La Scala (Milan) or Disney's New Amsterdam (New York), for example.

< **www.antaeus.org/Antaeus5.html** > The Antaeus Company's "classical theatre links," which extend well beyond the classical.

not all that different. They laughed and wept, applauded and hissed, got bored by bad performances and gave standing ovations to great ones. To understand this fact—that the theatre is a great force and that its audience is a great, vital constant—is to understand why the theatre is an art that stands at the center of human concerns.

Studying theatre history is valuable in its own right to grasp one context in which plays and styles of the past can be understood. Such knowledge, for example, is particularly needed by anybody who is going to make theatre. As well, however, theatre history is valuable as a means to understand wider history and as an example of that wider history. Art often predicts the near future of a society; theatre history sometimes reveals such forecasts.

At the same time, theatre history is no more free of fads, hidden agendas, and unstated assumptions than any other kind of history. In the United States, it is heavily tilted toward American subjects, then to British or at least European ones, fairly indifferent to theatre of Asia and Africa.

As you read what follows, then, you should notice where emphases have been put and where omissions have been made. You should ask yourself why these are as they are—remembering that in history of all sorts, a lack of evidence in one area and an over-supply in another greatly affects how much appears on the page. The modern period, for example—especially since the invention of photography and cheap printing—has so much information about itself that we have a hard time limiting it. Remember, too, that time is a quirky editor—through accident, war, intentional erasure, and neglect, it drops masses of information that would be thought vital if we could have it. Remember, too, the old adage of historians: it is the winners who write history. And remember, finally, that until quite recently, most people went unrepresented in history, including theatre history, which took as its subject people very like the ones who wrote the history: educated, male, close to the center of power, white, often affluent.

Each section in what follows is organized along similar lines. Where we have little information, or where the information is thought unimportant to introductory study, it may be left out; you can compare periods in terms of these emphases and omissions. The basic structure is as follows:

Background (i.e., the period, other than the theatre)

Subheadings

The [Subject] Period

Physical Theatre (i.e., architecture and buildings)

Audience

Production Practices

Costumes and Masks

Acting

Plays and Playwrights

Other (i.e., subheadings peculiar to this period)

An American scholar has said, "Art validates the center of power." He might have said, as well, that power validates art. No more important understanding, then, can come from the study of theatre history than to learn how the art of the theatre and social-political power come together and drift apart, validating and then becoming invisible to each other. To understand that relationship is to understand how theatre history is history.

Facade Stages: Greece and Rome

OBJECTIVES

When you have completed this chapter, you should be able to:

- Explain why there are different theories of the origins of theatre, and what some of those theories are

- Discuss the relationship between theatre and religion in Greece and Rome

- Discuss the role of competition in Greek theatre festivals

- Trace the development of the Greek and Roman physical theatres and their plays and playwrights

- Identify the major periods of Greek and Roman theatres, with approximate dates

- Explain how a Greek or Roman performance would have looked in the principal periods—what masks and costumes were used, what a chorus did, what acting space was used

- Explain the important differences between tragic and comic performances and occasions

THE UNCERTAIN ORIGINS OF THEATRE

Scholars disagree about the origins of theatre, in part because they do not agree on what constitutes theatre and in part because evidence is too scanty to permit certainty on many points. Everyone agrees that theatrical and dramatic elements exist in life and therefore in many societies. Scholars do not agree, however, whether such theatrical and dramatic elements should be included within what we call *theatre*.

Issues of definition are important because they have both political and artistic implications. Two examples can clarify the political stakes: If *theatre* is understood to be one of several forms of ritual, then theatre probably originated in many cultures; if *theatre* is defined as a self-conscious work of art, then theatre probably originated in Athens. If *theatre* is understood to encompass informal, improvisational performances at community gatherings, then women probably participated in theatre from its beginnings; if *theatre* is defined as an institutional activity supported by church or state, then theatre has been an all-male event for most of its 2500-year history. Questions of definition are important, then, because they exclude or empower certain groups of people. As you will see in the following chapters, the theatre's history as traditionally studied has been the history of an institution of mostly white, European males who taught that it originated in Athens and was supported by church and state.

Different definitions of theatre obviously predispose toward different theories of the origins of theatre. The conservative definition (and the one that we have adopted in this textbook—see Chapter 1) is that theatre is a self-conscious activity whose aim is a work of art. While acknowledging the many paratheatrical (theatre-like) activities in everyday life, this conservative definition seeks ways of distinguishing among life, ritual, ceremony, dance, music, theatre, games, and so on. In this context, the question of theatre's origin becomes, "Where, why, when, and by what means did the various theatrical and dramatic elements that are routinely found in life and in religion become transformed into activities whose primary aim was artistic (as distinct from religious or instructional)?"

Even if we can agree on this definition of theatre, we still cannot agree on the origins of theatre, because evidence does not allow us to offer clear answers to central questions. In the absence of certain answers, therefore, a number of theories have emerged.

The Storytelling Theory

Some scholars have proposed that Western drama developed from storytelling. Telling and hearing stories, according to this theory, are pleasurable and natural; so too is the tendency of a narrator to elaborate parts of the telling by impersonating the various characters, using appropriate voice and movement. From here, it seems merely a short step to having several people become involved in the telling of a story; and from this, it is thought, drama and theatre arose.

FIGURE 11.1 Dionysus.
Whatever its origin, early theatre in Greece was associated with the god Dionysus, envisioned in this painting with a satyr who plays a double pipe.

The Dance Theory

Other theorists suggest that movement rather than speech was at the core of the drama. By imitating the physical behavior of animals and humans, and by donning appropriate skins or garments, a dancer first impersonated them and later embroidered this performance with sounds and words. The single dancer was joined by others who likewise impersonated and dressed themselves, and a form of theatre was born, it is supposed.

The Judicial Theory

A few scholars have sought the form of drama in the judicial system of Athens, Greece. Alluding to the many instances in which debates and arguments occur in the plays and to the instances in which judgments are required, such theorists have sought the beginnings of Greek drama in the courts of its early societies.

The Ritual Theory

Probably the most fashionable, but not necessarily the most correct, view of the origin of theatre is the so-called ritual theory. A ritual is an activity that is repeated to gain a specific and predictable outcome. Religious rituals developed in primitive cultures as a means of affecting events, propitiating gods, transmitting information, educating the young, and so on. The ritual theory of drama proposes that from primitive religious rituals, in particular those connected with fertility and the spirits of the seasonal cycle, dramas evolved. Although few respectable scholars still accept the idea that drama "evolved" in some organic, necessary way from religious ceremonies, most acknowledge that ritual probably influenced emerging theatrical forms.

The "Great Man" Theory

Finally, some scholars view the appearance of tragedy and comedy as a supreme creative act of an unidentified artist. Arguing that art neither evolves like a biological organism nor happens by chance, such scholars look for the birth of drama in a revolutionary discovery made by a human being. They posit the synthesis of many elements already established in society (dance, music, storytelling) to produce a work of art.

Aristotle's Evidence

Two statements by Aristotle, the fourth-century B.C. philosopher, bear on the question. He claimed, in Chapter 4 of the *Poetics,* that "tragedy was produced by the authors of the dithyramb, and comedy from [the authors] of the phallic songs." Dithyrambs were choral odes; phallic songs were rites whose precise nature is not known. Although tantalizing, Aristotle's account does little to clarify for what reasons or in what manner the authors shifted from dithyramb to tragedy or from phallic song to comedy. He also observed that "imitation is natural to men from childhood and in this they differ from the other animals . . . and then everybody takes pleasure in imitation." Because Aristotle was writing closer to the event than any of those advocating other theories, his account deserves consideration; still, it should be remembered that Aristotle was himself writing more than two hundred years after the known appearance of tragedy.

In its essence, the argument over the origin of theatre is an argument over the most important element of theatre. To the anthropologist who looks at mimings or impersonations as different as the Mandan Buffalo Dance, the Iroquois False Face Society, and the Egyptian "Passion Play," the essence of theatre is ritual, and the ritual theory will be favored. To the critic who finds the bedrock of drama in conflict, mythmaking or legal battle will seem most like dramatic action, and the storytelling or the judicial theory will be favored. To the artist who looks at world theatre and sees a form rich in human meaning and almost indescribable in complexity, only a nonrational (artistic) leap will explain its beginnings.

In fact, we do not know how theatre began. Nonetheless, it is important to theorize and to argue, for in that thinking and that argument we preserve our sense of the extraordinary richness of a great art that will not allow itself to be reduced to simple explanations.

SHARED FEATURES OF GREEK AND ROMAN THEATRE

The first phase of theatrical and dramatic history for which we have records began in the sixth century B.C. and ended around A.D. 500, a period of about one thousand years. Despite important differences, the theatres of Greece and Rome shared important traits:

1. *A facade stage,* where actors performed in front of a neutral background.

2. *A relationship with religion,* in which plays were presented as a part of larger, religious celebrations.

3. *A sense of occasion,* because performances were offered only on special occasions and never often enough to be taken for granted.

4. *A noncommercial environment,* in which wealthy citizens or the state itself bore the costs as part of the obligations of citizenship.

5. *A male-only theatre,* in which women participated only as audience.

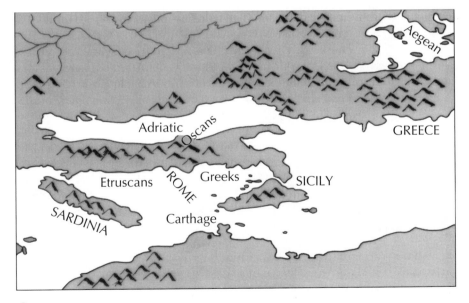

FIGURE 11.2   Greece and Rome.
Early Greek city-states influenced much of the Mediterranean, including the Italian peninsula. By the time of Christ, however, power had shifted to Rome, which then dominated formerly Greek territory.

THE GREEK THEATRE

Background

Although civilizations had existed in Greek lands for thousands of years, the civilization that produced the first recorded theatre and drama dated from about the eighth century B.C. By the fifth century B.C., the society had developed a sophisticated system of government and culture. The basic governing unit was the city-state, or *polis,* which consisted of a town and its surrounding lands. Many were important (e.g., Corinth, Sparta, Thebes), but Athens emerged during the fifth century B.C. as the cultural and artistic leader of Greece. The Athenians established the world's first democracy (508 B.C.) and provided a model for the participation of citizens in the decisions and policies of government. Under Pericles (c. 460–430 B.C.), Athens headed an empire in the Mediterranean, providing protection and trade in exchange for tribute. Buildings like the Parthenon were major achievements of the period, and art and philosophy reached a level that made them dominant in European culture for more than two thousand years. Athenian political power declined after 404 B.C.; the invasion by Alexander (336 B.C.) changed power on the Greek peninsula for good. The Roman Empire moved in two centuries later.

Greek theatre and drama lasted for more than a thousand years. Records of organized theatrical activity date from the sixth century B.C. and continue well into the Christian era. The unquestionable impact on the audiences of its day can be explained, at least in part, by four qualities that characterized this vital theatre:

1. Greek theatre was closely associated with Greek religion.
2. Greek theatre was performed only on special occasions.
3. Greek theatre was competitive.
4. Greek drama was choral.

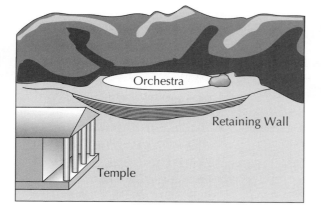

FIGURE 11.3
Early Athenian Theatre.
The earliest theatre for the extant Greek plays used a hillside for the audience area, and, at its base, a large circle (interrupted by a boulder) for the performing area. A temple stood nearby.

Greek Theatre and Greek Religion

Greek theatre was closely associated with Greek religion, a form of polytheism ("many gods"). Private worship was part of daily life; public worship occurred at festivals. Three such festivals—the Great or City Dionysia; the Rural Dionysia; the Lenaia—regularly included plays. For at least two hundred years after the first record of such plays, all drama in Greece seems to have been done only in Athens and only at these festivals dedicated to the god Dionysus.

The close association of Greek religion and Greek theatre is further shown by the presence of an altar within the playing area and, later, by places of honor in the theatres for the priests of Dionysus. Although the intimate connections between religion and theatre had been loosened by the end of the fourth century B.C., their relationship persisted; for example, when an actor's union was formed in the third century B.C., it took the name "Artists of Dionysus" and drew its officers from the ranks of Dionysian priests.

Occasions of Theatre

The fact that a festival is religious does not make it solemn; Mardi Gras and Halloween are, after all, religious festivals. Indeed, the fact that drama was performed at religious festivals in Greece seems not to have inhibited its joy or power, not least because the event was relatively rare and therefore special. In trying to capture the effect of the festival arrangement, it might be well to compare it with celebrating a birthday or attending Mardi Gras, rather than with attending a play or a movie.

Competitive Theatre

Dramatic works in the festivals were competitive, with dramatists competing for awards in writing and actors competing for prizes in performing. The audience was interested not only in hearing the individual plays but also in learning who had won the various contests. Greek theatre, then, probably had some of the elements of a long-standing football rivalry, as well as those elements associated with drama and theatre.

Choral Drama

In addition to actors, Greek drama required a *chorus,* a group of men who dressed alike, who were masked alike, and who moved and spoke together most of the time. The chorus often figured in the working out of the play's action and was important to the total theatrical experience.

The presence of the chorus in the performing area throughout the performance provided spectacle, its costumes, songs, and dances adding to the visual experience of the production. Because the chorus danced as it spoke, chanted, and sang, its rhythms indicated changing moods and shifting fortunes. By focusing at-

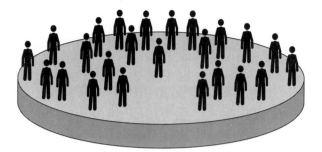

FIGURE 11.4   Chorus.
Originally as large as, perhaps, fifty, the chorus in the Classical period probably settled at twelve and then fifteen members for tragedy, twenty-four for comedy. Costumed alike, often speaking and moving together, the chorus worked mostly in the orchestra circle.

tention on certain characters and events and avoiding others, by supporting some actions and denouncing others, the chorus provided a point of view for the audience, serving often as an "ideal spectator." The chorus established the ethical system operating in the play and indicated the moral universe of the characters. Finally, and perhaps most important of all, the chorus—like an actor—participated often and directly in the action of the play, providing information and making discoveries and decisions. Whether in comedy or tragedy, the chorus was an invariable fact of the performance and influenced a number of practices. Chorus size varied but was commonly fifteen for tragedy and (probably) twenty-four for comedy.

Because the chorus usually came into the performing space soon after the play opened and remained there until the end, its presence had to be considered in both the physical layout of the theatre and the action of the drama. The chorus required a space large enough to move about in; and the presence of the chorus had to be justified and its loyalties made clear when secrets were shared. Because the vocal and visual power of the chorus was great (the contribution of each chorus member was, after all, multiplied by fifteen or twenty-four), the actors adjusted their style so as not to be overwhelmed by the impact of the chorus.

The Classical Period (c. 534–336 B.C.)

Beyond the facts that Greek drama and theatre were closely associated with religion, were performed on specific occasions, and were competitive and choral, little else is certain. Evidence is scanty and often contradictory. Most of what is known comes from five kinds of sources:

- The extant plays
- Scattered dramatic records of the period
- Commentaries such as those of Aristotle
- Archaeological remains of theatre buildings
- Certain pieces of visual art, most notably painted vases

Most of the extant plays date from the *fifth* century B.C., but most of the other evidence dates from the *fourth* century and later. The result is that for the

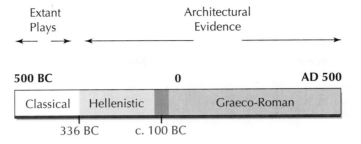

FIGURE 11.5 Time Line: Greek Theatre and Drama.
Extant dramas date from the Classical period, but architectural
evidence dates from the Hellenistic and Graeco-Roman periods.

period in which we know most about the theatre *buildings,* we know least about
the *plays;* and for the years for which we have plays to study, we know very little about the buildings in which they were done or the techniques used to produce them.

Unfortunately, some have "solved" this problem by grouping all of the evidence together and speaking of "the Greek theatre" as though its practices remained invariable throughout its thousand-year history. But Greek theatre
changed as markedly during its existence as the modern theatre has changed in a
thousand years. And so it is necessary to identify which period of the Greek theatre is meant when considering production practices.

We divide the Greek theatre into three periods: the Classical, the Hellenistic,
and the Graeco-Roman. Because most of the extant dramas date from the Classical Age, its practices will be described first and in greatest detail.

Physical Theatre

In Greek, *theatre* meant "seeing-place" or "spectacle-place." The Theatre of
Dionysus, Athens' first important theatre (c. 500 B.C.), was situated on a hillside,
where the audience sat, with a circular playing area (the *orchestra*) at its base; a
path or road separated audience and playing area and provided entrances (*parodoi*). This arrangement—hillside, orchestra, parodoi—was fundamental to all
Greek theatre arrangements (Fig. 11.3).

By 458 B.C., a scene house (*skene,* "tent" or "booth") had been added at the
edge of the orchestra opposite the audience. Its original layout is unknown, but it
probably had two or three openings and was first needed as a changing room for the
actors, only later becoming a kind of setting. It may first have been cloth (a tent)
but was certainly wood in short order, becoming stone only centuries later.
Whether wood or stone, it provided background and acoustical support and allows
us to call the Athenian theatre a *facade stage*—a conventional form in which actors
perform in front of a neutral facade, with the audience arcing to three sides or less.

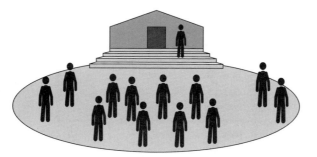

FIGURE 11.6   Early Athenian Theatre.
The actors probably had a separate acting area, perhaps including a
raised stage; the chorus probably played in the orchestra. If so, the
actors would have been the farthest from the audience, although
backed by the skene—originally probably a tent or booth for changing,
as shown here. See also Figure 11.3.

Thus, the principal characteristics of the Athenian theatre were:

- Facade conventions
- System of orchestra, skene, parodoi, hillside

Much is still not known about this theatre, above all:

- How much the skene may have been decorated to provide setting
- Whether or not there was a *raised stage* (for the actors, possibly for the chorus) between skene and orchestra

Audience

The outdoor theatre put the audience at the mercy of the weather; certainly, individuals must have used cushions, sunshades, umbrellas, etc. The hillside could hold fourteen thousand; the audience was as visible as the performers. The theatre was open to all; the social makeup of the audience is not known. Records suggest it was sometimes unruly.

Production Practices

The essential setting was the skene. We do not know if it was changed to suggest location; a kind of "flat" existed, but it is not understood. Two important theatrical machines were used:

- The *eccyclema,* a movable platform capable of being rolled or rotated out of the skene to reveal a result of offstage action (e.g., dead bodies)
- The *mechane,* some sort of crane that allowed people and things to fly in and out (e.g., dragons, clouds)

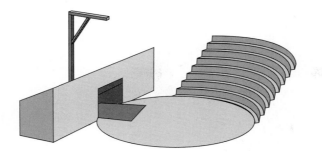

FIGURE 11.7   Skene, Eccyclema, Mechane.
By the middle of the fifth century B.C., the Athenian theatre
had a wooden skene with roof and doors, and two pieces
of stage machinery: the eccyclema, a platform, shown here
in the center doorway; and the mechane, a crane to fly
actors and properties in and out of the playing area.

Properties were numerous, and we hear of altars, tombs, biers, chariots, staffs, swords, and so on in tragedy; comedies often required domestic furniture as well as food, clubs, and so on.

Costumes and Masks

Costumes and masks helped to differentiate characters and to identify individuals. Costume variations included:

- Ethnicity—references are made to Greeks and to others dressed as foreigners.
- Color—black indicated mourning; in one comedy, a god was dressed in yellow to suggest effeminacy.
- Gender
- Social role—military heroes, servants, rural shepherds, and so on were visually identifiable.
- Formalization—some historians have argued for a "tragic costume," but some version of Athenian clothes seems likelier; in comedy, it was made laughable by being ill-fitting, exaggerated, and so on.
- Comic fantasy—to the costume of many male characters in comedy was attached a stuffed, oversized penis (*phallus*); fantastic characters and choruses—birds, wasps—seem to have been gorgeously costumed.

Masks were worn by all performers. They were full-face and had a hairstyle and a set facial expression. During the Classical Age, they seem not to have been exaggerated. The masks (and costumes) of the actors distinguished one from another; those of the chorus probably stressed their groupness.

FIGURE 11.8   Comic Performers.
This detail from a vase (right) apparently shows a scene from the story of Amphitryon and uses comic nudity and the oversized phallus seen on many male comic figures. Details of costume may be shown in the tights and the (padded?) torsos.

Acting

The first victor in the Athenian tragic contest was supposed to be Thespis, who also acted in his play (c. 534 B.C.)—hence *thespian* for actor. Acting, like playwriting, remained a competitive activity during the Classical Age, and rules governed its practice. For example, all actors were male. Apparently no more than three *speaking* actors were allowed in the tragedies and five in the comedies, although any number of extras might be used. Because the leading actor, or *protagonist,* was the only one competing for the prize, he was assigned to the playwright by lot, so that chance rather than politics decided who got the best roles. The second actor and the third actor were probably chosen by the playwright and the protagonist in consultation. With only three actors, doubling of roles was required, for the plays themselves often had eight or more characters. If the protagonist had an exceedingly demanding role, like the title role in *Oedipus Rex,* he might play only one character, but the second and third actors were expected to play two or more secondary roles. Doubling, the use of masks, and the use of only male actors suggest that the style of Greek acting was more formal than realistic; that is, although the acting was true and believable *on its own terms,* its resemblance to real life was of considerably less importance than its fidelity to the dramatic action. Given the size of the audience, the physical arrangement of the theatre, and the style of acting, it should be no surprise that vocal power and agility were the actor's most prized assets.

Plays and Playwrights

Of the thousands of plays written during the thousand years of Greek theatre, only forty-six survive. Most of these date from the Classical Age and can be attributed to four authors: Aeschylus (seven), Sophocles (seven), Euripides (eighteen), and Aristophanes (eleven).

Thespis.   The semilegendary Thespis supposedly wrote tragedies using only one actor and a chorus. Although none of Thespis' works survived, they probably were based on the intensification of a single event rather than the development of a story, because stories require changes to occur. With only one actor and a chorus, the opportunity to introduce new information into a scene (and thus to introduce change into a situation) was severely limited. The continual disappearance of either the actor or the chorus to fetch new information would obviously have been awkward and was thus necessarily curtailed.

Aeschylus.   Aeschylus (c. 525–456 B.C.) probably introduced a second actor, thereby permitting change to occur within the play. Although a second actor would also allow conflict between two characters, Aeschylus still tended to depict a solitary hero, one isolated and facing a cosmic horror brought about by forces beyond his control. With such a grand tragic conception, Aeschylus required great scope, and so he often wrote *trilogies,* three plays on a single subject that were intended for performance on the same day. One of his trilogies, the *Oresteia* (comprising the *Agamemnon,* the *Choëphoroe,* and the *Eumenides*), has survived intact along with several single plays. All display characteristics for which Aeschylus is admired: heroic and austere characters, simple but powerful plots, lofty diction. His general tone is well summarized by an ancient commentator: "While one finds many different types of artistic treatment in Aeschylus, one looks in vain for those sentiments that draw tears." (See Figures C-4 and C-22.)

Sophocles.   Sophocles (496–406 B.C.) was credited with adding the third actor and with changing practices in scenic painting and costuming. Less interested than Aeschylus in portraying solitary heroes confronting the universal order, Sophocles wrote plays that explored the place of humans within that order. The tragedy of Sophocles' heroes typically erupts from decisions made and actions taken based on imperfect knowledge or conflicting claims. Various aspects of the hero's character combine with unusual circumstances to bring about a disaster caused not by wickedness or foolishness but merely by humanness. For Sophocles, to be human was to be potentially a hero of tragedy.

The role of the chorus in Sophocles' plays remained important but not so central as in Aeschylus'. Conversely, the individual characters in Sophocles tend to be more complex, to display more individual traits, and to make more decisions. The result is that in Sophoclean tragedy, the actors, not the chorus, control the rhythm of the plays. Unlike Aeschylus, Sophocles did not need a trilogy to contain his tragedies; his plays stood alone. Of the more than one hundred attributed to him, seven have survived. Of these, *Oedipus Rex* is recognized by most critics as among the finest tragedies ever written.

Euripides.   Euripides (480–406 B.C.) was never very popular during his lifetime but came to be highly regarded after his death. Growing up at a time when Athens was embarking on policies of imperialism and expansionism, Euripides became a pacifist and a political gadfly. Although the populace viewed him with considerable distrust, the intellectual elite apparently admired him. It is reported, for example, that Socrates, one of the wisest men of the age, came to the theatre only to see the tragedies of Euripides and that Sophocles dressed his chorus in black on learning of the death of Euripides.

In comparison with the plays of Aeschylus and Sophocles, those of Euripides are less exalted and more realistic. His characters seem less grand and more human; their problems are less cosmic and more mundane. Euripides tended to ex-

FIGURE 11.9   Greek Playwright.
Greek dramatists wrote for masked actors, the number of actors limited so that the masks made doubling possible. This is supposed to be the comic playwright Menander; the masks seem fairly late.

amine human relationships and to question the wisdom of social actions: the purpose of war, the status of women, the reasons for human cruelty.

In keeping with Euripides' changed outlook came changes in dramatic technique. Replacing the philosophical probings common in the plays of Aeschylus and Sophocles, Euripides substituted rapid reversals, intrigues, chase scenes, and romantic and sentimental incidents of the sort later associated with plays called *melodramas*. (Euripides is said by some to be the father of melodrama.) He further reduced the role of the chorus, until sometimes it was little more than an interruption of the play's action. As the role of the chorus declined and the subjects became more personal, the language became less poetic and more conversational. Many of the changes that Euripides introduced into Greek tragedy, although denounced in his own time, became standard dramatic practice during the Hellenistic Age.

Comedy. Comedy was introduced into the Great Dionysia in 486 B.C., fifty years after tragedy. It seems never to have been comfortable there, perhaps because the festival was an international showcase for Athenian culture and thus often visited by foreign dignitaries. The real home of comedy was the winter festival, the Lenaia, where a contest for comedy was established in 442 B.C. At both festivals, an entire day was set aside for competition among the comic playwrights, five of whom competed.

Of the twelve extant Greek comedies, all but one are by Aristophanes (c. 448–c. 380 B.C.); therefore, information about comedy during the Classical Age necessarily comes from these plays. It is possible, of course, that Aristophanes was atypical, and so the conclusions drawn from his works may be incorrect.

So far as we know, however, comedy was satirical and political and was filled with references to real people and events (a tougher, funnier, religious *Saturday Night Live*). Near the end of the period, as Athens lost power, some kind of censorship may have been imposed, and comedy became less satirical. Aristophanes' later plays eased off on topical references and the sometimes bitter attacks of his earlier plays. This change is so radical that scholars see it as a turning point that separates *old comedy* from a safer, gentler kind now called *middle comedy*.

Although no two are exactly alike, surviving examples suggest a set structure for old comedy:

- Division into two parts separated by a direct address by the chorus or choral leader to the audience, breaking the dramatic illusion

- A first part consisting of a prologue, during which an outrageous idea is introduced, and a debate as to whether the idea should be adopted, ending with a decision to put this "happy idea" into action. (In Aristophanes' *The Birds,* for example, the happy idea is to build a city in the sky.)

- A second part made up of funny episodes and choral songs showing the happy idea at work

Thus, the happy idea is the heart of old comedy: it is outrageous and usually fantastic, and it contains social or political satire. In *The Birds,* for example, building the city in the sky is an attempt to get away from the mess on earth. The happy idea also enables the spectacular costuming and behavior of the chorus, which often gives the play its name (the birds found in the sky).

Contest Rules

During the Classical Age, plays were produced in Athens by the city-state in cooperation with selected wealthy citizens. (Women were not considered citizens.) At the Great Dionysia, three tragic writers (always male) competed each year for the prize. To compete, each submitted three tragedies and one *satyr play* (a short comic piece that followed the tragedies and occasionally burlesqued them). One day was set aside for the work of each tragic author; therefore, each year nine tragedies and three satyr plays were presented at the Great Dionysia. At the Lenaia, only four tragedies competed each year, each by a different playwright. At both festivals, five comic playwrights (always male) competed for a prize, and a single day was set aside for this competition.

How the competitors were selected is unknown, but, once chosen, each author was matched with a wealthy citizen-sponsor, who was then responsible for meeting the costs incurred by the chorus. The city-state provided the theatre in which the plays were performed and the prizes that were awarded to the winners.

The Hellenistic Age (c. 336–c. 100 b.c.)

Background

The new age marked by the conquests of Alexander the Great is now called the *Hellenistic.* The old system of city-states was replaced by a more centralized government. The center of political power moved from Athens to Alexandria, Egypt. Religion and intellectual life continued, but Athens' fifth-century complex of international power, democratic politics, art, and religion was gone.

Theatres were built throughout the eastern Mediterranean area. Performances were now given on many occasions, military and social as well as religious; in general, the civic, religious nature of performance lessened as theatre became more professional. Citizen-sponsors gave way to state support.

Physical Theatre

Theatres were built of stone now; archaeological evidence therefore remains. The primary features of the Hellenistic theatre were:

- A two-storied skene
- A long, narrow, high stage attached to the skene, usually with steps or ramps at each end, but sometimes with entrances only through the skene

- A circular orchestra, as before, but now of uncertain use. Was the chorus there, and the actors on the stage? Both in one place or the other? Or did practices vary?

Costumes and Masks

A formalized high boot with a platform sole may belong to tragic costume in this period, although it is not certain. A larger tragic mask is sometimes associated with this period, as well: It had a higher headdress than formerly and a larger, often distorted mouth. (See Figure 11.9.)

Acting

Actors remained exclusively male, but in the Hellenistic age they became a separate profession that organized into a performing guild called the Artists of Dionysus. The hints we have about costume and the higher, more separate stage suggest that the tragic acting style may have become showier, bigger; the comic style, on the other hand, may have become more representational to match the changes in comic plays.

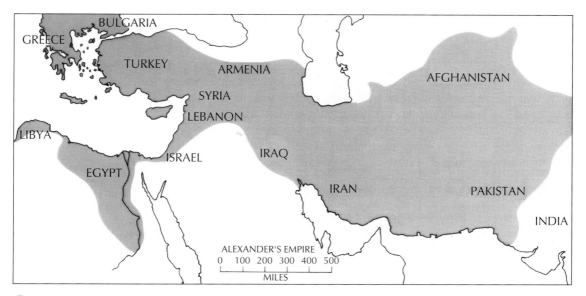

FIGURE 11.10   Hellenistic Greece: Alexander's Empire.
Alexander's conquests extended Greek influence but shifted power away from Athens.
Theatres began to appear throughout Greek areas, and acting became professionalized.
Greek drama may have had an influence as far away as India.

FIGURE 11.11 **Hellenistic Theatres.**
Stone remains, including those at Epidauros (top),
have led scholars to reconstruct the typical
Hellenistic theatre to look like the drawing
(bottom).

Plays and Playwrights

Tragedy. Tragedy appears to have declined in popularity in this period. Those
we know of seem to show the influence of Euripides, including the reduced importance of the chorus and the increased emphasis on sensation and melodrama.
Satyr plays disappeared.

Comedy.   Comedy, on the other hand, remained popular. Its political flavor now gone, it changed to a type now called *new comedy,* which showed domestic situations of the Athenian middle class. New comedy focused on such things as love, money, and family, often including intrigues involving long-lost children and happy reunitings. The formal structure of old comedy was gone, leaving merely a series of episodes and rather unrelated choral songs, with the chorus often incidental to the action. One example of new comedy has survived: *The Grumbler,* by Menander (c. 300 B.C.).

Theory: Aristotle

During the Hellenistic Age, the world's first and probably most influential dramatic theorist appeared. In his *Poetics* (c. 335 B.C.), Aristotle provided a theoretical definition of the form *tragedy.* (Aristotle defined neither comedy nor mixed forms in *The Poetics.*) Outstanding points include: "tragedy . . . is an imitation of an action that is serious, complete, and of a certain magnitude . . . in the form of action, not narrative . . . producing pity and fear and the catharsis of such emotions." The meaning of the definition has been endlessly debated, especially the phrase about catharsis, which some scholars believe refers to the response of audiences (though elsewhere Aristotle said he did not intend to talk about audiences) and other scholars think refers to emotions embedded within the episodes of the play itself.

He then defined and discussed the six parts of a play (See Chapter 3). Of the six parts, plot was the most important to Aristotle. He therefore discussed it in the most detail, considering its *wholeness* (having a beginning, a middle, and an end,

---

LINKS to more about theatre

James H. Butler, *Theatre and Drama of Greece and Rome,* 1972.

H. D. F. Kitto, *Greek Tragedy,* 1939. Brilliant and profound.

Mary Renault, *The Mask of Apollo,* 1966. Novel about a Hellenistic actor.

Satyricon. Directed by Federico Fellini. Some theatre, much decadence.

< **www.warwick.ac.uk/THEATRON** > Dazzling site of a project to create computer simulations of ancient theatres. Check out also *warwick.ac.uk/didaskalia,* the website of *Didaskalia,* an online journal of classical theatre with lots of links.

connected by causality); its *unity* (so that if any part is removed, the whole is disturbed); its *materials* (suffering, discovery, and reversal); and its *form* (complication and dénouement).

He argued that the best tragic protagonist is one who causes his own downfall through some great tragic error (*hamartia*), that the play's language should be both clear and interesting, and that spectacle is the business of the stage machinist rather than the poet.

Because *The Poetics* is so packed with ideas and its translation so difficult, its meaning has been debated for two thousand years. Certainly, it remains the base from which most discussions of dramatic theory must proceed, through either acceptance or rejection of its primary tenets.

The Graeco-Roman Age (c. 100 b.c.–a.d. 500)

By about 100 B.C., the expanding Roman Empire was exerting influence on Greece. Trends begun in the Hellenistic Age continued but were altered to bring them more into line with Roman practices. For example, Roman theatres were built in Greek lands, and Hellenistic theatres were remodeled to resemble Roman theatres, producing hybrids now called *Graeco-Roman.* Although some records show that theatre in Greek lands persisted, the center of influence shifted to Rome around the time of Christ.

FIGURE 11.12
Graeco-Roman Theatre.
Roman influence on Greek theatres reduced the orchestra to a half-circle and emphasized the elaborate facade represented by the pillars in this photograph of the theatre at Leptis Magnis. *Photo by Mert Hatfield.*

THE ROMAN THEATRE

Background

Rome was unparalleled among great Western civilizations because it remained intact so long. From a small prehistoric settlement, it grew to become the center of a far-flung empire that touched Asia and Africa as well as Britain and western Europe. At its height, a system of roads and a military and civil power stretched from northern England to Egypt and eastward to Syria.

The city, although founded in the eighth century B.C., did not control the Italian peninsula until the third century B.C. By that time, Rome had developed a republican form of government, the leaders of which were praised for their economy, discipline, loyalty, and rhetorical prowess. In technology and military matters, moreover, Rome had no contemporary equal. By the first century B.C., its territory was vast and included much of western Europe as well as many of the lands once within the sphere of Greek influence. Whenever Romans made contact with another culture, they freely borrowed its arts, religion, technology—anything that seemed useful. Roman culture, then, in many ways was an amalgam of attitudes and practices drawn from other lands but always adapted to the particular needs and interests of Rome and Romans.

In 27 B.C., the republican form of government was abandoned in favor of an imperial form; that is, power once vested in many representatives now resided in the person of the emperor. By that time, too, the energies of the government were becoming increasingly directed at maintaining control of the conquered territories, which were both numerous and distant. Its size and territorial complexity led in 330 A.D. to the formation of a second (Eastern) capital of the Empire, Constantinople, which shared responsibilities with Rome. Internal struggles and attacks from the north led to the collapse of Western Rome by the sixth century.

THINKING ABOUT CLASSICAL THEATRE

About 50 B.C., Pliny, a Roman, in his *Natural History* described a spectacular (and perhaps nonexistent) structure: *"two large wooden theatres built close together; each was nicely poised, turning on a pivot."* He explained that the theatres could be used either separately or *"the two theatres [could] swing together to face each other with their corners interlocking and, with their outer frames removed, they would form an amphitheatre."* Sketch or make a model of this theatre. Be certain to account for the place of both actors and performers in each configuration.

Although the Eastern Empire, centered at Constantinople, continued until 1453, Rome's influence was no longer a significant factor in the political life of Europe after about A.D. 500.

As the time line shows (Fig. 11.13), Greek and Roman theatres coexisted and influenced each other for about eight hundred years. In Rome as in Greece, the periods for which we have plays (mostly B.C.) do not correlate well with the periods for which we have information about the theatre buildings (mostly A.D.).

Unlike Greece, Rome did not leave us a drama that is a cornerstone of our idea of dramatic literature, nor did it create a theatre that is an example to us when we try to define the art of theatre or determine the origins of theatre. Rather, we value Roman theatre for two reasons:

- Roman theatre was enormously popular in its own day, as important a historical artifact as modern movies.

- Roman theatre, criticism, and drama were the models upon which the Renaissance built its ideas of theatre, criticism, and drama.

In the case of Greece, we have reasons for believing that we were handed down some of the best of tragedy and comedy. In Rome, however, we believe only that we were handed down representative comedies, while the tragedies we received were late literary imitations not even intended for production.

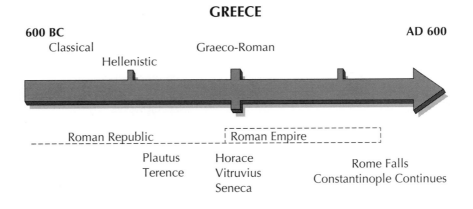

GREECE

600 BC   AD 600

Classical   Graeco-Roman

Hellenistic

Roman Republic   Roman Empire

Plautus   Horace   Rome Falls
Terence   Vitruvius   Constantinople Continues
                 Seneca

ROME

FIGURE 11.13   Time Line: Greece and Rome.
The theatres of Greece and Rome overlap, but their extant plays do not. In Rome as in Greece, the period of the extant dramas does not correspond to the period of surviving (stone) theatre buildings.

◉FIGURE 11.14   Roman Life.
The Romans put up elaborate buildings both to
celebrate their glory and to make life pleasurable.
At the same time, life was hard for many. Left, the
ruins of monumental Roman baths; right, an
intensely realistic sculpture of a Roman shepherd.

The Occasions of Roman Theatre

The Romans were borrowers of other cultures. From a people to their north, the
Etruscans, they got the practice of combining many forms of entertainment (including theatre) in *ludi,* state celebrations devoted to one of Rome's several gods.
Ludi were managed by a magistrate who got a government grant to cover the festival's expenses. He would, for example, deal with the heads of several acting
troupes and establish fees for their performances. For much of the Roman period,
these festival days continued to multiply until performances, although still "occasional," were common.

Theatre remained popular as the number of performances increased, from
one per year in 240 B.C. to more than a hundred per year during the third century
A.D., although the kinds of *drama* changed. Typically, several troupes played at
each festival. On performance days, plays were presented continuously, without
intermissions.

Characteristics of Roman Theatre

For convenience' sake, Roman theatre is divided into two large blocs of political history, the *Republic* (c. 5th century B.C.–27 B.C.), and the *Empire* (27 B.C.–c. 500 A.D.). (It may be easier to remember that the first Roman emperor was ruling when Christ was born.)

Physical Theatre

The first *permanent stone theatre* was not built in Rome until 55 B.C., very near the end of the Republic. Almost immediately, construction began on other theatres, until, by the end of Roman influence, more than one hundred theatres existed around the Roman Empire. (Most historians assume, perhaps incorrectly, that Roman theatres of the Republic were similar to those of the Empire, but, as evidence is limited and often perplexing, the appearance of the earlier wooden theatres remains a mystery.)

Like Greek theatres, known Roman theatres were facade stages. Unlike Greek theatres, known Roman theatres were typically built on level ground, and the seating was built up, stadium style. At the rear of the Roman auditorium was a wide, covered aisle, whose roof joined that of the scene house to form a single architectural unit. The orchestra remained, but, unlike that in Greece, was only a half circle, whose diameter was marked by the front of a stage raised to a height of about five feet and extended to a depth of up to forty feet. The stage was very long (100–300 feet) and was enclosed at each end by side wings jutting out from the scene house. At the back of the stage was the scene house, whose elaborate facade

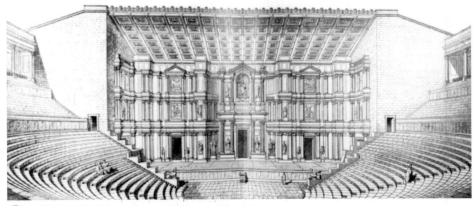

FIGURE 11.15   Roman Stone Theatre.
Imaginatively reconstructed from ruins, this drawing shows the major changes from Greek theatres: the orchestral half-circle, the elaborate architectural facade, the deep and roofed stage, and the architectural connection between stage house and auditorium.

was decorated with numerous statues, porticoes, columns, and so on. Perhaps to protect this elaborate structure from the weather or perhaps to improve acoustics, a roof extended from the top of the scene house over part of the stage. The corridors between the scene house and the audience area were covered and used as audience exits.

Architectural evidence suggests that a front curtain may have been used. Its use is unclear.

Vitruvius. The Roman architect Vitruvius wrote a ten-volume work detailing Roman architectural practices (c. 15 B.C.), including ways to build both theatres and scenery. He described the theatre, the scene house, and three types of scenes, tragic, comic, and satyric. Although (mis)interpreted, Vitruvius's work influenced both theatrical and scenic design of the Renaissance (after c. 1450 A.D.).

Audience

Accounts suggest that Roman theatres could seat between ten and fifteen thousand and that considerable care was taken to ensure audience comfort. Aisles were apparently wide and numerous, permitting easy comings and goings. An awning was used as protection against the sun, and at least in one theatre, a primitive air-conditioning system was contrived that used fans and ice brought down from nearby mountains. Important people could reserve seats in the orchestra or in the special boxes atop the audience exits. Theatre of the ludi was free and open to everyone. It is not clear how many women were in the audience.

Production Practices

The basic setting in the Roman theatre was apparently the scene house itself. For comedies, its several doors represented entrances to separate homes; for tragedies, its doors were entrances to various parts of a palace or a temple. The stage itself represented either a street running in front of dwellings (in comedy) or a gathering place before a temple or a palace (in tragedy). *Periaktoi* were used to suggest changes of place. According to one ancient commentator, they were located near the ends of the stage and could be rotated to reveal one of three scenes: a tragic scene (e.g., columns and statues), a comic scene (e.g., balconies and windows), or a satyric scene (trees, caves, and "other rustic objects"). Because the *periaktoi* could not possibly have hidden the facade of the scene house, they probably served simply to inform the audience of location, not to portray the place in a realistic way.

Also tantalizing are contemporary accounts of wondrous special effects. The accounts may be exaggerated, but for one event there were reportedly "sliding cliffs and a miraculous moving wood," and for another, a fountain of wine springing from a mountain top just before the mountain sank into a chasm and out of sight. These were, perhaps, not typical.

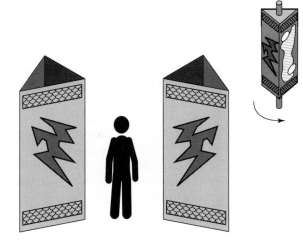

FIGURE 11.16 Periaktoi.
Probably Greek in origin, periaktoi were three-sided structures that allowed a change of "scenery" by rotating to show a new face to the audience.

Costumes and Masks

Roman masks, costumes, and scenic practices resembled those of Hellenistic Greece. Roman masks for tragedy and comedy were full and exaggerated, with high head-dresses and large mouths; the costumes resembled either Roman or Hellenistic fashions, depending on the kind of comedy or tragedy being done. Masks for *pantomime* (see p. 251), however, were made with closed mouths (because the dancers had no need to speak). As in Greece, all actors wore masks, except for the *mime* performers (see pp. 251–252). Clearly, as the popularity of mime increased, the use of masks on the Roman stage declined.

Plays and Playwrights

Tragedy.   Although no tragedies survive from the Republic, titles and fragments indicate that they resembled Hellenistic Greek tragedy: Sensational and melodramatic elements took precedence over philosophical inquiry, and the role of the chorus was peripheral rather than central to the development of the action. Depending on the subject matter and the costumes worn by the actors, Roman tragedy was divided into two types: (1) those written about Greeks, in which the actors dressed as noble Greeks, and (2) those written about Romans, in which actors were dressed as upper-class Roman citizens.

Seneca.   From the Empire, ten tragedies are extant, nine by *Seneca* (c. 5 B.C.–A.D. 65). None was intended for production in a public theatre. The importance of Seneca's tragedies rests neither on their literary excellence nor on their position among contemporary Roman audiences but on their monumental effect on later writers, who discovered, translated, and copied them (see pp. 282, 296), probably because they were both linguistically and physically more accessible than the earlier Greek tragedies.

FIGURE 11.17
Roman Tragic Actor.
Interpreting some evidence is difficult. This statue, once thought to be a Greek actor, is now believed to be a Roman tragic actor. The large blocks under the feet, once thought to be parts of platformed boots, are now interpreted as the means by which the statue was attached to its pedestal.

Seneca's plays display characteristics assumed to be typical of Greek Hellenistic tragedy. The chorus is not well integrated into the action, and so the (usually four) choral odes (songs) serve to divide the plays into five parts. His protagonists are often driven by a single dominant passion that causes their downfall. His minor characters include messengers, confidants, and ghosts. His language emphasizes rhetorical and stylistic figures, including extended descriptive and declamatory passages, pithy statements about the human condition (*sententiae*), and elaborately balanced exchanges of dialogue. Many of his plays feature spectacular scenes of violence and gore. Although Seneca's plays are now rarely done, their influence on the later development of tragedy in Italy, France, England, and even Germany was great.

Comedy. Comedy, like tragedy, was divided into that written about the Greek middle class and that written about Romans. Although many titles, names, and fragments remain, only twenty-seven comedies survive, all from two authors: Plautus and Terence. Both wrote during the second century B.C., and both wrote about the Athenian middle class. Both drew heavily from Greek "new comedies" for their materials and stories, and *neither used a chorus.* Despite these obvious similarities, however, the plays of Plautus and Terence are very different from one another and suggest a considerable range within Republican Roman comedy.

Plautus (254–184 B.C.) made a good deal of money as an actor-manager before turning to playwriting at about forty. He become a prolific and popular author. Of the more than one hundred works credited to him, twenty-one have survived, doubtless a tribute to the esteem in which he was held.

Plautus's sense of humor was always evident. The three names by which he was officially known (Titus Maccus Plautus) translate roughly as "big, splay-footed clown," perhaps a reference to his acting a clown. Probably his experiences as an actor accounted for the *theatrical* (as opposed to literary) qualities of his comedies. Plautine comedies are noted for their loosely linked episodes, which are filled with visual gags, verbal wordplay, and characters who are ludicrous in appearance as well as behavior. Never one to pass up an opportunity for a laugh, Plautus often broke the dramatic illusion, addressed his audience directly, and incorporated references to contemporary Rome in his comedies about the Athenian middle class. Among his many plays, *The Braggart Warrior, The Menaechmi, Pot of Gold,* and *Amphitryon* have been copied by Shakespeare, Molière, and others. (See Figure C-7.)

FIGURE 11.18   Roman Temporary Theatre.
A setting for a Roman play, based on research by Richard C. Beacham into a painting at
the Villa of Oplontis, constructed under his direction at the J. Paul Getty Museum. The
Republican theatres of Rome are believed to have been of this type. *Courtesy of Richard
C. Beacham.*

Terence (d. 159 B.C.) was less boisterous than Plautus. His use of language, for
example, was so careful and elegant that his plays were used in schools throughout
the Middle Ages as models of Latin eloquence. His plots, although based on those
of the Greek Menander and his contemporaries, often combined two or more of
the Greek comedies into a single, highly complicated dramatic action. He avoided
the episodic quality of Plautus's plots in favor of more carefully contrived actions
that proceeded by means of seeming cause and effect. His characters, too, appeared more normal and human, and thus more sympathetic. The result was, of
course, comedies that were more elegant and refined but less robust and free, more
thoughtful but less fun than Plautus's.

Finally, Terence's use of the prologue was unusual. Unlike Plautus, whose
prologues contained exposition, preparation, and summary, Terence used his to
argue matters of dramatic theory, to encourage audiences to behave politely, and
to defend himself from the attacks of critics. In a prologue that is as revealing of
republican audiences as of Terence's playwriting, for example, he complained that

the first performance of the play had been spoiled because the audience got more interested in a nearby troupe of acrobats.

Although comedy had always been more popular than tragedy in Rome, even its popularity waned within fifty years of Terence's death. Thus, by the time the first stone theatre was built (55 BC), the great period of Roman tragedy and comedy was over.

Theory: Horace

About the time that tragedy and comedy were fading from public theatres, Horace (65–8 B.C.) wrote his *Ars Poetica,* a work that exerted even more influence on the Renaissance than Aristotle's *Poetics* (on which it was loosely based). *Ars Poetica* is concerned with the standards and procedures to be followed in writing poetry, with special references to comedy and tragedy. Unlike Aristotle's work, which is a philosophical inquiry into the nature of the form *tragedy,* Horace's is a practical guidebook intended for people wanting to write. As such, it is considerably more prescriptive than Aristotle's work about such matters as the unities, the separation of the genres, and the appropriate arrangement of language. *Ars Poetica* seems to have expressed current dramatic theories, but it was irrelevant to practice in the popular theatre; therefore, Horace's importance (like Seneca's) rests on his appeal to later writers of the Renaissance.

Nonliterary Drama

Despite the theories of Horace and men like him, drama and theatre during the Empire became increasingly nonliterary. The two most popular forms, *pantomime* and *mime,* depended on spectacle, not language, and thus can scarcely be appreciated at a distance of two thousand years.

Pantomime.   A pantomime was a solo dance that told a story by means of movement alone. Accompanied by an orchestra and a chorus, a dancer enacted a serious story taken from history or mythology. Although pantomime for a time took the place of tragedy as a serious, popular entertainment, it too was overwhelmed by the popularity of *mime.*

Mime.   Paralleling the rise of Christianity, the success of mime marked several changes:

- *Mime included women* among its performers, the only theatrical entertainment in Greece or Rome to do so.
- Performers in the mime did not usually wear masks, and so their faces were both noticeable and important. Indeed, mime performers were often successful because of their looks: the very handsome or beautiful and the extraordinarily grotesque or ugly had the best chance of success, for they could more readily appeal to the audience as sympathetic or comic characters.

Mimes could be either comic or serious, simple or spectacular, but, whatever their form, they usually dealt with contemporary life. They became both Rome's most popular and its most notorious theatrical entertainment during the Empire (both East and West). Some mime actresses set fashions in clothes and behavior; one (Theodora) married an emperor; some became the equivalent of movie stars. Despite this popularity, no complete mime scripts have been passed down to us; the assumption is that they, perhaps like sitcom scripts, were thought (by those who kept libraries) to have no lasting value.

Christian Opposition

Because some mimes included real sex and violence as part of the performance, and because many of them mocked Christianity, Christian writers and believers demanded—unsuccessfully—the outlawing of theatre. Mime was not alone in its excesses, however; equally popular were chariot racing, gladiatorial contests, animal fights, and sea battles in which violence and death were also expected and applauded. Although these entertainments took place in special buildings like *amphitheatres* (e.g., Rome's Colosseum) and *circuses* (the Circus Maximus), theatres were occasionally appropriated for such events, reinforcing the arguments of those who wanted to ban theatre. The real issue, however, was culturally determined morality, of which mime was one expression.

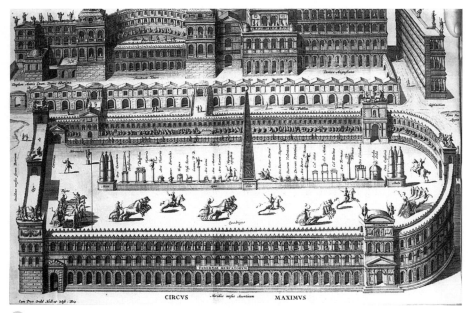

FIGURE 11.19   The Circus Maximus, Rome.
Such huge structures and their exciting chariot races competed with the theatre for the imperial Roman audience.

FIGURE 11.20 Naumachia.
The staged sea battle was another competitor for the theatre audience, offering slaves on real ships fighting, often to their real deaths, on real water.

Decline and Fall

A series of barbarian invasions first dissipated and finally destroyed the power of Rome. The "fall of Rome" managed to accomplish what the opposition of the Christian Church could not: the end of formal and organized theatrical activity in Western Roman lands, an event usually dated from about the middle of the sixth century A.D. With the collapse of Rome, its theatre disappeared, only to be reborn, not in the period immediately following (the "Middle Ages"), but in the more distant Renaissance, whose scholars studied Roman theories and plays, imitated them, and thus ensured a Roman legacy to the theatrical world.

THE PERIOD IN THE MODERN REPERTORY

Greek and Roman plays are rare, in fact almost nonexistent, on Broadway—although a comedy by Plautus was the basis for the musical *A Funny Thing Happened on the Way to the Forum.* Aristophanes is sometimes seen on university campuses, despite a scarcity of translations that are actually funny—Aristophanes was very topical—and high production demands (costumes, effects). *Lysistrata* is probably

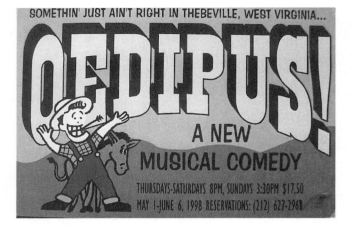

SOMETHIN' JUST AIN'T RIGHT IN THEBEVILLE, WEST VIRGINIA...

OEDIPUS!

A NEW
MUSICAL COMEDY

THURSDAYS-SATURDAYS 8PM, SUNDAYS 3:30PM $17.50
MAY 1-JUNE 6, 1998 RESERVATIONS: (212) 627-2961

FIGURE 11.21
Modern Performances.
An advertising postcard for a musical parody of Sophocles' *Oedipus Rex,* attesting to the story's durability. Greek tragedies have remained in the repertory more than comedies or Roman plays. *Advertising graphic/postcard for the New York City/Wings Theatre/Off-Off Broadway production of* Oedipus! A New Musical Comedy, *illustrated by and with the permission of Colin Stokes.*

the most common, perhaps because of its subject (war and peace) and its high sexual content. Roman tragedy means Seneca, whose plays are not supposed to be stageable; a version of one Senecan play was done some years ago by Peter Brook, however. It is Greek tragedy that is most often staged, and one is to be found in many university seasons. Most likely to be seen are the plays of Euripides and Sophocles: Euripides' *Medea* is currently popular because of its roles for women and its subject. His *Bacchae* was popular in the 1960s and is also the basis of an adaptation by the Nigerian playwright Wole Soyinka, *The Bacchae.* Sophocles' *Antigone* has attracted a number of modern playwrights as adaptors (Anouilh, Martha Boesing) and is often seen; *Oedipus Rex* is sometimes done, when an Oedipus can be found. Laurence Olivier did a memorable production in the 1940s—without the chorus, an understandable cut, the chorus being the single greatest problem in Greek drama for the modern director.

CURRENT ISSUES

Not only the drama, but also the philosophy, the architecture, the literature—some would say, the deep culture—of Greece and Rome have influenced subsequent civilizations in Europe and America. Until recently, it was difficult to imagine a Western society that would not proclaim its reliance on at least Greek democracy and Roman law. Until recently, "everybody" knew, or was supposed to know, Greek mythology and Roman legend. Until fairly recently, "everybody" studied at least Latin, and until a couple of centuries ago, "everybody" had at least a little Greek. As "everybody" agreed, Greece and Rome were the foundations of genuine civilization, and their great works were part of the necessary education of "everybody." These great works comprised a "canon"—a body of essential cultural authorities.

Today, however, many people argue with this canon. First, they point out, "everybody" who used to know Greek and Roman literature and culture turns out to have been mostly well-to-do whites, almost all male. Too, they argue, the societies of Greece and Rome were less free and noble than "everybody" thought, both having practiced slavery, ethnic superiority, and the subjugation of women. Just as importantly, they argue, the authors of the canon were all-male, not because of any innate superiority of males, but because of social manipulation at the time (women were not educated) and erasure by male historians since.

Yet, supporters of the canon assert, it is undeniable that Greece and Rome, and therefore their literatures, undergird much of Western culture, from the architecture of the U.S. Capitol to such ideals as public service and democracy itself. They argue that all educated people should know the canon so as to understand their culture and to share a common body of works. Opponents, however, see the perpetuation of Greek and Roman influence as questionable: To what degree, they ask, are problems in Western culture the result of this heritage? And to what degree is the canon guilty of giving those very problems dignity and credibility? How profoundly, for example, shall we take a Greek tragedy that depends on male dominance and the subjugation of women for its hidden subject? How seriously will we view a theatre that barred women from the stage and depended for much of its comedy on male interpretation of female behavior? How highly shall we prize a political system whose serious plays dealt only with an entrenched upper class? How far can we trust a culture that denied a voice to most of its people, however wonderfully the chosen ones spoke?

These and similar questions have led to challenges of the canon and changes, or requests for change, in many college curricula. Should the works of the canon be dropped entirely? Or, as some critics suggest, should it be expanded to include other works (by women, for example) to balance them? Or should the canon be kept as it is but taught critically, with equal emphasis given to its flaws? Or should we keep the canon as it is and teach it as one means of providing a binding force for our culture and our democratic politics?

KEY TERMS

Check your understanding against this list. Brief definitions are in the Glossary; page references there will direct you to appropriate pages. (Persons are page-referenced in the Index.)

City Dionysia	mime
chorus	new comedy
eccyclema	old comedy
facade stage	orchestra
Graeco-Roman	pantomime
Hellenistic	periaktoi
ludi	physical theatre
mechane	skene
middle comedy	theatre history

Emblem and Simultaneity: Middle Ages and Golden Ages

OBJECTIVES

When you have completed this chapter, you should be able to:

- Explain how and when a new kind of theatre came into being several hundred years after the fall of Rome

- Discuss how the medieval theatre was part of its culture

- Trace the changes in medieval theatre from its beginnings to its end, including its influence on the theatres of Shakespeare and Spain

- Describe the physical types of medieval theatres, and the influence they had on theatres that followed; and discuss how the various theatres were funded and organized

- List principal kinds of drama, important playwrights, and plays from the age of Shakespeare and the Spanish Golden Age

- Describe the physical theatre of Shakespeare and the Spanish Golden Age and use the correct terminology for their parts

257

The second phase of theatrical and dramatic history began in the tenth century and ended about 1650 (approximately one hundred years earlier in Italy). Despite important differences, the theatres of the Middle Ages and those of the Golden Ages of England and Spain shared important traits:

1. A staging convention of *simultaneous settings,* where several widely separated locations could be presented simultaneously to the audience.

2. The sharing of meaning through *emblems,* shorthand embodiments of richer content (a flag standing for a country, a crown for a king).

3. *Complicated plays* with numerous characters, many lines of action, and elastic time and place (traits seldom found in classical dramas).

4. A mostly male theatre, in which women participated mostly as audience.

Over the last two centuries of this period, rapid change led to overlap between this theatre and a new one then coming into being. This overlap was possible because of social and economic stratification of the theatre into such layers as a theatre of the court, a popular theatre, and an embryonic commercial or professional theatre.

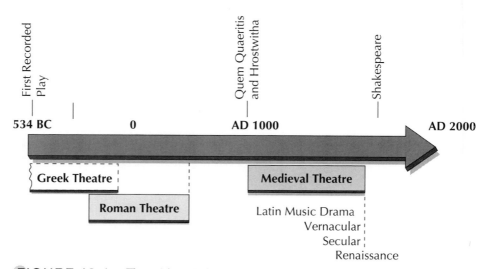

FIGURE 12.1   Time Line: Middle and Golden Ages.
Theatre left little record in the four hundred years after the collapse of Rome, reappearing in the 900s in Germany and England. This medieval theatre ended in western Europe in about 1550 but was followed by the golden ages of English and Spanish theatre, which in turn ended about 1650.

Until the advent of the embryonic commercial theatre, there were few professionals—that is, people who both devoted their lives to theatre and made their livings from it. Typically, these few were attached to a court or a rich nobleman as servants.

THEATRE IN THE MIDDLE AGES

Background

Although civilization in the Eastern Empire continued, that in western Europe was in a state of increasing confusion after the fourth century A.D. From then until the eighth century, western Europe experienced political disarray, out of which emerged a different kind of Europe, one based on new societies and diverse languages and traditions.

With the collapse of Western Rome in the sixth century, various forces that had before served to unify Europe weakened or disintegrated. The Roman system of roads and waterways fell into disrepair, and transportation and communication became at first troubled and at last almost impossible. Laws were ignored and order broke down, replaced by the rule of force: bands of pirates and brigands grew wealthy and influential enough to challenge rulers. Without the support of a government, the monetary system failed, and barter, with all of its cumbersome trappings, was the basis of trade.

Into the power vacuum created by Rome's defeat came a variety of competing interests, each sparring for political and economic clout. The Christian Church exerted increasing influence, especially after the tenth century, in part because its hierarchy ensured an orderly governance and in part because its influence in the daily lives of people gave it a substantial base. The other prevailing social organization was feudal, whose primary social unit was the manor. On the manor, each serf owed absolute allegiance to the lord, who, in turn, owed allegiance to more powerful lords, and so on. Similarly, in the Church, the priests ranked below the bishops, who ranked below the archbishops; at the top was the bishop of Rome, the pope, who spoke with authority on Church matters. Both power hierarchies were essentially pyramidal, with one (male) person at the top, relatively few (male) persons immediately under him, and so on until, at the base of each pyramid, were the peasants, that great mass of people who tilled the land and provided all those above them with the necessities and amenities of life. The two pyramids interlocked when Church leaders were drawn from the noble classes; the peasants provided goods and services for both Church lords and secular lords.

The life of the medieval peasant was one of work, ignorance, and want; that of people above the peasant varied. Because earlier historians saw this extended period as a lower one between two higher ones (Rome and the Renaissance—the "rebirth"), they called this the *Middle Ages* or the *medieval* (middle) period.

A series of crusades after the twelfth century against Muslims and others (including Constantinople) served to encourage trade and the opening of new sea

FIGURE 12.2   Medieval Life.
Peasants of the Middle Ages lived harsh lives of work and want.

routes. Increased trade, in turn, encouraged the development of towns, a movement well underway by the eleventh century. These towns and the merchants and tradesmen in them existed outside the feudal structure and gradually undermined it. As tradesmen organized themselves into *guilds* (trade brotherhoods), they were able to confront the feudal lords and eventually to challenge them successfully. With the rise of towns and the weakening of feudalism, nations began to take shape, and kings emerged to govern them. By the fourteenth century, the domination of the Church was under attack and its monopoly on matters of faith was being eroded. With the decline of feudalism and the authority of the Church, and with the emergence of towns and nationalism, the era metamorphosed into a different one (the Renaissance).

Continuity with Rome: Hroswitha

For many years, historians believed that no theatre or drama outlived the collapse of Rome in the sixth century, but it is now certain that, after the empire divided into two parts (about A.D. 330), plays continued to be performed in the Eastern Empire, and that, even in the West, remnants of the professional performers traveled about Italy, France, and Germany. Scattered references to *mimi, histriones,* and *ioculatores* (all words used to describe actors) surfaced periodically in medieval accounts, but the degree to which such performers performed actual plays, as distinct from variety entertainments like juggling, tumbling, dancing, and rope tricks, is not known. Clearly, if traditional dramas were performed between the sixth and the tenth centuries, their scale was much reduced.

Two events in the tenth century marked the reentry of theatre into western Europe.

Hroswitha, a religious leader (and noblewoman) attached to the Benedictine monastery near Gandersheim (in modern Germany), wrote seven plays (c. 950), the first still-extant dramas since the early days of the Roman Empire. Based on the comedies of Terence, Hroswitha's plays sought to celebrate "the laudable chastity of holy maidens" and *may* have been performed at court and at the monastery. Hroswitha is important on three counts: as the first female playwright, as the first known post-Roman playwright, and as proof of an intellectual continuity from Rome to the Middle Ages. For reasons not entirely clear (but perhaps related to the fact that men have written most histories), Hroswitha's contributions have been largely overshadowed by a different strand of theatre, one that also emerged in the tenth century and also at a Benedictine monastery.

Innovation in the Church: Ethelwold

Ethelwold, Bishop of Winchester, England, issued in 975 the *Regularis Concordia,* a monastic guidebook, which, among other things, described in detail how one part of an Easter service was to be performed. For about a hundred years before Ethelwold, the Church had been decorating and elaborating various of its practices. Music, calendar, vestments, art, architecture, and *liturgy* (rites, public worship)—all had changed in the direction of greater embellishment. One sort of liturgical embellishment was the *trope* (any interpolation into an existing text). One Easter trope was sung by the choir antiphonally and began, *"Quem quaeritis in sepulchro, o christocole."* Translated into English, the trope read in its entirety:

> *Whom seek ye in the tomb, O Christians?*
> *Jesus of Nazareth, the crucified, O heavenly beings.*
> *He is not here, he is risen as he foretold;*
> *Go and announce that he is risen from the tomb.*

It was this trope to which staging directions were added in Ethelwold's *Regularis Concordia:*

> *While the third lesson is being read, four of the brethren shall vest, one of whom, wearing an alb as though for some different purpose, shall enter and go stealthily to the place of the "sepulchre" and sit there quietly, holding a palm in his hand. Then, while the third response is being sung, the other three brethren, vested in copes and holding thuribles in their hands, shall enter in their turn and go to the place of the "sepulchred," step by step, as though searching for something. Now these things are done in imitation of the angel seated on the tomb and of the women coming with perfumes to anoint the body of Jesus. When, therefore, he that is seated shall see these three draw nigh, wandering about as it were and seeking something, he shall begin to sing softly and sweetly,* Quem quaeritis.

TRANSLATED BY THOMAS SYMONS

The passage is worth examining for its clues to costume, acting, properties, setting, text, and "stage directions," which are clear enough to call it a drama.

During the tenth century, then, the major directions for medieval drama were pointed. Some religious dramas (like the *Quem Quaeritis*) were part of the liturgy; others were performed under other conditions. Some plays showed classical influence (Hroswitha); others drew from different traditions. All were staged, however, within similar ideas of theatre space and convention.

New Conventions: Simultaneity and Emblem

Certain basic principles underlay the staging of medieval plays, whether the plays were given inside or outside the Church, for religious or secular purposes. Staging was *simultaneous* (several different locations were presented simultaneously to the audience); and it was *emblematic* (its meaning rested in visible signs that were understood by the audience).

FIGURE 12.3
Artistic Conventions.
Medieval art was usually religious, its primary conventions simultaneous and emblematic. This painting shows three locations simultaneously—heaven, earth, hell—and the emblems of hell, angel, bishop, and so on.

Simultaneous staging depended on two uses of scenic space, *mansion* and *platea:*

- *Mansions* were small scenic structures that served to locate a specific place.
- The *platea* was a neutral, generalized playing area.

In complex plays, many mansions could be arranged around the platea. Actors might first establish their specific location by reference to the appropriate mansion, after which they moved about the platea.

Emblematic staging depended on a shared understanding of many signs and symbols. Among mansions, for example, an animal mouth signified hell; a revolving globe stood for heaven, and so on.

Within these general staging conventions, some variations occurred.

Characteristics of Medieval Theatre

Physical Theatre

No medieval buildings were specifically reserved for use as theatres. Instead, two primary kinds of space were used: churches and a variety of nonchurch spaces.

Staging in the Church.   In staging in churches, existing church architecture was often used. For example, the choir loft might represent heaven, the crypt hell, and the altar the tomb of Christ. For elaborate plays, special mansions might be constructed, some small but others large enough for several persons to be hidden in. Special effects required machinery capable of flying objects and actors in and out of the playing area. For example, angels and doves flew about, Christ rose to heaven, and the three kings followed a moving star that led them to the stable of the Christ child and there stopped to mark the spot.

Staging in Nonchurch Venues.   The staging of religious plays outside the church took two major forms within the same conventions:

- *Fixed staging,* which occurred throughout Europe, except in parts of Spain and England
- *Movable staging,* which was used most importantly in parts of Spain and England

In fixed staging, mansions (or *scaffolds*) were set up, usually outdoors, in whatever spaces were available (e.g., courtyards of noble houses, town squares, the remains of Roman amphitheatres). Depending on the space, the mansions were arranged in circles, straight lines, or rectangles, and the platea and the audience

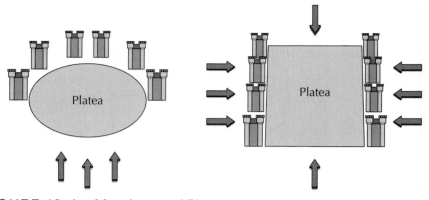

FIGURE 12.4 **Mansions and Platea.**
The principal medieval performance space was the platea in the midst of structures—mansions—that suggested locations. Space within the platea was elastic; the mansions were all present simultaneously.

area were established accordingly. Although the individual arrangements varied, heaven and hell (ordinarily the most ornate mansions) were customarily set at opposite poles.

In movable staging, *pageants* (pageant wagons) allowed the audience to scatter along a processional route while the plays were brought to them and performed in sequence, much like a parade with floats. Each play, then, was performed several times. A likely pattern was for the first play (e.g., Creation) to be presented at dawn at the first station; when it moved to the second station to perform, the second play (e.g., the Fall of Man) was presented at the first station. For most of the day, several plays were performing at once. The word *pageant* is important in a discussion of movable staging because it was used to describe the play itself, the spectacle of the plays in performance, and also the vehicle on which the presentation was staged.

The appearance of pageant wagons has been much discussed, but, as available evidence is scant, few firm conclusions are possible. Only one English description, dating from slightly before 1600, has survived, and its reliability is suspect:

> *Every company had his pagiant, or parte, which pagiants weare a high scafolde with two rowmes, a higher and a lower, upon four wheeles. In the lower they apparelled themselves, and in the higher rowme they played, beinge all open on the tope, that all behoulders mighte heare and see them. The places where they played them was in every streete.*

An obvious problem with the description, and one of the reasons its accuracy has been questioned, is that the wagons as described would need to be more

FIGURE 12.5
Movable Staging.
Wagons—their exact appearance not known (but see Figure 12.18)—brought plays and actors to designated audience locations along a processional route. This is a nineteenth-century artist's idea of what a wagon stage looked like.

than twelve feet tall to allow for the wheels and the two levels, yet narrow enough to be pulled by horses through the medieval streets. The resulting structure would be highly unstable and perhaps unable to turn corners as required in its trek from station to station.

The staging of secular dramas followed the same conventions: simultaneous and emblematic. Some plays, like those associated with great tournaments, might be staged out of doors; others, like those between courses of a banquet, were staged indoors. Movable staging might be adopted either outdoors or indoors, as might fixed staging.

Audience

The audience for early in-church theatre was largely religious—monks or nuns, lay brothers or sisters, novices. It grew more general as the plays moved out of monastic venues; in a few cases, it became general when in-church plays became annual events (occasionally combined with town plays), but this was rare.

Plays in nonchurch venues, on the other hand, always had mostly secular audiences and mostly mixed audiences (men and women). Obviously, the audience for a performance at a royal banquet was very limited (courtiers), as was that of a rural village (peasants). The great outdoor performances of the towns, however, played to a broad spectrum, from local religious figures to town officials to ordinary citizens. The audience was not universal, however: a fee was usually charged, and so a large part of the population was excluded. The well-to-do paid extra to sit in stands or special scaffolds or, when pageant wagons were used, in the windows of selected houses. Those who paid the least stood to watch the plays. Those who paid nothing may have been able to see the processions, if not the plays.

Audiences were subject to the weather, and they saw the plays against a backdrop of their fellow citizens and their own town. Food and drink were probably available. Toilet facilities were provided in at least some sets of stands erected for the gentry.

Production Practices and Sponsorship

Plays done in church were produced by the church. Outside the church, however, plays were supported in various ways. Sometimes, town officials took charge; sometimes, special committees did the job. Sometimes labor and religious organizations (*guilds* or *confraternities*) assumed responsibility, often under the town's protection.

Guilds were frequently called on to produce a single play in a group, sometimes on the basis of particular skills or association with the play's subject: Noah plays, which required a real (perhaps half-size) ship, went well with shipbuilding, for example. Because of both financial investment and tradition, plays tended to stay with the same guild for many years. As the plays and processions showed the wealth of the town, so the play and its properties showed the wealth of the guild.

The enormous complexity of some late medieval dramas also required specialists to oversee the production and to serve as the medieval counterpart of the

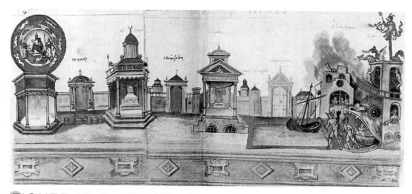

FIGURE 12.6   Fixed Staging.
Here, the mansions are placed behind and at the end of a platea. The mansions are elaborate, including Hell (right) and Heaven (left). Special effects include a practical ship and fire. (Valenciennes, France.)

modern producer. Although responsibilities differed with circumstances, the tasks of one medieval producer in France included:

- Overseeing the building of a stage and the use of the scenery and machines
- Overseeing the building and painting of scenery and the construction of seating for the audience
- Checking all deliveries to ensure accuracy
- Disciplining the actors
- Acting in the plays whenever necessary
- Addressing audiences at the beginning of the play and at each intermission, giving a summary of what had happened and promising greater marvels to come

Because special effects in the dramas were so extraordinary, some men, called *masters of secrets,* became specialists in their construction and workings, which included:

- Flying: angels flew about; Lucifer raised Christ; souls rose from limbo into heaven on Doomsday; devils and fire-spitting monsters sallied forth from hell and back again; platforms made to resemble clouds (*glories*), bore choruses of heavenly beings aloft
- Traps: appearances, disappearances, and substitutions, as when Lot's wife was turned into a pillar of salt, and tigers were transformed into sheep
- Fire: hell belched smoke and flames (in 1496 at Seurre, an actor playing Satan was severely burned when his costume caught fire), and buildings ignited on cue

Costumes and Masks

Costumes were primary carriers of meaning within the convention we have called emblematic: They indicated, symbolically and clearly, the nature of the wearers. Early on, a key identified Saint Peter; hoods signified women; wings meant angels; wallets and staffs identified travelers. At its most sophisticated, this convention became a rich source of both meaning and spectacle: In a parade of the seven deadly sins, Pride was dressed entirely in peacock feathers (the feather's "eye" symbolizing the love of display and self-admiration); a costume recorded for a late morality had symbols of coinage embroidered all over it. In the guild-produced plays, large sums were spent on such costumes, which were then used year after year.

Masks were rare in medieval theatre, probably being restricted to devils.

Acting

Roles in the plays were open to all male members of the community (in France, occasionally, women might perform) and were generally performed without compensation. As in any primarily amateur operation, the quality of the performances varied considerably, and it was probably in an attempt to upgrade the general level of acting that many cities hired professional "property players" to take the leading roles (after c. 1450) and to instruct the others. Although these few actors were paid, they were not looked down on as socially undesirable, as were professional actors in secular plays.

We have no textbooks of medieval acting. We believe that it was, like the costumes, emblematic. It probably depended on reducing character to large, symbolic strokes, without "inner" work or "psychology." We do not know how ama-

FIGURE 12.7
A Medieval Theatre in the Round.
This late (1470) medieval manuscript of the works of Terence shows knowledge of Roman theatre in the names Terentius (Terence) and Calliopius (an interpreter of Terence) and the words theatrum (theatre), joculatores (players), and scena (stage). The dress is medieval; the masks on the actors may come from Latin sources or may have an unknown medieval origin. What is apparently shown is a reading by Calliopius as the players mimed—a (mistaken?) medieval interpretation of a Latin account. It probably means to show a Roman theatre but shows instead a medieval one, with one mansion.

teurs handled the problem of being heard and understood outdoors. Some pictures of the period show prompters or directors, book in hand, standing among the actors; this professional may literally have been cueing gestures and turns of voice.

Some plays and some roles suggest a tradition of satirical or comic playing, with caricature an established technique. The traveling actors of the countryside probably emphasized low comedy and certainly passed on techniques and traditions that would flourish later with Shakespeare's clowns.

Plays and Playwrights

Most medieval drama was written anonymously. It is typical of medieval society that individual ego was not part of creativity—just as it was typical of later ages that authorship, artistic ownership, and ego were vital.

Medieval Drama

Religious Drama in the Church.   Many dramas like the *Quem Quaeritis* were performed inside monastic and cathedral churches as a part of the liturgy, and so are also called liturgical drama. Such plays were chanted or sung (rather than spoken) and were given in the language of the Church (Latin), and so are called Latin music drama. They were acted by clergy, choirboys, monks, and occasionally traveling scholars and schoolboys (and, occasionally, nuns); the actors, then, were almost always male (except in convents).

From the very short *Quem Quaeritis,* Latin music drama blossomed into many plays of varying lengths and varying degrees of complexity. The subjects of most such plays were Biblical, usually drawn from events surrounding Christmas and Easter: the visit of the three Marys to the tomb, the travel of the Magi, Herod's wrath. Other Latin music dramas, however, depicted such diverse stories as the life of the Virgin Mary, the raising of Lazarus, and Daniel in the lion's den. Almost all were serious, but at festivals like the Feast of Fools and the Feast of the Boy Bishops, the usual dignity was abandoned and in its place was substituted considerable tomfoolery. Latin music dramas continued to be performed in churches well into the sixteenth century, overlapping other types by hundreds of years.

Religious Drama Outside the Church.   Why drama came to be done outside the Church has been endlessly debated. Some argue that abuses like those at the Feast of Fools caused the Church to force the drama outdoors. Others argued that the appearance of drama outdoors merely reflected the changing needs of the plays and their audiences for more space and freedom. More likely is the increasing power of towns, which fastened on plays and other public shows as expressions of their new status. Whatever the reason for the development, records of religious plays given outside of churches appear by 1200 and are common by 1350, when relatively abundant accounts describe a civic and religious theatre of magnificent proportions throughout most of western Europe.

The new tradition differed from the old in several important ways:

- The plays outdoors were spoken rather than chanted or sung.
- The plays were in the vernacular (e.g., French, English, German) rather than in Latin.
- Laymen, rather than priests and clerics, served as actors.
- The stories and themes, no longer limited to liturgical sources, became more far-ranging.
- The performances tended to cluster in the spring and summer months, especially around the new Feast of Corpus Christi, rather than spreading throughout the church year, as before.

Of these changes, the most significant was the shift from a universal language (Latin) to the various national tongues, for with this shift came an end to an international drama and the beginning of several national dramas, a trend important to the future of both theatre and drama.

The plays remained decidedly religious, if not always scriptural. In general, they dealt with:

- Events in the life of Christ (*The Second Shepherd's Play*) and stories from the Old Testamant (*Noah*)—plays often called *mysteries*
- The lives of saints, both historical and legendary, called *miracles*
- Didactic allegories, often about the struggle for salvation (*Everyman*)— so-called *moralities*

Although the plays differed in subject matter and form, they shared several characteristics. First, they aimed to teach or to reinforce belief in Church doctrine.

FIGURE 12.8   Medieval Drama.
This shows relationships among several kinds of medieval drama. Only Hrostwitha showed clear connections with Roman drama. The urban cycles ended as the Renaissance was reached, but other forms cross-pollinated, producing the dramas of the golden ages.

Second, they were formulated as melodramas or divine comedies; that is, the ethical system of the play was clear, and good was rewarded, evil punished. Third, the driving force for the action was God and His plan rather than the decisions or actions of the dramatic agents. To a modern reader, the plays often appear episodic, with their actions unmotivated, their sequences of time and place inexplicable, and their mixture of the comic and the serious unnerving.

In fact, their traits expressed the medieval view. The plays presented the lure and strength of sin, the power and compassion of God, and the punishment awaiting the unrepentant sinner. They called for all people to repent, to confess, and to atone for their sins.

Because history was God's great lesson to humankind, the drama that expressed His plan was nothing less than the entirety of human history, from Creation to Doomsday. Any combination of events, any juxtaposition of characters, and any elasticity of time or place that would illuminate God's plan and make it more accessible and compelling was suitable drama. The great dramas of the fifteenth and sixteenth centuries that showed this history are called *cycles,* or *cosmic dramas,* and some took days, even weeks, to play from end to end.

Secular Drama.   The first records of secular dramas appeared at about the same time that religious dramas appeared outside the Church. At about the same time that these great religious plays were at their zenith, this other tradition was moving tentatively toward maturity.

Several principal venues of secular drama existed:

- At court and in the homes of the very wealthy, performances were given at tournaments and on holidays (especially Christmas and Mardi Gras). There, theatre pieces might be presented within another activity—for example, between the courses of a formal banquet; such a short dramatic entertainment was called an *interlude.* Short plays might also be given in connection with gift-giving by costumed revelers, as in entertainments called *mummings* and *disguisings.* The most spectacular of the noble and court entertainments, however, was the *masque,* in which allegorical compliments to the guests of honor were framed by intricate dances involving the courtiers themselves.

- Towns staged *street pageants* and *entries* in connection with various special occasions, often during the visit of an important dignitary. As a part of these events, plays were combined with elaborate processions. The plays were given for the instruction and entertainment of the visiting dignitaries, whose procession through the town constituted the major entertainment for the townspeople who watched it.

- In schools and colleges, *Roman comedies and tragedies* were studied, copied, translated, and emulated during much of the fifteenth century.

- For ordinary people in the towns and countryside, *farces* poked fun at all manner of domestic tribulations, particularly infidelity and cuckoldry.

- In many instances, secular *morality plays* featured classical gods and heroes rather than Christian virtues and vices, and occasionally morality plays were drawn into the religious battles of the Reformation: For example, anti-Catholic moralities costumed devils as Catholic prelates and Christian figures as Protestant ministers; anti-Protestant moralities did just the reverse. (See *The End of Medieval Theatre and Drama*, p. 273.)

Toward the end of the period (after c. 1450), a class of professionals appeared to put on such shows, including writing and staging them; they were often attached to courts or noble houses but, despite their skills and success, were servants.

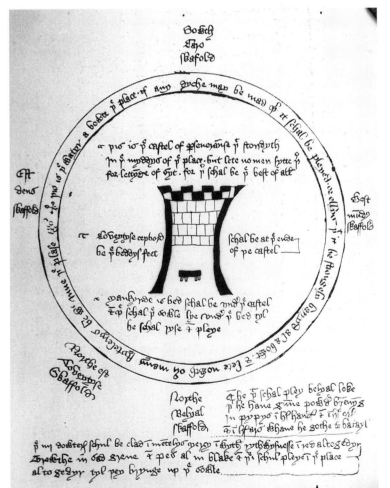

FIGURE 12.9 Medieval Theatre-in-the-Round.
From the medieval manuscript play *The Castle of Perseverance,* this "ground plan" shows a circular theatre with a major mansion in the center and five others around the periphery. The audience was to be inside the circle, as in Figure 12.7. For a detailed discussion and reconstruction, see Richard Southern's *Medieval Theatre in the Round.*

Popular farces were sometimes toured by tiny troupes, often families, who performed wherever they could get permission—no easy thing in the tight medieval world. They have left little record.

Although secular theatre seems to have existed throughout the Middle Ages, its increase and the rise of professionals to perform it after 1450 may themselves be taken as symptoms of change—the coming of the Renaissance.

The Register.   Because of a lack of mechanical printing, copies of playscripts were rare, and sometimes a single handwritten copy, with production notes, was maintained. This master copy, or *register,* was held by a responsible person or office. All parts were copied from it; some registers were occasionally lent to other towns so that they could produce the play.

The downside was that anyone who could get the register had the potential for stopping production—one reason that the book was so carefully controlled. In the sixteenth century, when religious dramas were being censored and then banned, there were moves by central governments to "call in" registers for "correction"—from which they never reappeared.

The End of Medieval Theatre and Drama

By the sixteenth century, a series of factions splintered away from the Roman Church; this religious Reformation quickly became political as rulers and nations found reasons to break from Rome or stay with it. The religious theatre was a visible annoyance to both Protestant and Catholic authorities, offending the one with doctrines already rejected, offending the other with doctrines better kept in church, at least until things quieted down. Worse, zealots on both sides were writing morality plays that cast their opponents as devils. In place after place, religious

---

THINKING ABOUT MEDIEVAL THEATRE

Medieval theatres were not simple, as this account from Valenciennes (1547) makes clear. "Truth, the angels, and other characters descended from very high. . . . Lucifer was raised from Hell on a dragon without our being able to see how. . . . Devils carried the souls of Herod and Judas through the air. . . . The fig tree, cursed by Our Lord, appeared to dry up, its leaves withering in an instant. The eclipse, the earthquake, the splitting of the rocks, and the other miracles at the death of Our Lord were shown with new marvels." Explain how such effects could be achieved. In addition to information in this and earlier chapters, books explaining magic tricks may be helpful.

plays were therefore outlawed by both Protestants and Catholics: Paris, 1548; England, 1558; the Council of Trent, 1545–1563.

The end of medieval drama was thus very quick. It had reached its height only within the century before the bans; indeed, much of the best and most elaborate of medieval theatre came in the first half of the sixteenth century. Briefly, in Italy, Renaissance court theatre co-existed with the medieval theatre of the street and church. Ironically, medieval theatre's final flowering was in part a benefit of the very forces—Renaissance wealth and ideas—that would destroy it. Yet, it left a legacy of production technology, acting, and playwriting, and the early professionals who had worked in it were the forebears of a great upsurge of professionalism after about 1550.

Theatre, denied the support of church and town, became a commercial venture. Regular performances in capital cities replaced occasional performances in cities and towns and private halls; permanent theatre structures replaced the streets or the town common; the professional actor replaced the amateur.

THEATRE IN THE GOLDEN AGES OF ENGLAND AND SPAIN

Background

Beginning in Italy around 1300, new ideas, social organizations, attitudes, and discoveries began to peek through the medieval order of Europe. For the next two hundred years, these new ideas gradually took hold and, in country after country, heralded the arrival of the *Renaissance* ("rebirth"). By the beginning of the sixteenth century, it had revolutionized many former attitudes and practices.

Humanism

People of the early Middle Ages had supposed that the temporal world would be destroyed, that the unrighteous would be purged, and that the righteous would be transported to a world of bliss. By 1300, however, new secular and temporal interests joined earlier divine and eternal ones. A love of God and His ways, long the basis of human behavior, was joined by a newfound admiration for humankind, whose worth, intelligence, and beauty began to be celebrated. This new concern for people and their earthly lives was called *humanism.*

Secularism

The older theology, a complete system based on divine revelation, gave way to competing philosophical systems that stressed *secularism* (that is, they advocated

FIGURE 12.10   Renaissance Life.
Rebirth of interest in Greece and Rome paralleled major discoveries in science. Among the most far-reaching was the proposal by Copernicus that the earth moved about the sun instead of the sun around the earth, as Ptolemy had asserted; the discovery challenged ideas of humans' place in nature.

ethical conduct as an end in itself rather than as a prerequisite to heaven, and they argued for logical systems of thought independent of divine revelation). In science, an earth-centered astronomy was challenged by a sun-centered universe in which human beings were relegated to life on a relatively minor planet, no longer at the center of creation.

The Reformation

Within the Church, demands for reform led to breaks with Rome: some Christians (like Martin Luther, fl. 1546) protested against the Church at Rome and launched what came to be called the *Reformation.*

In sum, although God, His Church, and His theology remained the central fact of human life in the Renaissance, they were no longer absolute and unquestioned. Humanism and secularism were competing with them for acceptance. But the emergence of new ideas and attitudes was only part of the phenomenon. Vital, too, were factors that encouraged the widespread dissemination of the new spirit. Two elements in particular were critical: the growth of trade and the arrival of the printing press in Italy.

Trade

Trade, both national and international, permitted and even encouraged a flow of ideas as well as of goods, an effortless exchange not possible as long as self-contained agricultural units dominated the economic life of Europe. At the center of most of the various trade routes of the fourteenth century were the city-states of Italy, which soon became centers of a commerce in ideas, skills, and products. When Constantinople fell to the Turks in 1453, many scholars and artists came to Italy. Thus, plays and treatises from ancient Greece and Rome, rescued from endangered libraries, arrived in Italy, where their study and interpretation began almost at once.

Printing

The introduction of the Gutenberg printing press to Italy at about the same time (1467) allowed the rapid reproduction of documents arriving from the East as well as of the interpretations and imitations of these documents. Certainly, the printing press allowed a veritable explosion of accessible information, so much so that, by 1500, numerous academies in the city-states of Italy were devoted to the study and production of Roman plays. Shortly thereafter, Italians began writing their own plays in imitation of the Roman models.

Patronage of the arts during the Renaissance was a major and acknowledged source of prestige, and, because the nobles' courts engaged in rivalries over which was to become the cultural center, painters, musicians, sculptors, architects, and writers flourished.

The appearance and effects of the Renaissance were markedly different in northern and southern Europe. The impact of the northern Renaissance on the medieval theatre in England brought about a golden age of theatre, that of William Shakespeare.

FIGURE 12.11   Printing. Probably no invention did more to spread new ideas than the printing press. Arriving in Italy as scholars sought refuge from the collapse of the Byzantine Empire, the presses disseminated writings brought by the scholars, made knowledge accessible, and made comparative criticism easier.

The Renaissance in the North: The Age of Shakespeare

The reign of Elizabeth I (1558–1603) brought greatness to England. With her ascent to the throne, the nation achieved the political and religious stability that permitted its arts and literature to thrive. When, in an attempt to mute religious controversies, the government outlawed religious drama, it opened the way for the rapid development of a secular tradition of plays and playgoing. When the queen finally agreed to the execution of Mary Stuart (1587), her chief rival for the throne and the center of Catholic assaults on the church and throne, Elizabeth's political situation was secured, and the domination of Anglican Protestants within the Church of England was affirmed. The English navy defeated the Spanish Armada in 1588 and established itself as ruler of the seas and leader among the trading nations. England, for the first time in generations, was at peace at home and abroad and was filled with a national confidence and a lust for life seldom paralleled in history.

Physical Theatre

In 1576, two commercial theatres opened in London, one an outdoor (or "public") theatre and the other an indoor (or "private") theatre. Thus, when Shakespeare arrived in London about fifteen years later, these two sorts of theatre were well established, and he wrote for and acted in both. Although their precise appearance cannot be known, their general features can be deduced from several kinds of evidence. First, and most important, perhaps, the architectural remains of two public theatres were uncovered in London in 1989. These newly discovered remains added to the information about public theatres that scholars had previously drawn from other sources like the extant plays, a contemporary building contract for the Fortune (public) Theatre, a contemporary sketch of the Swan (public) Theatre, a contemporary drawing of the Cockpit at Court (private) Theatre, and from various accounts taken from contemporary diaries, letters, and financial records (particularly those of Philip Henslowe, an entrepreneur).

Public Theatres. The outdoor, public theatres (of which nine were built between 1576 and 1642) consisted of a round or polygonal, roofed, multileveled auditorium that surrounded an open *yard,* into which jutted a platform raised to a height of four to six feet. The entire yard (or *pit*) and part of the stage platform were unroofed. The audience, probably numbering as many as 2500, surrounded the playing area on three sides, some standing in the pit, and others seated in the *galleries* or the still more exclusive *lords' rooms.* (Compare both the Roman and the Medieval theatres.)

The actors worked on the raised stage and apparently awaited cues and changed costumes in the *tiring house,* located at the rear of the platform. Covering part of the stage was a roof (the *heavens*) supported by columns resting on the stage and apparently decorated on its underside with pictures of stars, planets, and signs of the zodiac. Gods and properties flew in from the heavens.

FIGURE 12.12

The "Swan drawing" is one of the most important documents in English theatre history, although not an entirely clear one. It shows the interior of an Elizabethan theatre; its labels, here translated, are in Latin. It seems to show a partly medieval arrangement of circular "plain or arena" and surrounding audience. Compare it, however, with the "Theatrum" on the right, a slightly earlier interpretation of a Roman theatre, which also has "nobles" (aediles), a structure analogous to the "actors house" (proscenium), pillars, and circular audience.

The stage floor was pierced with *traps,* through which characters could appear and disappear. Connecting the tiring house with the stage were at least two doors, which often represented widely divergent locations (as, for example, when one led to the fields of France and the other to the shores of England). Atop the tiring house, a flag flew on days of performance, and at a level just below, in an area called the *hut,* were probably housed the various pieces of equipment and machinery needed for special effects. A *musicians' gallery* was apparently located just below the hut, at the third level above the stage.

FIGURE 12.13 Bankside.

The approximate location of the original Globe, seen from across the River Thames. The New Globe is the small, white building, center.

Other points are less certain. The plays clearly required two playing levels, an upper and a lower, and some sort of *discovery space,* a place where objects and characters could be hidden from view and discovered at the appropriate time. Most scholars agree that the discovery space was located between the two doors, but some conceive of it as a permanent architectural part of the theatre, whereas others conceive of it as a portable unit to be added or deleted as required; some picture the discovery space as a recessed alcove (a kind of miniproscenium theatre), whereas others see it as a pavilion that jutted out into the stage. Obviously, any decision about the conformation of the space at stage level had implications for the upper level as well. Obviously, too, the degree of permanence of the discovery space would radically affect the general appearance of the theatre. The whole problem has been made thornier by the absence of such a space in the Swan sketch (Fig. 12.12) and by the appalling problems with sight lines that any sort of discovery space seemed likely to introduce. Because the available evidence will not permit the issues to be resolved, ideas about the appearance of Shakespeare's playhouse must remain tentative.

Private Theatres. About the indoor, or private, playhouses, even less is known. They were roofed, smaller, and therefore more expensive to attend than the public playhouses. Despite their name, they were open to anyone caring to pay. Initially, the private theatres attracted the most fashionable audiences of London, who came to see erudite plays performed by troupes of boy actors. By 1610, however, as the popularity of children's troupes waned, the adult troupes that performed in the public theatres in the summer took over the private houses for their winter performances. The fact is significant because it indicates that the arrangement of the stage spaces in the theatres was probably similar.

Audience

The Shakespearean audience in the public theatres was like the medieval one, but more urbanized and probably more sophisticated. It did not include the poor or the very rich. It was sometimes rowdy, easily distracted. It was probably heavily male. A good part of it was educated enough to get jokes and learned allusions; most of it was fascinated by language, and so sat rapt through long soliloquies and much lyric poetry.

The private theatres supposedly attracted a more discerning and probably a more affluent audience. They sat indoors, were warmer in winter, less bothered by rain and slush. Probably mostly male, they were self-aware as embodiments of the new.

Production Practices

Elaborate scenery was unlikely in the Elizabethan theatres. Small properties were therefore important, and we find stage directions for the use of ladders, chairs and tables, tapestries, a free-standing arbor, and so on. The underlying conventions were medieval, and so we are mistaken to look for "scenery" that sets locale and surrounds the action. Nonetheless, such things as "a view of Rome" were included in a list of properties, so it may be that exotic locations were shown in paintings. It is also likely that some productions used simultaneous settings—putting the pieces for several scenes onstage at one time.

Costumes and Masks

Costuming was probably more important to spectacle than scenery. Contemporary accounts mention rich fabrics in many colors. Again, the basic convention was medieval, undoubtedly emblematic, with real Elizabethan dress the basic look. Nonetheless, other periods, countries, and races were signified by individual costume pieces—a turban, a Roman breastplate—but historical accuracy was unknown.

Most actors wore contemporary dress, some of it the castoffs of patrons or wealthy friends. Actors mostly supplied their own costumes, and building up a stock would have been important to an actor; however, unusual characters—devils, angels, allegorical figures, Turks, savages—would have called for help from the theatre company. This was a society emerging from medieval ignorance of the great world, and the theatre was one place where sophisticated London saw its new knowledge in three living dimensions.

Masks were used rarely, and then for specific reasons; masks were no longer a major convention of theatre.

Actors and Acting

A royal official, the Master of the Revels, licensed acting companies. The license protected actors from harsh medieval laws against players ("rogues and

FIGURE 12.14 **Elizabethan Performance.** Male actors perform Kyd's "revenge tragedy," *The Spanish Tragedy.* The properties include a real torch and a sword; a special effect has a body hanged in an arbor. Costumes were specific enough that the character with the torch, who is supposed to be ready for bed, is wearing a nightcap and shirt.

vagabonds"). Actors in the London troupes were further protected by nominal servant status in noble households: servants "belonged" to a household and found a medieval (feudal) shelter there. Despite this status, a few actors became wealthy: Shakespeare was able to retire as a gentleman.

The troupes themselves were organized as self-governing units—*sharing companies*—whose members shared expenses, profits, and responsibilities for production. A very few members owned a part of the theatre building itself; these were called *householders.* The most valuable members of the company held a whole share in the costumes, properties, and other company possessions; lesser members owned only half or quarter shares, with their influence and income reduced accordingly. In addition, each company hired some actors and stagehands (*hirelings*), who worked for a salary rather than for a share of the profits. Because all members were male, the roles of women were taken by men or young boys, many of whom were apprenticed to leading actors in the troupe. Among the actors, most specialized in certain kinds of roles (e.g., clowns, women, or heroes), and some were widely admired in Shakespeare's day: Richard Tarleton as a clown, Richard Burbage as a tragedian.

The precise style of acting is unclear, but vocal power and flexibility were prized. Plays of the period offered ample opportunity to display breath control and verbal dexterity in the monologues, soliloquies, complicated figures of speech, and symmetrical and extended phrases. On the other hand, oratorical and rhetorical techniques did not seem to overpower the actors' search for naturalness. Contemporary accounts, including lines from Shakespeare's *Hamlet,* spoke of an acting style capable of moving actors and audiences alike. The goal was apparently a convincing representation of a character in action performed by an actor with a well-tuned vocal instrument.

Status of the Theatre

By Shakespeare's day, the importance of drama and theatre had been argued and demonstrated by leading literary figures. In response to attacks on the theatre as an instrument of the devil, Sir Philip Sidney countered that drama was a most effective way of providing moral instruction and encouraging worthwhile actions in ordinary people, and this defense quieted many critics for a time.

By the time that Shakespeare arrived in London about 1590, then, his was a proud and growing nation whose power wanted to be celebrated. In place in the capital was a native theatre with permanent buildings, professional actors, and a legitimacy based on its own identification with capital and court.

Plays and Playwrights

The University Wits.   Added to the general well-being of the nation was the vigor of the court, the schools, and the universities, where scholars were remaking Italian humanism and classical documents with an eye to English needs and preferences. In particular, university students (the *University Wits*) were applying classical scholarship to the English public stage and laying the foundations for the vigorous theatre to come. These University Wits brought the erudition of humanistic scholarship to the English stage.

Thomas Kyd and Christopher Marlowe, in particular, broke new ground in tragedy; both adapted techniques from Seneca, and Marlowe created a "mighty line" of sonorous blank verse. Kyd is remembered for his revenge tragedy, *The Spanish Tragedy,* Marlowe for *Doctor Faustus* and the history play, *Edward the Second.*

Shakespeare (1564–1616).   Born in provincial Stratford-Upon-Avon, a day's journey from London, in 1564, Shakespeare was a middle-class boy who grew up as

FIGURE 12.15
The New Globe.
Completed in the late 1990s, the structure seeks to replicate Shakespeare's Globe in a distinctly modern setting.

the nation moved from medieval to Renaissance. Not university-educated, Shakespeare nonetheless had the solid basics of village schools: Latin, the classics, the foundation of writing style. His early life appears to have included acquaintance with powerful local families; his father, although a tradesman, was a man of position in the town.

Shakespeare married a local woman but did not stay long in his hometown. By his mid-twenties, he had gone to London to take up the perilous profession of acting, putting his father's trade behind him. He took with him, however, the rural England and the English characters of his youth, which would inform his plays and his poetry for his entire life.

When, rich and famous, he retired about 1612, it was to Stratford that he returned, there to purchase a handsome house and display the gentleman's coat-of-arms his success justified.

William Shakespeare was the greatest playwright of the English-speaking world and one of the greatest dramatists of Western civilization. Between 1590 and 1613, a period now acknowledged as the golden age of English drama, Shakespeare wrote thirty-eight plays, which for convenience are customarily divided into three types:

- History plays (those treating *English* history), like *Henry IV* (Parts 1 and 2), *Henry V, Henry VI* (Parts 1, 2, and 3), *Henry VIII, Richard II,* and *Richard III*

- Tragedies, like *Romeo and Juliet, Julius Caesar, Hamlet, King Lear, Othello, Macbeth,* and *Antony and Cleopatra*

- Comedies, ranging from popular romantic works like *Love's Labor's Lost, As You Like It, Twelfth Night, Much Ado About Nothing,* and *A Midsummer Night's Dream,* to the darker tragicomedies like *All's Well That Ends Well* and *Measure for Measure*

Features that tended to recur throughout his plays and those of his contemporaries include the following:

1. Shakespeare generally adopted an *early point of attack;* that is, he began his plays near the beginning of the story, with the result that the audience sees the story develop onstage rather than learning about it secondhand through messengers or reporters.

2. Shakespeare customarily developed several lines of action ("subplots"). Early in his plays, the various lines appear to be separate and independent, but as the play moves toward its resolution, the several lines gradually merge so that, by the play's end, the unity of the various lines is evident.

3. Shakespeare filled his plays with a large number and variety of incidents. The mixing of tears and laughter is not uncommon, nor is the close juxtaposition of tender scenes of love with brawling scenes of confrontation.

FIGURE 12.16   Shakespeare.
Playwright, actor, and part owner of the theatre building, Shakespeare was a man of the theatre and the greatest of playwrights in English.

4. Shakespeare ranged freely in time and place, allowing his actions to unfold across several months or years and in several locales.

5. Shakespeare used an unusually large number and range of characters. Casts of thirty are common, and among the characters can be found kings and gravediggers, pedants and clowns, old people and youths, city dwellers and rustics, rich people and poor ones.

6. The language in the plays is infinitely varied. Within the same play are found passages of exquisite lyricism, elegant figures of speech, ribald slang, witty aphorisms, and pedestrian prose, all carefully chosen to enhance the play's dramatic action.

In sum, the art of Shakespeare was an expansive one that filled a very large dramatic canvas with portraits of a wide cross-section of humanity engaged in acts ranging from the heroic to the mundane. The texture of the plays is rich, detailed, and allusive.

Shakespeare's plays shared more features with those of the Middle Ages than with those of classical Greece and Rome. Whereas classical plays like *Oedipus Rex* had late points of attack, unity of action, and relatively few characters, locations, and incidents, Shakespeare's plays told their stories from the beginning and included many rich details in several developing lines of action, each with its own characters. Whereas classical plays adopted rather restricted patterns of time, place, and language, Shakespeare ranged freely. Whereas the power of classical tragedy rested on intensity achieved through concentration and sparseness, Shakespeare's power emerged through the wealth of detail, the range of emotion, the sweep of his vision.

Other Dramatists.   With Shakespeare's death in 1616 came a decline in the quality, if not the quantity, of drama. Although many playwrights were esteemed in their own day, most notably Ben Jonson (1572–1637), none has achieved the modern admiration accorded Shakespeare. Thus, the golden age of English theatre was already in decline after 1616.

The Court Masque and a New Kind of Scenery: Inigo Jones

Not all theatre was done in the public and private playhouses. By invitation only, some individuals formed a courtly audience for plays and spectacles staged in royal and noble houses. Although both Henry VIII (Elizabeth's father) and Elizabeth had supported theatrical entertainments, it was the Stuart kings who followed them, James I (r. 1603–1625) and Charles I (r. 1625–1642), who perfected splendid court *masques.* Stuart masques were allegorical stories designed to compliment a particular individual or occasion. Their texts were little more than pretexts for elaborate scenic displays and lavish costumes. Although the major roles and all of the comic or villainous characters were played by professionals, the courtiers themselves performed the heart of the masques, three spectacular dances. Great sums of money ensured the splendor of the entertainments; one such masque cost a staggering 21,000 pounds at a time when the average *annual* wage for a skilled worker was about 25 pounds.

Although many leading dramatists wrote masques, Ben Jonson was the most significant. Jonson became annoyed that the text assumed such a clearly secondary position to the scenery, and so he stopped writing masques in 1631.

The star of the masques was not Jonson but the scenic designer, *Inigo Jones.* An Englishman by birth, Jones studied in Italy, where he learned the newest techniques of stage painting, rigging, and design. He introduced many of these into the English court when, in 1605, he staged his first masque for James I. *By the end of his career, Jones had introduced into the English courts* (but *not* into the theatres) *all the major elements of Italianate staging then developed* (see pp. 297–302).

Stuart masques, then, have a significance that exceeds the number of persons who saw them:

- First, they were using Italianate systems of staging during the first half of the seventeenth century, at a time when the English public and private theatres still relied on scenic practices that were essentially medieval.

- Second, the close association of the masques with the monarchy, added to their expense, were major factors in the closing of theatres when a shift in power occurred.

FIGURE 12.17 **Inigo Jones and the Masque.**
Jones was England's first major designer of scenery and costumes. Trained in Italy, he brought Renaissance staging to the court (but not the public) theatres of England after Elizabeth's death. Shown here are a number of his costume sketches.

The Closing of the Theatres, 1642–1660

In 1642, a civil war broke out and the winning side deposed the king, seized power, and closed the theatres. However, as music was not banned, a writer of masques named William Davenant produced "operas" and thus introduced Italianate staging to the public. When, in 1660, parliament restored the monarchy, theatre was again allowed; Davenant—and the new staging system—were waiting.

The Spanish Golden Age (c. 1550–c. 1650)

In the sixteenth and early seventeenth centuries, Spain vied with England for supremacy on the seas and in the New World. With a strong navy and a strong monarch, Spain sought to subdue England, first through marriage and, failing that, through war (the Spanish Armada). Unsuccessful on both counts, Spain shortly thereafter withdrew from the mainstream of Europe to pursue its own view of government, life, and society. During the Middle Ages and the early seventeenth century, however, Spain and its theatre were vital forces.

Medieval religious theatre in Spain had included Latin music drama and religious street theatre. The 1540s had seen the rise of *Corpus Christi plays* and processional theatres. At almost the same time, Spanish professional actors began organizing as sharing companies and traveling to major towns, where they performed on temporary stages in many locations. Religious plays, comedies and farces, school and university plays, and even court interludes formed their repertory.

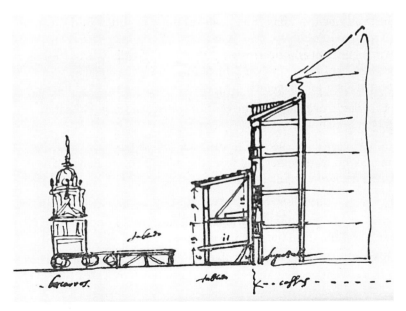

FIGURE 12.18
Spanish Movable Stage.
Spain, like England and France, had a vigorous medieval religious theatre, most of it processional. This *carro* (wagon) of 1644 is pulled up to a stage in front of a temporary, two-story audience stand built against a house front. Even this rough sketch of the wagon probably gives a better idea of its correct appearance than Figure 12.5. *Courtesy of the Ayuntamiento de Madrid.*

Women on the Stage

These companies differed from the English companies, however, in their use of women as actors. Exactly when women first appeared on the Spanish stage is unclear, but they were certainly there by the time of the first two permanent theatres in Madrid: the Corral del Cruz (1580) and the Corral del Principe (1584). Thereafter, some actors were able to settle in the city, touring only when the permanent theatres were closed.

Physical Theatre

Spanish theatres of the Golden Age shared several features with the public theatres of Elizabethan England:

- They were outdoors.
- A five- or six-foot-high platform jutted out in front of a background pierced by entrances.
- On the stage platform were two columns holding up a roof that covered part of the acting area.
- There was a raised, secondary acting area.
- An audience area existed slightly below and in front of the stage, with additional audience areas provided by galleries above and around it.
- Flying machines and stage traps were available, probably remnants of the medieval stage.

Spanish theatres, however, had some features not encountered in England:

- The permanent Spanish theatres were set up in *corrales* (yards in the center of blocks of houses), over which an awning stretched as protection against the elements.
- Some of the audience stood in the central courtyard (*patio*) or sat on covered benches along the sides.
- Opposite the stage at the second level was a gallery (*cazuela*) set aside for women, who were segregated from the men in the audience. The *cazuela* had its own entrance to the street.
- Windows in adjoining houses were rented to the audience members.
- Above the *cazuela* were two additional galleries, the second level divided into boxes, and the third holding the cheapest seats.
- The stage itself was somewhat smaller than the Globe's and had a back curtain that, when opened, revealed an additional acting area (discovery space).

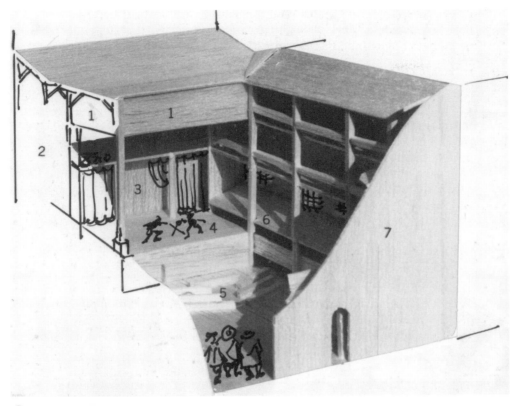

FIGURE 12.19 Spanish Corral.
Sharing many traits with the Elizabethan theatre, Spanish urban theatres were outdoors, with raised, partly roofed stages (1), two acting areas (3, 4), a tiring house (2), and an audience on three sides and in a pit below the stage (5, 6). Unlike the free-standing Elizabethan theatres, the Spanish corrals were built between houses and used their walls.

Production Practices

Spanish scenery and costuming conventions were similar to those in England, although larger scenic pieces were probably common. Large properties (e.g., a fountain, a tomb, or a ship's rigging) were sometimes set behind the curtain. Costumes were emblematic, with a mixture of contemporary garments and special dress. There was no attempt at unified "design."

Plays and Playwrights

The Spanish Golden Age produced thousands of plays, including secular tragicomedies (*comedias*), plays on religious subjects (*autos sacramentales*), cloak-and-sword plays (*capa y espada*), and farces. The earliest important playwright, Lope de Rueda, specialized in farces and religious plays. Another, Lope de Vega, may have originated the cape-and-sword plays, swashbucklers that subsequently influenced both English and French dramatists. The author of more than five hundred works, Lope de Vega is now best known for his play *Fuenteovejuna.*

The best-respected Spanish playwright of the Golden Age, however, was Pedro Calderon de la Barca, whose *Life is a Dream* epitomized the poetry and intellect of his best works. Calderon stopped writing for the stage about 1640; the theatres were closed shortly thereafter for royal mourning (1644–1649). When they reopened, the Golden Age had passed, although the *corrales* remained in use into the eighteenth century.

Like other countries, Spain also had a court theatre, and, somewhat belatedly, Italianate scenery. It is, however, for the public theatres and plays that the Golden Age is important.

THE PERIOD IN THE MODERN REPERTORY

Medieval plays were once rare in the North American repertory, but they have enjoyed a minor resurgence since the 1960s, spurred by production of entire cycles in cities like York, England, which has been producing the city's medieval cycle yearly since just after World War II. Certain places in North America have become

FIGURE 12.20 Shakespeare Today.
As You Like It at the University of South Carolina, directed by Jim Patterson, setting by Dennis C. Maulden, lighting by Ann Courtney, costumes by Rebecca Dosen.

centers of medieval study (e.g., Toronto, Canada), and there entire cycles have been produced, as well. *The Second Shepherd's Play* and *Everyman* are the most likely to be seen on a university campus. Latin music drama continues to enjoy a revival, more for its music than its theatre, but actually seeing a production is a rarity. (*The Play of Daniel* was a notable production that is still available in video and sound recording.)

Shakespeare, of course, is the backbone of most university repertory; the plays are also common in regional theatre and in London but are rare on Broadway. Spanish plays of the Golden Age are, on the other hand, rare all over North America, in good part because of a lack of modern translations. *Fuenteovejuna* was fashionable in the 1930s with Leftists because of its group protagonist, but politics have changed. Lacking the magic of Shakespeare's name in English-speaking countries, the Spanish plays are questionable bets because of large casts, heavy production demands, and old translations—too bad, because the best of them are superb plays.

CURRENT ISSUES

Scholars of the nineteenth century treated medieval theatre as "naive" and "simple-minded"—probably a deliberate attempt to dodge the problem of religious drama in a secular age. Later analysts, however, have found complexity, intelligence, and high art in these plays, and so a valid question can be asked about why we do not produce them more. Some practical reasons can be given, to be sure—large casts, special theatre spaces, technical demands. None of these is more severe than for the average musical, however. In that case, some suggest, the plays are too distant because of elapsed history; but experience, especially in England, shows that in fact the plays are quite accessible to modern audiences.

It seems likely that the biggest problem for modern producers is the plays' religious content, which is sometimes strident and which includes an ethnic and religious narrow-mindedness that includes occasionally overt anti-Semitism and references offensive to Muslims. None of these things is monolithic—that is, none of the medieval plays in English is *merely* pro-Christian or anti-Semitic or anti-Islamic—and many individual plays of the cycles are free of the last two things. Nonetheless, the plays' failure to find a solid place in the modern repertory raises an important issue about what we will tolerate in a public art: that is, to what extent does *content* determine what we will or will not put on the stage?

If, for example, a play is an acknowledged artistic masterpiece, we should feel some obligation to its artistry. But if its content is offensive, should we not do the play? Suppose, for example, we had a first-rate play from Hitler's Germany that happened to be pro-Nazi. Should we stage it anyway? Or should we avoid it? Or to put it the other way, should we stage a bad play with content we approve of?

As it happens, most medieval drama in English is not anti-Semitic but is pro-Christian. Does this render it unfit for public production in a secular society? How about using public money to produce it? Or is American society "mostly Judeo-

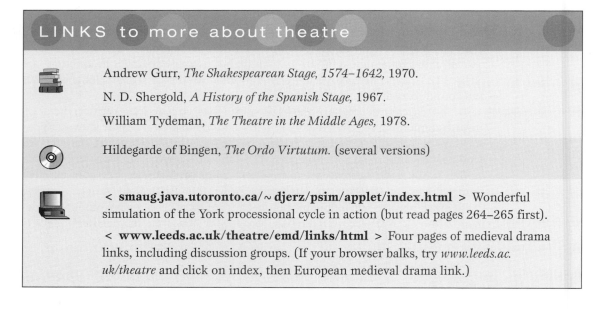

LINKS to more about theatre

Andrew Gurr, *The Shakespearean Stage, 1574–1642,* 1970.

N. D. Shergold, *A History of the Spanish Stage,* 1967.

William Tydeman, *The Theatre in the Middle Ages,* 1978.

Hildegarde of Bingen, *The Ordo Virtutum.* (several versions)

< **smaug.java.utoronto.ca/~ djerz/psim/applet/index.html** > Wonderful simulation of the York processional cycle in action (but read pages 264–265 first).

< **www.leeds.ac.uk/theatre/emd/links/html** > Four pages of medieval drama links, including discussion groups. (If your browser balks, try *www.leeds.ac. uk/theatre* and click on index, then European medieval drama link.)

Christian" and therefore a logical home for such plays? But, remembering that these very plays became the focus of controversy in the Reformation, what are our obligations to Protestant sectors of the public? Or to Roman Catholic ones, for that matter?

Lest we think that this issue applies only to matters of religion and ethnicity, consider the American record in producing plays from the old Soviet Union. We produced virtually none. Was this because all the plays were bad, or because we were uncomfortable with the plays' political content? If the latter, were we right to deny good plays production? Who was the loser, the American audience or world communism? When is a good play too uncomfortable to be staged?

KEY TERMS

Check your understanding against this list. Brief definitions are in the Glossary; page references there will direct you to appropriate pages. (Persons are page-referenced in the Index.)

cazuela	liturgy	public theatre
confraternity	mansion	*Quem Quaeritis*
Corpus Christi play	masque	register
discovery space	Middle Ages	Renaissance
emblem	miracle play	scaffold
Golden Age	morality play	secular (play)
guild	mystery play	simultaneous staging
householder	pageant	tiring house
interlude	patio	yard
Latin music drama	private theatre	

Illusionistic Theatres I: Neoclassicism and Italianate Staging

OBJECTIVES

When you have completed this chapter, you should be able to:

- Define and discuss Neoclassicism, Italianate staging, and the Renaissance

- Explain why Neoclassicism was such a departure from medieval theatre

- Trace Italianate staging in Italy, France, and England

- Cite and explain the principal early examples of Neoclassical theatre in Europe

- Discuss the importance of Roman ideas, and their interpretation, to Renaissance theatre

- Name and discuss the principal playwrights and kinds of plays in France and England in this period

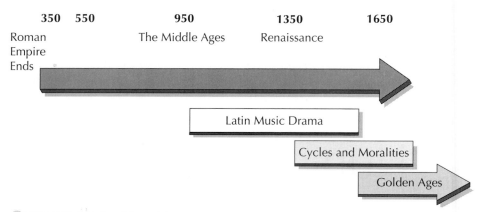

FIGURE 13.1   Time Line.
The Italian Renaissance overlapped the Middle Ages and the golden ages of England and Spain. It brought Italy's most important period in theatre and led to the golden age of French theatre.

THEATRE IN ITALY (1550–1750)

The Renaissance in Italy, unlike the period in England and Spain, revolutionized theatre and drama. In their efforts to recapture the practices of Greece and Rome, Italian artists set theatres in Europe on a new path—a path toward *illusionism.* Theatre was thereafter to seek an illusion of real life.

Three contributions of the Italians were to have far-reaching effects:

1. The Neoclassical ideal in playwriting and criticism
2. The Italianate system of staging and architecture
3. The popular theatre known as *commedia dell'arte*

Mainstream Theatre

Theory: Neoclassicism

Neoclassicism literally means "new classicism," but in fact it was based far more heavily on Rome than on Greece. Neoclassicism, as first developed by the Italians and later adopted throughout most of western Europe, rested on five major points:

1. Verisimilitude, and the related decorum
2. Purity of genres
3. The "three unities"
4. The five-act form
5. A twofold purpose: to teach and to please

Verisimilitude.   Central to Neoclassical doctrine was a complex concept called *verisimilitude*—literally, "truth seeming." But the meaning of *verisimilitude* is more involved than its facile definition might suggest, for artists have always aimed to tell the "truth." Thus, the critical problem for a student of Neoclassicism is to understand what "truth" meant to the Neoclassicist.

Truth for the Neoclassicist resided in the essential, the general, the typical, and the class rather than in the particular, the individual, and the unique. To get at truth, a Neoclassical artist had to cut away all that was temporary or accidental in favor of those qualities that were fundamental and unchanging. To be "true" meant to be *usually* true, *generally* accurate, *typically* the case. The humanness of one person, for example, rested in those essential qualities that he or she shared with all other people, regardless of place, century, or ethnicity. Individual differences were not important, because they were not essential to humanness. Such a view of truth placed a premium on classification and categorization, and *verisimilitude* had a meaning very different from that ascribed to it by our own age's view of the importance of individuality and uniqueness: fidelity to essences.

Neoclassical truth implied other matters as well. Verisimilitude in drama required the elimination of events that could not reasonably be expected to happen in real life. Although an exception was made when ancient stories or myths incorporating supernatural events were dramatized, even then the dramatist was expected to minimize the importance of such events, perhaps by putting them offstage. Because in real life people generally talk to one another rather than to themselves, monologues and soliloquies were customarily abandoned in favor of dialogue between major characters and their *confidants* (see p. 49).

The tendency of people to behave in certain ways because of age, social rank, occupation, gender, and so forth could be observed; therefore, characters in drama were also expected to behave with the same *decorum* (that is, they were to embody the traits normally held by members of their group) or, if they did not, they would suffer ridicule or punishment for their deviations.

Finally, because it was believed that God ruled the world in accord with a divine plan and that He was a good God, verisimilitude required that dramatic actions be organized according to *morality*—so that good was rewarded and evil punished. Although in daily life good occasionally went unrewarded and evil unpunished, such

FIGURE 13.2   Renaissance Life.
Medieval life changed as Europe moved into the Renaissance: Trading rivaled agriculture; cities rivaled manors; gunpowder and cannons eclipsed the armored warlord.

observable events were believed to be aberrational and therefore to be unsuitable subjects for drama.

Purity of Genres.   Verisimilitude also inspired *purity of genres,* meaning that the two major forms, tragedy and comedy, must not be mixed. The injunction against mixing did not mean merely that funny scenes were improper for tragedy or that unhappy endings were inappropriate for comedy. Both tragedy and comedy were far more rigidly defined than today, and the rule against mixing the forms meant that no element belonging to the one should appear in the other. For example, tragedy was to depict people of high station involved in affairs of state; its language was to be elevated and poetic; its endings were to be unhappy. Comedy, on the other hand, was to display persons of the lower and middle classes embroiled in domestic difficulties and intrigues. Its language was always to be less elevated, often prosaic, and its endings were to be happy. Purity of genres meant, then, that a prose tragedy or a domestic tragedy could not exist—both were a contradiction in terms. It also meant that kings and queens could not appear in comedies, and affairs of state were not suitable subjects for comedy.

The Three Unities.   Verisimilitude and interpretations of classical examples created the Neoclassical notion of "the three unities"—time, place, and action. Although Aristotle had argued cogently for plays with a unified action, Neoclassical theorists were more concerned that their plays unfold within a reasonable time and a limited place, so that verisimilitude would not be strained. No audience would believe, the Neoclassical argument went, that months had passed or oceans had been crossed while the audience sat in the same place for a few hours. Theorists varied in the strictness of their requirements for unity (some argued for a single room, others for a single town; some required that the playing time of the drama equal the actual time elapsed, others that no more than twenty-four hours elapse). Most Italian theorists accepted some version of the three unities after about 1570.

Five-Act Play.   By then, as well, Neoclassicists had adopted the *five-act play* as standard for drama, a norm probably derived from the theories of Horace and the practices of Seneca (five sections separated by choruses), although neither had used the "act" as a dramatic unit.

Purposes of Drama.   The Neoclassicists found a justification for drama and theatre in their ability to teach morality while entertaining an audience. *To teach* and *to please* were defined as the *dual purposes of drama,* and playwrights took care that their plays did both. The idea of a drama's existing only for its own sake or as an expression of an individual artist was not accepted.

After about 1570, Neoclassical ideas became the standard in Italy. By 1600, they were being accepted in other parts of Europe. They remained dominant for the next two hundred years among educated and courtly audiences. Neoclassicism's

FIGURE 13.3   Renaissance Life.
This consultation of physicians captures not
only the renewed interest in science but also
the change in men's fashion that came with the
Renaissance in Italy.

propriety and concentration may account for its lack of appeal to many people, who sought more spectacle than the three unities permitted. Thus, despite the acceptance of Neoclassicism as an ideal, its tenets were undercut in a variety of ways— by spectacle, for example.

Physical Theatre: Illusionism

The Italianate theatre and its system of staging, like Neoclassicism itself, developed as a mixture of ideas and techniques from ancient Greece, Rome, and contemporary Italy. Most important from the ancients was the work of Vitruvius (see p. 246).

Vitruvius in the Renaissance.   In 1486, Vitruvius' Roman work on architecture, which had existed only in manuscripts, was printed. By 1500, it was the acknowledged authority in the field, and interpretations and commentaries in Italian followed. Although he had written about architecture and scenery, Vitruvius had provided no illustrations. As a result, the Italians translated him and provided illustrations in terms of *their* practices, most notably a fascination with *linear perspective*—a means of representing spatial depth (three dimensions) on a two-dimensional surface. On the stage, perspective became a means of representing greater depth than in fact existed.

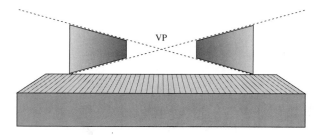

FIGURE 13.4   False Perspective.
Behind the Renaissance forestage, a vanishing point
(VP) was the apparent meeting place of lines (dotted)
that, by defining the tops and bottoms of "returns"
(scenic faces at angles to the front of the stage),
created an illusion of greater depth than the actual
theatre offered.

Perspective.   Although known to the Romans, perspective, when rediscovered by Italian painters, caused an artistic revolution. Artists worked to master the "new" technique, and spectators hailed its ability to trick the senses. The "vanishing point," to which objects receded away from the viewer, became, in stage design, the key to false, or forced, perspective, in which a stage depth of thirty feet could be made to seem three hundred. On the stage, achieving this sense of depth often meant actually constructing three-dimensional objects (usually buildings) in false perspective, so that the actor—whose real size could not be changed—would dwarf the upstage buildings if he appeared up there.

In 1545 an Italian, *Sebastiano Serlio,* published *Dell'Architectura,* thereafter the authoritative interpretation of Vitruvius. Serlio's work dominated theatre architecture and design for the next century. Vitruvius, of course, had described the circular, outdoor Roman theatre. But wealthy Italians wanted plays done indoors in wealthy homes. Thus, when the first indoor theatres were designed, the task was to adapt Vitruvius to rectangular spaces and to accommodate them to linear perspective.

An early solution was the *Teatro Olimpico,* which had five onstage doorways (corresponding to Vitruvius' five stage openings), but with a vista in perspective constructed behind each doorway (and each with its own vanishing point). This early solution used a Roman facade and doorways, and it satisfied the Italian demand for perspective. Its multiple vanishing points satisfied its patrons, a wealthy gentlemen's academy: With five vanishing points, there were five "perfect" places to sit rather than one.

Later theatres used a proscenium arch that framed and separated the false perspective; some had other arches farther upstage, each increasing the illusion of depth.

Production Practices: Illusionism

Vitruvius' scanty descriptions of tragic, comic, and satyric scenes became, in Serlio's books, detailed illustrations in false perspective. A brief comparison of Vitruvius and Serlio will show their differences.

Of the satyric scene, Vitruvius said, "Satyric scenes are decorated with trees, caverns, mountains, and other rustic objects delineated in landscaped style." Of the same scenes, Serlio (as translated into English in 1611) said, "The Satiricall Scenes are to Represent Satirs, wherein you must place all those things

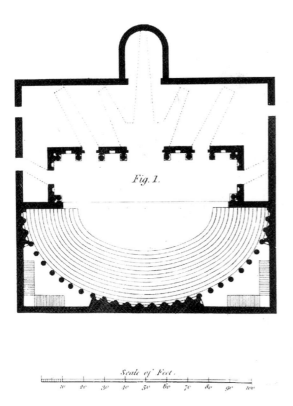

FIGURE 13.5 **The Teatro Olimpico.**
This was one of several attempts to recreate a Roman theatre while indulging the Renaissance passion for perspective. Each of the five doorways (left) had a three-dimensional vista in false perspective behind it, giving the audience in the curved auditorium some sort of view down at least one (right).

that be rude and rusticall." He then went on to quote Vitruvius as calling for "Trees, Rootes, Herbs, Hils, and Flowers, and with some countrey houses. . . . And for that in our dayes these things were made in Winter, where there were but fewe greene Trees, Herbs, and Flowers to be found; then you must make these things of Silke, which will be more commendable than the naturall things themselves."

In the remainder of his book, Serlio provided tips on the use of colored lights, fire effects, fanciful costumes, and the use of pasteboard figures in a perspective setting. Serlio's scenography was thus the basis for what we now call *Italianate staging.*

FIGURE 13.6   Serlio.
Combining Vitruvius on the Roman theatre with Renaissance interest in perspective, Serlio created his own ideal scenery for tragedy, comedy, and pastoral (satyric). *Courtesy of Rare Books and Special Collections, Bowling Green State University.*

Italianate Staging.   With certain modifications related to place and date, Italianate settings throughout Europe shared the following features during the sixteenth, seventeenth, and early eighteenth centuries:

1. Scenery painted in *single-point perspective* (all objects recede to the same vanishing point), as calculated from one seat toward the back of the orchestra (usually the seat of the most important noble or patron)

2. Scenery consisting of *wings,* or paired flats (wooden frames covered with fabric and painted), each pair closer together as they were farther from the audience, so that the lines of the inner edges of the flats receded toward the vanishing point. The setting culminated upstage in a backdrop or a *shutter,* a pair of wings

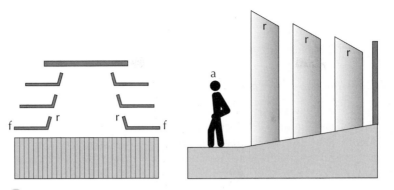

FIGURE 13.7   Serlio's Theatre.
Serlio's settings were meant to emphasize depth through false
perspective. Pairs of flats with angled returns (f, r) receded toward a
common vanishing point. The stage floor was raked (angled) upward to
accomodate the false perspective line of the bottoms of the returns.
Actors (a) worked in front of the scenery rather than in it, where they
would have destroyed the illusion: As the scenery seemed to grow
rapidly smaller, the actor would only slightly have done so.

pushed together. Shutters could be opened to reveal even deeper perspective space,
or pierced to make a *relieve* through which greater depth was glimpsed

3. Scenery placed behind a proscenium arch *and* behind the actors, forming
a background rather than an environment to surround them

4. A *raked stage,* slanted upward from front to back to increase the sense of
depth. Sometimes only the stage behind the proscenium arch was raked, sometimes the entire stage, causing the actors to climb or descend (and hence our terms
"upstage" and "downstage")

5. Machinery and rigging hidden overhead by *borders,* framed or unframed
fabric painted like sky, clouds, leaves, and so on

Movable Scenery: Torelli.   Having developed this system, Italian artists set about
almost at once to give it movement, to shift scenery, and to allow rapid changes of
place. The most effective system was shown in 1645 when Giacomo Torelli as-
tonished audiences with fluid, fast, apparently magical changes. The secret was
his *chariot-and-pole system.* Small wheeled wagons ran on tracks under the stage,
each with a pole that extended through a slit in the stage high enough to support
a flat. The idea was elegant and simple: As the chariots moved, so the flats moved;
pulling a chariot toward the center brought a flat into view; pulling the chariot
away from the center caused a flat to disappear. With the chariots harnessed by
ropes and pulleys to the same winch, stage mechanics could turn one wheel to

change an entire setting. Torelli—no stranger to self-promotion—earned the title "The Great Wizard" by coordinating these changes with special effects (flying, lightning, explosions).

Contradiction in Mainstream Theatre

A contradiction clearly existed, however, between the ideals of theory—the unities of time, place, and action; and an avoidance of the supernatural—and the ideals of scenic design, whose artists increasingly emphasized rapid change of place and spectacle. This tension was resolved by keeping an austere style for Neoclassical plays while expending creativity and money on operas, ballets, and lavish *intermezzi* (entertainments given between the acts of a Neoclassical play)— a way of having their cake and eating it at the same time.

By the mid-seventeenth century, Italian opera had thus become the most popular (and spectacular) form of entertainment in Italy. As it was exported to the rest of Europe, so were its scenic techniques. (In London, remember, Davenant had staged *operas* after the theatres were closed in 1647; even in English, the word probably signified as much about scenery as it did about music.)

An Alternative Theatre: Commedia dell'Arte

Neoclassical dramas and elaborately staged operas were primarily the entertainment of the noble, the wealthy, and the educated. Among other classes, another, very different kind of dramatic entertainment flourished in Italy: the *commedia dell'arte* ("professional playing"). Although neither the origins nor the sources of *commedia* are well understood, its major characteristics were well established by 1550, and Italian troupes were touring western Europe by 1600.

Commedia players—both male *and* female—worked from a basic story outline (*scenario*) within which they improvised much of their dialogue and action. Each actor in the troupe played the same stock character in almost every scenario

---

THINKING ABOUT *COMMEDIA*

The avant-garde director and playwright Alfred Jarry (1873–1907) said that an actor *"should use a mask to envelop the head, thus replacing it by the effigy of the CHARACTER."* Invent a modern set of *commedia* characters for a contemporary acting troupe of four. They should represent common types today (e.g., nerd, politician). After naming each character, sketch (or describe carefully) their costumes and masks: What traits should go with the type? What nose? Hairstyle? Eyes and mouth? Color and cut of fabric, etc.?

Pulliciniello · Siĝª Lucretia · Scapino. Cap: Zerbino.

FIGURE 13.8 Commedia dell'Arte.

Troupes had both male and female actors and both masked and unmasked characters. The unmasked Lucretia is an *inamorata* (lover); the masked characters are two servants and a boastful soldier.

and therefore wore the same costume and mask, reused the same bits of comic business (*lazzi*), and even repeated some of the same dialogue from scenario to scenario. Most troupes had ten or twelve members; each troupe had one or two sets of young lovers (*innamorati*) and a number of comic "masks" (characters)—Capitano (the captain), Pantalone (the merchant), Dottore (the doctor), and several *zanni* (servants) like Arlecchino (Harlequin), Brighella, Scaramuccio, and Pulcinello. Male actors outnumbered female. Both mask and costume became traditional for each character (except the lovers, who wore no mask).

Organized as sharing companies, such troupes toured constantly as they tried to scratch out a living without the protection or the financial support of noble houses. Although the influence of *commedia* extended throughout Europe, its ephemeral nature militated against its leaving a lasting record (especially scripts), although this popular Italian comedy has been revived and imitated in many more recent cultures.

Italy: Eclipse

Despite Italy's unquestioned leadership in dramatic theory and scenic display, and in spite of its unique popular comedy, by 1750, except for opera, Italy was no longer a world leader in theatre. Both England and France had outstripped their teacher and had attained an international reputation by the end of the seventeenth century, and both achieved a lasting acclaim never given the Italians, from whom they drew.

THEATRE IN FRANCE (1550–1750)

The ideas and practices of the Italian Renaissance reached France early. However, France was politically unstable until the early seventeenth century, and so its permanent, public theatre came later than England's.

Until about 1600, farces performed by traveling actors were the mainstay of the scattered French theatre. With some political stability thereafter, Paris increasingly became the center, with the first professionals establishing themselves permanently about 1625. Their theatre was the so-called Hôtel de Bourgogne, a space built seventy-five years earlier for the production of religious plays (just as they were being banned). Thus, at a time when the English and Spanish theatres were vigorous and the Italian theatre was revolutionizing scenery, the French theatre was only establishing itself.

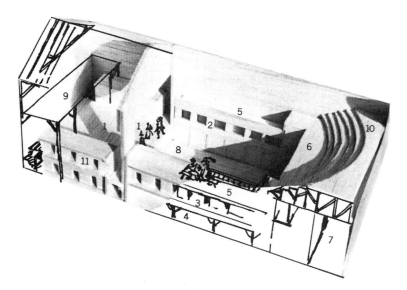

FIGURE 13.9 The Hôtel de Bourgogne.
Originally a medieval theatre, it was rebuilt as a sixteenth-century theatre with stage (1) and upper stage (9), a pit with benches (8), audience *loges* down the long sides (2–5), and two elevated seating areas opposite the stage (6, 10). The medieval *loges* behind the new stage front (11) were kept for dressing rooms and storage.

Before 1650

Physical Theatre

When rival professionals began to settle in Paris after 1625, the buildings they chose for theatres were indoor tennis courts. About one hundred feet by thirty, these buildings had seats down one side and a covered structure at one end; the rest was open. The tennis court was converted to a long, narrow auditorium with a small stage at one end, probably with an upper level (as in both London and Madrid) and some sort of "inner" stage below it; usually, shallow boxes were put down both sides of the auditorium and a set of bleacher-like seats was put at the end opposite the stage; between the bleacher-like seats and the stage were benches. These converted tennis courts were small, tight, intimate theatres that might hold six or seven hundred people. Scenery was still simultaneous (medieval), despite the limited stage space.

Audience

Audiences for the early farces had been famous for their unruliness, and the theatre was a pretty rough place before about 1600. Gradually, however, it became more regular and more genteel; audiences came to include many women as well as people from the court. By the 1630s, theatre and its audience were sufficiently important to make them a focus of government interest.

FIGURE 13.10   Medieval Scenery, Renaissance Stage.
Medieval simultaneous settings (mansions) were still used in France during the early sixteenth century, including on the stage of the Hôtel de Bourgogne. This is a performance of 1656.

FIGURE 13.11   Renaissance Scenery, Renaissance Stage. This frontispiece of a French play first produced in 1636 suggests commitment to single-point perspective and Italian influence—on the part of the illustrator, at any rate. We do not know what the scenery actually looked like.

Plays and Playwrights

Alexandre Hardy.   The first French playwright of note was Alexandre Hardy (c. 1572–1632), a prolific writer of non-Neoclassical plays. His tragedies, despite their Renaissance awareness, were staged in medieval simultaneous settings.

Corneille and Le Cid.   When political stability made permanent theatre possible in Paris after 1625, a number of educated men began to write for it. Chief among them was Pierre Corneille (1606–1684), whose play *Le Cid* (1636) marked a turning point. Based on a Spanish play of the Golden Age, *Le Cid* was reshaped by Corneille to bring it closer to Neoclassical ideas but not into strict conformity with them: The original six acts were reduced to five; its several years were compressed into a single day; the many locales were squeezed into a single town. Still, the play had a happy ending, and its numerous incidents strained Neoclassical verisimilitude. The recently formed French Academy—itself an example of aggressive Neoclassicism, a literary society supported by those in power—praised *Le Cid* where it conformed to the rules but condemned it where it strayed. French playwrights, including Corneille, got the message: Critical acclaim (and approval from those in political, financial, and social power) would come from lining up with Neoclassicism. After 1636, Neoclassicism would dominate French drama for more than a hundred years.

FIGURE 13.12 Italianate Scenery in France.
In 1641, pushed by Cardinal Richelieu, a French court theatre attempted this Italianate
production, *Mirame*. It was the precursor of the magic of Torelli.

Production Practices: the Coming of the Italianate System

In 1641, the first Italianate theatre was built in Paris. Giacomo Torelli (see p. 301)
was brought to Paris in 1645 to install a chariot-and-pole system. His productions
marked the acceptance of all Italianate scenic practices in Paris: almost immediately, the tennis-court (public) theatres had to adapt or die; they installed some
form of Italianate scenery. Thereafter, simple Neoclassical settings competed with
lavish operas, ballets, and *machine plays,* plays written specifically to exploit the
new scenery.

From the Neoclassical evolved a distinct French style (in the *public* theatre),
austere and tense. At the other extreme, exemplified by costly entertainments, was
a *court* theatre where plays from the public theatres were restaged with ballet interludes, movable scenery, and gorgeous costumes, and where king and courtiers
played heroes of romance and mythology in purpose-written entertainments that
moved out into parks and gardens, sometimes with mock tournaments and battles.

The Age of Louis XIV

In 1659, the man who would say "I am the State" and who would take the sun
for his symbol, Louis XIV, came to the French throne. Absolute power, ego, and
show were summed up in the word *gloire,* which carried over into the theatre
from war and extended to the building of great follies like the palace of Versailles.

An aggressive campaign of national self-display was pursued, principally through the arts and military adventures. The theatres flourished and got both royal subsidy and royal patronage, but not enough to survive without public support, and so they were sometimes in the position of serving two masters at once. Displeasing the king *or* the people could be very costly.

In the theatre, Louis XIV's reign meant:

- The continuing dominance of Neoclassicism
- The continued enthusiasm for Italianate staging
- The emergence of two great playwrights to join Corneille
- The expansion of professional theatre to five permanent theatres in Paris, later reduced to three, with strict government control through monopolies

Plays and Playwrights

Racine. Although Pierre Corneille wrote important plays until after 1675, his fame was eclipsed by that of Jean Racine. Born three years after the first production of *Le Cid,* Racine was educated by Jansenists, a Catholic sect with an overriding

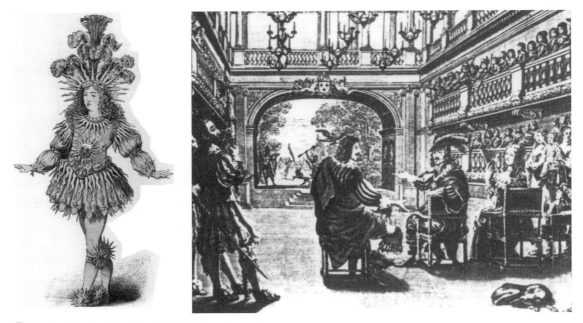

FIGURE 13.13   Louis XIV, the Sun King.
Louis performed in a court ballet, costumed as the sun (left). With Richelieu and the queen, he attended a performance in a rebuilt court theatre, transformed from the medieval to the Italianate. (See Figure 13.12.)

preoccupation with sin and guilt, concerns that permeated Racine's major plays. Trained in the classics, Racine based his only comedy, *The Litigants,* on Aristophanes' comedy *The Wasps,* and his most esteemed tragedy, *Phèdre,* on Euripides' *Hippolytus.*

Phèdre is a model of Neoclassicism. Because the play's major conflicts occur within the character of Phèdre, the Neoclassical requirements for unity are easily accommodated; and, because Phèdre's passion leads to her downfall, Neoclassical commitment to the punishment of evil is satisfied. *Phèdre,* unlike *Le Cid,* is Neoclassical through and through, and its achievement in plot, character, and diction placed it among the masterpieces of dramatic literature. France had accomplished what England would not: lasting and popular drama based on Neoclassical theory.

Molière. French comedy found its genius in the actor-dramatist Molière. At about the time that theatres were closing in England, Molière was leaving home to join a traveling theatrical troupe in France. By 1660, he was head of the troupe, wrote most of its plays, and had firmly established it as a favorite of Louis XIV. Perhaps the greatest comic writer of all times, Molière used his own experiences as an actor as well as his knowledge of Roman comedy, Italian *commedia,* and French farce to create comedies that ridiculed social and moral pretentiousness.

Molière's comedy typically depicts characters made ludicrous by their deviations from decorum. Although his dialogue is often clever, verbal elegance and wit for their own sake do not form the core of his plays; instead, the comedies depend heavily on farcical business (like *commedia's lazzi*) and visual gags. Of his more than twenty plays, the best known are probably *Tartuffe* (1669), *The Miser* (1668), and *The Imaginary Invalid* (1673), whose leading role Molière was playing when he was stricken. Denied last rites by the Church because he was an actor, he was granted Christian burial only through the direct intervention of Louis XIV.

Actors and Acting

The life of French actors was not easy. Some troupes were granted royal subsidies, and the king tried to improve their reputation and social acceptability by royal edict. Nonetheless, French actors were denied civic and religious rights throughout most of the seventeenth and eighteenth centuries, a situation that led many actors to adopt pseudonyms (e.g., Molière) in order to spare their families. Forced to tour continuously until 1625, only the most talented actors were gradually able to settle in Paris as members of a permanent troupe. By 1660, there were five such troupes in Paris, including Molière's, a *commedia* troupe from Italy, and the opera, music, and dance troupe headed by Jean-Baptiste Lully (1632–1687). All were sharing companies, and all included women. Unlike England, however, France had no householders—no actors who owned parts of the theatre building.

With Molière's death (1673), his troupe was joined with two others to form the *Comédie Française,* which became France's national theatre. Membership in this sharing company was fixed; therefore, new members could not be elected until others had retired or died. Because of its financial rewards, including a substantial pension for retired members, the list of applicants was long.

FIGURE 13.14 French Actors.
Molière became famous but was almost denied Christian burial; most French actors lived semi-outcast lives. These frontispieces from works about actors show them on and off the stage.

Sponsorship: Monopoly Theatre

The Comédie Française was granted a monopoly on (legal) performance of tragedies and comedies in Paris. Lully's company held a monopoly on musical entertainments and spectacles. The Italian troupe—after a short banishment for a political indiscretion—got exclusive rights to what came to be called comic operas. Thus, less than a century after the free-wheeling days of the first professionals, French theatre was rigidly structured, with three legal troupes that were expected to continue their traditions, not to initiate the new. The result was a highly polished but conservative theatre—and the suppression of competition.

Audience

The court withdrew from Paris when Versailles was opened. The theatres continued to depend on the general public, however. Vigorous criticism of plays reflected an intense interest, and both men and women were active audience members. Favored male audience members even sat *on* the stage. At its best, this theatre offered great variety and superb quality, satisfying an audience that became the most demanding and sophisticated in Europe.

LINKS to more about theatre

Scaramouche. Not great history, but fun.

Pierre Louis Duchartre, *The Italian Comedy. The Improvisation, Scenarios, Lives . . . of the Commedia dell'Arte,* 1966. Lavish and fascinating.

Stephen Orgel, *The Illusion of Power: Political Theatre in the English Renaissance,* 1975.

Molière, *The Versailles Impromptu.* Molière's play about himself and his troupe, rehearsing under pressure.

Drama and Theatre, 1700–1750

Around 1700, a new conservatism was noticeable as Louis XIV grew old and cautious. Dramatists, intimidated by the reputations of Corneille, Racine, and Molière, strove to copy them. A modest shift toward what came to be called the sentimental occurred (see p. 316). Voltaire (1694–1778) tried to loosen Neoclassicism's hold by introducing some Shakespearean features to the French stage, including more spectacle and wider subject matter, but his efforts were mostly frustrated. (Shakespeare was almost unknown on the Parisian stage until the nineteenth century.)

In comedy, virtue replaced Molière's social sanity as an ideal, and audiences wept at comedies as much as they laughed—a far cry from Molière's theatre.

Theatres got bigger, their scenic potential greater. In production practice, *angle perspective* (moving the vanishing point away from the center) let actors work closer to the scenery. *Changed scale* allowed monumental interiors that disappeared overhead, suggesting palaces that dwarfed the human beings who occupied them—a probably unconscious reflection of the French court and French government.

Costumes continued to be contemporary, not historical, and lavish, not realistic. Even the *commedia* actors' costumes were prettified, sentimentalized.

With no outlet for the talents of the many actors and writers who did not get into the Comédie Française, and with dwindling enthusiasm for Neoclassicism, French men and women began to work in illegal theatres—that is, theatres other than the monopolies. Joining jugglers, dancers, and others who had worked at fairs for centuries, theatrical troupes began to play outside the law, practicing all kinds of tricks to avoid open conflict with the monopolies. (The fairs, for example, had held special legal status since the Middle Ages, some even having their own judicial systems.) From the experiments of these "illegitimate" theatres came the forms and practices that would flourish in Paris itself in the next century, taking their name from their location—the boulevards.

In sum, the French theatre for the first half of the eighteenth century looked back on its past glory, when the genius of Torelli, Corneille, Racine, and Molière had helped make France the self-proclaimed leader of European culture. Change was rare and usually in the direction of elaborating Neoclassical and Italianate practices. Thus, by 1750, the legal French theatre was probably out of touch with French life—a mirror of the monarchy on which it depended.

THEATRE IN ENGLAND (1660–1750)

Transitional Theatre

We left the English theatre at the moment when the monarchy was restored in 1660—the *Restoration*—the theatres having been closed since 1642; William Davenant had produced a few "operas" in the Italianate style first brought to England by Inigo Jones.

Until new theatres could be built in 1660, companies used old ones that still stood, or they adapted tennis courts. Their model was no longer the theatre of Shakespeare's and Jonson's England; now, it was the theatre of Paris. The new English theatre's characteristics included:

- A new theatre architecture consonant with Italianate scenery

- A new commercial structure: Two monopoly *patents* were granted by the king to Davenant and Thomas Killigrew. Although often challenged, these patents were reaffirmed through most of the eighteenth century, limiting London to only two "legitimate" theatres.

- Inclusion of women. Women were allowed to act for the first time; their presence apparently encouraged, fairly or not, the risqué reputation of the Restoration theatre. After 1661, women assumed all female roles except witches and comic old women, which continued to be played by men.

The Restoration to 1750

Physical Theatre

When English theatres opened in 1660, they combined Shakespearean and French features. The auditorium was divided into box, pit, and gallery. As in France, certain favored audience members sat on the stage itself. The stage now had a proscenium arch and a raked stage behind it, where *grooves* were installed to facilitate scene changes. Most of the acting, however, took place on the

Italianate Scenery in England.
This is the Duke of York's Theatre in 1673, with Italianate scenery, a musician's gallery (?) above the stage, and (shaded) side boxes, perhaps not accurately shown. There was also a forestage, not shown.

forestage, which jutted into the pit. Most of the scenery, on the other hand, was located behind the proscenium. Initially, the forestage was as large as the stage behind the proscenium, probably an attempt to synthesize earlier Elizabethan practice with currently fashionable Italian practice. In time, however, the forestage decreased and the stage space behind the proscenium increased, so that, by 1750, little difference existed between English and French or Italian stages. The Restoration theatres seated about 650, whereas, by 1750, some theatres could accommodate 1,500.

Audience

The first Restoration playhouses were intimate places, with as little as thirty feet from forestage to the rear boxes. The audience was fairly cohesive—young, courtly, and self-confident, many of them veterans of exile in France with the king. Royalty and the upper aristocracy came to the theatre. Women came, too; it was a place to see and be seen, as well as to enjoy the plays. Some women in the audience wore masks, as much to increase their attractions as to hide them.

Between 1660 and 1750, both stage and auditorium grew as the composition of the audience and the repertory of the plays changed. After 1675, non-aristocratic power increased and more noncourtiers took up the theatre. As the number of middle-class citizens in the audience increased, the audience's taste changed, growing less cynical, perhaps more pragmatic, less snobbish. By the early eighteenth century, this new audience was dominant.

FIGURE 13.16 English Audience. Part caricature, this engraving captures some of the variety of the post-Restoration audience: beaux in the boxes, paying no attention to the play; much-entertained, middle-class men and women in the pit; musicians, foreground.

Production Practices

Scenic practices were Italianate. Wings, borders, and shutters were standard. A group of stock sets appropriate for each form of drama (comedy, tragedy, pastoral) provided scenery for most plays. New settings were commissioned from painters of the day. Because lighting was still by candles, audience and actors were equally illuminated, although by the early eighteenth century some modest attempts were being made to dim and color lights. Costuming continued to be the major source of visual excitement, and most actors wore an elaborate and sumptuous version of contemporary fashion.

Actors and Acting

The earlier tendency of actors to specialize in certain kinds of roles became gradually more rigid until, by 1750, clearly defined *lines of business* emerged. New actors or actresses were hired as *utility players* and gained their experience by playing a great number of small and varied roles. They then declared a specialty in a specific kind of role: a "walking" lady or gentleman (third line); a specialist in low comedy, or "stage eccentric" (second line); or a hero or heroine (first line). Once committed to a particular line of business, actors did not stray far from it, regardless of age. (Shakespeare's teen-aged Juliet, for example, was often played by women in their fifties because they were "first-line" players.)

Along with lines of business came a practice known as *possession of parts,* an agreement that an actor who played a role in the company possessed that role for as long as he or she remained in the company. Both practices placed a premium on tradition—and, often, on age—and inhibited innovation.

The acting style depended heavily on vocal power and versatility and on formality and elegance rather than "truth to life." For example, some actors apparently intoned or chanted the poetic and lyrical passages of tragedies, much as the recitative of opera is delivered today, and many actors played for *points,* expecting to receive applause for passages particularly well delivered (in which case, the actor might repeat the passage).

Although some acting troupes continued to be organized as sharing ventures, some performers by the early eighteenth century preferred a fixed salary that they could augment by *benefit performances.* For *benefits,* the designated actor received all of the profits from the evening, a sum that occasionally equaled or exceeded a year's salary.

Plays and Playwrights

Many plays written during the age of Shakespeare continued to be produced (usually in adapted versions), but the new plays, both comic and serious, were closer to continental Neoclassicism than to Shakespeare. From 1660 to about 1700, the plays tended to depict a highly artificial court society, probably influenced by life at the court of Louis XIV.

Comedy of Manners. Most famous today are the Restoration "comedies of manners," plays whose witty dialogue and sophisticated sexual behavior reflect the highly artificial, mannered, and aristocratic society of the day. The heroes and heroines are "virtuous" if they succeed in capturing a lover or tricking a husband. "Honor" depends not on integrity but on reputation, and "wit," the ability to express ideas in a clever and apt way, is prized above all. The admirable characters in the plays are those who can operate successfully within an intricate social sphere; the foolish and laughable are those whose lack of wit or upbringing denies them access to social elegance. In short, the comedies depict the mores and conventions of a courtly society where elegance of phrase and the *appearance* of propriety were more highly prized than morals and sincere feelings. Among the most famous authors of Restoration comedies were William Congreve (1670–1729) and William Wycherley (1640–1715).

Heroic and Neoclassical Tragedy. "Heroic" tragedies presented a conflict between love and duty. In a world far removed from that of the Restoration comedies, tragic heroes were flawless and heroines chaste. The dialogue was based on "heroic couplets," two-line units of rhymed iambic pentameter. The idealization and formality of this kind of tragedy made it unusually susceptible to parody, and so burlesques of it soon appeared.

Succumbing both to the onslaught of burlesque and to the changing tastes of audiences, heroic tragedies declined in public favor, their place being filled by Neoclassical tragedies like John Dryden's *All for Love* (1677), a rewriting of Shakespeare's *Antony and Cleopatra* that brought it closer to the principles of Neoclassicism.

Sentimental Comedy.   The eighteenth century brought with it a change of values. Between about 1700 and 1750, society grew steadily more conservative, middle-class, moralistic, and *sentimental.*

Sentimentalism asserted the basic goodness of each individual. This doctrine contrasted with the previous, Neoclassical, view that human existence was a continuing struggle between good and evil. According to the sentimentalist, evil came about through corruption; it was not part of human nature at birth. Sentimentalism thus implied that, although people might not be perfect, they were perfectible. Literature should therefore show virtuous people acting virtuously in their daily lives. Heroic behavior and ethical perfection need not be restricted to some idealized world of pastoral poetry or exotic tragedy. Sentimentalism affected both comedies and serious dramas in England (as in France).

The amoral tone of the Restoration comedy of manners became offensive to many by the early 1700s. In its place came the view that drama should teach morality. At first, the change was merely in the plays' endings: Young lovers philandered and cuckolded throughout four acts of the play but, in the fifth, repented and declared their intention to lead a moral and upright life henceforth. By the 1730s, however, heroes and heroines were becoming embodiments of middle-class values, struggling cheerfully against adversity until, at the end, their courage and persistence were rewarded.

Prized especially were characters able to express their insights into human goodness in pithy statements (which came to be called *sentiments*). Thus, the label *sentimental hero* implied not only one who embodied virtue but also one whose speech was rich in sentiments. The audiences of the day experienced "a pleasure too exquisite for laughter," and so the term *sentimental comedy* predominated in the comic literature by the middle of the eighteenth century.

Serious Drama, 1700–1750.   George Lillo's *The London Merchant* (1731) was also a major break with the Neoclassical ideal: A middle-class hero is led astray by love and is ultimately punished. Although the play aimed to teach morality by showing the punishment of evil, it was nonetheless a far cry from strict Neoclassicism because it was written in prose, featured a middle-class hero, and dealt with affairs of the heart and the marketplace rather than affairs of state.

New Forms of Drama.   None of these plays, however, satisfied the English taste for scenic splendor and spectacular effects. Thus, opera and a number of so-called minor forms developed to provide outlets for visual display. Native English opera was gradually replaced by spectacular Italian opera, whose popularity soared in the eighteenth century. As well, English *pantomimes* combined elements of *commedia dell'arte,* farce, mythology, and contemporary satire with elaborate scenes of spectacle in short *afterpieces,* that is, short entertainments to be performed after the evening's play. Often, the dialogue was merely an excuse for major scenes of transformation, in which Harlequin, by a wave of his magic wand, changed places and people into new and dazzling locales and characters. Because new scenery was often commissioned for pantomimes, many innovations in the design and execution of settings in England can be credited to pantomime.

FIGURE 13.17 **Early Theatre in America.**
An engraving supposed to be the John Street Theatre in New York at about
the time of the Revolution; probably re-drawn.

THEATRE IN AMERICA, c. 1750

Many English actors and actresses found themselves squeezed out of the London
theatre. Some sought a living in the English provinces, but one group, headed by
William and Lewis Hallam, chose to go to America, instead. In 1752, the troupe
arrived in Virginia and, after building a theatre, opened with Shakespeare's *The
Merchant of Venice.* This group (although reorganized and enlarged after the
death of Lewis Hallam and renamed The American Company in recognition of
America's break with England) toured the towns of the East Coast with almost
no competition until the 1790s. Its repertory, acting styles, and production conventions were English, with appropriate adjustments made for the needs of almost constant touring.

THE PERIOD IN THE MODERN REPERTORY

Italian plays of the Neoclassical period are now almost unknown on the English-
speaking stage, with one exception—Niccolò Machiavelli's comic *Mandragola,*
which occasionally shows up on a college bill. In the same way, most French Neoclassical tragedies and English heroic tragedies are neglected, with the occasional
exception of Racine's *Phèdre,* a London success in 1998, for example. At the

FIGURE 13.18
Commedia dell'Arte in Modern Performance.
Atsa Matta You Commedia Troupe, performing at the University of Maryland. *Courtesy of Peter Avery, Artistic Director.*

Comédie Française, however, which is still a vigorous part of the French theatre, both Racine and Corneille are performed regularly, and both are done at other theatres, as well: they form part of the national heritage.

It is in comedy, however, that the period is best represented. Molière's plays are probably second only to Shakespeare's in university and regional theatre seasons, and they are sometimes performed in New York at places like Lincoln Center and the Circle in the Square. *Tartuffe* and *The Miser* are regulars all over North America. Restoration comedy, too, is a staple in universities and regional theatres, with Wycherley's *Country Wife* and Congreve's *The Way of the World* probably best represented.

CURRENT ISSUES

We noted at the beginning the observation that "art validates the center of power." Nowhere is this seen more clearly than in the Renaissance and Neoclassical period. Partly because of the buoyancy of the Renaissance itself, there is an aggressiveness to much public art, a love of display. This alone, however, does not account for the way in which theatre was taken up by political and economic power and caused to take certain shapes.

The best example is probably France from *Le Cid* through the age of Louis XIV. Here, a competitive, somewhat ragtag theatre was given status (by the French Academy and the court) and turned into one of the great theatres of all time. The gain, from the artists' point of view, was immeasurable. It can be argued, for example, that without the personal enthusiasm of Louis XIV, Molière could not have lasted in Paris; not only would the Parisian audience have been denied one of the great comic actors of all time, but we would not have his plays. It can be argued that, like the great porcelains and the great tapestries of this period, like Versailles itself, the French theatre was possible only because it was funded and given priority by power.

At the same time, it can be said that monopolies over the long haul are bad for art; that forcing an actor like Molière or a dramatist like Corneille to please those in power or perish puts an intolerable burden on them (and Corneille retired early; Molière died fairly young); and that, worst of all, supporting and pushing an art to help an agenda that is not apparent at the time is immoral. Corneille, by submitting to the judgment of the French Academy, was unwittingly encouraging all of France to submit to judgment from above and to accept arbitrary rules.

If art "validates" the center of power (embodies its agenda, or gives it credibility, or makes it seem admirable for its generosity), is the art tainted by whatever may taint power? What are the limits of what art can accept or agree to without losing its own credibility? Is the acceptance of corporate or governmental or aristocratic support a deal with the devil, or is it a value-free, win-win deal?

Molière, we suppose, wanted only to write and act and keep his theatre going; there is no evidence that he had any great concern for the deep structure of Louis XIV's power. Yet, he became a representative of that power; he is *still* a representative of that power, and of a world in which art (the porcelains, the tapestries, Versailles) belonged to the wealthy but helped put an intolerable burden of taxation and graft on the nation. Did he validate something that should not have been validated?

What of a symphony orchestra that is supported by a company that is a major polluter? A sculptor who designs a memorial to a hated war? A photographer who takes grant money from a government agency that refused a grant to another photographer because her work "violates community values"?

Should art validate the center of power?

Key terms

Check your understanding against this list. Brief definitions are in the Glossary; page references there will direct you to appropriate pages. (Persons are page-referenced in the Index.)

angle perspective	patent
benefit	perspective
chariot-and-pole	raked stage
commedia dell'arte	scenario
comedy of manners	sentimental comedy
decorum	shutter
illusionism	single-point perspective
intermezzi	three unities
lazzi	verisimilitude
machine plays	wing
Neoclassicism	

Illusionistic Theatres II: Romanticism, Commercialism, and Realism

OBJECTIVES

When you have completed this chapter, you should be able to:

- Define Romanticism and explain what was new and revolutionary about it

- Explain Richard Wagner's place in theatrical history

- Define Realism and explain what was new and revolutionary about it

- Trace major movements in commercial theatre and drama after 1850

This is a very long chapter. It is so because it covers complicated changes within the dominant paradigm we have called *illusionism.* These changes are:

- The rise of a new style, *Romanticism,* that displaced Neoclassicism

- The rise of a new economic structure, *commercialism,* which turned the increasingly popular theatre into an industry

- The overuse and trivialization of the new style, Romanticism, by commercial theatres, leading to

- The rise of a rebellious new style, *Realism,* outside the commercial theatre

- The adoption, over-use, and trivialization of *this* new style, Realism, by the commercial theatre

These changes did not, of course, happen so neatly or so clearly.

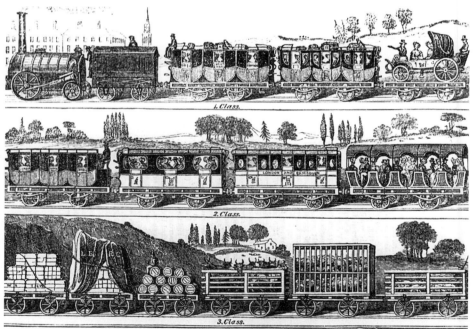

THE LONDON AND BIRMINGHAM RAILWAY CARRIAGES.

FIGURE 14.1   The Age of Industrialization.
The coming of steam power made railroads practical; they eased transportation of goods to market and of people from town to town.

ROMANTICISM

Background

The American Revolution began in 1776, the French in 1789. One electrified Europe; the other terrified it. Both, however, were significant of their times (1750–1850), which were a turmoil of conflict between old and new.

Not least, 1750–1850 is the age of the beginning of industrialism. It is also the beginning of the movement of population from countryside to cities. Toward the end of the period, it sees the coming of steam power, of cheap printing and the penny newspaper, and—perhaps most important to the theatre—of photography. For the first time, the mass of people saw themselves; for the first time, they could keep pictures of themselves and relatives, as the rich did. For the first time, they could see distant places as they really were. One of the significant effects would be to put a priority on the real world and its images.

This was also the period that saw the end of Neoclassicism. Its decline after 1750 was rapid and pronounced. Sentimental views gained and joined with new ideas of beauty, art, and truth. Artists and theorists increasingly rejected the "rules" of Neoclassicism. When their new ideas coalesced, the result was called *Romanticism.*

Romanticism took many forms. Its extraordinary diversity caused one critic to suggest that we should speak of Romanticism*s* to remind ourselves of its shifting nature. Certainly, the English Romanticism of Keats and Shelley was different from that of the French playwright Dumas or the German Schiller.

In spite of this complexity, Romanticism, as it peaked in the first half of the nineteenth century, had certain basics:

1. Equality, individualism, and the rejection of rules. It was an age of revolutions—besides the American and the French, there were uprisings in 1830 and 1848 that radically changed Europe. There were social revolutions, too: antislavery societies flourished; women's rights organizations were formed. Most of these struggles can be understood as conflicts between the status quo and efforts to change society in the direction of individual freedom and democratic process.

In art, Romanticism rejected rules and authority, including Neoclassicism. In an equally revolutionary leap, criticism moved the basis of judgment of a work of art from the work to the perceiver of the work. An obvious effect was to democratize art by making one person's response as valid as another's (but see 4, below).

2. A profound interest in nature. Natural feelings, instincts, were accepted as more reliable guides than authority or opinion. Reason became distrusted because it was the product of civilization and education and was therefore corruptible; instinct was natural and therefore reliable.

These ideas led to the idealization of "natural" peoples—"noble savages." Children, common people, and rural peasants were admired because they were least corrupted (Cooper's "Leatherstocking," for example).

DOLBY'S BRITISH THEATRE.

FATHER AND SON.

I. R. Cruikshank, Del.   *White, Sculpt.*

Ant. She's mine—approach and die!
Paul. Thine! miscreant, tremble!
[*Music.—they fight a decided combat*—ANTOINE *strikes* ROSEN
FORD *a violent blow.*

ACT II. SCENE 2.

FIGURE 14.2
Romanticism: Love of Nature.
Romantic theatre featured many plays set outdoors and beyond the newly sprawling cities, with heroic natural characters (peasants, "savages") and villainous aristocrats. This frontispiece shows a number of these traits.

3. Detail. In the particular lay the truth. The specific and the unique were important, because any detail could lead to a better understanding of the universe, whose parts were related. To establish uniqueness was, therefore, to establish identity.

4. The idealization of art. Most people (because of civilization, education, and such false priorities as manners and class) could not understand truth. The artist, on the other hand, was in direct contact with it through special feelings and instincts. The artist, therefore, came to be thought of as a misunderstood genius. In this sense, it may be said that the Romantics invented the artist—someone inevitably out of tune with society, above all with materialism. This tendency was sometimes pushed to an extreme: oddballs, misfits, and even psychopaths were given special status (e.g., Frankenstein's "monster").

5. Anti-industrialism. Romantics used the word "sublime" in talking about art and artists. The idea was near-mystical. Artists, by their nature, and those who "understood" art, were closer to the sublime, to that which transcended the material. In part, this—like the value put on nature—was a response to the industrial revolution and the growth of cities; in part, it was a response to industrial capitalism and the first generations of self-made entrepreneurs, who, without labor laws, consumer protection, or taxes, seemed to be embodiments of life without sublimity. Artists recoiled from things like child labor, brutal factory work, and noise that destroyed contemplation; one called factories "dark, Satanic mills."

Characteristics of the Romantic Theatre

The effect on theatre was significant, if erratic. Settings moved toward the exotic, either in the past (especially Greece and the Middle Ages) or primitive cultures. Stories dealt with children, commoners, rustics, and savages, set in detailed backgrounds of forests, caves, dungeons, jungles. Plays appealed more to the emotions than the intellect, with spectacle becoming more important than poetry.

Aristocrats flocked to the opera and ballet. The middle and lower classes all but took over the theatre.

In England and America, Shakespeare became a cultural icon. His plays were seen everywhere, from London's Drury Lane to the mining camps of California; he was read, recited, declaimed, and learned by heart. With the Bible, Shakespeare's works became a binding force of English-language culture, giving it a common frame of reference and a common elevated language.

FIGURE 14.3   Theatre Buildings in the Romantic Age.
As interest in seeing, rather than hearing, plays grew, audiences began to prefer the orchestra (the old pit) to the boxes. The cheapest seats continued to be in the galleries, farthest from the stage. Theatres grew larger early in the nineteenth century, as well. Here, an audience watches and hears *As You Like It* at London's Drury Lane Theatre. Compare this version of the wrestling scene with Figure 8.3. Courtesy of the Department of Rare Books and Special Collections of the University of Rochester.

The major trends in the theatre between 1750 and 1850 were the following:

1. The middle and lower classes came into the theatres in increasing numbers.

2. The number and the seating capacity of theatres increased.

3. The size and complexity of stages and support areas increased (although the size of the forestage decreased).

4. The number, accuracy, and consistency of visual details (scenery, properties, and costumes) increased, as emphasis shifted from the aural to the visual aspects of production.

5. The theatre divided into "legitimate" and "illegitimate"—the official on the one hand and the popular on the other.

Physical Theatre

Because theatre was the form of entertainment preferred by vast numbers of people and because Romantic plays stressed spectacle, new theatres between 1750 and 1850 featured ever-larger auditoriums and ever-more-sophisticated stages and support areas. For example, London's Covent Garden Theatre seated fewer than 1500 people in the 1730s but could accommodate 3000 by 1793. In America, the original Chestnut Street Theatre of Philadelphia (opened in 1794) was built to house 1200 but was soon enlarged to accommodate more than 2000. In France, all the major theatres were enlarged and modernized between 1750 and 1800. Between 1775 and 1800, more than thirty permanent theatres were built in Germany, most of which incorporated elaborate machinery to permit rapid and simultaneous changes of setting; by 1850, the number had grown to sixty-five.

THINKING ABOUT NINETEENTH-CENTURY THEATRE

When Drury Lane (London) was rebuilt in 1812, a contemporary tells us that it had *"three circles of boxes, each containing 24 boxes. . . . The boxes will hold 2100 individuals; the pit about 850; the lower gallery 820; and the upper gallery 480."* Calculate the seating capacity of this remodeled theatre. Compare both the seating arrangements and capacities of this theatre to those of a typical movie theatre, sports arena, and legitimate theatre today. What conclusions does this evidence suggest?

Audience

The standard configuration for the audience area was box, pit, and gallery, with boxes originally the most prized and expensive seats. As *seeing* the spectacular effects gradually became more important than *hearing* the vocal displays of the actors, the advantage shifted to the pit (later called the *orchestra*), and so box seats gave way to orchestra seats as the most favored and expensive in the theatre. The cheapest seats were always those of the upper galleries (in large theatres, there might be as many as five levels). Called the *gods,* the audience in the upper galleries were primarily working-class people who were criticized (by the elite) for their bad manners. About 1760, spectators were no longer permitted to sit on the stages in England and France, for onstage spectators clearly destroyed the illusion of reality and took up spaces now needed for scenery and acting.

Production Practices

By the 1770s, with the spectators gone from the stage, designers were free to create a complete stage picture. Phillippe Jacques de Loutherbourg (1740–1812), England's leading designer, began to reproduce familiar English locations on the stage and thus created a vogue for "local color" settings. In France, the scenery at the boulevard (non-monopoly) theatres used French local color as well as "authentic" reproductions of the Orient, the Americas, Russia, and so on.

Scenery consisted of a combination of wings, drops (large pieces of fabric suspended from above the stage to the floor), borders, and ground rows (cut-away flats adapted to stand free on the stage floor), the overall arrangement being called *wing-and-drop scenery.* All scenic pieces were painted to achieve the illusion of reality, and some were cut away (in the shape of leaves at their edges, for example) or layered (in gauzes or other fabrics) to enhance the illusion. Because many plays of the Romantic period were set outdoors, the borders often consisted of sky, clouds, and leaves, while the flats and drops were natural scenes. For plays set in medieval castles, all flats, drops, and borders might be painted to imitate large stones.

Whenever required by the play's action, three-dimensional details were included; for example, a bridge would be built if characters had to walk on it. But most of the scenery was two-dimensional, with details painted on it.

Scenery and special effects were governed by three overriding and interrelated assumptions:

1. The stage picture should present the illusion of reality (thus, the term *pictorial illusionism* was used for the scenery).

2. Many details should be included in order to particularize the settings.

3. Because time and place were important, historical and geographical accuracy of detail should be sought. Attention to such details increasingly won public acclaim and so became increasingly practiced during the nineteenth century. By 1850, even in America, whose theatre was late in getting under way, *antiquarianism* had made its mark, and historical accuracy in theatrical settings and costumes was, if not achieved, at least approached.

Although there was a considerable gap between these goals and their realization, designers moved steadily in the direction of their ideals from about 1750 to 1850.

Lighting.   The scene was lit by candles or oil lamps (or, after 1830, in some theatres, by gas) placed at the front of the stage as *footlights* and behind the several sets of wings. In no case was the illumination high, and so scenery and actors were not brightly lighted.

Special Effects.   Settings were enlivened by an enormous variety of special equipment and effects. Characters and objects flew about by means of elaborate systems of ropes and pulleys; they disappeared and appeared magically through various traps in the floor and, less often, through rotating wall panels. Fountains

FIGURE 14.4   Special Effects.
Theatrical machinery grew more and more sophisticated, even when still manually operated. This is a late eighteenth-century device for a moving waterfall. By the mid-nineteenth century, special effects would dominate some productions.

and waterfalls gushed and flowed by means of specially installed water systems. By unwinding a large painted cloth from one giant spool onto another, the landscape behind an onstage boat or carriage could be made to unroll and the vehicle would seem to move. When, late in the nineteenth century, such panoramas were combined with treadmills, even horse races and chariot races could be staged. Volcanic eruptions, fires, thunder, lightning, rainstorms, explosions—all were part of the theatre's spectacle, and all were popular with mass audiences.

Actors and Acting

Professional Structures.   Some troupes, like the Comédie Française, continued to operate as sharing companies, but most performers now worked for a fixed salary that was supplemented by the gate receipts of one or more "benefit" performances.

For a time, the *stock company* dominated—that is, a group of actors who stayed together over a period of years, performing appropriate roles in a variety of plays and each contributing to the reputation of the company as a whole. After about 1830, however, perhaps as a consequence of the Romantics' growing attachment to the idea of "individual genius," and most certainly because of improved transportation networks (particularly the expanding system of railroads), the company system gradually declined.

In its place came the *star system,* which meant that leading performers moved from stock company to stock company, where they played the plum parts, supported by resident players. The star system, although exceedingly popular with audiences, caused numerous problems for the acting profession. One French actress, for example, demanded and received a salary equal to that of her country's prime minister (leaving little for her fellow artists). For a time, there was a rage for child stars, who played not only Shakespearean roles like Hamlet but also the heroes in various melodramas of the day, where they single-handedly foiled the villains. Some female stars specialized in *breeches roles,* that is, women playing men's roles in men's clothing.

Thurston, del.   *Fittler, sc.*

FIGURE 14.5   Acting in the Romantic Era.
Frontispiece of a Romantic play, suggesting the importance of demonstrations of emotion.

Acting Styles.   Like other elements of theatre, acting style changed. At the beginning of the period, the style was *formal,* emphasizing vocal power and physical dignity, obviously indebted to Neoclassicism. The greatest English actor of the eighteenth century practiced a pre-Romantic style that was called "easy and familiar, yet forcible." *David Garrick* (1717–1779) was praised in both comedy and tragedy. (He was also a playwright.) Abandoning the formal, Garrick pushed his personal style toward what he considered the natural—although he would probably seem artificial today. He played Macbeth, for example, in eighteenth-century military dress; his vocal delivery, although far closer to regular speech than the formal actors', was undoubtedly based on ideas of "correct" accent and delivery.

The revolution in English acting appears to have occurred when Edmund Kean (1787–1833) made his London debut in 1814. Kean abandoned dignity and intellect in favor of flamboyance and passion. To see Kean act "was to read Shakespeare by flashes of lightning." Passionate outbursts and novel interpretations then marked the actors labeled "Romantic" during the period that followed.

FIGURE 14.6   Edmund Kean.
Kean's acting was turbulent, emotional—
"flashes of lightning." Here, his Hamlet.

Plays and Playwrights

Revivals of Shakespeare were a mainstay of the Romantic theatre, which produced them in new theatrical settings designed to illustrate the locales mentioned in the dramatic texts and to stress the plays' exotic qualities. Some Neoclassical works remained in the repertory, but new plays that defied Neoclassical conventions predominated.

Serious Drama.   During the Romantic period, a recognizable difference appeared between "important" plays and popular ones. Among the critically important works can be found plays ranging from domestic tragedies to philosophical inquiries. In the popular theatre, only melodramas mattered.

The earliest of the critically important plays were sentimental ones that dealt with the everyday problems of the middle class. In France, Denis Diderot defined the *drame* (a serious play treating domestic matters), and he provided a model for it in *The Illegitimate Son* (1757).

Germany produced major *philosophical dramas.* Following the publication of Gotthold Ephraim Lessing's *Nathan the Wise* (1779) and a surge of dramatic experiments under a group of writers called the *Storm and Stress* (fl. 1770–1790), two leaders emerged: Johann Wolfgang von Goethe (1749–1832) and Friedrich Schiller (1759–1805). Goethe's final work, *Faust,* in two parts (1808 and 1831), came to epitomize for many the Romantic dilemma. Never intended for the stage, the work is an episodic presentation of a philosophical point of view and an acknowledged literary (as distinct from theatrical) masterpiece. Of Schiller's many works, the best known now are *The Robbers* (1782), whose immediate success created a vogue for other "Robin Hood" plays, and *William Tell* (1804), a celebration of individual worth and democratic government.

Less philosophical were French *Romantic tragedies* like *Hernani* by Victor Hugo (1802–1885). Its first production in 1830 caused a riot. The battle of *Hernani,* fought in both the pit of the Comédie Française and the literary circles of Paris, was resolved in favor of the Romantics, and so 1830 is the date now given for the acceptance of Romanticism into the mainstream of France's theatrical life (several years after it had been accepted in England, Germany, and America).

Perhaps because the English found in Shakespeare the traits they most prized, English Romantics produced no new serious dramas of consequence. Some poets wrote *closet dramas*—plays to be read, not staged.

Melodrama.   The most popular form was *melodrama.* Although not new (such plays have probably existed in all ages), melodrama attained new stature and significance in the theatre of the late eighteenth and the nineteenth centuries.

Melodrama means literally "music drama," a name derived from the extensive use of music within the plays. Much like popular television and movies of today, nineteenth-century melodramas used *emotional music* to provide the proper mood and background for the action and to underscore moments of suspense and surprise. Music was also often used to identify characters for the audience. Such

Disaster
Action
Success

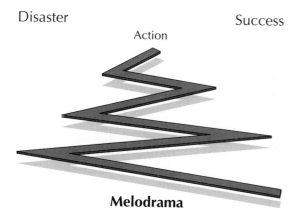

Melodrama

FIGURE 14.7 Romantic Drama: Melodrama.

One of melodrama's defining characteristics is its sequence of reversals from near-disaster to salvation and back. These reversals increase in intensity as the action goes forward. (It is still the pattern of many movies and television shows.)

music, called *signature music,* was played when a character was about to enter or leave or to perform some astounding feat.

Melodrama presented a simplified moral universe in which good and evil were clearly defined and embodied in recognizable stock characters. A physically attractive hero and heroine (often in love) possessed a kindness and virtue that were as unmistakable as they were unblemished. These characters, along with their friends and servants, represented the forces of good. Propelling the action of the play was a villain, whose physical appearance as well as behavior expressed evil. The remaining characters were most often friends or sidekicks of the three defining characters and almost always included at least one comic character. The villain initiated the action of the melodrama by posing a threat to the hero or the heroine; he or she escaped, and the villain posed another threat; he or she again escaped; and so on. The episodic play thus progressed by a series of threats and escapes, each reversal becoming more extreme than the last, until the final incident, when the hero or heroine might move from almost certain death to a happy marriage in a matter of minutes.

Many melodramas depended heavily on special effects—fires, explosions, drownings, earthquakes—both as threats to the sympathetic characters during the action of the play and as obstacles to the villain in the final scenes. As well, many melodramas developed around the use of various animals: most common were *equestrian dramas* (horses) and *canine melodramas* (dogs). The interest of the Romantic writers in sea stories gave rise to *nautical melodramas.*

Between 1750 and 1850, two writers of melodramas were especially important. The German playwright August Friedrich von Kotzebue (1761–1819) wrote more than two hundred plays, many translated into English and French and performed throughout the world. René Charles Guilbert de Pixérécourt (1773–1844) was the French author of more than one hundred plays. He set a fashion for canine (dog) melodramas and disaster melodramas, which might require a flood to sweep through the stage, uprooting a tree and bearing the heroine away on a board, or might use a volcanic eruption to foil the villain. Because the physical requirements were often so demanding, Pixérécourt insisted on directing his own plays in order to ensure their success. Pixérécourt, therefore, figured prominently in the history of French directors as well as of French playwrights.

Comedy.   During the Romantic period, at least three different types of comedies competed for public favor: sentimental comedy, "laughing" comedy, and the "well-made play."

Probably closest in tone to the early romantic ideas of innate human goodness were the *sentimental comedies,* those written to appeal to the audience's sense of virtue rather than to its sense of humor. Although most contained some laughable situations and an occasionally funny character, the plays' primary appeal depended on their depiction of the successful struggles of virtuous characters whose laudable goals ensured their ultimate success.

In the second half of the eighteenth century, there was a strong urge to return to the witty, or at least funny, *laughing comedy* of the late seventeenth century. Three authors in particular excelled in it:

- Beaumarchais (Pierre Augustin Caron, 1732–1799), whose *Marriage of Figaro* (1783) captured comically some of the resentments that would explode in the French Revolution six years later

- Oliver Goldsmith (c. 1730–1774), also a noted novelist, best known for *She Stoops to Conquer* (1773)

- Richard Brinsley Sheridan (1751–1816), whose *The Rivals* and *The School for Scandal* (1777) used aspects of sentimentalism while making fun of it

The most popular comic writer of the hundred years between 1750 and 1850 was Eugène Scribe (1791–1861), a Frenchman who wrote more than three hundred plays for the Parisian theatres. Their translation into German and English and their frequent production throughout the nineteenth century caused French comedy to set the standard for the world by mid-century.

Scribe's techniques (e.g., careful preparation, meticulous networks of relationships) were designed to give the appearance of an action tightly unified by cause and effect when, in fact, the plays were built around multiple lines of action that unfolded by chance and coincidence. The phrase *well-made play* was used first as a compliment to describe the particular kind of play that Scribe perfected, but because later scholars deplored the superficiality of his works, the term became one of derision during the twentieth century. Scribe and the well-made play exerted considerable influence on later writers.

Summary: A Century of Change

The profound changes that can be seen between 1750 and 1850 were the result of changes in what audiences would accept as "real" or "true."

FIGURE 14.8
Out with the Old.
The Romantic theatre replaced actors like Charles Macklin (1697–1797), shown here as Macbeth, with the pyrotechnics of actors like Kean, and Macklin's elegant version of an eighteenth-century officer's uniform with more authentic costume.

In 1750, generalized scenery and costumes formed a sparse background for the actors. Audiences, still largely upper class, were unperturbed by its lack of detail or its inaccuracy, for they thrilled to the verbal displays of excellently trained and elegantly attired actors. They sought and found their artistic truth in the formal, generalized portraits of an upper- or middle-class hero that formed the basis of most of the new plays.

In 1850, carefully painted settings and historically accurate costumes provided a richly detailed picture. The audiences, now mostly middle and lower class, sought lavish spectacle and special effects. They expected reasonably authentic sets and costumes, and they appreciated actors who could grip the emotions. Such audiences found truth in the detailed representations of individual people and places.

POST-ROMANTICISM
RICHARD WAGNER AND THE BAYREUTH THEATRE

Although Richard Wagner (1813–1883) is most often associated with music and opera, he was an important theorist and practitioner of the theatre as well. Two contributions in particular assured Wagner his place in the history of theatre: (1) his call for a *unified work of art* and (2) his development of a *classless theatre.*

Wagner argued that the artist should be a mythmaker who presents an ideal world to the spectators, providing them with a communal experience that highlights for them their shared culture. The best drama, according to Wagner, was one that combined music and poetry to achieve a total art, one that fused the emotional with the intellectual.

For Wagner, the experience of the audience was the critical factor in planning and shaping a work of art. He sought a stage production so compelling that spectators would be drawn in and would believe in and empathize with the world behind the proscenium arch. Indeed, for Wagner, the success of a production was measured primarily by its ability to capture the emotions of the audience and to transport them to a new sense of shared purpose.

Master Artwork

To achieve the ideal production, one capable of entrancing an audience, Wagner proclaimed the need for a *master artwork,* or "unified artwork," by which he meant a work in which all elements of the drama and of theatrical production were carefully synthesized into a unified whole. Such unity could be achieved only, according to Wagner, when a single person, a supreme artist, controlled every aspect of the production. Indeed, it was Wagner's concept of the *master artist,* the single controlling force behind a work of art, that did much to establish the role of the director as the central artist in the theatre.

Classless Theatre

Wagner was able to build a theatre that allowed him to put his theories into practice. Opened in 1876, the Bayreuth Festspielhaus included features that helped Wagner establish his ideal world of the stage. Rather than one proscenium arch, the theatre at Bayreuth had several; the orchestra pit, customarily in full view of the audience, at Bayreuth extended partway under the stage and was entirely hidden from the audience. Steam jets installed at the front of the stage permitted special effects like fog and mist to establish mood and to mask the changes in scenery. Such unusual architectural features were joined by new practices—darkening the auditorium during the drama and forbidding the musicians to tune their instruments in the pit—to separate the real world of the audience (in the auditorium)

FIGURE 14.9   Wagner's Classless Theatre.
In addition to increasing the separation between stage and auditorium through a series of proscenium arches, Wagner's Bayreuth theatre also democratized the audience area by eliminating box, pit, and gallery in favor of "continental seating," in which all seats were equally good and equally expensive.

from the ideal world of the drama (on the stage). This separation of the two worlds Wagner referred to as the "mystic chasm."

Unusual as some of these features were, they were less innovative and influential than changes that Wagner introduced into the auditorium at Bayreuth. Whether because of a desire to democratize the theatre or because of the increasing importance of seeing (rather than hearing) a play, Wagner eliminated the box, pit, and gallery in favor of a new "classless" theatre in which every seat had an equally good view of the stage and each ticket cost the same amount of money. The seats at Bayreuth were arranged in the shape of a fan, with the shorter rows closer to the stage and with entrances at the end of each row. This kind of arrangement came to be called *continental seating,* and some version of it was widely adopted as new theatres were constructed during the twentieth century.

Although, in fact, Wagner's productions seldom strayed far from the sort of illusionism common during the last years of the nineteenth century, his theories and architectural innovations placed him outside the mainstream of his day and made him a precursor of later experimenters.

COMMERCIAL THEATRES (c. 1850–1900)

The Rise of Commercialism

Wagner was unique. His influence was to be felt gradually. Of far more immediate and widespread importance was a change in the business side of the theatre—the rise of commercialism. Commercial theatre had several characteristics:

1. Replacement of stock and sharing companies with hired companies headed by an *actor-manager* (e.g., England's Henry Irving) or a *producer* (e.g., America's Augustin Daly)

2. Centralization in large cities (New York, Paris, London), including central control of touring circuits ("the road"), culminating in trusts like New York's Syndicate (c. 1896–1905)

3. Identification of a nation's theatre with an area of a large city—London's West End, Paris's boulevards, New York's Broadway

The division noted earlier (p. 311) between official and popular theatre was emphasized by the rapid increase in urban populations and the fascination of the popular theatres for middle- and working-class people. The old theatrical monopolies could not maintain their control, and they finally gave up their opposition to competition. The Comédie Française survived; the English monopoly theatres did not. Theatre buildings got bigger and their number increased, many new theatres going up in new working-class neighborhoods. Increasingly, the people who made theatrical decisions were concerned with catering to these big audiences. Those who controlled theatres were more and more businessmen, less and less members of an artistic group. They embraced the new style, Romanticism, because it was popular, not because of any artistic or philosophical conviction. As a result, commercial Romanticism became a form of spectacle that drove all the other parts of the play.

Thus, commercial houses in France, England, and America in the last half of the nineteenth century thrived on plays, production practices, and acting of the sort popularized by the Romantic theatre. The most popular plays now ran for dozens, even hundreds of nights and played to audiences of many social levels and artistic tastes. It was a theatre of enormously popular performances and—to some—increasingly trivial concerns. It was a paradox: the more it succeeded, the more it created pressure for a noncommercial, non-Romantic opposite.

Plays and Playwrights

Revivals.   Shakespeare's plays were still produced often and were given elaborate settings designed to reproduce faithfully the illusion of specific locales mentioned in the text. "Illustrating" Shakespeare became popular, and so *The Merchant of*

Venice used real water for onstage canals, and *Romeo and Juliet* reproduced in detail the historical Juliet's tomb. Countless plays from the first half of the nineteenth century and a few from the eighteenth century were also revived. Most popular, of course, were the spectacular melodramas.

Comedies.   The most popular commercial playwright of the period was probably the Frenchman Victorien Sardou (1831–1908), who is best remembered for well-made plays like *A Scrap of Paper* (1860). Eugène Labiche (1815–1888), with *The Italian Straw Hat* (1851), and Georges Feydeau (1862–1921), with *A Flea in Her Ear* (1907), set the style for plays based on a highly complicated set of adventures unfolding at rapid-fire pace amidst rooms with many doors. They were the forerunners of "French bedroom farce."

Melodrama.   Among the most important popular writers of melodramas was the Irish-American Dion Boucicault (1822–1890). Boucicault fused sentimentality with sensationalism, against a background rich in local color. He captured large audiences on two continents with works like *The Octoroon* (1859). (See Figure 14.10.) He demanded and received a percentage of receipts for each performance of his plays, thus instituting the practice of *paying royalties to playwrights.* By 1886, an international copyright agreement had been instituted, in part because of Boucicault's influence—a significant aspect of commercialization.

Although none was so well known as Boucicault, a number of other dramatists of the time thrilled audiences with plays that featured heroes tied to railroad tracks, heroines trapped in burning buildings, onstage eruptions of volcanoes, chariot races, and other spectacular effects.

Probably the most popular commercial play in the world during this period was the American melodrama *Uncle Tom's Cabin* (1852), based on the novel by Harriet Beecher Stowe. A sentimental view of slavery in the Old South, the play included scenes of slaves escaping across the ice-clogged Ohio River pursued by dogs and slave traders, a dead child being carried to heaven by angels amidst the weeping of her family and friends, and Uncle Tom being beaten by the white villain, Simon Legree. The success of the play was unprecedented. Various versions played in Germany, France, and England, and twelve different American versions were in print in 1900. The play's popularity remained strong through World War I, when more than a dozen companies still traveled about performing only this one play.

Musical Entertainments.   Although operettas like those of Jacques Offenbach (1819–1889) were popular, they were eclipsed by the work of two Englishmen, William S. Gilbert (1836–1911) and Arthur Sullivan (1842–1900), whose *H.M.S. Pinafore* (1878), among others, remains popular to this day.

In America, burlesque (and its cousin, vaudeville) were popular. Originally little more than parodies and variety acts, both were well established in the American theatre during the first half of the nineteenth century. Burlesque became

FIGURE 14.10 Melodrama.
Melodramas often treated contemporary social problems, although they seldom tried to resolve them. Here, two famous American melodramas on slavery. Top, a slave auction scene from Dion Boucicault's *The Octoroon;* bottom, Eliza crossing the ice-clogged Ohio River, escaping slavery, in the most popular melodrama of the century—perhaps of all time—*Uncle Tom's Cabin.* (This production was French. From *Le Theatre.*)

overwhelmingly a male entertainment after Lydia Thompson's "British Blondes" visited America in 1869. Increasingly thereafter, the popularity of burlesque depended on a combination of spectacle, song, dance, and female bodies. Soon after World War I, "striptease" was added, and burlesque moved still further to the outskirts of respectability. Vaudeville, on the other hand, flourished as a family entertainment, some of its stars moving to radio and the movies in the 1930s.

Actors and Acting

The pleasure of theatregoers was not entirely bound up with the plays themselves, for the commercial stage featured theatrical stars of the highest rank. Many leading actors traveled from city to city to play starring roles with resident stock companies; others traveled with their entire productions (cast, costumes, and scenery) across continents to satisfy audiences who thronged to the theatres to see the latest star. Sarah Bernhardt (1844–1923), although French, was virtually an international super-star. England's most famous actor was Henry Irving (1838–1905), whose performances in a now-forgotten melodrama named *The Bells* (1871) spanned thirty-four years and eight hundred performances. That, together with his Shakespearean successes, led to his being knighted, the first English actor to be so honored. In America, the leading actors were Joseph Jefferson (1829–1905), whose fame rested primarily on his portrayal of the title role in *Rip Van Winkle;* Edwin Booth (1833–1893), regarded by his contemporaries as Shakespeare's finest interpreter but probably remembered today by more people as the brother of President Lincoln's assassin; and James O'Neill (1847–1920), who made an acting career in *The Count of Monte Cristo* (1883) and fathered playwright Eugene O'Neill (see p. 358).

REALISM

After Romanticism, the split between "serious" drama and entertainment became permanent. From 1850 through the 1950s, significant drama and staging were in a style called *Realism*. Commercial theatre and drama lagged decades behind but finally embraced a diluted and trivialized Realism by the end of World War I.

Background

By the 1850s, certain problems that had grown out of society's shifting bases of wealth and its developing industrialization were becoming clear. The products of industry were being distributed unevenly, and the gap between those who did the work and those who reaped the profits was widening, a development that led Karl Marx (1818–1883) to propose an alternative method of social and economic organization for society. Urban poverty was on the rise and, with it, urban crime. Political instability gave way to political repression, which, in turn, fanned latent dissatisfactions that demanded correction.

At roughly this same time, science offered new theories that threatened to undermine previously accepted views of humanness. Charles Darwin (1809–1882)

THE WHITE SLAVES OF ENGLAND.

FIGURE 14.11
The Problems of Industrialization.
As factories multiplied, workers—including women and children—were often exploited, with few legal protections from managers and owners. Thus, both the problems and the benefits of industrialization affected society and became the subjects of writers from Marx to Dickens.

proposed that human beings had evolved from simpler forms of life and that they were not a separate, special act of creation. He therefore seemed to suggest that people were more like animals than angels and that their capacity was limited by environmental forces. Gregor Mendel (1822–1884) showed that certain traits were passed from generation to generation in statistically predictable ways. From there, it was only a short step to the conclusion that people, like plants and other animals, were defined by their genes and that they were neither free agents nor special creatures. Sigmund Freud (1856–1939) proposed that behavior was not rational and so motives were not understandable, even to ourselves. His emphasis on subconscious desires and repressed responses hinted that people were trapped into patterns of behavior by forces (often sexual and aggressive) that they neither controlled nor understood. One result of such developments in science was to dislodge humankind from the philosophic pedestal on which it had rested since the Middle Ages.

Finally, revolutionary technological advances had the effects of changing both the way people lived and the way they saw the world. Impressive changes in transportation (steamboats, railroads, automobiles, and airplanes) and communication (telegraph, telephone, radio, and television) speeded up the flow of information, goods, and people. Improved medical science slowed down death rates. Science and technology seemed to ensure eventual answers even to complex questions. History, therefore, seemed to be progressing inexorably toward a better world.

FIGURE 14.12   Realism: Materialism and Objectivism.
If truth depends on fidelity to material reality—and for the realists it did—then a realistic setting will include many material objects and many details. Here, a realistic setting of 1893.

Realism—and its more extreme relative, *Naturalism*—arose in part as responses to these new social and philosophical conditions. Realists and Naturalists were *materialists:* They believed that truth resided in the material objects observable in the physical, external world. They were also *objectivists:* They believed that truth could be discovered through the application of scientific observation and could be replicated by a series of objective observers.

According to the Realists and the Naturalists, the function of art, like that of science, was the betterment of humankind, and so the method of the artist should be that of the scientist. Because truth resided in material objects, art had to depict the material world. Because problems could be solved through application of the scientific method, dramatists should copy scientists and strive to become objective observers. Plays should be set in contemporary times and places, for only they could be observed firsthand by the playwright. As the highest purpose of art was the betterment of humanity, the subject of plays should be contemporary life and its problems.

Naturalism

While sharing with Realists a belief in science as a solver of problems, the Naturalists differed in their definition of what problems most needed attention and in their hope for the future. The Naturalists stressed the problems of the poor and tended to be pessimistic about the solution of these problems. According to the Naturalists, people were victims, not actors in life. Their destiny was controlled by factors like heredity and environment, factors over which they had little if any influence. Because the Naturalists attempted to give the impression that their plays were an actual record of life, the dramas often appeared formless and unstructured, traits that gave rise to the phrase "a slice of life" to describe some Naturalists' plays.

Socialist Realism

Based on nineteenth-century Realism but coming a generation later, *Socialist Realism* was a serious attempt to construct a critical theory appropriate to international communism in the 1930s and after. As first proposed in the Soviet Union, it rejected the pessimism of Naturalism and called for a heroic Realism that would show models of behavior (a surprising return to one aspect of sentimental comedy). Character was to be conceived socially and not psychologically (as in Western, or "critical," realism). Socialist-realist plays should have happy endings—as seen from the point of view of Communism, not its characters. The theory came under severe strain as the observable reality of Soviet life got further from the heroic ideal; from a Western point of view, it could not work because it was based on a system that did not work.

On the other hand, another Marxist theorist, Georg Lukacs, questioned whether Western Realism could work for long, either. He suggested that a Realism that found its characters in average individuals, and its focus in psychology, could be made interesting only through exploring quirks, special problems, and oddities. Lukacs saw this as an art based in "pathology."

FIGURE 14.13 Socialist Realism.
The details of costume, of properties (the firearms) and scenery (the railroad tracks, the station) identify the style as Realism. The story, with socialism triumphant, marks it as socialist—hence, Socialist Realism. (From P. A. Markov, *The Soviet Theatre.*)

Leading Figures in Realism and Naturalism

Despite the period's interest in the mass of people, and despite democratizing forces, this was an era of self-defined great men (and a few women). As a result, most significant events are identified with individuals. In part, this is a kind of historical shortcut, representing complex forces in one person, but in part it was the nature of the period, when optimistic, forceful people, aping Wagner, tried to change the world—and occasionally succeeded. The master artist appeared in several guises.

Georg II, Duke of Saxe-Meiningen

One of the first important contributors to the *realistic staging of prerealistic drama* was Georg II, Duke of Saxe-Meiningen (fl. 1870s-1880s). In some ways, the duke was merely perfecting and popularizing ideals of staging promulgated much earlier; nonetheless, it was he who influenced later, important Realists.

Saxe-Meiningen objected to many practices of the commercial theatrical mainstream because they resulted in productions that lacked unity (internal consistency) and that seemed artificial and unreal. For the duke and his court theatre, the art of the theatre was the art of providing the *illusion of reality;* he therefore sought methods of production that would lead to "an intensified reality and [would] give remote events . . . the quality of actuality, of being lived for the first time." To this end, the duke stressed accurate scenery, costumes, and properties; lifelike acting; and unity.

Production Practices. The Duke believed that all elements of a production required coordination. The setting must be an integral part of the play, and so he encouraged his actors to move *within* the setting rather than merely playing in front of it (as was currently fashionable). If actors were to move within an environment, the scenic details had to be three-dimensional rather than painted, and so actual objects were used in the settings. Simultaneously, the duke strove to provide several levels (e.g., rocks, steps, and platforms), so that the scenic design would not stop abruptly at the stage floor. In these ways, he did much to popularize the use of real, three-dimensional details.

Historical accuracy in both scenery and costumes was important. Georg II designed and supervised every aspect of the physical production. To increase accuracy in the selection of details, he divided each century into thirds and differentiated among various national groups within each period. To increase accuracy of construction, he used authentic fabrics instead of the cheaper substitutes often resorted to in the commercial houses of the day. Many items were made in his own shops.

Acting. In Saxe-Meiningen's group, there were no stars. Each member of the company was eligible to play any role; and each member, if not cast as a major character, was required to play in crowd scenes, something a commercial star would never have done. Moreover, each actor in a crowd scene was given lines and actions that were carefully rehearsed. To make the crowds seem real, the duke divided his actors into several groups, each led by an experienced actor. To increase a sense of realism in crowd scenes, the actors were to avoid parallel lines on stage, to make crosses diagonally rather than parallel with the curtain line, to keep one foot off the ground whenever possible (by placing it on a step or by kneeling on one knee), and not to copy his neighbor's stance. Actors were told to look at one another rather than the audience, to react to what was said and done onstage, and to behave naturally (even if it meant delivering a line while not facing the audience). Moreover, the Duke required all actors, from the most to the least important, to wear the costumes that were designed for them, regardless of the current fashions, and to acquaint themselves with the postures and stances of the period. Makeup was based on historical portraits.

Influence.   Beginning in 1874 (eight years after the duke took over the theatre), the Meiningen plays began touring western Europe and Russia. From then until its last tour in 1890, the troupe gave more than 2800 performances in thirty-six cities. From these performances came the group's international reputation and its influence.

André Antoine and the Théâtre-Libre

André Antoine (1853–1943) abhorred the commercial theatres of Paris, disapproved of the way actors were trained at the Paris Conservatoire (France's leading school for actors), objected to the scenic practices of the major theatres, and decried the flimsiness of contemporary popular drama. What was needed, Antoine

LINKS to more about theatre

Heller in Pink Tights. Touring the Old West with Sophia Loren.

Funny Girl. Barbra Streisand as Fanny Brice.

Gerald Bordman, *American Musical Theatre,* 1992 (2nd edition).

Charles Dickens, *Nicholas Nickleby.* No one will ever create a better—or funnier—picture of a fifth-rate theatre troupe.

Henry T. Sampson, *The Ghost Walks,* 1988. "Blacks in show business, 1865–1910." Essential to an understanding of African Americans vis-à-vis the commercial theatre of the period.

concluded, was a theatre where new and controversial plays could gain carefully mounted and realistically acted productions. Thus, when an amateur group to which he belonged balked at producing a daring new play, Antoine undertook the production himself and, spurred by early success, became the full-time director of his own new theatre in 1887. He named it the Théâtre-Libre (Free Theatre) and described it as nothing less than "a machine of war, poised for the conquest of Paris."

Production Practices—The "Fourth Wall."   Antoine believed with the Naturalists that environment determined, or at least heavily influenced, human behavior. Stage setting was therefore very important. For this reason, Antoine took great care to make his stage settings as believable and as much like real life as possible. He designed a room, placing the furniture and accessories in it, only then deciding which "wall" of the room was to be removed so that the audience could see in. Antoine depended heavily on actual, three-dimensional objects rather than their painted substitutes. For one play, he brought real sides of beef on his stage; for another, real trees and birds' nests; and for another, a real student's actual room furnishings. The attention that he paid to realistic detail and his reliance on actual objects led to his being called by many the father of naturalistic staging. Jean Julien, a contemporary of Antoine's, seemed to sum up the goal of Antoine: "The front of the stage must be a fourth wall, transparent for the public, opaque for the player."

Acting.   Antoine believed that actors should appear to be real people, not actors in a play. He believed that actors trained at the Paris Conservatoire could not portray real life on stage because they had been trained to use their voices in special, theatrical ways, to align their bodies in unlifelike poses, and to play to their audiences directly. Antoine wanted his actors to say their lines naturally, just as one might engage in a conversation with friends and, at the same time, to move about the furniture and accessories as in real life. Sincerity and conviction were the qualities he sought, and so he advised his actors to ignore the audience and to speak to one another in conversational tones—in short, to try to *be,* rather than to *act,* the characters in the play. Perhaps for these reasons, Antoine often used amateur actors in his theatre, actors who had not received conventional training for the commercial theatre and who were therefore more receptive to the experimental, new style of naturalistic acting.

Plays.   Although Antoine produced a wide range of plays while at the Théâtre-Libre, he seemed most comfortable with plays in the Realistic and Naturalistic styles. Because Antoine organized his theatre as a subscription house, he was able to bypass threats of censorship. Consequently, he was able to introduce to Parisians a wide range of French and foreign authors whose works were considered too scandalous for production in the major theatres of the day.

Influence.   The major contributions of Antoine and the Théâtre-Libre (1887–1896) were

1. To popularize acting techniques leading toward naturalness on stage

2. To gain acceptance for scenic practices now known as "fourth-wall realism," with all that implies about scenic detail and literal objects

3. To introduce a new generation of playwrights (both French and foreign) to the theatregoing public of Paris

4. To establish a model for a censor-free theatre

The most significant experimental theatre of its day, the Théâtre-Libre gave rise to a number of similar noncommercial theatres throughout the world. Called the *independent theatre movement,* this blossoming of small theatres in several countries almost simultaneously gave the impetus to, first, an international idealism, and then an ultimate acceptance of Realism as the mainstream of the commercial theatre, an acceptance completed by early in the twentieth century.

Konstantin Stanislavski and the Moscow Art Theatre

When the Meiningen company toured Russia in 1885 and 1890, Konstantin Stanislavski (1863–1938) and Vladimir Nemirovich-Danchenko (1858–1943) saw it and were impressed. They decided to establish a new kind of theatre in Moscow, an experimental theatre whose goals were to remain free of the demands

FIGURE 14.14   The Moscow Art Theatre.
Maxim Gorky's masterpiece of naturalism, *The Lower Depths,* at the Moscow Art Theatre, with Stanislavski on the table, right center. (From Oliver Sayler, *The Moscow Art Theatre Series of Plays.*)

of commercialism, to avoid overemphasis on the scenic elements of production, and to reflect the inner truth of the play. For this theatre, Nemirovich-Danchenko was to select the plays and handle the administration, while Stanislavski was to serve as the production director.

From its opening in 1898, the Moscow Art Theatre was known for its careful, realistic-naturalistic productions. During its early years, the greatest attention was given to the accuracy of historical detail in all areas of the physical production, but, within ten years, Stanislavski's interest moved from a largely external Realism toward finding an inner truth for actors. External Realism from this time on became, for Stanislavski, merely a key to opening the inner reality of the plays, and he strove to develop techniques that would help the actors achieve an inner truth.

Acting. By 1917, he had developed, from personal experience and observation of others, his major ideas for training actors, ideas that he codified in a series of books that have since been translated into more than twenty languages (the dates are for the American editions): *My Life in Art* (1924), *An Actor Prepares* (1936), *Building a Character* (1949), and *Creating a Role* (1961). Together, these books represent what has come to be called the Stanislavski "system" of actor training, although Stanislavski himself insisted neither that his was the only way to train actors nor that his methods should be studied and mastered by everyone.

Although today Stanislavski's reputation rests largely on his contributions to actors' training, he was in his own time considered an innovative director. During the early years of the Moscow Art Theatre, Stanislavski worked in a rather autocratic fashion, planning each detail of his actors' vocal inflections, gestures, movements, and so on. But as his interest in the problems of the actor grew, and as his actors became more skillful, he abandoned his dogmatic approach and became an interpreter and helper to the actors. His ideal became for the director and the actors to grow together in their understanding of the play; therefore, he no longer appeared at rehearsals with a detailed production book containing minute directions for the actors. Only after the group had grasped the psychology of the roles and the complex interrelationships (often a three-month process) did the actors begin to work on the stage. Beginning with very small units in the play and moving gradually to acts and finally to the whole play, the actors and the director built a performance, a process often requiring six months or longer.

It was probably this careful attention to psychological detail that permitted Stanislavski's company to succeed with the plays of Anton Chekhov (see p. 351) where others before had failed. On the other hand, it should be clear that such rehearsal procedures are seldom possible in commercial theatres.

Influence. What began in 1898 as an experiment in external Realism and was by 1906 an experiment in psychological Realism had become an established tradition in Russia by the time of the Russian Revolution (1917). Because a number of Russians trained in "the system" left their country after the revolution, the teachings of Stanislavski came to the attention of the outside world. Mikhail Chekhov and

Vera Kommissarzhevskaya worked in Europe and the United States and brought their own versions of "the system" with them. Richard Boleslavsky and Maria Ouspenskaya came to the United States and led the American Laboratory Theatre, where they had as students Harold Clurman, Lee Strasberg, and Stella Adler, founders of the Group Theatre, America's major propagators of Stanislavski's system of actor training (although by their time somewhat altered and renamed the "Method"). (See p. 361.)

Characteristics of Realistic and Naturalistic Theatre

Physical Theatre

Theatres that were built for Realistic plays or those remodeled to improve their spaces for Realistic productions tended to be intimate proscenium houses without apron or proscenium doors. Because the scenic requirements were relatively simple, few provided elaborate machinery for shifting scenery. The best seats were in the orchestra. The auditoriums often abandoned box, pit, and gallery arrange-

FIGURE 14.15 Theatres for Realism. The Madison Square Theatre in 1884, on the verge of American Realism. It still has boxes and gas light, but the audience is in semi-darkness; realistic lighting effects are being attempted; and the proscenium arch makes a well-defined stage picture despite the vestigial forestage. Slightly later Realistic theatres would go to continental seating and a darkened auditorium.

ments in favor of some modification of Wagner's seating plan. The audiences consisted primarily of the middle classes, perhaps because it was most often their problems that were being addressed. The availability of electricity for theatrical lighting after the 1880s had two major results. It made the control and therefore the artistic manipulation of lighting possible, and it extended the life expectancy of theatre buildings by reducing the number of theatre fires, a plague of theatres during the first half of the century.

Production Practices

As staged, Realistic and Naturalistic plays shared many traits. Both styles set their plays in the contemporary world; both included numerous details; both relied on three-dimensional objects rather than their painted representations; and both adopted conventions of acting that focused the actors' attention onstage and discouraged them from moving in front of the arch or openly acknowledging the audience (which now sat in a darkened auditorium). Both abandoned wing-and-drop scenery in favor of a *box set,* a stage "room" built of flats but with one wall missing so that the audience could look through it (Antoine's "fourth wall").

Although agreeing on these basic conventions, the two styles often looked quite different onstage, mostly because their dramatic subjects and characters differed. The Realists, who treated problems of the middle class, set their plays in well-appointed living rooms with standard furnishings (e.g., lamps, ashtrays, portraits) and costumed their characters as the prosperous people they were. The Naturalists, dealing with the problems of the underclass, set their plays in factories and bars and costumed their characters in the clothes of poverty.

Plays and Playwrights

Realism in the drama began tentatively and cautiously. Although French writers like Scribe presaged Realism, it was the Norwegian Henrik Ibsen (1828–1906) who launched Realism as a major artistic movement.

Ibsen. With plays like *A Doll's House* (1879), Ibsen broke with the sentimentalized "problem plays" of earlier days and assumed his controversial role as the attacker of society's values. Structurally, his plays were fairly traditional: They told a story and moved logically from event to event, just as well-made plays had done for years. But their content was shocking: When individuals came into conflict with society, they were no longer assumed to be guilty and society blameless. Indeed, social customs and traditional morality were exposed by Ibsen as a tangle of inconsistencies and irrelevancies. Questions like the proper role of women, the ethics of euthanasia, the morality of business and war, and the economics of religion formed the basis of serious probings into social behavior. Theatrical producers throughout the world who believed that drama should be involved in the social issues of the day applauded the Norwegian dramatist, and soon other artists began to translate, produce, and, later, emulate his plays.

Ibsen's plays became a worldwide phenomenon. Here, *Neela,* based on *A Doll's House*
and Ingmar Bergman's adaptation of it, in India,
with Swatilekha and Rudraprasad Sengupta.
*Courtesy of Farley Richmond and Nandika
Theatre of Calcutta.*

Shaw. In England, George Bernard Shaw (1856–1950) became one of Ibsen's
most vocal and influential supporters. A prolific writer and a (Fabian) socialist,
Shaw delighted in puncturing time-honored assumptions about human behavior
and exposing various forms of social posturing. In an early play, *Arms and the
Man* (1894), he spoofed romantic notions of love and war and satirized the then-
popular comic form, the well-made play. Later, he turned to consider contemporary social situations in plays like *Major Barbara* (1905). Unlike many Realists,
Shaw always retained his sense of humor; he almost always wrote comedies, and
their popularity did much to ensure the final acceptance of Realistic drama in England before the close of World War I.

Chekhov. In Russia, Realism took a different form. Anton Chekhov (1860–1904)
scored his first success in 1898 when *The Seagull* was produced at the Moscow Art
Theatre. Chekhov's plays differed from those of Ibsen and Shaw in their tendency
toward poetic expression and symbolic meanings. Chekhov's manipulation of language, with careful rhythms, measured pauses, deliberate banalities, and artful rep-
etitions, produced a sense of reality based on compelling psychological truths as
well as a degree of music and allusion uncommon in prose dramas. His incorpora-
tion of symbols into the texts (often the plays' titles) extended the plays' significance beyond the lives of the central characters. In some ways, he foretold the
Russian Revolution by depicting the isolation of the aristocracy and its inevitable
extinction. In another sense, he portrayed the loneliness and the comic desperation

of people who continue to hope while living in a hopeless situation, who persist in believing that help will come when none, in fact, is to be had.

Naturalistic Playwrights.   Émile Zola (1849–1912), although a playwright, is better known today for his novels and his essays promoting Naturalism. He called for "living characters taken from real life," who spoke everyday language and offered "a material reproduction of life"; he called for playwrights who scientifically analyzed and faithfully reported the social problems of the world with a view to their correction.

Among the most successful playwrights in the Naturalistic style were August Strindberg (1849–1912), Gerhart Hauptmann (1862–1946), and Maxim Gorky (1868–1936). Strindberg's *Miss Julie* (1888) shows two complex characters, an aristocratic woman and her male servant, who are locked in a sexual battle of wills and whose actions derive from their heredity, their environment, and their class-conscious society. Hauptmann's *The Weavers* (1892) uses a group protagonist to show the devastation that comes to already impoverished workers when industrialization threatens their way of life. Gorky's *The Lower Depths* (1902), by depicting the seemingly hopeless lives of people living in a flophouse, explores whether religion or political reform offers the best chance for change.

COMMERCIAL THEATRE AND SOME ALTERNATIVES IN THE UNITED STATES (1900–1960)

Commercial theatre in the United States was a big business by 1900. It continued to be the dominant type throughout the period (1900–1960), easily adapting Realism to its needs as Realism became popular. Even when reactions were made against commercial theatre in the form of alternative theatres (see pp. 359–362), plays, actors, and the standards of the art came from the commercial theatre. By and large, playwrights who began in some alternative to the commercial theatre found their real success in, and wrote their best plays for, the commercial industry.

Broadway

Broadway boomed early in the twentieth century. At the end of World War I (1918), there were two or three hundred productions a year. Costs of production were reasonable (as low as $2000 for a small show, rarely more than $10,000). Ticket prices were modest—for about $3.00, a patron could have the best seat in a Broadway house. Tourists joined New Yorkers in flocking to Broadway, whose growing audiences early in the century encouraged the building of several new theatres, usually featuring a proscenium arch.

This theatre's vitality, including the large number of new plays produced, included many plays that were trivial—and some that were downright awful. But many of the plays had long runs as producers tried to recover the costs of produc-

FIGURE 14.17
Commercialism in America.
The myth of "Broadway" is really the myth of commercialism—the centralization of American theatrical economics and operation.

tion and turn a profit. Long runs rather than rotating repertory were well established by the 1920s.

Trouble on Broadway

By the end of the 1930s, however, the vigorous commercial theatre of the 1920s was in trouble. Despite occasional bright spots, Broadway's commercial theatre continued to decline through World War II and beyond. In 1930–1931, there were 187 new productions; in 1940–1941, there were only 60; in 1950–1951, only 48. Increasingly, theatres were abandoned, torn down, or converted to movie houses or "girlie shows." Many others were dark (closed) as often as they were open.

Several causes may be given for this decline of the commercial theatre during the second quarter of the twentieth century. The Depression (the 1930s) hit theatre hard. Not only was money scarce, but also new forms of entertainment began to compete with theatre for the public's entertainment dollars, especially after sound film (1927) proved popular. As spectator sports and movies demanded a bigger share of the entertainment dollar, theatrical unions grew strong enough to demand higher wages—from a theatre less able to pay them. Soon thereafter, the price of land in downtown Manhattan soared, making theatre buildings extremely expensive to rent or to buy. Fire regulations grew more strict, and the cost of remodeling a building to meet the new codes went up. As the cost of producing plays escalated, so did ticket prices; therefore, some former patrons found themselves priced out of the theatre. And just when it appeared that things could not get worse, television (1948) became an important national entertainment. Clearly the commercial theatre was in trouble, and its death was regularly—if inaccurately—predicted.

The American Musical

Music has always been part of the theatre, and music was common in various forms of European and American theatre through the end of the nineteenth century. However, from about World War I (c. 1915) on, the United States put so much energy into musical commercial theatre that many critics now speak of "the American musical" as a distinct form, even as America's only distinctive theatrical creation. This form, however, had its roots in European music and African American music, although the latter was for a long time minimized. Although the European base was undoubtedly broader, the impact of African American rhythms on theatrical music was very important.

Antecedents.   As the American musical developed after about 1900, it separated itself gradually from European operetta, on the one hand, and the musical revue, on the other. The operetta was a romantic, story-based musical with emphasis on the waltz, its antecedents the great Strauss creations. The musical revue was a nonstory mosaic of songs, dance numbers, comic skits, and vaudeville turns, epitomized by the "Ziegfeld Follies" produced by Florenz Ziegfeld from 1907 through 1931—opulent productions that "glorified the American girl" and featured such stars as Fanny Brice and Will Rogers. From its beginnings, then, the American musical had a double appeal in melodic music and spectacle; "spectacle" was often the female body, gorgeously costumed, often dancing—"Follies girls," chorus girls.

Composers.   Most of the top Broadway composers of the first half of the twentieth century wrote for operetta or revue (or both), even while (perhaps unconsciously) helping to create the new, story-based, integrated form that became American musical comedy. They worked with *lyricists* (writers of words to songs) and *librettists* (writers of the play or "book"). These composers included:

- Victor Herbert (1859–1924), *Babes in Toyland,* 1903; *The Red Mill,* 1905; *Naughty Marietta,* 1910 (operettas)
- Jerome Kern (1885–1945), *Oh, Boy!,* 1917; *Sally,* 1920; *Show Boat,* 1927
- Sigmund Romberg (1887–1951), *Blossom Time,* 1921; *The Student Prince,* 1924; *The Desert Song,* 1926
- Irving Berlin (1888–1989), *Music Box Revue,* 1921; *Annie Get Your Gun,* 1946; *Call Me Madam,* 1950
- Cole Porter (1891–1964), *Anything Goes,* 1934; *Red, Hot and Blue!,* 1936; *Kiss Me, Kate,* 1948
- George Gershwin (1898–1937), *Lady, Be Good,* 1924; *Strike Up the Band,* 1930; *Of Thee I Sing,* 1931 (first Pulitzer Prize for a musical); *Porgy and Bess,* 1935
- Richard Rodgers (1902–1979), *Garrick Gaieties,* 1925, 1926; *On Your Toes,* 1936; *Pal Joey,* 1940; *Oklahoma!,* 1943; *Carousel,* 1945; *The Sound of Music,* 1959

FIGURE 14.18 The American Musical: A Theatre of Stars.
Ethel Merman became perhaps the greatest of musical comedy stars in the period when a star's name could fill a theatre. Here, she is seen in Cole Porter's *Anything Goes* in the 1934 Broadway production. *Corbis/Bettman-UPI.*

A slightly later group of composers (with their lyricists, librettists, and directors) brought the integrated story musical to its optimal form:

- Frederick Lowe (1901–1988), *Brigadoon,* 1947; *My Fair Lady,* 1956; *Camelot,* 1960

- Jule Styne (b. 1905), *Gypsy,* 1959; *Funny Girl,* 1964

- Leonard Bernstein (1918–1990), *On the Town,* 1944; *Candide,* 1956; *West Side Story,* 1957

Neither these composers' backgrounds nor their music was entirely "American," however. Herbert was born in Ireland, Romberg in Hungary, Berlin in Russia, Lowe in Germany, Styne in England. Their musical training was often European and classical, not American and popular—Gershwin with a private teacher; Romberg, Herbert, and Lowe in Europe; Kern at the New York College of Music and in Europe; Porter at Yale and Harvard. What distinguished their music as the century progressed, however, was the adoption of rhythms that were the rhythms of popular dance music. Such music had its roots in nineteenth-century black musical forms that, by 1900, had their own literature and their own artists and that were known throughout America. Probably popularized in theatrical types that were themselves patronizing to blacks (e.g., the minstrel show, blackface vaudeville acts, "coon singing"), this music—cakewalk, ragtime—was already in the American grain by the time the American musical was ready to begin its evolution. Over the next half-century, jazz, blues, and then rock were also welcomed. Such music's creators, however, were not adequately credited, and black composers rarely made it to Broadway. (Exceptions included Marion Cook and Eubie Blake).

This new American music was sung by new American characters. The characters of operetta had been stock European figures, usually with upper-class backgrounds (Romberg's *Student Prince* is typical); the characters of the new musical were untitled—although sometimes rich—and American.

Lyricists. Essential to such change were the lyricists who wrote the words to the songs and, sometimes, the scripts of the musicals. With increasing frequency, the top composers were associated with the same lyricists in musical after musical, and the lyricists clearly shaped the tone and often the style of the music. In no composer is this clearer than Richard Rodgers. Until 1940, his lyricist was the witty and inventive Lorenz Hart, and their musicals show Hart's unsentimental mind (*Pal Joey*). Rodgers later connected with Oscar Hammerstein II, and the musicals became more romantic, sometimes saccharine—*The Sound of Music,* for example. Hammerstein had had much the same effect on Jerome Kern, with whom he collaborated after 1925; the result was *Show Boat,* a more serious and sentimental musical than Kern's earlier work with others. George Gershwin, on the other hand, worked throughout his career with his brother Ira. Frederick Lowe had his greatest successes when teamed with Alan J. Lerner (*Brigadoon* and after). Cole Porter wrote his own lyrics.

Melody and Song. Both the operetta and the revue faded after the 1920s; the "book musical" (drama with music, but not operetta, first seen in the second decade of the twentieth century) took their place. Still usually frivolous and with songs often more stuck in than developed from the action, such musicals were meant as entertainments whose scripts were excuses for glorious melody. As a result, they produced many of the great songs of the American theatre. Jerome Kern, for example, poured out beautiful melodies seemingly endlessly; George Gershwin, in his short life, wrote many songs that became "standards." What is perhaps most significant about these composers is that they were primarily *song*-writers. Many of them wrote songs on order for a moment in a script ("song cue here!")— love songs, novelty songs, Southern songs, patter songs, "show-stoppers." These songs became part of the national cultural life at a time when many middle-class homes had a piano, and sheet music was sold at the five-and-dime. Songs were detached from the musicals and popularized via sheet music and radio, and they were sung and played in nightclubs and supper clubs—and in homes.

FIGURE 14.19   The American Musical: A Theatre of Spectacle and Song.
George Gershwin's 1935 *Porgy and Bess* remains an outstanding work whose songs were complex, melodic, and near-operatic. This is the 1952 Broadway revival with William Warfield. *Photo courtesy of Brown Brothers.*

The Integrated Musical.   Only gradually did a more serious dramatic purpose appear, foreshadowed in *Show Boat,* fully realized in *Pal Joey* and *Oklahoma!*. The movement thereafter—that is, after 1940—was toward a serious comedy with a happy ending, usually centered on romantic love, mostly dealing with contemporary people, and having song arising from character and moving the plot along (integrated). The appearance of serious social content was sometimes important (*West Side Story*), but it was a rare musical that dealt so harshly with tough subject matter that it demanded a downbeat ending (*Gypsy*).

Gender and Race.   It should be noted that all the composers and lyricists named above were white men; so were most musical producers and directors. (A few white women—Dorothy Fields, Betty Comden—were notable lyricists; Mary Rodgers was a composer.) Many of the composers and lyricists were also European immigrants or children of immigrants; most revered European culture but were caught up in American commercial culture. Their assumptions were reflected in the musicals, which, until at least the 1970s, were mostly about a white America obsessed with romantic love and material success. The "glorification of the American girl" was a very white-male undertaking.

Mostly invisible but essential to the music were black musicians of both sexes. Although individual white composers often acknowledged a debt to African American music, the industry did not, and some black musicians resented such cooptings as Gershwin's *Porgy and Bess*—a white's version of Southern black life, using the white's version of black music. Yet, Gershwin's work is now an American classic, and one that has provided great roles for black musical performers. Since the 1970s, the imbalance has somewhat corrected itself.

Plays and Playwrights

Perhaps by 1900 but certainly by the end of World War I (1918), Realism (somewhat trivialized and popularized) was widely accepted in the commercial theatres of France, England, and the United States. By the 1920s, the Parisian boulevard theatres regularly played serious plays treating social problems, and audiences no longer found them controversial. Commercial theatres in London found audiences ready to accept both Ibsen and Shaw as well as sophisticated plays (both serious and comic) by authors like Noel Coward (1899–1973). In the United States, comedies and musicals dominated the commercial houses, but playwrights of serious drama earned international reputations, the first American playwrights to do so.

Comedies. During Broadway's boom years before the Depression, theatre thrived with large-cast plays filled with wisecracking characters. Such plays included *You Can't Take It With You,* a comedy of family life, by George S. Kaufman (1889–1961) and Moss Hart (1904–1961). As the costs of production rose, however, the sizes of casts shrank—and with them some of the comic exuberance.

Serious Plays. Few serious plays were commercially successful on Broadway, and even many of these have faded with the years. Lillian Hellman (1905–1984) and Thornton Wilder (1897–1975) are still regularly produced. Lorraine Hansberry's *A Raisin in the Sun* (1959) remains an important work. But probably only three playwrights active before 1960 retain a prominent place in today's theatre: O'Neill, Williams, and Miller.

Eugene O'Neill (1888–1953), son of the actor James O'Neill, became America's first internationally acclaimed playwright. Nurtured by alternative theatres, O'Neill showed that significant serious drama could find an audience and compete with commercial theatre. A writer not afraid to experiment with new ideas and new forms, O'Neill wrote plays that set several new directions for later writers to follow (*The Great God Brown,* 1926; *Desire Under the Elms,* 1924; *Strange Interlude,* 1928). In *Long Day's Journey Into Night* (1956) he offered a searing autobiographical drama of his own family, in which the mother's drug addiction and the father's weakness shaped the lives of the sons. Although flawed, O'Neill's plays remain significant because of the theatricality of his visions and the intensity of his passion. O'Neill's plays are still regularly read and occasionally produced, usually in regional theatres.

Tennessee Williams (1914–1983) won the Drama Critics Circle Award for his first major Broadway production, *The Glass Menagerie* (1945), a wistful memory play vaguely reminiscent of the impressionists and Chekhov. *A Streetcar Named Desire* (1947) won both the Pulitzer Prize and the Drama Critics Circle Award and established Williams as a major American playwright. The same

FIGURE 14.20
American Tragedy:
Arthur Miller.
Death of a Salesman,
Miller's finest play. *Directed
by Nigel Maister at the
University of Rochester
International Theatre
Program, Todd Theatre.
Joe Gawlowicz photo.*

production established Elia Kazan as a major American director, and Selective (or simplified) Realism as a major style among American designers.

Arthur Miller (b. 1915) is, like Williams, a Realist of sorts, but whereas Williams's work tended toward the dreamlike and impressionistic, Miller's moved in harsher, more expressionistic ways. *All My Sons* (1947) told of an American businessman who knowingly sold inferior products to the American military in order to turn a profit. In *Death of a Salesman* (1949), realistic scenes are interspersed with scenes remembered by the disordered protagonist, Willy Loman. *Death of a Salesman,* as directed by Elia Kazan and designed by a major American designer, Jo Mielziner, won both a Pulitzer Prize and the Drama Critics Circle Award and further promoted the conventions of American Realism.

Alternatives to Broadway

As commercial American producing became more expensive, producers understandably became more cautious. Good business practice recommended minimizing risk; in the theatre, this meant trying to find something that would be sure to please audiences. Entertainment, it was believed, sold better than art. Commercial theatre thus spent more and more money on fewer and fewer productions and longer and longer runs.

Others, however, tried to find ways to stress art instead of business. They created new producing arrangements that would allow higher risk, usually by cutting costs. For example, the United States had its belated version of the independent theatre movement: between about 1915 and 1925, a number of self-styled "little theatres" opened all across the country; the most famous began in Provincetown,

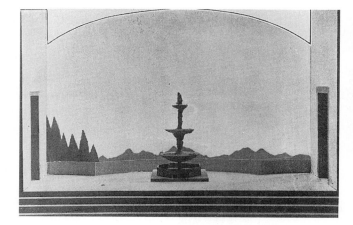

FIGURE 14.21
Alternatives to Broadway.
The New Stagecraft movement that began in 1915 coincided with the first wave of American avant-gardism, the Art Theatre Movement. This early example of the New Stagecraft, by Sam Hume, is noteworthy for the simplicity and nonrealistic lack of detail.

Massachusetts, and moved to New York as the Provincetown Players. Amateur, idealistic, and noncommercial, the little theatres did not last. Some closed, and many settled into being community theatres. Yet they had influence both on non-commercial producers and on the educational theatre.

Other alternatives were more like Broadway and often overlapped Broadway, sharing audiences, actors, directors, and other artists. The most important of these were, in New York, the Theatre Guild, the Group Theatre, and Off-Broadway; and, beyond New York, the Federal Theatre Project and the regional theatre movement.

The Theatre Guild

Founded in 1919, the Theatre Guild was the earliest and most dynamic new pro-ducing organization of the 1920s. It attacked the provincialism of American theatre by staging a series of foreign works by important (and controversial) playwrights like Ibsen and Shaw. It supported as well the works of those American playwrights whose plays treated serious social issues, among them Eugene O'Neill.

Between 1926 and 1928, the Theatre Guild produced fourteen plays whose success almost persuaded Broadway that there was an audience for serious American drama. By the Depression, however, the Guild's influence waned. As its own finances became more precarious, it moved closer to the practices of other commercial producers in an attempt to improve its balance sheet. By 1940, the Theatre Guild was almost indistinguishable from those commercial Broadway producers against which it had originally rebelled.

The Group Theatre

Founded in 1931, the Group Theatre was at first a militant voice for non- or anti-commercial theatre in New York. Through its repertory it focused attention on various social causes, especially those related to poverty and oppression. It also popularized an American version of Stanislavski's acting techniques. Called the *Method,* this American style came to dominate both stage and film. (See pp. 133–135.)

In production, the Group favored a kind of Realism, one based more on psychological truth than on detailed settings. Perhaps as a result, the Group helped popularize a style of design called Simplified (or selective) Realism, a style also associated with American design. Financial and political problems caused the Group Theatre to fade before the end of World War II.

The Federal Theatre Project (FTP)

Launched in 1935, the FTP was a program of the federal government aimed at aiding theatre artists who had been thrown out of work by the Depression. Part of the program's excitement came from its national character (units were established in almost every state); part came from its commitment to cultural diversity (there were, for example, both Jewish and black theatre companies); and part came from its innovative artistic practices. In New York, for example, the first *living newspaper* in the United States premiered. A kind of staged documentary, living newspapers soon spread throughout the country, dramatizing society's most pressing problems: housing, farm policies, venereal disease, war. During an anticommunist government probe, however, living newspapers were denounced as communist plots. In 1939 the government failed to appropriate money for the FTP, and so ended the nation's first far-reaching experiment in support of the arts. Before its demise, however, the FTP introduced a number of major new artists and theatres, among them Orson Welles (1915–1985).

The Regional Theatre Movement

This movement is usually dated from 1947, when Margo Jones opened a professional theatre in Dallas, Texas. Her goal was not only to decentralize the theatre (to bring professional productions to the heartlands of America) but also to encourage the production of original and classical plays. (She nurtured the talent of Tennessee Williams, for example.) Before Jones's death in 1955 there were professional theatres in Washington, D.C.; Houston, Texas; and Milwaukee, Wisconsin. With the 1960s came a surge of such theatres in places like Minneapolis, Los Angeles, Baltimore, New Haven, and Louisville. In a departure from current New York practices, some of these theatres built spaces without proscenia, preferring theatres in the round (e.g., Dallas and Washington, D.C.) or thrust stages (e.g., Minneapolis).

The Off-Broadway Movement

This movement is usually said to have begun in 1952, when Tennessee Williams's *Summer and Smoke* (first produced by Margo Jones in Dallas) earned critical acclaim in a production at Circle in the Square—the first major hit in a theatre located below Forty-second Street in thirty years. From then through the 1960s,

Off-Broadway served as a showcase for new talent and for plays whose experimental style or controversial subjects made them unsuitable for the big business of Broadway. Off-Broadway, however, finally succumbed to the pressures of commercialism, and today it is little more than a tryout space for Broadway.

THE PERIOD IN THE MODERN REPERTORY

It is significant that virtually the only plays from 1750–1850 that are still performed widely in the United States are the laughing comedies of Sheridan and Goldsmith, which are staples of universities and regional theatres. Forms enormously popular at the time—melodrama, sentimental comedy, and the well-made play—might as well never have been written for all the impact they have on current production. This situation may be temporary, the result of twentieth-century parochialism, not the least in acting style. Individual European countries keep a few serious dramatists of the period in their repertories (e.g., Goethe and Schiller in Germany).

Otherwise, the plays of Realism, Naturalism, and commercial realism are the backbone of many repertories. Ibsen is still staged, not least because he wrote good roles for women; Strindberg, Chekhov, Shaw, and Coward are often seen. Eugene O'Neill is not so often staged as his reputation would seem to recommend, but *Long Day's Journey Into Night* is still done; some of the earlier plays now seem dated and overdone. Miller and Williams are, of course, staples, especially Williams.

A number of works from the commercial theatre of two generations ago are now the big titles in American high schools: e.g., *You Can't Take It With You* and the musicals of Rodgers and Hammerstein. They share the common traits of no bad language, no overt sex, and no controversial subject matter—until 1960, key elements of commercial realism.

CURRENT ISSUES

The era of Realism is also the era of motion pictures, and then of television. Realism, shorn of its reforming zeal, became a mainstream style after 1900; within a decade, crude movie theatres were beginning to draw away some of the audience. By 1915, multi-reel feature films were being shown; by the 1920s, "picture palaces" and neighborhood movie houses had replaced many theatres. Audiences—including a new audience of children—filled the new structures, only to leave them for private houses when television took hold in the 1950s.

Some critics look at television and movies and see a "dumbing down" of both audience and the thing they look at, and some see the dumbing down as progressive. It was common in the 1930s, for example, for Hollywood cynics to proclaim that movies were made for fourteen-year-olds; cynics in television now contend that sitcoms and soap operas are made for ten-year-olds. In the early 1960s, a government official called television "a vast wasteland." Recent critics attack both

FIGURE 14.22 "A Vast Wasteland."
Although Newton Minnow was talking about television, his expression, "a vast wasteland," might equally well have applied to most popular theatre of the last century and a half. Violence and spectacle dominated the best-loved melodramas, as the one shown here amply demonstrates. Indeed, much of popular theatre can be thought of as a kind of television without the commercials.

movies and television for violence and sex. Few of even Hollywood's staunchest supporters would suggest that intellect and art are its main products.

However, is this a dumbing down, or is it a change in medium, or is something else going on? The changes in medium, for example, have meant a change in distribution: A hit play may be seen by two million people over several years, a hit movie twenty million over a couple of months, a hit television show thirty million in an hour. Is it this increase in the size of the audience that explains the increased sensationalism, the oversimplification (as some people see it) of ideas, the lack (as some people see it) of daring? Or is it some change in the makeup of the audience—an increase in the number of children, for example?

Does massification imply an inevitable dumbing down? Is there some magic number of audience size, beyond which lower taste, or lower intelligence, or dulled perception must be expected?

Opponents of this view would point to the theatre of 1900 and ask what about it showed either good taste or intellect. It was, they say, a theatre mostly of sensation and spectacle, not all that different from today's television. Where did the dumbing down occur? If there has been a dumbing down, they say, it started with the decline of Neoclassicism; the dumbing down, they would contend, has come not from the new media of movies and television, but from democratization, urbanization, and industrialization, which brought a new class into the theatres.

What is the relationship between massification (or democratization) and theatre? Is dumbing down inescapable as an audience base is expanded? If so, why? Or if not, why do critics observe what they think are a parallel dumbing down and massification since 1900?

KEY TERMS

Check your understanding against this list. Brief definitions are in the Glossary; page references there will direct you to appropriate pages. (Persons are page-referenced in the Index.)

actor-manager	musical
box, pit, and gallery	Naturalism
breeches role	Realism
continental seating	Romanticism
formal acting	Socialist Realism
fourth wall (realism)	starring system
laughing comedy	stock company
little theatre (movement)	unified work of art
long run	well-made play
master artwork/master artist	wing-and-drop
melodrama	

Reactions Against Realism: The Avant Garde, 1890s-1960s

OBJECTIVES

When you have completed this chapter, you should be able to:

- Explain why Realism inspired opposition, and what theatrical forms or "isms" that opposition took

- Explain why commercialism inspired opposition, and what forms the opposition took

- Name the major theatrical theorists of the twentieth century and discuss their theories and the kinds of theatre they created

- Define avant gardism and show why it appeared c. 1890–1975

Background

The division that had opened between legitimate and popular-commercial theatres in the eighteenth century became, in the nineteenth, something rather different. The old theatre monopolies finally withered away, and the formerly illegitimate theatres gained status and position. The surviving monopoly theatres, especially the Comédie Française, kept a special status as bearers of a tradition important to the national culture, but all theatres after c. 1860 were in effect competing for the same audience. In the United States, which had never had an official or national theatre, the commercial theatre *was* the theatre.

The audience was middle and lower class. Cities by late in the nineteenth century were big, crowded, noisy; each nation had a cultural capital—New York, London, Paris, Berlin—that set the style and defined sophistication for the nation. The commercial theatre was part of this culture-selling, both through extensive touring networks and through new magazines and newspapers in which theatre people were arbiters of fashion, food, ideas, and language.

However, a new split opened with the coming of the independent theatres of the late nineteenth century. Thereafter, anticommercial (or *independent,* or *art*) theatres existed in opposition to the commercial and its role in the culture. They made many significant contributions, despite usually short lives—contributions (e.g., Realism) that the commercial theatre cheerfully coopted when it was clear they would enhance sales, visibility, or critical esteem.

The anticommercial movements are usually called the "avant garde," literally, the vanguard—that which is in advance of a main body. In theatre, they have mostly worked in opposition to the commercial *style,* as well as its subjects and methods. No commercial style has so inspired the avant garde as Realism has—despite the fact that Realism had itself been the style of the independent theatres.

Even before Realism became the mainstream style in Europe and America, its limitations became apparent. Four questions were the focus of avant-garde concern:

1. *How can Realistic drama be kept interesting?*

Before Realism, most serious dramatists had depicted characters who were considerably removed from everyday experience—princes, kings, demigods—who participated in events that were out of the ordinary: a war, a national crisis, a cosmic struggle. The plays were set in faraway times and places, environments that were, in themselves, often mysterious and compelling. When confronting a crisis, these exalted characters burst into passages of extreme lyricism in which the full resources of the language (rhythm, rhyme, and metaphor) were marshaled to produce heights of emotional intensity.

But Realistic drama, by definition, portrayed ordinary people involved in mundane situations. Their language necessarily resembled everyday conversation and their clothing reflected their middle- or lower-class status. What then, made them interesting? Audience pleasure seemed to depend largely on the factor of *recognition* alone. Although this new factor is a very potent one, it was being asked to carry the entire weight of provoking and maintaining interest, a burden that proved too heavy for many dramas.

FIGURE 15.1 Anti-Industrialism.
Industrialization and mass production offended many people in the middle class, who saw it as "dehumanizing" and "deadening." Activists began to urge a reform or even rejection of the factory system; at the same time, others were urging a new kind of art.

2. *How can Realistic drama be made significant?*

Traditionally, serious playwrights depicted serious actions that were of consequence to a large range of people—a nation or even a world. But Realistic dramas typically dealt with men and women as they lived out rather humdrum lives. If no more was at stake than the happiness of a single individual or a small family, who beyond their immediate friends would find it significant?

Some Realistic dramatists increased the significance of their plays' actions by having the protagonist represent something bigger. Willy Loman in *Death of a Salesman,* for example, was made to stand for all working men. Such a solution, however, pulled against the very philosophical assumptions on which Realism was based. Perhaps more seriously, abstractions are often undramatic. Poetry and the novel, where the reader can return time and again to study and consider the text, are usually better media for abstractions and symbolizations than are plays, where the living presence of the actors encourages specificity and where the basis of the form is action rather than idea or word.

3. *What is the role of the audience in a Realistic theatre?*

Even though the stage in Realistic drama was a close reproduction of the real world and the actors were a replication of everyday people, the separation of the audience from the dramatic action in "fourth-wall Realism" was greater than ever. The conventions of the style required the audience to sit in a darkened auditorium and to watch silently as a separate world unfolded behind the proscenium arch. The actors, for their part, behaved as if the audience were not there, turning their backs and mumbling lines in an attempt to reproduce the inarticulateness of everyday conversation. The result was a world on the stage quite separate from the real world where the audience sat. It is ironic that Realistic drama and staging, which had seemed to bring the world of the stage closer to that of the audience, ended by separating them to a degree unparalleled in the history of the theatre.

4. *How can the theatrical event be kept probable (or believable)?*

All playwrights, of course, must construct plays that are probable, or believable, if they are to capture the interest and the commitment of an audience. But only the Realist additionally required that the world in the play resemble, on a one-to-one basis, the world outside: The theatrical scenery was to be a photographic likeness of the outside world, and the actors were to be the embodiment of everyday people. To produce the familiar and to make it believable *and* dramatic proved too demanding a chore for many Realistic playwrights.

Because of these problems, a variety of alternatives to Realistic plays and staging were being proposed and tested by the 1890s. The years between 1890 and 1960 saw a proliferation of *isms:* Neoromanticism, Formalism, Symbolism, Impressionism, Expressionism, Constructivism, Futurism, Absurdism, and so on. Each strove to address and solve one or more of the problems inherent in Realism. As each developed, grew, and declined, the mainstream of Realism shifted slightly to accommodate various attributes of the competing styles. As a result, although Realism remained the mainstream of theatre from about 1900 through 1960, it shifted perceptibly throughout that period as it incorporated first one and then another new approach to playwriting or staging.

IMPRESSIONISM

Impressionism (fl. 1890s) was a style that sought to capture and reproduce the fleeting moments of awareness that were believed to constitute the essence of human existence. By reproducing faithfully these fleeting glimpses, art could provide insights into the truth that lay underneath the external world. Probably the playwright who wrote most successfully in the style was Maurice Maeterlinck (1862–1949). In short plays like *The Intruder* (1890), Maeterlinck presented a world far removed from reality. Subjectivity permeates the plays, which are typically moody and mysterious, hinting at a life controlled by unseen and inexplicable forces. The actions seem hazy, distant, out of focus; indeed, in the theatre, the plays were often played behind gauzes (*scrims*) or clouds of fog, and they moved between patches of light, dark, and shadow.

For Impressionists like Maeterlinck, a play aimed to convey intuitions about a truth more profound than the tangible, objective, external world of the Realists. Through symbols, it alluded to a significance beyond the immediate, and through its language and stories it aspired to arouse interest by its exoticism. Some of its techniques, however, were adopted by Realists like Ibsen (in his later plays), Chekhov, and Tennessee Williams.

FIGURE 15.2   Impressionism. Maurice Maeterlinck was probably the most famous of the Impressionists. His *The Blue Bird* is shown here; among its departures from Realism are the shimmering, dreamlike quality of the setting, the lack of detail, and such unrealistic elements as the long fingernails, the remarkable costume, center, and the symmetrical construction.

SYMBOLISM

The Impressionists were closely allied with the *symbolists,* of whom the most famous were the designer-theorists Adolphe Appia (1862–1928) and Gordon Craig (1872–1966).

Appia

Appia believed that artistic unity was the fundamental goal of theatrical production and that lighting was the element best able to fuse all other elements into an artistic whole. Like music, light was capable of continual change to reflect shifting moods and emotions within the play. Like music, too, light could be orchestrated by variations in its direction, intensity, and color to produce a rhythm designed to underscore the dramatic action. Because he found an aesthetic contradiction between the three-dimensional actor and a two-dimensional floor set at right angles to two-dimensional painted scenes, Appia gave the stage floor and scenery mass. He solved the problem in part by devising three-dimensional settings composed of steps, ramps, and platforms, among which the living actor could comfortably move.

Craig

Like Appia, Craig opposed scenic illusion and favored instead a simple visual statement that eliminated unessential details and avoided photographic reproduction. His emphasis was on the manipulation of line and mass to achieve, first, a unity of design and, ultimately, a unity for the total production. Although Craig

FIGURE 15.3
Symbolism.
Gordon Craig, one of whose designs is shown here, was an idealist who sought unity in the manipulation of mass, light, and shadow rather than in reproduction of surface reality.

placed less emphasis on the importance of the actor and the text than Appia, they agreed on the importance of the visual elements of the production. Perhaps it would not be an injustice to designate Appia as the formulator of the theories that Craig later popularized. The theories of Appia and Craig gained a secure foothold in theatrical practice following World War I.

EXPRESSIONISM

Whereas Impressionism sought to present echoes of a transitory and mysterious truth, *Expressionism* (fl. 1910–1930s) usually focused on political and social questions. If Impressionism produced a dreamlike vision, Expressionism created a stage world close to nightmare. The plays were often didactic and cautioned the world against impending cataclysms caused by uncontrolled industrialism, rampant impersonalization, and the modern industrial state. Seldom did the plays tell a simple story; more often, they developed as episodic examinations or demonstrations of a central thesis. They customarily unfolded in a world of bizarre and garish colors, jagged angles, and oddly proportioned objects (perhaps because they were often told through the mind of the protagonist, whose mental vision was distorted). Actors, often dressed identically, moved in mechanical or puppet-like ways and often spoke in disconnected or telegraphic conversations. They bore names of types rather than people: The Mother, The Son, The Cipher, and so on. Conventional ideas of time and space collapsed; in their place were elastic units where years could fly by as seconds crept and adjacent objects appeared as if seen through the opposite ends of a telescope.

FIGURE 15.4
Expressionism.
If Impressionism resembles a dream, Expressionism resembles a nightmare, with humanity trapped by forces beyond its control. Here, Toller's *Man and the Masses.*

Expressionism as a movement was most developed in Germany. Its two leading playwrights were Georg Kaiser (1878–1945), author of *From Morn to Midnight* (1916), and Ernst Toller (1893–1939), whose best-known work is *Man and the Masses* (1921).

Expressionism has been influential for three reasons:

- First, many of the techniques were adapted and used by the growing film industry (*The Cabinet of Doctor Caligari*).

- Second, some Expressionistic techniques were adopted by important playwrights in the Realistic mainstream, notably (in the United States) Eugene O'Neill and Arthur Miller.

- Third, German Expressionism was an early influence on Erwin Piscator's and Bertolt Brecht's "epic theatre" (see pp. 374–376).

CONSTRUCTIVISM

In Russia, the practices of Vsevolod Myerhold (1874–c. 1940) paralleled those of the German Expressionists. Although early in his career Myerhold directed experimental works for Stanislavski, during the 1920s he devoted himself to developing

FIGURE 15.5   Constructivism.
Associated with Vsevolod Myerhold (whose production is seen here), Constructivism is a visual style in which settings are conceived as machines on which actors can work; it also tends to reveal rather than to hide its own physical structure. For Myerhold as director, Constructivism had more to do with a mechanistic theory of acting.

a theatrical art suitable for a machine age. He relied on two major techniques: *biomechanics* and *constructivism*. *Biomechanics* was a training system and performance style for actors based on an industrial theory of work: They were to be well-trained "machines" for carrying out the assignments given them, and so they needed rigorous physical training in ballet, gymnastics, and circus techniques. *Constructivism* was a theory of visual art in which scenery did not attempt to represent any particular place but provided a "machine" on which actors could perform. In practice, sets designed for Myerhold were often elaborate combinations of platforms, steps, ramps, wheels, and trapezes. A goal of both biomechanics and constructivism was to retheatricalize the theatre.

ABSURDISM

Just after World War II, several new playwrights caused a temporary flurry of excitement. Not comprising a self-conscious movement, these playwrights were nonetheless grouped together and given the name *Absurdists* by a contemporary scholar, Martin Esslin. *Absurdism* (fl. 1940s and 1950s) was itself a blend of earlier abortive experiments of the French avant garde. With *Dadaism* (fl. 1920s), it shared an emphasis on life's meaninglessness and art's irrelevancy and a commitment to irrationality and nihilism as appropriate responses to life and living. With *Surrealism* (fl. 1920s), it viewed the source of insight as the subconscious mind. Most important, with *existentialism* (fl. 1930s and 1940s), it sought an answer to the plaguing question: What does it mean to exist and to be? Jean-Paul Sartre (1905–1980), a philosopher turned playwright (*No Exit*) and a major advocate of existentialism, sought to establish a code of life based on a consistent atheism, where the absence of moral laws left human beings adrift in a world without order or purpose: Each person must define his or her own value system and then act accordingly.

Absurdism stressed that the world was unreasonable, illogical, incongruous, and out of harmony. The word *absurd,* then, meant not *ridiculous* but *without meaning.* The Absurdists abandoned telling a story in favor of communicating an experience; they abandoned a dramatic unity based on causality and replaced it with one whose source, and indeed whose very presence, was not always clear.

The plays were often constructed as a circle (ending just where they began, after displaying a series of unrelated incidents) and as the intensification of a single event (ending just where they had begun but in the midst of more people or more objects). Usually, the puzzling quality of the plays came from the devaluation of language as a carrier of meaning: In the plays, *what happens* on stage often transcends and contradicts *what is said* there. Absurdists included Samuel Beckett (1906–1989), who won the Nobel Prize; Eugène Ionesco (b. 1912); and Edward Albee (b. 1928); they influenced later playwrights like Harold Pinter.

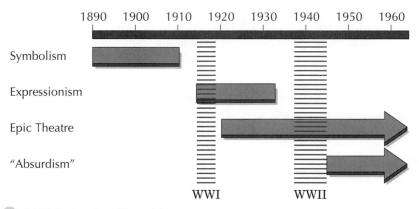

FIGURE 15.6   Time Line.
Impressionism and Symbolism predated World War I; Expressionism peaked between the world wars; Epic Theatre, growing out of Expressionism, began before and continued past World War II. Absurdism followed World War II.

BRECHT AND ARTAUD

Although all of the styles described here have had an impact on today's theatre, the theories and practices of Bertolt Brecht and Antonin Artaud have probably been more influential than others. These two theorists operated from quite different sets of assumptions about the nature of theatre and the purpose of art, but they shared a disdain for Realism. Although it may be a falsification, at least in part, it may be useful to regard Brecht as developing from the Expressionistic German traditions and Artaud from the Impressionistic and Surrealistic traditions of the French theatre. Together, their theories can help account for much experimentation during the 1960s and 1970s.

Bertolt Brecht and Epic Theatre

Bertolt Brecht (1898–1956) believed that theatre should educate *citizens* (participants in a political system) in how to bring about socially responsible change. He saw theatre as a way of making a controversial topic easier to consider. His commitment to a socially responsive theatre doubtless came, in part, from his being both Jewish and leftist at a time when Hitler was rising to power in Germany.

Traditional German theatres, whether those of Wagner or Saxe-Meiningen, sought an illusion that allowed the members of the audience to believe in and identify with the onstage actions. In such theatres, Brecht observed, audiences reached a state of self-oblivion: "Looking around, one discovers more or less motionless bodies in a curious state . . . they have their eyes open, but they don't look, they stare . . . they stare at the stage as if spellbound." As Brecht was a Marxist and viewed theatre as an instrument for change, he objected to a theatre that mesmerized its audience and made them passive. Brecht therefore strove to redefine the relationship among the theatre, its audience, and the society at large. He proposed that if he jarred audiences periodically out of their identification with the action, he would succeed in shaking their complacency and in forcing them to think about what they saw onstage. He sought, therefore, alternately to engage and

---

THINKING ABOUT THE AVANT GARDE

"The theatre is a humble materialistic enterprise which seeks to produce riches of the imagination, not the other way around."

—Charles Ludlam (1943–1987), avant-garde playwright and director.

Study the illustrations in this chapter. Compare them with those in Chapter 14. In what ways has the imagination been called on to reduce material riches in the avant-garde productions?

estrange his audiences, a technique he called *Verfremdungseffekt* (usually translated as the *alienation effect* or, simply, the *A-effect*).

Alienation

To achieve alienation required artists to work in new ways. Actors were encouraged to hold themselves distant from their roles by speaking the stage directions out loud during the rehearsal process, to think of their characters in the third person rather than in the first person, and to use the past tense rather than the present tense when talking of their work. Such procedures made an actor a *commentator* as well as an impersonator, an *evaluator* of the action as well as a demonstrator of it.

Brecht urged lighting designers to expose the instruments to remind the spectators that they were in a theatre and that the illumination was coming from a high-wattage lamp rather than from the sun. If a set was to represent a town, it should look like a town that had been built for the theatre; it should not be built with the goal of "fooling" the audience into accepting it as a real town.

Theatrical elements should be juxtaposed in unexpected ways so that each could make an independent contribution and comment on the ideas of the play. Thus, if the set was to make one point, the costumes should make a different one; a grisly story of war and atrocity might be set to a lively tune with a lilting melody; the seeming incongruity would force the audience to consider the apparent conflict of elements and to draw conclusions about the absurdity of war. This is the opposite of the unity demanded by Wagner, Appia, and Craig.

In short, Brecht proposed that each artist make an independent contribution to the production and to the didactic purpose of the script, and that each element be used not to create an atmosphere that encouraged the audience to identify with the action (as in traditional theatre) but to reinforce the didactic purpose of the drama.

Brecht was a playwright (e.g., *Mother Courage and Her Children* [1938]) as well as a theorist and a director. His plays typically consisted of a series of short episodes connected by songs, narratives, or signs. The purpose was to engage the interest and belief of the audience (within each episode) and then to break the spell by forcing the spectator to think about and evaluate the meaning and implications of the episodes (by manipulating various materials between them).

Epic Theatre

The complex of staging and playwriting used by Brecht came to be called *epic theatre. Epic* captured many of the qualities that Brecht prized: the mixing of narrative and dramatic episodes, the telescoping of time and place, and the spanning of years and countries (similar to epic poetry).

Although Brecht was not the first to use either these techniques or the term *epic* (Erwin Piscator, 1893–1966, had been active in the same kind of experimentation several years earlier), Brecht popularized the term and the practices through his own plays, his theoretical writings (particularly the "Little Organon for the Theatre," 1948), and his productions at the Berliner Ensemble, after 1954 East Germany's most prestigious theatre.

Antonin Artaud and the Theatre of Cruelty

Antonin Artaud (1895–1948) fit the Romantic stereotype of the misunderstood and tormented artist. Artaud was an influential theorist immediately following World War II; by the 1960s, he was virtually a cult hero in Europe and the United States.

Although Artaud was an actor, director, playwright, poet, and screenwriter, it was as a theorist that he made his greatest impact. *The Theatre and Its Double,* a compilation of Artaud's major essays, was published in France in 1938 but was not translated into English until the late 1950s. Because Artaud believed that important ideas came not from logical reasoning or rational thinking but from intuition, experience, and feelings, he developed his major ideas by means of images and metaphors. For this reason, many people have found him irrational. Nonetheless, Artaud's major points seem clear enough, particularly if the reader attends to the major metaphors that appear: the theatre as *plague,* as *double,* and as *cruelty.*

FIGURE 15.7 Theatre of Cruelty.
Peter Weiss's *The Persecution and Assassination of Marat as Performed by the Inmates of Charenton Under the Direction of the Marquis de Sade* ("*Marat/Sade*") was the basis of a landmark British production of the 1960s. Directed by Peter Brook, it was "theatre of cruelty" in its relentless assault on the audience, although some elements of the play that seem "cruel"—persecution, assassination, inmates, the Marquis de Sade—may not themselves be what Artaud meant. *Here, a performance of* Marat/Sade *at the University of South Carolina, directed by Richard Jennings.*

FIGURE 15.8 Postmodern Drama: Samuel Beckett.
First lumped among the "absurdists," Beckett is more accurately seen as a postmodernist and minimalist. These costume designs for his *Waiting for Godot* capture the essential natures of his principal characters, Vladimir and Estragon, who are both clowns and sufferers in a nonrealistic play beyond genre. *Designs by Martin Thaler.*

The Theatre as Plague

First, Artaud called for theatre to return to its rightful place as a great force in humanity, a force for putting people back in touch with the intensity of living. Comparing theatre to a plague, Artaud said, "It appears that by means of the plague, a gigantic abscess, as much moral as social, has been collectively drained, and that like the plague, the theatre has been created to drain abscesses collectively." He declared that theatre caused people to confront themselves honestly, letting fall their individual masks and confessing their social hypocrisies.

The Theatre and Its Double

Second, Western theatre had lost its magic and its vibrance and had become merely a pale imitation, a *double,* of the true theatre (that is, the Eastern theatre). In order to regain its power, the Western theatre must reject logical demonstrations and causal actions and instead seize and impel its spectators toward truth, forcing them to apprehend meaning through the whole of their bodies. To this end, Artaud proposed "a theatre in which violent physical images crush and hypnotize the sensibility . . . as by a whirlwind of higher forces."

The Rejection of Language

Third, Artaud wanted to remove the script from the center of his theatre, for he believed that words and grammar were insufficient carriers of meaning. Truth came instead from spiritual signs whose meaning emerged intuitively and "with enough violence to make useless any translation into logical discursive language." Artaud wished to substitute gestures, signs, symbols, rhythms, and sounds for ordinary language; he advocated "a superabundance of impression, each richer than the next." He was convinced that theatre was neither logical nor paraphrasable nor rational; it was intuitive, primitive, magical, and potentially powerful.

The Centrality of Audience

Fourth, the audience was central to the theatre. Artaud dismissed notions of art as a kind of personal therapy for the artist. Theatre was good only when it profoundly moved its audiences, when it returned them to the subconscious energies that lay under the veneer of civilization and civilized behavior. Whereas Brecht wished to cause an audience to *think* about a social or political issue, Artaud wanted to move an audience to *feel* or *experience* a spiritual awakening, to participate in something that might be called a *communion* (in its real sense of a *coming together*).

The Theatre of Cruelty

Fifth, Artaud called for a *theatre of cruelty,* a theatre that showed the "terrible and necessary cruelty which things can exercise against us. We are not free. And the sky can still fall on our heads. And the theatre has been created to teach us that first of all." Cruelty, then, was primarily psychic rather than physical.

To achieve his theatre of cruelty, Artaud developed a number of techniques seldom used in commercial productions. Because he wanted to bombard the senses with various stimuli in order to cause the whole organism (not merely the mind) to be moved, he experimented with ways of manipulating light and sound: In both, he adopted the abrupt, the discordant, the sudden, the shrill, the garish. Lights changed colors quickly, alternated intensity violently; sound was sudden, often amplified. Scenery was subservient to the other elements of production, with the audiences placed in an environment created by actors, lights, sound, and space (Artaud preferred barns and factories to conventional theatres). The actors were encouraged to use their bodies and their voices to provide scenery, sounds, and visual effects and not to be bound by notions of psychological realism and character analysis. Actors were to address the senses of the spectators, not merely their minds.

Artaud's theories, in many forms and with many distortions, were appropriated and applied after 1960 by theatre artists, makers of movies, and especially rock musicians. Whatever one may think of his pronouncements, it is clear that, although long in coming, their acceptance has been widespread.

THE AVANT GARDE IN THE MODERN REPERTORY

One of the facts of avant gardism is that it dates quickly. For this reason, very few avant-garde plays survive; instead, they do what they are supposed to do and then get off the stage. When, however, they become part of a successful movement and enter a national culture, as Brecht's plays did, they become "classics."

Few of the early *isms* left plays that are still staged. Maeterlinck may be seen occasionally in a college's "experimental theatre," and plays by Kaiser and Toller are staged in Germany. Constructivism has not really left any plays, but it has proven an influential design style whose effects are still visible (although constructivist acting, as conceived in the 1920s, is dead). Absurdism, on the other hand—perhaps because its plays are part of the early theatre careers of people now

LINKS to more about theatre

Shari Benstock, *Women of the Left Bank: Paris, 1900–1940*, 1986.

C. D. Innes, *Avant Garde Theatre, 1892–1992*, 1993.

James Schevill, *Break Out! In Search of New Theatrical Environments*, 1973.

teaching—is alive in American university and regional-theatre bills—above all, Samuel Beckett's *Waiting for Godot.*

It is Brecht, however, who remains in the world repertory from these movements. A major theatre (the Berliner Ensemble) is still dedicated to him; he remains a pillar of German culture. The collapse of communism may make him temporarily less important, but he will stay on university bills and elsewhere if only because he and Marxist critical theory are still so influential; perhaps, too, his creation of roles for women will help.

Artaud's Theatre of Cruelty persists in many kinds of performance, although not much in the traditional theatre and never with Artaud's name attached. What remains are rock concerts and some aspects of MTV, and, perhaps, shock horror films.

CURRENT ISSUES

It is, or was, common to hear the avant garde dismissed as mere complaining, or amateurism, or exhibitionism. The most telling dismissal, however, has usually been the insistence that the avant garde has no real status because it cannot compete (artistically, critically, popularly) with the mainstream—it cannot win an equal share of the audience. This view sees the theatre as a market and the various producers as sellers, the audience as buyers—a concept admired by commercial theatre people and one more or less correct, probably, within the commercial theatre itself. By extension, this idea makes a rough implied equation between the "free market" and democracy: That which sells has been "elected" as buyers vote with their pocketbooks; that which fails has been "voted down." Market forces then equal democratic forces—which are by definition a good thing.

For the avant gardists, however, this metaphor was itself suspect. Some avant gardists have challenged the idea of commercialism itself; some have challenged what they see as commercialism's monopoly of access to audience; some have challenged a commercial structure that, they say, makes art impossible. Usually, these challenges have got mixed up with other challenges—political ones, social ones, behavioral ones—and they are hard to sort out. Antoine's Free Theatre, for example, was partly a challenge to the then-dominant commercial style

(Neo-Romanticism), partly a challenge to official censorship, and partly a challenge to professionalism (in a sense, the individual's version of commercialism). Yet, at base it was a challenge to a system that viewed art (or what was art to Antoine, at least) as a commodity, with the assumptions that, first, art that failed to win an audience was bad art; and, second, that art that won the biggest audience was the best art.

Some avant gardists, on the other hand, have concluded that the commercial audience is itself antiart, unable to tell good from bad, over-cautious or narrow-minded, and they reject the very idea of popularity. A story is told of the playwright Eugène Ionesco in the early 1950s; asked how his new play was going, he said, "A triumph! Nobody came!"

What, then, in a democratic, capitalist society, is the relationship between theatre and popular audience? Is a ticket a kind of ballot? Does the population vote with its wallet? Is the most popular the best? Or is the habitual audience of the commercial theatre, as some avant gardists see it, numbed, brain-dead, smug, interested only in the comfortable—and, therefore, to be dismissed?

What is the relation of market forces to art? Is it even possible to talk about market forces and art in the same context, or is art in a different value system? Or is art redefined by a market system, where devices familiar and necessary to the market—advertising, sales gimmicks, competition, the bottom line—cause art to change? Or, as the Little Theatre Movement saw it, is art by nature antithetical to commerce, and destructive of it? Or is art not democratic?

Key terms

Check your understanding against this list. Brief definitions are in the Glossary; page references there will direct you to appropriate pages. (Persons are page-referenced in the Index.)

Absurdism	existentialism
A-effect	Expressionism
alienation	Impressionism
avant garde	Independent (or art) theatre
Constructivism	plague (as metaphor)
Dadaism	Surrealism
double	Symbolism
epic theatre	theatre of cruelty

chapter 16

Changing World, Eclectic Theatre: 1960s–Y2K

OBJECTIVES

When you have completed this chapter, you should be able to:

- Trace lines of commercial and noncommercial theatre in the United States since 1960, with specific examples of artists and theatres

- Discuss in detail black and women's theatres and their relation to the social history of the period

- Define and give examples of performance art

BACKGROUND

The period since 1960 has been one of fast and powerful change. The 1960s were a watershed, the clearest dividing lines the Vietnam War and the civil rights struggle. The 1960s were also the consolidation of the electronic age. In that age, not only could things happen quickly, but also the rate of change kept accelerating and is still doing so. In the United States, these changes came at the end of a brief period of apparent calm, even dullness. The end of World War II (1945) led to the transformation of American life; however, a "cold war" between the West and the Soviet Union split the world. The Cold War ended with the collapse of the Soviet Union in 1989. The United States declared that it had "won." New difficulties arose almost immediately, however, as ethnic and nationalistic passions, long suppressed by communism, erupted.

The electronic age brought two new influences: unprecedented quantities of information, and points of access that kept people at home instead of sending them out. The results were, on the one hand, self-realization by all kinds of groups—ethnic, religious, political, sexual, social—and a shift from "engagement," or direct individual experience, to observation, or the life of the "couch potato," to virtual relationships via the Internet.

The quantity of information also led to self-awareness; millions of people discovered that they were not alone in what they had thought was an isolated morality or sexual orientation or belief: Both conservative Christianity and feminism were fueled by the new communications and both became movements, with formal institutions, national agendas, fund-raising capacities, and issues. Electronic communications "democratized" institutions by making it far more difficult to hide information or to ignore constituencies. They also gave new power to individuals, who could e-mail their views to elected representatives. "Identity

FIGURE 16.1 Contemporary Life.
In the world of the beginning of the twenty-first century, advertising and popular culture leap across national boundaries, yet economic and cultural disparities are huge. Left, a rural road in southern Africa; right, a street in New York's Greenwich Village.

politics" caused individual awarenesses to coalesce around common concerns—ethnicity, gender, belief. Changed laws and changed social ideas allowed formerly closeted realities like homosexuality to come out, including in the theatre. The AIDS epidemic after the early 1980s became a cause for which the theatre often supplied a forum.

As well, big contradictions existed within and between nations. Americans were many pounds overweight; millions died of starvation in Africa. The United States, one of the richest countries in the world, was also one of the most violent. The former communist-bloc countries were now democratic and capitalist; they were also broke, bitter, and crime-ridden. Capitalism triumphed worldwide, and economies crashed.

In the United States, as a result, contradictions and uncertainty seem rampant, despite a political stability and economic power that much of the world envies.

THEATRE, 1960s–2000s

Whenever society is uncertain about its goals and its values, art is apt to display uncertainty. As society seeks a paradigm capable of explaining the age, its theatre will also seek a model that allows it to capture the essence of the age.

And indeed, if anything could be said to characterize the theatre during the period, it was its *eclecticism*—that is, its use of many, diverse styles. The theatre buildings of the period were variously shaped and variously located. The theatrical

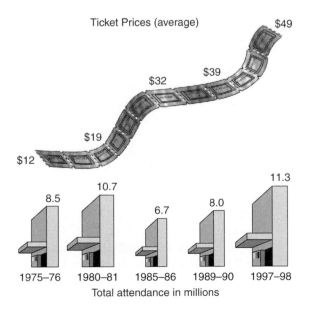

Ticket Prices (average)

$49

$39

$32

$19

$12

11.3

10.7

8.5

8.0

6.7

1975–76   1980–81   1985–86   1989–90   1997–98

Total attendance in millions

FIGURE 16.2   Ticket Prices and Attendance.

Recent ticket prices have risen steadily; attendance fell but has recently risen to the highest total in a quarter century. Figures from *Variety*.

productions were variously conceived and funded (see pp. 96–97). Plays were of mixed forms.

For purposes of discussion, however, we can still divide contemporary theatres into commercial and noncommercial. Both sorts of theatre existed in the major theatrical centers of the United States and abroad. Although reference will be made to western and eastern Europe, our major focus will remain on practices in the United States.

Commercial Theatre

Large profits continued to be the goal of theatres on Broadway, on the boulevards of Paris, and in London's West End. As costs for these productions continued to escalate, long runs grew ever more important and ticket prices rose still higher. The average Broadway ticket cost about $10 in 1975, about $30 in 1985, more than $35 by 1990, and more than $45 by 2000. In 1993, the average *regional* theatre ticket cost $20, with a high of $48. As prices rose, both audiences and repertories tended to grow more conservative. In the United States, musicals dominated the Broadway repertory. An occasional serious drama appeared, but none captured Broadway's audience for long.

Musicals

Musicals of the early 1960s were mostly optimistic—*Camelot, Mame*—but they gave way to darker works as the era itself darkened. The two following decades were dominated by composer-lyricist Stephen Sondheim. His lyrics for *Gypsy* and his music and lyrics for *Follies* (1971) took a bittersweet look at the musical stage itself. *Company* (1970), *A Little Night Music* (1973), *Sunday in the Park with George* (1984, Pulitzer Prize), and others were totally integrated works in which character and song were organically bound, and songs could often not be detached from the drama. To some, the gain in dramatic power was won at the loss of tunefulness and the old zesty, punchy musical show. The theatre had changed, too, however; no longer were there 200 shows a season or stars whose names could sell out a theatre for months. Other changes came, as well: *Hair* (1967) brought a counter-culture and rock to Broadway; *A Chorus Line* (1975) brought a group protagonist and a new Broadway love affair with spectacular dance, still evident in dynamic tap shows like *Bring in Da Noise, Bring in Da Funk* (1996); black composers and performers broke through the commercial theatre's glass ceiling.

The musicals of the 1990s emphasized spectacle. Dance, costume, and high-tech effects stood out. An influx of British musicals in the 1980s (*Cats, Phantom of the Opera*) encouraged the shift, as did the expensive and elaborate Disney production, *The Lion King* (1997). Melody and the memorable song were no longer so important: The age of sheet music and the home piano had given way to the age of the CD and karaoke.

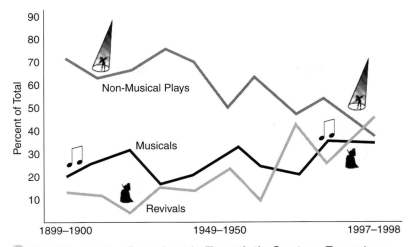

FIGURE 16.3 **Broadway's Twentieth-Century Repertory.**
During this century, the kinds of plays on Broadway have changed. Expressed as percentages of the total, revivals have increased; new musicals have increased; nonmusical plays have declined. Data from *Variety.*

Comedy

Commercial theatres also relied heavily on comedies to attract audiences and enrich box office receipts. During most of the period, Neil Simon was the playwright most successful with audiences. Major plays from the 1960s (*The Odd Couple*) established his reputation as the master gag writer of the theatre. During the 1970s, that reputation was solidified with works like *Last of the Red Hot Lovers.* In the 1980s, Simon produced semiautobiographical plays that were acclaimed by audiences and reviewers alike (*Brighton Beach Memoirs*). In 1991, he won the Pulitzer Prize for *Lost in Yonkers.*

Serious Plays

The proportion of serious dramas declined, but successful serious plays were still important. Older playwrights (Miller, Williams) had done their best work but continued to write at a high level. During the 1960s, Edward Albee moved from Off-Broadway and infused new life into Broadway with plays like *Who's Afraid of Virginia Woolf?* (1962), and he has remained as an important force, writing, encouraging younger writers, and creating such highly praised works as *Three Tall Women* (1994). Arthur Kopit, too, began Off-Broadway (*Indians,* 1969); although less prolific than Albee, he has been a consistently serious, thoughtful playwright.

In the 1970s and 1980s, David Rabe (*Sticks and Bones,* 1971), David Mamet (*Glengarry Glen Ross,* 1984), and Sam Shepard (*Buried Child,* 1978) had outstanding New York careers; they were joined by Beth Henley (*Crimes of the Heart,*

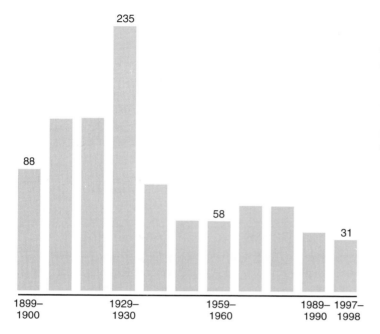

235

88

58

31

| 1899– | 1929– | 1959– | 1989– | 1997– |
| 1900 | 1930 | 1960 | 1990 | 1998 |

FIGURE 16.4
Broadway Openings in the Twentieth Century.
The number of new productions reached a peak in the 1929–30 season and fell thereafter, with slight increases between 1960 and 1980 before falling again. Data compiled from *Variety.*

1981), Charles Fuller (*A Soldier's Play,* 1982), Marsha Norman (*'Night, Mother,* 1983), and August Wilson (*Fences,* 1987).

In the 1990s, the outstanding drama was the multi-part *Angels in America* by Tony Kushner, which won prestigious prizes in both 1993 and 1994.

Imported Successes

Despite some promising American artists, the American commercial theatre would have been impoverished had it not been for imports. From the 1960s into the 1990s, some of Broadway's best productions were those whose success had already been demonstrated abroad. Early in the period, the British director Peter Brook brought his productions of *Marat/Sade* (by the German playwright Peter Weiss) and *A Midsummer's Night's Dream* to New York. England's Harold Pinter intrigued—and sometimes baffled—Broadway audiences with plays like *The Birthday Party.* More recently, plays by English feminist Caryl Churchill (*Cloud Nine*) and English farceur Michael Frayne (*Noises Off*) have joined English musicals on Broadway. By the 1990s, few shows opened on Broadway without having first proved successful elsewhere.

Noncommercial Theatre

The 1960s and 1970s saw the rise of a strong counterculture in the United States, one that questioned old values and traditional ways. The counterculture expressed itself in theatre through a vigorous avant-garde movement that began Off- and Off-Off-Broadway but quickly spread to many towns and cities, but, by 1980, some were proclaiming avant gardism dead in the United States.

Street theatre and *guerrilla theatre* were terms used to describe productions that brought theatre to people, recalling the resemblance of these theatres to street and guerrilla fighters. *Happenings* were non-linear, "meaningless" events that challenged the definition of *theatre.*

Others in the avant garde thought that theatre was so trivialized and demeaned by contemporary practices as to be impotent and irrelevant. Such groups sought primarily to revitalize the art, restoring its magical power, reintegrating it into the life of the community, and replacing it at the center of artistic life, a position it had once claimed.

Both sorts of avant gardists agreed that to make theatre once again important to the social, political, and spiritual life of people and their communities would require rethinking several basic relationships: of theatre to life, the other arts, and the media; of theatre to commerce; of actors to audience; of text to performance. Thus, the works of avant gardists bore resemblances whether their primary goals were political or artistic (indeed, in many groups the two goals were inextricably linked).

So long as political and social turmoil gripped society, as it did in the 1960s and 1970s, the avant garde remained vital. In the 1980s, however, society developed a more optimistic, if less searching, vision of itself. With less inflation and more national pride, popular presidents, an invigorated economy, and three quickly successful military adventures (Grenada, Panama, Iraq), society became disinclined to probe or to protest. In this environment, the avant garde declined. By the 1990s, only local vestiges of the once vigorous alternative theatre movement remained.

FIGURE 16.5   Open Theatre.
Jean-Claude van Italie's *Interview,* one of the major plays of the original Open Theatre. Boxes for furniture and almost no set focus attention on the actors. Production at Elmira College, directed by Jack L. Jenkins and designed by Peter Lach.

Major Noncommercial Groups

The rise and decline of this avant garde can be sketched through a brief summary of its major groups.

The Living Theatre (founded 1947; prime movers Julian Beck and Judith Malina) reorganized in the 1960s into a theatrical commune whose actors lived and performed together to promote revolution. Their international reputation came from their political agenda (benevolent anarchy), their incorporating of audience members into performances (through discussions, protests, and marches), and their often shocking tactics (including nudity).

The San Francisco Mime Troupe (founded 1959) reorganized in 1966 as a collective devoted to social change and thereafter performed original pieces devised around subjects like racism, sexism, militarism, and capitalism.

The Bread and Puppet Theatre (founded 1961) toured, offering plays outside traditional theatre buildings and using common (often found) materials. The company's name came from their use of bread (which it shared with its audience) and giant puppets (who told stories that tried to recapture simple values in a complex world). By the 1990s its influence had become mostly local.

The Open Theatre (founded 1963; prime mover Joseph Chaikin) is best known for its attention to ensemble, its use of theatre games and improvisations to build scripts, its use of transformations (actors playing several roles without changing costumes or masks and without clear transitions in dialogue), and its dependence on actors rather than scenery to build dramatic environments (by "becoming" trees, ambulances, tables). It dissolved in 1974 to avoid mere popular success.

El Teatro Campesino (founded 1965) took short skits (*actos*) into the fields of Southern California to organize migrant workers. After a riot-related death in 1970, the company became a religious commune devoted to revitalizing Chicano culture.

Charles Ludlam and the Ridiculous Theatrical Company (founded 1967) appealed mostly to a culturally and theatrically literate audience. Ludlam's scripts relied on "cultural recyclings": That is, he included snippets of dialogue, characters, and events from many sources and counted on the audience to recognize and appreciate the allusions. The company's performance style was highly theatrical, often camp, sometimes sexually ambiguous. Ludlam died in 1987.

Richard Foreman and the Ontological-Hysteric Theatre (founded 1968) sought to compel audiences through an accumulation of details, all controlled by Foreman himself: He wrote the scripts, designed the sets and costumes, recorded the sound track, directed the (usually untrained) actors, and ran the control boards. Foreman's goal was to cause audiences to create rather than merely to receive a performance.

Robert Wilson and the Byrd Hoffman School of Byrds was heavily influenced by practices in music, dance, sculpture, painting, and cinema. Wilson sought a "theatre of images" rather than of words. Through manipulating time, space, and sound, he developed works that had an incantatory, trancelike quality and myriad sensory impressions. Although Wilson is still working, his influence was strongest during the 1970s and 1980s, perhaps because his concepts have been so fully accepted. He is probably the most important of the old avant garde.

Major Noncommercial Movements

Related to, but separable from, the old avant garde were two theatre movements directly tied to political movements: black theatre, tied to the Black Power movement, and women's theatre, tied to the feminist movement. Although these two theatrical movements shared many basic assumptions, they differed profoundly in several ways.

FIGURE 16.6
Black Theatre of the 1960s.
Lonnie Elder III's *Ceremonies in Dark Old Men* was one of the important plays of the 1960s. Douglas Turner Ward (center) was actor, playwright (*Day of Absence*), and director, as well as being artistic director of the Negro Ensemble Company. Also shown is David Downing (left). *Corbis/Bettmann-UPI.*

Black Theatre. Although African-American performers in America date from well before the Civil War, and African-American theatre companies were firmly established within their communities by the end of the nineteenth century, their performers and plays seldom reached commercial theatres in the United States until midway in this century.

Before the 1960s, most *commercial* plays featuring African-American characters had been written by whites, who often stereotyped and placed them in inferior social positions, where they were patronized by wealthier, wittier, and more powerful white characters. Paul Green's *In Abraham's Bosom* (1926), Marc Connelly's *Green Pastures* (1930), and Carson McCullers' *The Member of the Wedding* (1950), although sympathetic treatments of African-American characters by white playwrights, nonetheless displayed many of the stereotypes.

Public images died hard, but they did die. The French playwright Jean Genet, in *The Blacks* (1959), reversed the traditions of the minstrel show and used African-American actors in white face to display abuses of power. Although many African Americans rejected the play's thesis—that blacks will come to power only by adopting the tactics of their white oppressors—few failed to realize that the play represented a turning point in the portrayal of black people. More important, Lorraine Hansberry's *A Raisin in the Sun* (1959) appeared, an early portrait of African-American family life in which the tensions between women and men were sympathetically and sensitively dramatized; it won the Drama Critics Circle Award.

With the racial turmoil of the 1960s and the early 1970s, blacks turned in large numbers to the arts as a way of demanding change and repairing their ruptured society: "Black Art is the aesthetic and spiritual sister of the Black Power concept." The black theatre movement is dated from 1964 and the Off-Broadway production of LeRoi Jones's first two plays, *The Toilet* and *Dutchman,* both of which presented a chilling picture of racial barriers, human hatred, and the senseless suffering that results from racism. Thereafter, the stereotypical stage Negro was increasingly replaced by more honest, if often less agreeable, black characters. Throughout the 1960s and the early 1970s, Jones (now Imamu Amiri Baraka) remained the most militant and best-known black playwright.

Alongside such antiwhite and separatist works were plays depicting the politics and economics of life within the African-American community. Douglas Turner Ward's *Day of Absence* (1967) poked fun at whites as they were outwitted by cleverer blacks, whose disappearance for a single day led to the collapse of the white social structure. Alice Childress's *Mojo* (1970) suggested that African-American men and women could work out their differences and exist happily as equals if they loved and respected one another.

By the mid-1970s, African-American authors felt free to criticize their own community. Ntozake Shange's *For Colored Girls Who Have Considered Suicide/ When the Rainbow is Enuf* (1976) explored the double oppression of being black and female and presented a most unflattering portrait of black males, some of whom were portrayed as brutalizing black women as they themselves had been previously brutalized. Originally staged in an African-American theatre, this powerful "choreopoem" eventually moved to Broadway, where it captivated audiences and earned the Tony Award. It became clear that plays once considered suit-

FIGURE 16.7
Black Theatre/Feminist Theatre.
Ntozake Shange's *For Colored Girls Who Have Considered Suicide/When the Rainbow Is Enuf* spoke not only of racism in white culture but also of sexism in black culture. *Here, in production at the University of South Carolina, directed by Bette Howard.*

able only for African-American audiences could be successful in the mainstream of America's commercial theatre.

A few of the major authors and their best-known works can serve to indicate the robust state of this theatre from the 1960s through the 1980s: Ed Bullins, *The Electronic Nigger* (1968); Lonne Elder III, *Ceremonies in Dark Old Men* (1968); Charles Gordone, *No Place to Be Somebody* (1969); Adrienne Kennedy, *The Owl Answers* (1969); Charles Fuller, *A Soldier's Play* (1981); and August Wilson, *The Piano Lesson* (1990).

Among the major theatres dedicated to producing African-American plays for primarily African-American audiences (1960s and after) were the Negro Ensemble Company, the New Lafayette Theatre, and Spirit House (all in the New York area) and the Watts Writers Workshop, the Performing Arts Society of Los Angeles, and the Inner City Cultural Center (in the Los Angeles and San Francisco areas).

African-American theatres, like their plays, served their audiences in very different ways. In Los Angeles, for example, while one theatre specialized in revolutionary pieces, another, across town, was producing a "black version" of *Death of a Salesman.* Both believed they were serving the particular needs of their specific audiences.

With new plays and special theatres came calls for a new criticism. Some African-American critics took the position that their audiences saw and understood art in ways different from whites. Traditional aesthetics were at best irrelevant and at worst corrupting. Those artists and critics sought an aesthetic that was moral and corrective, one that supported plays that, in a direct and immediate way, affected the lives of African-American theatregoers. An African-American critic explained, "The question for the black critic today is not how beautiful a melody, a play, a poem, or a novel is, but how much more beautiful [that] poem, melody, or play [has] made the life of a single black man." This attack on the accepted canon of Western drama raised issues that were still being debated in the 1990s.

Women's Theatre.   Whereas black theatre and drama arose from the social upheavals of the late 1950s and 1960s, women's theatres were a phenomenon of the 1970s, during which increasing numbers of people, mostly female, banded together into theatrical units that aimed to promote the goals of feminism, the careers of women artists, or both. By the mid-1970s, more than forty such groups were flourishing; by 1980, more than a hundred had formed. Unlike black theatres, which were usually found in urban settings and amid high concentrations of blacks, women's theatres sprang up in places as diverse as New York City and Greenville, South Carolina.

The theatres ranged in size from those depending on one or two unpaid and inexperienced volunteers to organizations of professionals numbering into the hundreds. Budgets, too, varied widely, with some groups existing on a shoestring and the good wishes of friends, and others displaying a financial statement in the hundreds of thousands of dollars. Organization, repertory, working methods, and artistic excellence were highly diversified, but the groups all shared the conviction

FIGURE 16.8
Women's Theatre.
Although many feminist plays were done in feminist theatres, some found mainstream production, as well. Elinor Jones's *A Voice of My Own* featured the writings of twenty-four women. This is a scene from the Acting Company's production, directed by Amy Saltz, with Laura Hicks, Frances Conroy, Leslie Geraci, and Claudia Wilkins. Photo by Nathaniel Tileston.

that women had been subjected to unfair discrimination based on their gender and that theatre could serve in some way to correct the resulting inequities.

Like the African-American theatres, the women's theatres attempted to serve different audiences and to serve them in different ways. Some groups, like the Women's Interart in New York City and the Los Angeles Feminist Theatre, existed primarily to provide employment for women artists. Such groups, seeing that women had inadequate opportunities, served as a showcase for the works of women playwrights, designers, and directors. Because their goal was to display women's art in the most favorable light, artistic excellence was a primary goal of each production. Critical acceptance by the theatrical mainstream was the ultimate measure of success. But other groups, like the now-defunct It's All Right to Be Woman Theatre (also in New York), believed the problems of women to be so deeply rooted in the society that only a major social upheaval could bring about their correction. Such groups were revolutionary and tended to adopt tactics designed to taunt, shock, or shame a lethargic society into corrective action. These groups cared not at all for the approval of the established critics, because they believed that traditional theatre was a male-dominated, and hence oppressive, institution.

Two techniques in particular came to be associated with revolutionary women's theatres: a preference for collective or communal organization and the use of improvised performance material, much of it uncommonly personal. Like guerrilla theatres, many feminist groups replaced the traditional theatrical hierarchy (a director leading a team of actors, designers, and technicians) with a leaderless group working together and with the audience to create a theatrical experience. The idea seemed to be that hierarchy suggests competition, and competitiveness is a masculine trait; collectivity, on the other hand, involves cooperation, a quality to be prized in the new social order.

Perhaps this view accounts as well for the groups' frequent preference for scripts that were cooperatively developed through improvisation. The actors, occasionally aided by their audiences, were encouraged to dip into their own experiences of being women in today's society and, from these shared personal experiences, to improvise dramatic presentations. Apparently such efforts, although naive, were capable of provoking audiences to awareness and action, for, in several instances, women reported changed lives as a result of encounters with a feminist production.

During the 1970s and 1980s, three feminist playwrights attracted special attention: Megan Terry (*Approaching Simone*, 1970); Myrna Lamb (*The Mod Donna*, 1970); and Martha Boesing (*Antigone Too*, 1984). By 1990, however, these playwrights had moved to other matters.

By the 1990s, women's theatres were also in flux. Some, like It's All Right to be Woman, had ceased producing, and some, like Omaha Magic, had moved away from feminism. Others moved in directions being newly pointed by feminism itself—emphasizing differences among women. Through both their composition and their repertories, women's theatres in the 1990s celebrated women's diversity—in age, race, ethnicity, and sexual preference. They renewed explorations of the function of gender in life and art, investigating through performance the ways in which society and theatre construct gender. These new directions (earlier pointed by Caryl Churchill) found expression in the works of playwrights like Simone Benmussa (*The Singular Life of Albert Nobbs*) and Hélène Cixous (*Portrait of Dora*) and in theatre companies like Split Britches and Spiderwoman.

Gay and Lesbian Theatre.   Many American cities had self-aware gay and lesbian communities before the 1960s, but these were largely covert, "in the closet." Homosexuality was illegal in most of the United States; public homosexual conduct, even language, was sometimes punishable under laws against indecency and obscenity. Thus, plays about homosexuality usually fell under the heading of prohibited speech. The exceptions were guarded, almost coded—for example, Lillian Hellman's *The Children's Hour* (1934). This situation changed in the 1960s, however, as court rulings extended free speech and concepts of privacy.

In 1968, Mart Crowley's *The Boys in the Band* was produced Off-Broadway and became the first homosexual hit comedy in a mainstream venue. Sympathetic to the lives and problems of gay men, Crowley's play made a place in commercial theatre for plays in which homosexuality was acceptable and non-threatening—and funny. Self-deprecating and sometimes self-destructive wit positioned homosexuals as victims, however, and thus ran the risk of sentimentality.

A year earlier, Off-Broadway had become home to Charles Ludlam and the Ridiculous Theatre Company (See page 388.) Ludlam's model was not commercial drama, as Crowley's was, but an anti-realism (now considered postmodern) that took much of its reference from pop culture—in Ludlam's case, especially movies and opera. This comic and subversive attack saved Ludlam's theatre from senti-

FIGURE 16.9
Recent American Drama.
Tony Kushner's *Angels in America* was one of the most honored works of the 1990s. It brought subjects and characters once found in gay theatre to the mainstream. Here, at Syracuse Stage, with Sue-Ann Morrow and Michael Malone. Directed by Robert Moss. Douglas Wonders photo.

mentality and gave it far wider meaning, even while insisting on its homosexuality. It made a place for gay theatre not in the commercial mainstream, but in the political avant garde.

In the 1970s, gay theatre companies found permanent homes in big cities (e.g., Theatre Rhinoceros in San Francisco, The Glines in New York). Sympathetic gay plays have since became common in mainstream theatre, the more so when the AIDS epidemic became national news, and "AIDS plays" became a subgenre (e.g., *As Is,* 1984). Lesbian theatres surfaced in the 1980s (e.g., Split Britches). Now, some theatres produce both gay and lesbian plays. Glines, for example, produced Jane Chambers's *Last Summer at Bluefish Cove,* a major lesbian work.

As with other political theatres, coherent theoretical bases are elusive. Problems of definition exist: What is a gay play—a play about gay men? By a gay man? Is a negative play about gay men a gay play? When is a woman's play a lesbian play? Where does a play by a gay or lesbian author but with a different subject fit? What of those plays of the past by homosexual authors (e.g., Oscar Wilde, Tennessee Williams) that have no ostensibly homosexual content?

Partly to deal with such problems, the idea of queer theatre and queer studies has evolved. "Queer" is both an umbrella and a political term, a weapon seized from, as it were, "the enemy" and turned around. Queer theatre announces itself and has pride in itself. Nonetheless, as a theoretical term it is no easier to define, and it has no clearer theoretical base, than gay and lesbian theatre. What is clear is that, having seized public space, these theatres are now vigorous and can sometimes give a new dynamism to the commercial theatre, as with Tony Kushner's *Angels in America* in the mid-1990s.

New Directions: Performance Art. *Performance art* probably began in European art circles of the turn of the century, among the dadaists, and it found echoes in the happenings of the 1960s. Its resurgence in the 1980s made performance art the most energetic expression within the avant garde. It is a form that defies traditional categories like theatre or dance or painting and that varies widely among its practitioners. As its name suggests, it depends on both performance and art, and despite its diversity it tends to share certain traits:

- A preference for a nonlinear structure, one unified more often by images and ideas than by stories

- An emphasis on visual and aural rather than literary elements

- A tendency to mix elements of several arts, especially music, dance, painting, and theatre

Although performance art includes many group works, a large proportion of the works are conceived and performed by individual artists working alone, often resembling standup comedians like Lenny Bruce.

Performance art probes the boundaries between life and art and among the several arts. Its frank experimentation has made it controversial not only among those who resist blurring the boundaries of arts but also among those who resent its often graphic portrayal of (to them) repugnant ideas or activities (e.g., feminism, homosexuality, pornography). Performance art is rarely Realistic, but many of its devices (the solo performer, the confessional mode, the lack of deliberate technique) seek to authenticate its reality. In a sense, it is the ultimate reduction of American Realism.

It is also part of the social shift that has made the talk show and "checkbook journalism" popular.

THINKING ABOUT THEATRE

Gwendolyn Brooks (1917–present), American poet, suggests that *"Art hurts."* On the other hand, Tommy Tune (1957–present), one of today's director-choreographers, believes that theatre's *"only a show...."* Which is closer to your view of what theatre should be? Which is closer to your view of what theatre is in America today? Is it possible to reconcile the two positions?

FIGURE 16.10   Recent Trends.
A Chorus Line used improvisation to help create its text, although the big finish was pure show biz. Directed by F. Scott Black, Cockpit in Court Theatre, Essex Community College.

Noncommercial Into Commercial

Except for performance art, relatively little experimental work was still underway by the 1990s. Some groups had ceased producing; some had moved toward the mainstream; some continued their earlier work, simply echoing themselves and their early experimentation. Indeed, except for the work of performance artists and some of the women's theatres, most of the vitality of the avant garde of the 1960s and 1970s has dissipated.

Nonetheless, several of the directions pointed by the avant garde in the 1960s and 1970s were visible, if modified, in the commercial theatres of the 1980s and 1990s. The commercial theatre of today, unlike that of the 1940s and the 1950s

- Exercises greater freedom with respect to language, dress, and subject. Nudity and profanity are readily accepted and previously taboo subjects are now freely treated—e.g., *Torch Song Trilogy* (1983, homosexuality), *'Night Mother* (1983, suicide), and *As Is* (1985, AIDS)

- Includes and awards prizes to plays by African-American authors—e.g., *A Soldier's Play* by Charles Fuller (Pulitzer, 1982), *Fences* (Tony, 1986; Pulitzer, 1987) and *The Piano Lesson* (Pulitzer, 1990) by August Wilson

- Includes and awards prizes to plays by female playwrights in larger numbers than before—e.g., *Crimes of the Heart* by Beth Henley (Pulitzer, 1981), *'Night Mother* by Marsha Norman (Pulitzer, 1983), *The Heidi Chronicles* by Wendy Wasserstein (Tony, 1989)

- Offers new opportunities for diversity among performers—e.g., *Zoot Suit* (1979, Chicano), *Children of a Lesser God* (1980, hearing impaired), *Driving Miss Daisy* (1988, African American), *M. Butterfly* (1988, Asian)

- Uses ensembles and improvisation as the basis of commercially successful scripts—e.g., *A Chorus Line* (1976) and *Quilters* (1985)

- Continues a long-recognized trend toward less literary and more visual and aural theatre

- Continues a trend toward mixing and merging theatre with other arts

THE PERIOD IN THE MODERN REPERTORY

Commercial plays from recent seasons make up a large part of many university seasons, a much smaller part of the bills of the regional theatres. They are probably the mainstay of community theatres in the United States.

Neil Simon, unquestionably the most successful playwright (in terms of commercial audience and commercial criticism), has probably had the most productions. Major musicals also make it to colleges and universities, although recent ones have enormous production requirements that limit their suitability. The comedies of Christopher Durang and Wendy Wasserstein have been much seen.

Plays by African Americans have become a major part of university and regional-theatre seasons (which sometimes now produce such plays before they go to New York). Shange's *For Colored Girls* was widely produced in the 1970s

---

LINKS to more about theatre

Margaret Croyden, *Lunatics, Lovers and Poets: The Contemporary Experimental Theatre,* 1974. The sixties avant garde.

William Goldman, *The Season,* 1969. Insight into a Broadway year.

Meryle Secrest, *Stephen Sondheim: A Life,* 1998.

Hair.

 < **http://nytheatre-wire.com/marquee.htm** > Site of *New York Theatre Wire,* an online magazine with lots on alternative and non-Broadway (and Broadway) theatre, ticket prices, what's playing, reviews, photos, more.

FIGURE 16.11   Rejuvenation in New York.

These photographs of the same block of Forty-Second Street were taken in 1989 and 1997. What was a depressed block with a derelict theatre (left) was, at the decade's end, the site of the rebuilt theatre where Disney's multi-million-dollar *The Lion King* was playing (right). Across the street, two theatres had been turned into one to house *Ragtime*.

and 1980s, the plays of August Wilson in the 1980s and 1990s. Plays by women are also much more common than formerly, but a distinction must be made between plays by women from the commercial theatre and plays from the feminist theatre; the latter receive many fewer productions around the country, in good part because they lack a distribution and information system.

Much of the influence of the recent avant garde has been through production techniques rather than plays. Both The Open Theatre and The Living Theatre have changed the way plays are staged and acted, as well as the way scripts are created (group work rather than individual work). The women's theatres have given examples of sometimes short-lived, self-contained groups that never sought wide publicity or big audiences. In fact, if there has been any single legacy from the very different avant-garde groups of the 1960s, 1970s, and 1980s, it is an indifference to the communications machinery of the commercial theatre, from reviewing to advertising. The buzz words of the commercial theatre—professionalism, good reviews, big houses, Broadway, big tickets, long runs—have been ignored; many of the avant-garde groups, especially the women's groups, have formed far from New York and remained there. Thus, rather than leave scripts for other theatres to put in their repertories, they have left only their own experiences, and their audiences'. This is a different idea of theatre.

Performance artists, too, do not leave replicable texts, therefore are not to be looked for in the repertories that imitate the commercial.

CURRENT ISSUES

When the forerunner of the Soviet KGB (the secret police) murdered Vsevolod Myerhold, the Constructivist director, in the 1930s, they showed how seriously avant-garde theatre can be taken (not to mention how seriously style can be taken). On the other hand, by the 1990s in the United States, the farthest reaches of avant-garde theatre hardly got a raised eyebrow from the center of power unless money was involved and unless one of a very few buttons was pushed (sex, family values, gay rights). This difference can be partly explained by the difference between an authoritarian state and an open one, but only partly. It can also be explained by the fading of avant gardism in the American theatre, to the point that the reaction to most efforts nowadays is a ho-hum. The avant garde, that response says, has no teeth.

But it may not be the avant garde alone that has no teeth. There is a serious question to be asked about the entire American theatre: has it been moved so far from the center of the culture that it has no teeth, either—in fact, no life? Is American avant gardism dead because the American theatre is dead?

We can see several things that suggest it is not—two thousand college and university programs in theatre, for example; a Broadway that, although diminished, still manages to get productions on and make some money; regional theatres, some of which are flourishing. These are not aspects of a dead theatre.

Or are they? It depends on what we mean by "dead." Does "dead" mean a theatre that no longer supplies common images, common language, and common heroes (role models, stars, idols—call them what you will) to its culture? Do these things come from the theatre in the United States as the millenium begins?

In the nineteenth century, people of all ages could mention certain characters, scenes, or lines from Shakespeare and be understood. Is that true now? In 1900, certain hairdos and dresses could be identified with a stage actor's name. Is that true now? As late as 1925, certain words, jokes, and punch lines from stage plays and vaudeville routines were shared by large sections of the nation. Is that true now? What, other than a very few songs, comes directly from the American theatre to the great mass of people and is recognized by them?

Those who believe that the theatre has been moved from its former centrality point instead to certain elements of popular culture that are electronically communicated and universally recognized: rock music, advertising lines and images, sports, notorious news events. Nowadays, they argue, people communicate by referring to these, not to the theatre. Role models and stars, they argue, come not from the theatre but from MTV and televised sports.

If it is true that the American theatre has been pushed to the margin of the culture, then what is the position of those two thousand university and college programs? In a practical sense, should they train people for jobs in a marginalized field? In a theoretical sense, do they have any responsibility to the importance (or lack of it) of their subject?

In the nineteenth century in France, people battled in the theatre over the play *Hernani.* In the twentieth century in Moscow, Myerhold and others lost their lives because of positions they took in the theatre. At the end of the twentieth century in the United States, does anybody even lift a voice over what happens in the theatre?

KEY TERMS

Check your understanding against this list. Brief definitions are in the Glossary; page references there will direct you to appropriate pages. (Persons are page-referenced in the Index.)

black theatre movement	Open Theatre
eclecticism	performance art
guerilla theatre	revival
happening	street theatre
improvisation	transformation
Living Theatre	women's theatre

World Theatre

OBJECTIVES

When you have completed this chapter, you should be able to:

- Explain how traits of ritual differ from similar practices in Western theatre

- List traits shared by most African dramas

- Cite major differences among the theatres of West, East, and South Africa

- Describe kinds of theatre and drama from Turkey, India, and China

- Differentiate among Kabuki, Kyogen, and Noh

The focus of this book has been the self-aware narrative theatre derived from that of ancient Greece, which is now the dominant theatre of Europe (including the former Soviet Union), North America, and Central and South America. But there are other important traditions of theatrical performance outside this one—the theatres of Africa, the Middle East, and Asia, for example. This chapter will introduce some representative work within these traditions. Obviously, a single chapter can offer only the briefest survey, but perhaps such an introduction can stimulate an interest to be pursued later in other courses and other readings.

Before moving to the theatres themselves, however, we need to provide a context for what follows by confronting two issues, cross-cultural currents and theatre-like activities.

BACKGROUND

Cross-Cultural Currents

International mass communication and high-speed, cheap transportation have made international cross-influences important factors in contemporary art. Cultural influence tends to follow political and economic influence. The present world position of the United States has given American culture great importance in non-Western cultures: McDonald's hamburgers appear in Moscow, Coca-Cola cans alongside roads in central Africa. With these come films, television, tapes, and, with them, ideas of impersonation and dramatization and theory different from indigenous ideas. The result is sometimes a mixture.

This cultural mixing has had implications for today's theatres. In country after country of Africa and the East, for example, there now exists a theatre much like that which we see in the United States and Europe and which we have been describing throughout this book. This theatre usually began as a form of entertainment for settlers of European or American extraction who lived abroad to do missionary work, undertake business, or run the government during colonial times (thus its name, "settler theatre," in much of Africa). The audience for this transplanted Western theatre now consists of both expatriates (Europeans, Americans) and locals (Indians in India, Turks in Turkey).

Alongside this theatre there continues to be an indigenous theatre that operates on quite different assumptions and displays quite different practices. This indigenous, traditional theatre often has deep cultural roots that stretch well back in time. Originally attended primarily by local people, these theatres are now attended by expatriates and tourists who seek to see and understand a kind of theatre quite unlike their own.

Alongside both these theatres are still others. One kind blends elements of both Western and indigenous theatres. Called by one scholar "syncretic," such a theatre brings together elements of both traditions to form another, attended by local and expatriate audiences. Another kind is the often highly political "theatre of

FIGURE 17.1

Despite Western-style economic development and urbanization, as in this street in the capital of Botswana, much of the world either holds to indigenous theatrical forms or seeks new, more culturally relevant ones.

development," a theatre that aims to reach villagers in their own language, treating such problems as land use, water policy, and women's equality.

It is not always possible now to identify a purely Western or purely indigenous form, so intertwined have they become in some locations. It is not even possible, especially in former colonial areas like Africa, to say what, if any, theatre existed before the Western idea of theatre arrived. This introduces our second major issue, the one with which this book began: What is theatre?

Theatre and Theatre-Like Activities

In many cultures outside the West, various rituals, ceremonies, and performances shared elements that we now associate with theatre:

- Masks

- Costumes

- Dance and music

- Some sort of text (although the "texts" were often improvised and transmitted orally rather than in writing)

Because of these shared traits, some scholars have blurred the distinctions among theatre and theatre-like activities. However, throughout this book we have

ⒻIGURE 17.2   Masks.
Masks are an important element of theatrical or quasi-theatrical activities. These are from native peoples in the United States, Mexico, and Africa. None is theatrical in the Western sense.

maintained a separation between them, and we do so here as well. Let us consider two important kinds of theatre-like activities: *rituals* and *paratheatricals.*

Rituals

In Africa, pre-Columbian America, Southeast Asia, and parts of the Pacific, many social and religious forms have been grouped together under the term *ritual* because they tend to share certain elements. Many of their shared elements, however, are often not those that in the West we typically associate with theatre. Major elements shared by rituals are listed here and then compared with practices more usually found in Western theatre.

Major elements shared by rituals are:

- Communal bonding of all those present
  —*In ritual,* the identifying element is "community."
  —*In Western theatre,* the identifying element is "art."

- No clear separation of audience and performer
  —*In ritual,* those in attendance participate in the activities.
  —*In Western theatre,* audiences typically watch and listen to activities performed by others.

- Indifference to permanently established space
  —*Rituals* take place in spaces made specially for the ritual but seldom permanently altered.
  —*Western theatre* typically has a space set aside and configured specifically to accommodate the event.

- Diffused focus
  —*Rituals* may take place over several miles of countryside, without an audience and with some people able to catch only occasional glimpses of the activities.
  —*Western theatre* typically takes place in one place arranged so that the audience's attention is focused on the event.

- Little or no "scenery" (visual clues to location)
  —*Rituals* make no attempt to recreate a location other than the actual location of the event.
  —*Western theatre* typically strives to represent and identify some place other than the theatre itself.

- Purposes that are cultural
  —*Ritual* aims to do things like heal, honor, or mourn.
  —*Western theatre* typically aims to do things like teach, entertain, or make money.

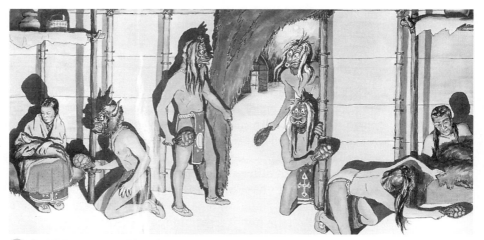

FIGURE 17.3   Ritual.
Using aspects of performing (e.g., masks and music), ritual has the additional characteristic of *efficacy,* the desire to effect a purpose—in this case, healing. This is a recreation of a ceremony of the Iroquois False Face Society by artist Ernest Smith. Courtesy of Donald G. Cameron. Photograph by the Rochester, New York, Museum of Arts and Sciences.

Both Western and indigenous scholars still debate whether rituals should be considered a kind of indigenous theatre.

Paratheatrical Forms

In addition to these still-debated rituals, there are other indigenous forms that are clearly related to theatre and that have received much attention from scholars. Important and representative among such forms are the following:

- Storytelling, often with music (or at least drumming) and mime; for example, the *griot* of West Africa and the *meddah* of Turkey

- Cultural transmission—the passing-on of knowledge in cultures without writing. This varies enormously, from simple but expert pantomime of birds and animals to elaborate instruction in traditions through pantomime, song, and dance

- Dance, often with narrative and elaborate theatrical effects, especially costumes and masks—for example, the elaborate temple dances of Southeast Asia

- Puppet theatre—for example, the shadow puppets of Turkey and the large Bunraku puppets of Japan

Neither ritual nor the paratheatrical forms are discussed in this chapter as forms of theatre, although elements of them appear clearly in several indigenous theatres that we do discuss.

AFRICA

Africa is a huge and diverse continent. Before the coming of the colonial powers, its people spoke many different languages, practiced many different religions, made their livings in many different ways, and otherwise represented a wide range of social and cultural practices.

The colonial period, although brief (c. 1870–1965), changed Africa radically. People with different languages, religions, and cultural backgrounds found themselves under one (European) government. In fact, the boundaries of modern countries of Africa often were set up by European colonizers for the convenience of the colonizers, without regard to the integrity of the indigenous groups living within them.

The colonial influence is important in part because of the effect that language has had on African life, and so on theatre. For example, many people in Africa have found themselves needing three languages in order to thrive: a local language in which to conduct their daily lives; a national language (like Kiswahili in East Africa), which diverse indigenous people speak as a way of communicating across tribal groups; and an international language (usually the language of

FIGURE 17.4 Africa: Nigeria. Nigerian universities were at the forefront of both theatre studies and theatre production. *The Prisoners* by Chris Nwamuo *at the Nigerian Universities Theatre Arts Festival.*

their colonizers—English, French, German, Portuguese) with which they conduct much of their business, especially international business.

Plays in Africa have been written in all three sorts of language. And it is not unusual for a play to be written in more than one language or for different parts of the same play to be written in different languages. Language has even taken on political meaning, the choice of language becoming itself a major political act. For example, to write in English or French may signal an effort to assimilate into the colonizer's culture or to gain international fame, whereas to write in a local or national language may signal an attempt to help solve a local or regional problem, as in much of the theatre for development. So controversial has the choice of language become for writers, that some now refuse to write in their international language, preferring to show, through language, their commitment to African rather than colonial culture.

However, because most people in Europe and the United States read or speak only Western languages, plays written in local and national African languages remain largely inaccessible to people in the West. For this reason, our discussion sketches only the English-language theatre within Africa.

The colonial influence is also important because of the effect it has had on education in Africa. Formal schooling was introduced by the colonizers and patterned along lines familiar in Europe. It took as its goal the preparation of African students for life in a colonial (European-influenced) social structure, and so most children received only minimal schooling, learning to read and write enough to work in low-level jobs. However, those young adults destined to enter the elite circles of government service or education were educated beyond the basic level. For them, African countries established their own universities (again modeled on European universities), but, even with the local universities, many of the most able students were—and still are—sent to Europe for their university and graduate educations.

African universities are extremely important in any study of African theatre because they have served as the center of theatre on the continent. Many have departments of theatre, and such departments often grant advanced degrees. Throughout Africa such universities take the place of commercial centers like Broadway or the West End in New York and London; that is, unlike the American situation, college and university theatres in Africa tend to be central rather than peripheral to the "real theatre" of the country. Indeed, where university theatre has been strong, African theatre tended to be strong, especially in Ghana, Nigeria, Kenya, and South Africa.

African theatres also share a tendency to use amateur rather than professional actors and to work willingly in a variety of performance spaces. In these ways, too, African theatres tend to differ from European and American ones. Probably these traits emerged in part from the practicalities of college theatres, but also from the limited budgets available for producing theatrical works in Africa and from the influence of various indigenous practices (rituals, paratheatrical forms).

Like their theatres, African dramas tend to share certain traits that set them apart from European and American dramas. The major similarities among African dramas can be listed:

- An epic quality: large casts, sweeping themes, loosely structured plots, free-ranging space and time

- A didactic purpose

- A mixture of Realistic and nonrealistic elements, especially music, dance, and drumming

- An extensive use of recognizable cultural elements: e.g., proverbs, gestures, history, symbols

- An openness to dramatic symbolism, especially symbolic characters

Regrettably, African plays are not so well known as they should be in Europe and the United States, in part because of difficulties with language but also because of their typical elements, which make African plays very different from plays written by Americans or Europeans and therefore often difficult to read and understand.

Despite similarities, each African country has its own theatrical traditions, and it is to the major of these that we now turn.

For our purposes, Africa can be considered in five geographical areas:

North Africa (mostly Islamic; few theatres)

Southwest Africa (German-influenced; few theatres)

West Africa (French-influenced; major theatres)

East Africa (English-influenced; major theatres)

South Africa (English- and Dutch-influenced; major theatres)

FIGURE 17.5 Africa: Botswana.
This sparsely populated nation in southern Africa has a modern capital in which the university has one of the principal theatres. An original production, *Vision in a Dance,* directed by David Kerr.

As we consider the theatres, we need to remember that when the new African nations gained independence (mostly in the late 1950s and 1960s), they had to cope with the conflicting realities of old and new, tribal and colonial, traditional and modern. The countries of this continent continue to have enormous difficulties, particularly as their populations increase and their need for industrialized goods grows. Thus, conditions in many African countries have not been conducive to the creation of theatre.

West Africa

The francophone (French-speaking) drama of several former French colonies is vigorous, in part because of continuing ties with Paris. In the mid-1980s, one scholar identified nearly three hundred francophone plays in print since independence. Of those published after 1980, half came from only two countries,

Senegal and Cameroon; another quarter came from Ivory Coast and Congo, with the remainder divided among seven nations, some of which (Zaire, for example) are more properly seen as Central than West African.

In formerly English-speaking areas, two nations stand out:

Ghana

"Concert Party Theatre is the only fully evolved indigenous form of theatre. . . . It enjoys a countrywide appeal." A native theatre form, concert party theatre, emerged in the 1920s. (*Concert party* is itself a British term.) It was narrative vaudeville, sometimes funny but sometimes serious, dealing mostly in subjects from domestic life. The leading figure was Ishmael Johnson, called the first professional actor in Africa.

In the 1950s, the Ghana Drama Studio was founded by Efua Sutherland. There, she produced new Ghanaian plays, including her own *Foriwa* (1967). Ama Ata Aidoo (also a woman) is the author of *Anowa* (1970) and other plays. Both dramatists, as well as others in Ghana's theatre, have had close connections with the University of Ghana. More recently, playwrights like J. C. de Graft (*Muntu,* 1976) have gained notice.

Nigeria

Nigeria is a very large nation with dense population centers and many universities. Out of one of its dominant languages, Yoruba, has come a traditional masked performance, the Alarinjo, on which the "father figure" of Nigerian theatre (as one Nigerian critic has called him), Hubert Ogunde, drew. Creator of a native concert party form, Ogunde wrote and produced many plays for his own traveling troupe and was a seminal figure in an indigenous form, *Yoruba opera.* Rich in music, Yoruba opera is performed by touring companies that are able to create with Yoruba audiences some of the communal feeling of ritual. In part, this commonality is possible because of the plays' use of traditional stories and moral ideas.

Unquestionably, however, the most important figure in Nigerian theatre has been Wole Soyinka, winner of the Nobel Prize for Literature in 1986. Soyinka's first play was produced while he was at the Royal Court Theatre in London; his later plays, like *The Trials of Brother Jero* (1964), have gained international acclaim and have (as with many African theatre people) got him into trouble with the government during periods of stress. Soyinka went into exile when government repression increased. In 1996, playwright Ken Saro-Wiwa was executed, apparently for anti-government activity. A change of government in 1998 led Soyinka to make a brief return.

East Africa

Markedly different from West Africa, the East African nation of Kenya is distinct in both culture and language. For example, masks, rituals, and paratheatrical activities, so popular in West Africa, were almost never as important in Kenyan society, and Kiswahili, the dominant national language of Kenya, is not common in West Africa.

The outstanding theatre figure of Kenya is Ngugi Wa Thiongo. In the 1960s, Ngugi's plays and novels were concerned with the problems of independence and freedom from Western influence and, in some cases, with much earlier historical conflicts of his Kikuyu people. However, plays like *I Will Marry When I Want* (written with Ngugi wa Mirii, 1980) have powerful implications for policies and practices in post-independence Kenya. As a result, Ngugi has had difficulty with the Kenyan government. His theatre company was forbidden to play in 1982, and for several years he was himself in detention. He finally decided to live outside Kenya and left the country.

Elsewhere in East Africa, Tanzania has tried to encourage the development of a Kiswahili theatre, and Uganda saw the beginnings of a native theatre. But political events—especially the waves of violence in Uganda from the late 1970s on—discouraged theatre. However, Uganda in the 1990s has again stabilized; there is a

FIGURE 17.6. Africa: Uganda.
Makerere University is one of the historical centers of East Africa theatre, although Uganda now has a national theatre in Kampala, as well. Here, a production of Brecht's *Mother Courage* at Makerere, *directed by Jessica Kaahwa.*

National Theatre in the capital, and theatre studies are again underway at Makerere University, once the center of East African drama.

South Africa

Until 1993, South Africa remained a colonial nation, with the majority black population ruled by a minority white population of mostly English and Afrikaaners (originally Dutch). The races were kept legally separated by a series of oppressive laws—the legal system called apartheid. As a result, South Africa's most visible art was, and still is, colonial, and theatre was mostly Western theatre in the white areas of the cities. The media, also controlled by whites and subject to apartheid, advertised and reviewed plays imported (or copied) from Broadway and London and largely ignored black theatre (thus making themselves allies of white domination).

Despite apartheid, a black "township theatre" came into being decades ago. Originally celebratory rather than confrontational, it highlighted musicals that combined elements of Broadway with indigenous dance and music (*King Kong*—NOT made from the movie—had a successful international tour); the leading figure was Gibson Kente. The increasingly heated atmosphere of the sixties and seventies saw more political theatre, which was repressed by the government. Out of it, however, by way of several universities, came an integrated, multiracial theatre not associated with the white establishment; its most successful examples were the Space Theatre in Cape Town and the Market in Johannesburg.

Because of apartheid and resistance to it, drama in South Africa was unique among African nations. Its subjects were most often apartheid, colonialism, oppression, and their social consequences. The casts were often very small because curfews made it difficult to assemble casts for rehearsals, and the plays were often written in somewhat discrete sections so that whichever actors could make it to a rehearsal could work, even when the entire cast could not assemble.

One playwright of great international importance has appeared in South Africa: Athol Fugard. Widely produced in Europe and the United States, Fugard is the author of plays that accept the current Western idea of drama as their base. Usually realistic, these plays have made powerful presentations of the South African racial crisis on the world's stages—for example, the 1982 success of '*Master Harold' . . . and the Boys*.

Although Fugard, who is white, has received by far the most international attention, black South African playwrights and artists like Percy Mtwa and Musemala Manaka are of great importance to the new South African theatre.

The end of apartheid had the potential for removing the theatre's main subject. (Something of the sort happened in Russia after the end of communism.) However, drama and theatre remain vigorous, as shown by international tours in the late 1990s of a new Fugard play (*The Captain's Tiger*—see Figure 6.3) and Jane Taylor's *Ubu and the Truth Commission,* whose title places it historically.

THE ISLAMIC WORLD

With the appearance of the prophet Muhammed in the late sixth century A.D., a new religion, Islam, spread rapidly from the Arabian peninsula: north into the Near East; west along all of Mediterranean Africa and down the East African coast; and east into India and Southeast Asia. For complex reasons, the world of Islam was hostile to theatre (although not to storytelling, puppetry, and dance). As well, it drastically limited the public life of women, including their appearance on the stage.

Islamic peoples developed a highly sophisticated literature, especially in Persian and Arabic, along with other arts; theatre, however, was largely ignored until the nineteenth century. Turkey was an exception.

Turkey

Contemporary Turkey has both professional theatre companies that perform Western and Turkish plays and a vigorous film industry. Turkey also had a popular, traditional theatre that has now effectively disappeared. A popular comic form called *orta oyunu* persisted into the twentieth century. Although its origins are not known, scholars suggest that it may be a continuation of Byzantine mime. Some similarities to Italian *commedia dell'arte*—comic regional types, improvisation, stock costumes and characters—suggest influence but may be the result of a common root or may be coincidence. Important characteristics of this form of theatre were

- Freedom from established theatre spaces

- Popularity of subject and language

- Lack of scenery, except for an all-purpose cloth enclosure or tent

- Continuity of characters over many years

Other Islamic Theatre

Other theatre in Islamic countries has been the result of Western influence or of imitation of the West. The development of an Islamic theatre apparently came about because of European domination of certain Islamic areas: France in Lebanon; Great Britain in Egypt, Syria, and what is now Jordan; and Italy in Somalia. Following European example, young dramatists began to write and produce plays in Damascus and Cairo, and Cairo became the center for a theatre heavily dependent on music.

THINKING ABOUT WORLD THEATRE

In 1991, Peter Brook, English director and theorist, explained that *"in India, in Africa, in the Middle East, in Japan, artists who work in the theatre are asking the same question: What is our form today? Where must we look to find it?"* List elements shared by today's theatre artists in the several countries discussed in this chapter. Which of these elements also appeared in Classical Greece? Rome? The Middle Ages of Western Europe? Contemporary theatre in the United States? What speculative conclusions are possible from these data?

A few women had appeared on the infant Islamic stage—most of them Christians and Jews—but after World War I, a liberal movement in Islam loosened some restrictions. In Cairo, a government-funded theatre was set up in 1948.

Nonetheless, theatre in Islamic countries cannot yet be called vigorous, although film flourishes, especially in Egypt. Particularly since the rise of Islamic fundamentalism in the 1970s and the economic hardships of the same period, theatre has had the status of a minor, and perhaps a threatened, art.

THE EAST

Major traditional theatres have appeared in a number of cultures of the Orient. The cultures themselves have often been conservative and religious, with the result that arts—including theatre—have often been preserved centuries after their initial creative energies were gone. Elites within the cultures have often prized these arts, seeing in their preservation an expression of their own continuity. As a result, the modern nations that have emerged from these ancient cultures now typically display a dual theatrical sensibility: one track is re-creative and backward-looking, displaying the sensibility of a museum; the other is creative and forward-looking, displaying the sensibility of Western art.

Neither track is "better" than the other. Appreciation of the traditional theatres has changed; like great works of painting or sculpture, they are preserved for their beauty, even though their languages may no longer be the languages of discourse and their styles may be almost foreign. In many cases, experienced audiences for some of these traditional theatres follow performances with annotated scripts open before them, as some Westerners follow operas.

As one Western scholar has pointed out, traditional Eastern theatre is an art of the "invisible world"—the world of religion, often a religion of demons, spirits, and multiple divinities. Generally, these Eastern traditional theatres are nonrealistic and share certain common elements:

- Highly stylized, dancelike movement
- Nonrealistic makeup or masks

- Non-Western dramatic form, meaning that they are not based on Aristotelian ideas of action, unity, and the interrelated parts of the play

- Acting styles far removed from Western ideas of impersonation, often with radically different uses of the voice (so that Westerners have called some forms "operas"), for which years of rigorous training are required

Despite similarities, however, traditional Eastern forms are so different from each other that one looks as foreign to an Easterner from another culture as it does to a Westerner.

The theatres that we shall consider come from three modern nations: India, Japan, and China.

India

The multilingual culture of India was already old when Alexander the Great reached it in 327 B.C. The Indian subcontinent stretched from the Himalayas to the Indian Ocean coast, broken politically into many units. Dominated early by Hinduism, India saw a major shift in the north to Islam after the twelfth century. Europeans set up trading enclaves in the sixteenth century, and England dominated the entire subcontinent from the mid-nineteenth through the mid-twentieth centuries. Independent again after World War II, the subcontinent is now made up of the nations of India, Pakistan, and Bangladesh.

It is the modern state of India that maintains an important tradition of theatre, as well as a minor modern theatre and a world-famous film industry.

Sanskrit Theatre

Sanskrit was the spoken and written language of India, then of its ruling and intellectual classes, until a thousand or so years ago. It was the language of an important treatise on the theatre, the *Natyasastra,* and of the drama.

The Natyasastra. Probably derived from oral tradition and ascribed to the "mythical" authority Bharata, the *Natyasastra* was a long treatise on theatre and drama, analogous to Aristotle's *Poetics,* probably written down between 200 B.C. and A.D. 200. Its basic assumptions were those of Hinduism: a universe of unity expressed through multiplicity, therefore aesthetically an art of multiple forms—dance, song, and poetry—unified through total performance into a form that would induce in the receptive audience a state of understanding—*rasa.* The *Natyasastra* is a valuable source of theatrical evidence, revealing an ancient India of touring professional acting companies that included both men and women; of permanent theatres built of wood and stone, with elevated stages and close connections to temples; and of rigid caste limits, restricting this kind of theatre to the elitist Brahmin caste.

The Drama.   Sanskrit drama included at least a thousand plays in the period A.D. 200–800. Of these, the plays of Kalidasa are best known in the West, and his *Sakuntala,* which reached Europe in the early nineteenth century, is the most often seen. In seven "acts," it follows a highly romantic love action between a king and the modest Sakuntala and includes the intercession of gods, a curse, and a ring that is lost and then found in the belly of a fish. *Sakuntala* is a play of many scenes, places, and moods, unified not by action but by *rasa,* the state of perception and emotion (in this case, love) induced in the audience. Like much of Sanskrit drama, it took as its source the *Mahabharata,* which, with the *Ramayana,* is the great source work of Hindu culture.

Popular Offshoots of Sanskrit Theatre: Kuttiyatam.   Sanskrit, already the language of a small elite, became archaic after about 800; popular languages took its place. In many places in India, Sanskrit theatre absorbed or was absorbed into other forms; the results were highly varied. The most important extant form is *Kuttiyatam,* still performed in southern India. It is characterized by:

- Inclusion of part or all of a traditional Sanskrit play.

- Interpretation of and comment on the Sanskrit by a popular figure, the Vidusaka, who can be satirical, comical, and parodic.

FIGURE 17.7
India: Kathakali.
One of the rich variety of theatre-dance forms of India. Photo courtesy of Farley Richmond.

- Performance by family troupes of the *Chakyar* lineage, traceable to the tenth century; these actors undergo years of rigorous training.

- Creation of an indigenous theatre architectural type, the *kuttambalam,* which has a square, raised stage with a pillar-supported roof; a rear wall with two doors and two copper drums (for rhythmic accompaniment); and an audience area surrounding the stage on three sides. The *kuttambalam* is built close to a temple so that the actors perform facing the deity.

Kuttiyatam performances go on for several, sometimes many, days. Like Sanskrit theatre, they include totally integrated dance, poetry, music, story, and impersonation. Although aesthetically based in the *Natyasastra,* Kuttiyatam violates Sanskrit purity (its clowning has been called obscene, for example) but offers the possibility of adaptation and change, which pure Sanskrit drama did not.

Non-Sanskrit Theatre: Kathakali

Because of the great importance of movement, especially highly controlled and traditional movement, most Indian theatre has close affinities with dance. Certain forms are often called *dance drama* or *dance theatre* because the dance element is so important. Because they include story and impersonation, some of these forms can be included here; of them, a spectacular example is *Kathakali,* which, like Kuttiyatam, had its origins in southern India.

Kathakali, like many Indian dramatic types, uses stories from the *Ramayana* and the *Mahabharata.* These are sung by one group of performers while others dance to the accompaniment of loud, fast drumming. No raised stage is used and there is no theatre structure: Performers work outdoors on a flat earth square about sixteen feet on a side. The only light is an oil fire. There is no scenery. While the singers recite the text and the drummers pound, the dancers, in astonishing makeup and elaborate but almost abstract costumes, mime, sign, and dance, impersonating characters with intricate hand symbols, facial expressions, and body movements.

Most spectacular of Kathakali elements is the makeup, which can take all day to apply. The entire face is colored, then decorated with lines and planes of other intense colors. False "beards" of rice paste are built up; the eyes are reddened by the insertion of a special seed. In this theatre of the demonic and the divine, such utterly nonrealistic makeup is essential.

All Kathakali performers are male, and the dancers' training takes many years.

Western-Influenced Theatre

British residents of India built Western theatres as early as the eighteenth century and began to perform Western plays, to which some Indians were invited. In the nineteenth century, Western theatre became one of the foci of antitraditionalism,

FIGURE 17.8   India.
Outdoor performance for a rural audience. Photo courtesy of Farley Richmond.

and a Western style of Indian drama emerged. The most influential among those who bridged classical and modern Indian styles was Rabindranath Tagore (1861–1941), India's first Nobel laureate. Tagore's ideal of a native drama that would provide a modern fusion of poetry, music, and movement, however, has not been realized.

The popular modern Indian form is film, not theatre, and outside cities like Calcutta and Bombay, professional secular theatre does not flourish. The Indian theatrical tradition is religious; the modern state—with its capacity for funding the arts—is secular. The gulf between the two is great.

Japan

Japan, situated on a chain of islands in the Pacific Ocean off the Asian mainland, developed early under Chinese influence and then, after about the fourteenth century A.D., rejected China and its ways. From then until the middle of the nineteenth century, Japan turned inward, deliberately turning its back on the outside, particularly the West, except for minor trading contacts. However, in the 1850s an American fleet "opened" Japan, and thereafter a pronounced political and cultural shift led to the rapid development of one of the world's great modern nations. Despite its defeat and heavy losses in World War II, Japan at the close of the twentieth century is a major technological and industrial power.

Several forces created traditional Japanese theatre: a feudal society with an emperor nominally at its top; a warrior ethic that made the samurai warrior a model and placed the military ruler at the actual head of state from the sixteenth through the mid-nineteenth centuries; and religion, including native Shinto ("the way of the gods"), Chinese Confucianism, and, above all, a form of Indian Buddhism, Zen.

Dance was probably fundamental to all Japanese theatre. Important dramatic theatre developed from or alongside it, incorporating movement forms that demanded special training. Like Indian theatre, then, Japan created an important dance form (Bugaku) and dramatic forms that were nonrealistic, preserved more or less in their ancient forms for hundreds of years.

Two of these forms are of particular interest.

Noh

Noh has been called "the oldest major theatre art . . . still regularly performed." Poetic and austere, it is a theatrical expression of Zen Buddhism. Its originators were a father and son, Kanami (1333–1384) and Zeami (1363–1444), both professional actors attached to a temple. They wrote most of the more than two hundred extant Noh plays, creating a body of work with certain rigid characteristics.

- A three-part structure of *jo, ha,* and *kyu*

- A form based on the interaction of two characters—the *waki,* an accidental confidant, and the *shite,* the protagonist—with a chorus

- Classification of plays into five subject categories: god, man, woman, insanity, and demon

FIGURE 17.9   Japan: Noh.
Compressed, poetic drama and symbolic, nonrealistic staging typify this traditional form with close ties to Zen Buddhism. Courtesy of the Japan Information and Culture Center, the Embassy of Japan, Washington, D.C.

Traditionally, a Noh performance took all day and consisted of five plays—one from each category, in the above order—and an introductory dance, the *okina,* which used an ancient Sanskrit (Indian) text. All five plays have the same active shape:

- *Jo:* the *waki* introduces himself and "travels" (to chorus accompaniment) to a destination symbolized by a pillar on the stage; the *shite* enters, and *waki* and *shite* engage in question and answer to reveal the *shite's* reason for being at that place and his or her concern.

- *Ha:* the *shite* dances; the dance is related (as expression, narrative, or symbol) to the *shite's* concern.

- *Kyu:* the *shite* appears in a new self called forth by the first two sections—for example, a possessing demon or a ghost. Resolution comes from this confrontation with hidden reality.

Noh plots are simple; their abundant exposition seems natural to a form that is concerned not with events but with the effects of past events. The protagonists are usually tormented figures—dishonored warriors, crazed women, guilty priests—whose appearance in the *kyu* section in a different form is, to a Westerner, a kind of exorcism. Profoundly influenced by Zen Buddhism, however, Noh's ideology is intuitive, not rational, and its goal is an understanding reached by a mental leap from appearance to reality.

Modern Noh performances rarely include five plays because of the plays' length and difficulty. The style and staging, however, remain largely unchanged:

- A small, raised stage, with all entrances made along a raised passage (*hashigakari*) at one side; at the rear is a wall with a pine tree painted on it

- Onstage musicians (three percussionists and flute) and chorus, soberly costumed and unmasked

- Male performers, with the male voice undisguised for female roles

- A very deliberate tempo

- Masks for certain characters

- Elaborate and beautiful costumes, but no scenery, and rare, often symbolic properties

Noh had an important offshoot: Kyogen.

Of later (fifteenth-century) creation but based in much earlier forms, *Kyogen* is a comic drama performed between Noh dramas. It seems a contradiction, for it mocks the very austerity and aristocratic spirituality that make Noh what it is.

The reason usually given is that Kyogen was written by commoners at a period when commoners attended Noh performances; Kyogen expressed their attitudes. Kyogen is funny, dealing in the universals of comedy. Its most typical character is a comic servant who serves a feudal lord and is, of course, smarter than he. Kyogen used the Noh stage but no orchestra or chorus.

Kabuki

Although related to Noh, the far more robust and spectacular form Kabuki, which appeared in the seventeenth century, quickly established itself as a different and far more popular form. Early censorship actually strengthened the form, leading to much more active and diverse texts (when music and dance were temporarily suppressed) and much more carefully defined acting (when first women, then young men, were banned from the stage).

In its developed form, Kabuki featured long and fully developed actions unfolding in many acts, with many characters and scenes. It was also marked by illusionism, with its direct imitation of contemporary (seventeenth-century) life.

FIGURE 17.10 Japan: Kabuki.
This nineteenth-century print shows an older form of Kabuki theatre, with two raised walkways through the audience. Men play female roles; scenery, costumes, and staging are often spectacular.

FIGURE 17.11   Japan: Kabuki.
A contemporary Kabuki performance on a more modern stage. Courtesy of the Japan
Information and Culture Center, Washington, D.C.

The Kabuki also developed its own theatre and style, which included:

- A large raised stage with a raised walkway to it, the *hanamichi,* through
  the audience (originally, there were two such walkways and a
  connecting walkway at the rear)

- Spectacular scenery, including a revolving stage, introduced c. 1750 (the
  first in the world); trap doors; and a front curtain

- Elaborate but fundamentally illusionistic makeup

- Complex, beautiful costumes, including a spectacular feature called
  hikinuki—costumes so constructed that at a gesture they completely
  change, literally turning themselves inside out to reveal, for example, a
  man in armor where a woman had stood

- All-male companies, with the art of the female impersonator carried to
  great detail; as a result, Kabuki became above all an actor's, rather than
  a playwright's, art. Great Kabuki actors have been declared national
  treasures, like great paintings or great buildings.

Kabuki stories were drawn from many sources and were often heroic and
"romantic." Whereas Noh is a theatre of resignation and withdrawal from the
world, Kabuki is a theatre of confrontation and an embracing of the world.

Western-Influenced Theatre

The abrupt influx of Western ideas into Japan in the nineteenth century corresponded roughly with the rise of dramatic Realism in the West. The result was the somewhat exotic blossoming of several imitations of Western theatre, some of them not very well understood by their practitioners.

A modern theatre that kept pace with theatrical changes in the West emerged after the turn of the century. Although not widely popular, it introduced major Western forms and encouraged a Japanese acting style distinct from Kabuki.

Until the 1930s, leftist and proletarian theatres were important; however, censorship under the war governments of the 1930s and 1940s virtually ended modern drama for that period. After World War II, the American occupation government imposed a new kind of censorship—this one prejudicial to Kabuki and traditional forms—and modern theatres began to appear again. A new Japanese play, Junji Kinoshita's *Twilight Crane* (1950), has been called "a milestone in the history of modern Japanese playwriting"; it successfully fused Japanese art with modern concerns and was widely produced.

Recent hits have emphasized plays as diverse as a musical version of *Gone with the Wind* and the plays of Shakespeare. A small avant-garde drama exists. European in influence, it has shown great concern with the theatre's ability to play on the shifting relationships between appearance and reality—the concern of such European avant gardists as Pirandello and Genet. Japan's large cities now have several professional troupes, but theatre is not a truly popular art; like India, Japan is in love with film.

LINKS to more about theatre

David Kerr, *African Popular Theatre*, 1995.

Victor Turner, *From Ritual to Theatre: The Human Seriousness of Play*, 1982.

David Henry Hwang, *M. Butterfly*.

< **www.welcometoindia.com** > Click on culture, then on leisure, then on theatre.

< **www.chinavista.com** > Click on English, then culture, then Beijing opera (under "Music").

< **www.darpana.com** > Website of the Darpana Academy of Performing Arts in India—enlightening hypertext re the school, performances, festivals, etc.

China

Like India's, China's is an ancient culture that developed in a region of diverse geography and languages. Nonetheless, while Europe was struggling to create order after the collapse of Rome, China was already a stable empire whose central administration effectively governed a vast area. Invaders changed the governors but not the institutions of government, and, until the early twentieth century, Chinese society and Chinese culture existed self-sufficiently, exerting influence on Japan and Southeast Asia.

Central to Chinese society were reverence for the past ("ancestor worship") and Confucianism, a moral system based in ideas of stability and family. Social order was strongly marked. Literacy was limited to a small group. Trade and the amassing of wealth were despised. Paradoxically, then, a popular theatre developed whose actors were social outcasts and whose patrons were often wealthy merchants.

The last imperial government of China fell in 1906. Thereafter, more or less stable, more or less democratic governments held on until the Japanese invasion in 1937 and World War II, when much of the country was overrun. In 1949, a communist government under Mao Zedong took over; despite liberalization, China remains cautious of outside influence.

One scholar estimates that more than three hundred regional styles of Chinese theatre exist. Nonetheless, they are represented by—and to some extent are being absorbed by—one of them.

Chinese Opera

The Western designation of Chinese theatre as "opera" suggests one of its major characteristics: reliance on song and musical accompaniment. Chinese music is very different from Western music, and the style of production is very different from that of Western opera, but the name persists. Significantly, too, it accurately reflects the minor role of dance in Chinese theatre.

Early precursors included a form of theatre known as early as the ninth century A.D., for which a palace theatre school, the Pear Garden, was established. In the fourteenth-century Yuan dynasty, China's most important dramas were written. Yuan drama included:

- Performance by both men and women

- Multiact dramatic structure, with one major song per act

- Division of characters into four types: man, woman, and two types of clowns

- Reliance on classical novels and history for stories and characters

A great play of the Yuan period, still performed, was Gao Ming's *The Lute Song* (c. 1360). Hundreds of other plays were written, produced by traveling troupes of actors in temporary theatres throughout southern China.

**FIGURE 17.12
China: Beijing Opera.**
A teacher and student in a class in clown techniques at the Beijing Opera Institute. Courtesy of the People's Republic of China. (See also Figures 3.9. and C-9.)

Classical Chinese theatre as it is now understood—called *Beijing opera* after the city where it appeared—developed in the nineteenth century on the foundation of Yuan and other forms. It is typified by:

- Multiact dramas

- All-male actors

- Song and music virtually throughout

- Division of characters into four major types: male, female, painted face, and clown (*painted face* referring to those using elaborate makeup, e.g., demons and warriors)

- A reliance on traditional sources for stories and characters

Beijing opera in the nineteenth century became an enormously popular form. Although the tradition of itinerant actors continued (troupes rarely stayed at the same theatre more than a few days, even in big cities), permanent theatres were built. Leading actors moved from one theatre to another in the way that Western opera stars move; the repertory was generally so well known that without rehearsal, they could step into a part in any theatre. The performances themselves relied on centuries-old conventions, on stages all of the same type. Outstanding elements included:

- A raised, pillared stage with an audience on three sides and entrances left and right

- No scenery, and restriction of large properties to chairs and tables (which could be used as walls, mountains, and so on)

- An acting style removed from reality, the result of up to twenty years of rigorous training in every gesture and slightest facial movement

- An onstage orchestra and property man

- Symbols and signs—for example, carrying a whip symbolized riding, and running with small flags symbolized wind

- Almost unbelievable acrobatics—used, for example, in battle scenes (see Figure 3.9)

Western accounts of nineteenth-century Beijing opera performances described noisy audiences—laughing, talking, and socializing—but these descriptions may have reflected a corrupt, late stage. However, authorities agree that Beijing opera, like Kabuki, was an actor's art: Audiences came to see the great actor at his great moments. By the late nineteenth century, the rest was a social event.

One name stands out in later Beijing opera: Mei Lan Fang (1894–1943). A superb actor of women's roles, he toured extensively in the West, restored some classical elements to Beijing opera, and was a force for the preservation of the form through World War II. His memoirs are an important record of actor training and theatre history.

Other Chinese Theatre

The fall of the last dynasty loosened antitraditional feelings; antitraditionalists turned West. *Uncle Tom's Cabin* was one of the first non-Chinese plays produced (1911). Others followed, bringing disturbing innovations: popular, rather than classical, language; non-Confucian social and moral questions; all-spoken (not sung) drama; and, after 1924, actresses in female roles. The first coeducational theatre school was created in 1930. A new drama emerged, typified by Ts'ao Yu's *Thunderstorm* and his play of World War II, *Metamorphosis,* which encountered difficulties with both the communists and the anticommunists.

With the communist rise to power in 1949, Chinese theatre went into a period of change, some of it under Russian influence (evident in the introduction of classical ballet, for example). A model revolutionary opera, *Taking Tiger Mountain by Strategy,* was produced, incorporating conventions of Beijing opera but relentless in its revolutionary emphasis.

Contemporary Chinese theatre includes traditional Beijing opera and modern theatre, as well as resurgent regional theatre forms. In addition, the Republic of China (Taiwan) preserves some traditional forms, and opera companies exist in the Chinese communities of Western cities like San Francisco.

A very small avant-garde movement has appeared in China; however, the repressions of 1989 and after have endangered it. With expression rigidly controlled, avant gardism is likely to withdraw into formalism.

CURRENT ISSUES

As we have seen, theatre often participated in the colonization of a culture, sometimes replacing and sometimes corrupting already existing modes of performance. It is perhaps unsurprising, then, that theatre has become a flash point for persons wishing to assert cultural independence from the West. Such people often urge a rejection of the West—its values, its politics, its culture, and its art, including its theatre. Much world theatre of the last twenty years has been theatre reacting against the remnants of colonialism. One such theatre is theatre for development.

In developing countries, those persons rejecting Western values have most often sought to distance themselves from Western theatre's reliance on causal plots and illusionistic settings, its artistic specialization and elitism, and, perhaps most of all, its commercialism. They seek instead a theatre that is by and for common people, one aimed at building community and improving daily life, one that rejects hierarchy and asserts the worth of personal experience. One transformation of Western theatre to meet local needs can be seen in changes made in theatre for development within the last decade or so.

FIGURE 17.13
Theatre for Development.
Chimbuzi (The Toilet), collectively directed by the Mulangali Theatre for Health Workshop, Malawi. Courtesy of David Kerr.

Theatre for development was once produced by experienced theatre people *for* villagers. For example, officials in a government or a university would see a problem (e.g., AIDS, marriage laws); they would study the problem and decide on an appropriate course of action for its solution or amelioration; they would work with actors to develop a script and production; finally, they would send a company of actors into the countryside to perform plays that would show the problem and solution in dramatic form, thus hoping to educate the villagers to take certain steps for their own good. This, the top-down model, has come to be viewed as arrogant, paternalistic, "Western," "colonial."

Theatre for development is now conceived cooperatively. A few actors go into a village, living there for weeks or months and talking *with* villagers about their problems and how they think they might solve them. Together, the activist/actors and villagers develop and rehearse a script in the local language. All villagers are encouraged to participate—watching rehearsals, performing, gathering costumes and properties. This bottom-up model assumes that people who have problems will be able to identify them and suggest ways of solving them. The theatre thus becomes a way of studying a problem, devising a solution, and showing all involved how to effect the solution. Opening up the processes of both making plays and exploring solutions is said to demystify both theatre and social problems and so to empower ordinary people, allowing them to control their own lives and art.

Theatre for development is not without its critics. Perhaps because it has been most often practiced by activists of the political left, theatre for development is often opposed by those on the right. Others argue that expecting uneducated villagers to analyze their problems and suggest feasible solutions is naive, unrealistic, and so unproductive. Still others maintain that, although theatre for development may be socially useful, it is neither artistic nor aesthetically pleasing and so is not really theatre at all. The issue is not hypothetical: it was Ngugi's move into a kind of theatre for development that caused his detention and exile.

What should be the role of theatre in a developing society?

Key terms

Check your understanding against this list. Brief definitions are in the Glossary; page references there will direct you to appropriate pages. (Persons are page-referenced in the Index.)

Beijing Opera	Kyogen	Paratheatrical
Kabuki	*Natyasastra*	ritual
Kathakali	Noh	theatre for development
Kuttiyatam	Orta oyunu	Yoruba opera

Glossary

(Discussion will be found on the page or pages indicated, where appropriate.)

A-Effect: See *Alienation.*

Abstraction: An artistic depiction that is different from a literal, photographic representation of the thing depicted, usually by being more generalized, less particular. (72)

Absurdism: A style of drama popularized in France after World War II that viewed human existence as meaningless and treated language as an inadequate means of communication. Major authors include Samuel Beckett and Eugène Ionesco. (372)

Academy: A group formed to further a specific artistic or literary end; for example, the French Academy and the rhetorical academies of the Renaissance. (298)

Acting: Creation of a character in action, through impersonation, for an audience. In formal acting, the actor seeks the truth of theatrical convention; in realistic acting, the actor seeks the truth of everyday life.

Action: According to Aristotle, a causally linked sequence of events, with beginning, middle, and end; the proper and best way to unify a play. More popularly, the single and unified human process of which a drama is the imitation. To some modern critics, an interaction (between dramatic protagonist and others).

Actor-Manager: A starring actor who is head and nominal artistic director of a company; for example, Sir Henry Irving in the late nineteenth century in England. (337)

Actors Equity: See *Unions.*

Actos: Very short, politically significant playlets. Term associated with Chicano theatre, particularly the work of El Teatro Campesino. (388)

Aesthetic Response: Audience reaction to art object as art, not as idea, meaning, and so on; implies some idea of "beauty." (8)

Aesthetics: Study of the nature of beauty.

Agitprop: Short for *agitation propaganda.* A kind of political drama popular in the 1920s and 1930s in America. Phrase subsequently used to describe all didactic drama whose social stance was unusually militant.

Alienation: Customary, but perhaps misleading, translation of the German *Verfremdung,* "to make strange." Term now almost always associated with Bertolt Brecht's epic theatre, which aims to distance the spectator from the play's action in order to force conscious consideration of the political and social issues raised by the play. Shortened often to A-effect. (375)

Alley Stage: Performance-area shape that puts audience on each side with the performance area, usually a long rectangle, between. (84)

Angle Perspective: Multipoint perspective; results when several vanishing points are located away from the center of the stage so that vistas appear toward the wings. (311)

Angle Wing: Wings consisting of two parts hinged together, one rectangular flat placed parallel with the proscenium arch and one (called the return) placed at an angle to it in order to increase the sense of distance. (On a raked stage, the return is not a rectangle but a trapezoid.)

Antagonist: The opponent in an *agon,* or contest; in drama, either of two opponents in conflict, or the character who opposes the protagonist. (49)

Antiquarianism: The study of the details of past civilizations, often with a view to reproducing historically accurate settings onstage. Movement was popular toward the end of the eighteenth century and is viewed as a precursor to Romanticism. (328)

Apron: That part of a stage that extends in front of the proscenium arch. (82)

Arena (Stage) Theatre: A theatre in which the audience completely surrounds the playing area. Also called *theatre in the round.* (84)

Art: Activity done for its own ends, separable from both life and practicality, although it may be applied to very practical as well as aesthetic purposes. (7)

Art Theatre: A theatrical movement of the late nineteenth and early twentieth centuries that tried to separate itself from commercial theatre and the reliance on box-office. (366)

Atellan Farce: A short, rustic, improvised, and often bawdy play especially popular in Rome during the first centuries B.C. and A.D. Possibly the forerunner of the *commedia dell'arte* (see entry).

Audition: A session at which a theatre artist, usually an actor, displays his or her craft in order to secure a job. (137)

Auditorium: "Hearing place"; audience section of theatre.

Autos Sacramentales: Vernacular religious plays of sixteenth- and seventeenth-century Spain. (289)

Balance: On the proscenium stage, the visual equalizing of the two halves of the stage picture as seen from the audience. In any stage moment, the attempt to achieve a sense of equal weight among the people and objects on stage. More a metaphor than an actuality. (172)

Balcony: Elevated audience area.

Ballad Opera: A "minor" form of musical drama especially popular during the eighteenth and nineteenth centuries in England and featuring political satire interlarded with familiar tunes for which new and topical lyrics were devised; for example, John Gay's *The Beggar's Opera.*

Beat: A rhythmic unit in a play; defined variously by different actors and directors. (177)

Beijing Opera: Traditional Chinese theatrical form, spectacular, nonrealistic. (424)

Benefit: A performance, the profit of which is set aside for a particular actor, company member, or cause. In the eighteenth and nineteenth centuries, a primary means of supplementing an actor's annual salary. Now, any performance done for charity. (315)

Biomechanics: The concept and the complex of techniques devised by Vsevolod Myerhold to train actors so that their bodies could be as responsive as a machine. (371)

Black Theatre Movement: A theatre movement of the 1960s and after, primarily for black audiences, actors, and playwrights, originally connected with the Black Power Movement, a political ideology. (389)

Blocking: Stage movement for actors, given in rehearsal (usually) by the director. (166)

Body Language: Communicable emotional states understood from posture and other conscious and unconscious use of the body. See also *Gesture.* (128)

Book: 1. The spoken text of a play or musical; early musicals with stories and dialogue were called *book musicals.* 2. Several flats hinged together and folded together form a *book of flats.* 3. To *book* a production is to schedule a performance of it.

Booth: Temporary structure for fairs, etc; *booth stage* has playing area in front of curtained booth.

Border: Curtain, or less often flats or cutouts, suspended at intervals behind the proscenium arch to mask the overhead rigging. Particularly important in Italianate settings. (301)

Boulevard: Historically the permanent home of the old fair theatres of eighteenth-century Paris, and later of the illegitimate houses where melodrama and comic opera flourished during the nineteenth century. Now refers to the district of the commercial theatres in Paris and means roughly what the word *Broadway* implies in the United States. (312)

Box: Historically the favored, and most expensive, seats in a theatre. Made by sectioning off parts of a gallery, boxes were spacious and outfitted with armed chairs, in contrast to the crowded galleries, whose seats consisted of backless benches, and to the pit, where originally no seats were provided. (327)

Box, Pit, and Gallery: Eighteenth- and nineteenth-century arrangement of audience with a ground-level pit, up to five levels of boxes or galleries surrounding it, with the cheapest seats at top. (327)

Box Set: Interior setting represented by flats forming three sides (the fourth wall being the proscenium line); first used around 1830 and common after 1850. (350)

Breeches Role: Role in which an actress portrays a male character and dresses like a man, presumably adding sexual titillation to dramatic interest. (329)

Broadway: In popular parlance, the area of New York City on and adjacent to the street named Broadway, where the commercial theatre of America is concentrated. (85)

Bugaku: Traditional Japanese dance form.

Bunraku: Traditional Japanese puppet theatre using half-life-size dolls manipulated by puppeteers visible to the audience.

Burlesque: In eighteenth- and nineteenth-century theatre, a form of "minor" drama popular in England and featuring satire and parody. In America of the late nineteenth century and the twentieth century, a kind of entertainment originally dependent on a series of variety acts but later including elements of female display (including striptease) in its major offerings. After moving to the fringes of respectability by the 1940s, burlesque disappeared in the United States by the late 1950s.

Business: Activity performed by actor(s) at given points in a performance; for example, the *business* of lighting a cigarette or cooking a meal. See also *Lines of business.*

Byplay: Business that takes place alongside the primary action and that is slightly different from it; for example, in *Tartuffe,* Orgon's behavior under the table while Tartuffe is trying to seduce Orgon's wife.

Casting Call: Public announcement of auditions or interviews for casting of a play. (163)

Catharsis: Aristotle cited as the end cause of tragedy "the arousal and catharsis of such emotions [pity and fear]," a statement popularly understood to mean that tragedy "purges" fear and pity from the audience; but alternative interpretations suggest that tragedy arouses and satisfies such emotions within its own structure and characters. Highly controversial and elusive concept. (241)

Causality: Belief that human events have causes (and therefore consequences); as a result, events are seen as joined in a chain of cause and effect.

Causal Plot: Plot of linked, internally consistent cause and effect. (47)

Cazuela: In Spanish Golden Age theatre, the women's area. (288)

Centering: Actor's term for localization of human energy source in the body, usually in the abdomen. (124)

Character: One of Aristotle's six parts of a play, the material of plot and the formal cause of thought; an agent (participant, doer) in the play whose qualities and traits arise from ethical deliberation. In popular parlance, the agents or "people" in the play. (48)

Chariot and Pole: An elaborate system for changing elements of the scenery simultaneously. Devised by Giacomo Torelli in the seventeenth century, the system involved scenery attached to poles that rose through slits in the stage floor from chariots that ran on tracks in the basement and depended on an intricate system of interlocking ropes, pulleys, wheels, and windlasses for their simultaneous movement. (301)

Chorus: In Greek drama of the fifth century B.C., a group of men (number uncertain) who sang, chanted, spoke, and moved, usually in unison, and who, with the actors (three in tragedy and five in comedy), performed the plays. In the Renaissance, a single character named *Chorus* who provided information and commentary about the action in some tragedies. In modern times, the groups that sing and/or dance in musical comedies, operettas, ballets, and operas.

City Dionysia: The major religious festival devoted to the worship of the god Dionysus in Athens. The first records of tragedy appeared at this festival in 534 B.C., and so it is called the home of tragedy. See also *Festivals.* (238)

Classical: Specifically refers to that period of Greek drama and theatre from 534 B.C. to 336 B.C. (the advent of the Hellenistic period). Loosely used now to refer to Greek and Roman drama and theatre in general (a period dating roughly from the sixth century B.C. through the sixth century A.D., about twelve hundred years). (230)

Climax: The highest point of plot excitement for the audience. (47)

Cloak and Sword Play *(capa y espada):* Romantic Spanish plays of love and dueling—swashbucklers. (289)

Closet Drama: Plays written to be read, not performed.

Comedy: A form (genre) of drama variously discussed in terms of its having a happy ending, dealing with the material, mundane world, dealing with the low and middle classes, dealing with myths of rebirth and social regeneration, and so on.

Comedy, Middle: See **Middle Comedy.**

Comedy, New: See **New Comedy.**

Comedy, Old: See **Old Comedy.**

Comedy of Manners: Refers most often to seventeenth- and eighteenth-century comedies whose focus is the proper social behavior of a single class. (315)

Comic Opera: A "minor" form of musical drama popular first in the eighteenth century and characterized then by sentimental stories set to original music. Later used to mean an opera in which some parts were spoken (in contrast to "grand opera," where everything was sung).

Commedia dell'Arte: Italian popular comedy of the fifteenth through seventeenth centuries. Featured performances improvised from scenarios by a set of stock characters and repeated from play to play and troupe to troupe. See also *Lazzi*. (302)

Community Theatre: Theatre performed by and for members of a given community, especially a city or town. Usually amateur, with sometimes professional directors, designers, and business staff. (93)

Complication: Ascending or tying action. That part of the plot in which the action is growing tenser and more intricate up to the point of *crisis* (turning point), after which the action unties and resolves in a section called the *dénouement* (see entries). (46)

Composition: Arrangement of visual elements for aesthetic effect.

Confidant(e): In drama, a character to whom another leading character gives private information. (49)

Conflict: Clash of characters, seen either as objectives that create obstacles for each other, or as actions, neither of which can succeed unless the other fails.

Confraternity: In France, a religious brotherhood, many of which sponsored or produced plays during the Middle Ages. One, the Confraternity of the Passion, held a monopoly on play production in Paris into the 1570s. (266)

Constructivism: A nonrealistic style of scenic design associated with Vsevolod Myerhold and marked by the view that a good set is a machine for doing plays, not a representation of familiar locales. Incorporated simple machines on stage and often revealed the method of its own construction. (371)

Continental Seating: First devised by Wagner in the late nineteenth century for his theatre at Bayreuth; eschews a central aisle in favor of entrances and exits at the end of each aisle. (336)

Convention: A way of doing things agreed on by a (usually unstated) contract between audience and artists; for example, characters' singing their most important feelings and emotions is a *convention* of musical comedy. (70)

Copyright: Legal concept of intellectual property rights.

Corpus Christi: A spring festival established in the fourteenth century in honor of the Christian Eucharist, at which medieval cycle plays and cosmic dramas (see entry) were often performed. Also see *Festivals*. (270)

Corrales: Spanish theatres of the late middle ages, sited in open courtyards among houses. (288)

Cosmic Drama: Long dramatic presentations popular in the Middle Ages that depicted religious events from the Creation to the Last Judgment. Short plays were combined until the total presentation could last several days or weeks and occasionally a month or more. See also *Cycle play*. (271)

Court Theatre: A theatre located at the court of a nobleman. After the Renaissance, Italianate theatre, whose perspective was drawn with the vanishing points established from the chair of the theatre where the ruler sat, making his the best seat in the house.

Crisis: Decisive moment at the high point of a rising action; turning point. (47)

Criticism: The careful, systematic, and imaginative study and evaluation of works of drama and theatre (or any other form of art). (211)

Cue: Immediate stimulus for a line, an action, or an effect.

Cycle Play: Medieval (especially English) dramas covering the "cycle" of history from the creation of the world to doomsday. See also *Cosmic drama*. (271)

Dadaism: Art movement of the first third of the twentieth century that rejected logic and tradition; often satirical, sometimes intentionally contradictory, silly. (373)

Decision: In Aristotelian criticism, the most highly characterizing trait of a dramatic agent; the trait that translates idea into action and thus, in Aristotelian terms, unites with plot (in the sense here of action). See also *Plot* and *Action*.

Declamation: A style of verbal delivery that emphasizes beauty of sound, speech, and rhetorical meaning rather than the realistic imitation of everyday speaking.

Deconstruction: A strategy in criticism for finding unintended meanings in a work. Popularized by Jacques Derrida, postmodern strategies have been adopted by feminists and Marxists for social as well as poetic analyses of scripts and performances. (211)

Decorum: In Neoclassical theory, the behavior of a dramatic character in keeping with his or her social status, age, sex, and occupation; based on the requirements of *verisimilitude* (see entry). (295)

Dénouement: That part of the plot that follows the crisis (turning point) and that includes the untangling or resolving of the play's complications. (46)

Determinism: Philosophical stance undergirding Naturalistic drama that asserts that human behavior and destiny are determined by factors, especially heredity and environment, largely beyond human control.

Deus ex Machina: Literally, "the god from the machine," a reference to a deity who flew in at the conclusion of some Greek tragedies (particularly those of Euripides) to assure the play's appropriate outcome. Popularly, any ending of a play that is obviously contrived.

Dialect: Regional or ethnic speech, sometimes necessary for an actor in a particular role. (131)

Diction: In Aristotle, one of the six parts of a play; also called language; the formal cause of music, the material of thought; the words of a play. Popularly the proper and clear formation of the play's words. (52)

Didacticism: "Teaching." In the theatre, plays are didactic when they emphasize ideological content rather than artistic form.

Dimmer: Instrument for controlling the intensity of light by manipulating the amount of electricity that reaches individual lamps. (199)

Dionysia: A Greek religious festival in honor of the god Dionysus. The City Dionysia and the Rural Dionysia both included drama as a part of the celebration, but the city festival was clearly the dominant one of the two. See also *Festivals.* (229)

Diorama: Distant scene viewed through a cutout or other opening in scenery. Also, a three-dimensional arrangement of figures and painted scenes.

Discovery: According to Aristotle, any passage from ignorance to knowledge within a play, by means of (for example) sign, emotion, reasoning, action. Good discoveries grow out of suffering (awareness) and lead to reversal (change of direction). (46)

Discovery Space: Permanent or temporary space in the Elizabethan (Shakespearean) playhouse that permitted actors and locales to be hidden from view and then "discovered" (or revealed) when needed. Location, appearance, and even invariable existence of the space are hotly disputed. (279)

Dithyramb: A hymn of praise, often to the god Dionysus, performed by a chorus of men or boys; a regular part of the religious festival of Athens after 509 B.C. (226)

Domestic Tragedy: A serious play dealing with domestic problems of the middle or lower classes. In the eighteenth century, a reaction against "regular" or Neoclassical tragedy. See also *Purity of genres.* (331)

Double: 1. To play more than one role. 2. *The Theatre and Its Double,* an influential book by Antonin Artaud, calls the Western theatre merely a shadow or *double* of the (to him) true and vital Eastern theatre.

Downstage: That part of the stage closest to the front. In early Italianate theatres, the stage floor was raked (slanted) up from the front to the back; therefore, to move forward on the stage was literally to move "down the stage." (168)

Drama: 1. In the eighteenth century, a serious play (*drame,* in France) that dealt with domestic issues and thus failed to conform to the standard Neoclassical definition of tragedy. 2. Any serious play that is not a tragedy. 3. The literary component of performance, the *play*—often contrasted with the *theatre.*

Dramaturgy: Practice and study of creation of plays for the theatre; the work of the dramaturg. (213)

Dress Rehearsal: A final rehearsal in which all visual elements of production, including costumes, are used. Typically a rehearsal that strives to duplicate, insofar as possible, an actual performance. (178)

Drop: Backdrop. Large curtain, usually of painted canvas, hung at the rear of the stage to provide literal and visual closure for the stage setting. (327)

Dual-Issue Ending: Double ending. Ending of a play when good is rewarded *and* evil is punished. Associated with melodrama particularly.

Eccyclema: In classical Greece, a machine used to thrust objects or people (often dead) from inside the scene house into view of the audience. Probably some sort of wheeled platform that rolled or rotated through the *skene's* central door. (232)

Eclectic(ism): Gathering of materials from many sources; popularly a mixture of styles and methods. In twentieth-century theatre, the idea that each play calls forth its own production style.

Educational Theatre: Theatre by and (in part) for students in an elementary, secondary, or collegiate setting. (92)

Emblem: A device (usually an object or picture of object) used as an identifying mark; something that stands for something else. In the Middle Ages, a key stood for St. Peter, a crooked staff for a bishop. (262)

Empathy: "Feeling into" another's state.

Ensemble: A performing group. Also, a group acting method that emphasizes unity and consistency of performances.

Environment: The visual and spatial surrounding of the play, influenced by such matters as mood and visual meaning.

Environmental Theatre: 1. Theatre whose performance is the audience's environment, so that the performance surrounds some or all of the audience and the line between performance space and audience space breaks down. 2. Theatre done in nontraditional space.

Ephemeral Art: Art that cannot be repeated exactly.

Epic Theatre: Term originated by Erwin Piscator and popularized by Brecht to describe a theatre where the audience response is objective, not subjective, and where such narrative devices as film projections, titles, and storytelling are used. See also *Alienation.* (375)

Epilogue: A short scene that comes at the conclusion of the main line(s) of action.

Episodic plot: Plot whose incidents are connected by idea or metaphor or character, not by cause and effect. (48)

Existentialism: A philosophical system that lies at the root of Absurdism (see entry) and whose basic assumptions are the absence of transcendental values, the isolation of humans and their acts, and the lack of causality in the universe. (373)

Experimental Theatre: Any theatre whose methods or goals depart markedly from the mainstream of its day; thus, in the eighteenth century, Romanticism was experimental; in the heyday of American Realism, Absurdism was experimental.

Exposition: Necessary information about prior events, or a part of a play given over to communicating such information; because it is a "telling" and not an enacting of narrative, it is usually nondramatic. (45)

Expressionism: A style of theatre popular in Europe after World War I and typified by symbolic presentation of meaning, often as viewed from the standpoint of the main character; distortions of time, space, and proportion are common. (370)

Facade Stage: One that puts the actors in front of a neutral (nonrepresentational) surface. (231)

Farce: Form of comedy "stuffed" with laughs that arise not from verbal wit or human profundity but (usually) mechanics: business, mix-ups, mistaken identities, etc. (56)

Feminist Criticism: Analyses of plays and productions in terms of gender and the consequent effects on audiences and society. (211)

Feminist Theory of Theatre: An attempt to explain the effects of gender in the workings of theatre and drama and, through them, on society and culture. (211)

Festivals: In Greece, religious worship took place in private and at major public festivals. In and around Athens, there were four festivals devoted to the god Dionysus. At three of these, records of drama appeared during the fifth century B.C. At the festival of no other gods can such records be found. See *City Dionysia, Rural Dionysia,* and *Lenaia.* During the Middle Ages, there were Christian festivals at which dramas were often produced. See also *Corpus Christi.*

Flat: A structure upon which scenery is painted, consisting of a wooden frame and canvas covering; usually of a size to be carried by one or two persons for shifting. Used in both Italianate staging and box sets (see entries).

Floodlights: Broad-beam stage instruments that "flood" a large area with light. (199)

Flying: Method of handling scenery for quick shifting by raising it out of sight over the stage with one of various systems of ropes, pulleys, counterweights, machines, and so on. Also, the illusion of flight in actors and properties through the use of concealed wires and the same system of ropes and pulleys.

Focus: The point or object that draws the eye of the audience to the stage picture. (171)

Foil: A minor character intended to set off another character through contrast. (49)

Followspot: Powerful, hard-edged lighting instrument mounted so that an operator can "follow" action with the light. (199)

Footlights: Light sources arranged along the front of a stage (between actors and audience) to throw light upward from stage level to eliminate shadows from harsh overhead lighting. Rarely used with modern lighting systems, but standard equipment with candle, oil, gas, and early electrical systems (c. 1650–1920).

Forestage: That level part of the stage in front of the scenery, especially in Renaissance stages, which used a slanted floor for forced perspective in the scenic area. See also *Apron.* (313)

Formalism: 1. Strict adherence to established ways (forms) of doing things. 2. In scenic design, use of nonrepresentational shapes and forms as the design base. 3. In criticism, attention to matters of dramatic form and structure as distinct from philosophical and sociological issues.

Fourth Wall (Realism): Nineteenth-century concept of a completely Realistic performance space that the audience looked into through a removed or invisible "wall" (the proscenium plane). (346)

French Scene: Scene division between entrance or exit of major character(s). (176)

Front of House: Activities relating to production that transpire in front of the curtain: e.g., promotion and publicity for performances, house management, box office sales. (214)

Functionalism: Aesthetic or artistic method that focuses on the function of objects (scenery, for example) instead of on prettiness.

Gallery: The highest audience areas in nineteenth-century theatres (box, pit, and gallery), hence, the cheapest seats; the balconies. (327)

Gel: In stage lighting, a medium for coloring the beam of light. (199)

Generic Criticism: Criticism by identification of genre (comedy, tragedy, etc.) (55)

Genre: In dramatic criticism, a category of plays: comedy, tragedy, melodrama, farce. Popularly, any category. (55)

Gesture: In one sense, any human act that conveys meaning (i.e., a speech is a gesture). In a more limited sense, a planned physical movement that conveys meaning, like waving a hand or pointing a finger.

Given Circumstances: In Stanislavskian vocabulary, those aspects of character that are beyond the character's or actor's control: age, sex, state of health, and so on. (133)

Given Circumstances (of performance): Basic facts that define the world of the play; conditions of place, period, social level, and so on. (68)

Glory: In medieval and Renaissance art, a cloud or sunburst in which divinities appeared. In the theatre of those periods, a flown platform made to look like a cloud or sunburst. (267)

Golden Age: The great age of any culture. In Spain, the period c. 1550–1650, the greatest age of Spanish drama; in France, the age of Louis XIV; in England, the age of Elizabeth and Shakespeare.

Gradas: Covered bleacher-style seats at ground level in the Spanish *corrales* (which see).

Graeco-Roman: That period in Greece and Greek lands when Roman domination had arrived, usually dated from c. 100 B.C. to the fall of the Western Roman Empire, c. A.D. 550. In theatre architecture, those Greek theatres that were remodeled to bring them in closer accord with the Roman ideals. (Not to be confused with Roman theatres built in Greek lands.) (242)

Griot: West African storyteller. (406)

Groove: A shallow channel in the stage floor in which a flat rode, for quick scene changes; a bank of several grooves would allow one flat to be pulled aside while another was pushed on in its place, seemingly in the same plane. (312)

Ground Plan: The "map" of the playing area for a scene, with doors, furniture, walls, and so on indicated to scale. (161)

Ground Row: A piece of scenery at stage level, often used to hide stage-level machinery or lights or to increase the sense of distance. (327)

Guerrilla Theatre: Didactic political theatre done in nontheatrical spaces—streets, factories, subways—without previous announcement; hit-and-run performances like guerrilla attacks. (387)

Guilds: Religious and, sometimes, trade or professional organizations in the Middle Ages that became the producers of civic medieval theatre. (266)

Hamartia: Aristotle's concept of error or failure of judgment by the tragic hero (sometimes translated inaccurately as "tragic flaw"). (242)

Hanamichi: In the Japanese Kabuki theatre, a walkway through the audience used by actors to get to and from the stage. (422)

Happening: Quasi-theatrical event of the 1960s, done outside the commercial theatre, usually done in nontraditional spaces and having no plot (in the Aristotelian sense); often, audience members moved through the event at their own rates and in their own sequences. (387)

Happy Idea: The basic premise on which a particular Greek old comedy was based. For example, the *happy idea* in *Lysistrata* is that women can prevent war by withholding sex. (238)

Hashigakari: In the Japanese Noh theatre, a walkway at the side of the stage for the actors' entrances and exits. (420)

Heavens: 1. Area above the stage: in the Elizabethan theatre, the underside of the roof that extended over the stage. 2. In the nineteenth century, the highest gallery. (277)

Hellenistic: 1. That period of Greek history dating from the coming of Alexander the Great (c. 336 B.C.). 2. In theatre architecture, those Greek theatres built during the Hellenistic period. (238)

Hero: 1. A figure embodying a culture's most valued qualities (for example, Achilles in *The Iliad*) and hence the central figure in a heroic tragedy. 2. Popularly the leading character in a play or, more precisely, the leading male character in a play. 3. In melodrama, the male character who loves the heroine. See also *Protagonist.*

Heroic: Of or relating to a hero; by extension, exalted. *Heroic couplets* are two lines of rhyming iambic pentameter, probably an English attempt to reproduce the French Alexandrine, the approved verse for Neoclassical tragedy. *Heroic acting* stressed the vocal and physical grandeur of the actor. *Heroic tragedy,* popular during the seventeenth and eighteenth centuries, customarily treated the conflict between love and duty and was written in heroic couplets.

High Comedy: Comedy of intellect and language, usually emphasizing upper-class characters and concerns. See also *Comedy.*

Hikinuki: In Japanese Kabuki performance, the sudden transformation of a costume into a completely different one. (422)

Hireling: In professional companies of the Renaissance and after, an actor or technician hired by the shareholders, to work for a set wage at a set task. (281)

Hit or Flop: Supposed condition of a commercial theatre that has no middle ground and no economic tolerance for plays that may earn back their costs slowly. (86)

Householder: Member of an acting company who owns a share of the theatre building itself. (281)

Humanism: That philosophy that believes that people should be at the center of their own deepest concerns. (274)

Idea: In Aristotelian criticism, the moral expression of character through language; more generally, the intellectual statement of the *meaning* (see entry) of a play or a performance. (50)

Identification: Audience attitude in which the audience member believes that important elements of himself or herself are to be found in a dramatic character; the audience "identifies" with the character. A suspect theory. (66)

Illusion of the First Time: An expression used by an English critic (late nineteenth century) to describe the effect of good realistic acting: That is, the event seems to be happening for the first time *to the character.*

Illusionism: Scenic practices (with analogs in acting, directing, and other theatre arts) that rely on a belief in the theatrical imitation of the real world. (297)

Imagination: In acting, inventive faculty of the actor. (See also *Instrument.*) More generally, that faculty of mind or feeling, usually thought to be nonlinear, imagistic, metaphorical, and playful. (122)

Impersonate: To pretend to be another.

Impressionism: A style of art that sought truth in fleeting moments of consciousness. Prevalent in the drama and theatre of the 1890s, Impressionism was noted for its moody and mysterious quality. (368)

Improvisation: Acting technique or exercise emphasizing immediacy of response and invention rather than rehearsed behavior. (133)

Independent Theatre Movement: In nineteenth-century Europe, the appearance of noncommercial theatres in several countries more or less simultaneously, most of them amateur or nontraditional and able to operate outside the usual censorship, "independent" of commercial demands. (347)

Instrument: The actor's physical self. See also *Imagination.* (121)

Interlude: A kind of dramatic fare performed between other events, as between the courses of a banquet. Important during the Middle Ages and the Renaissance and connected with the rise of the professional actor. (271)

Intermezzi: Italian entertainments usually given at courts and presented between other forms of entertainment. See *Interlude.* (302)

Italianate Staging: A kind of staging developed during the Renaissance in Italy and marked by a proscenium arch and perspective scenery arranged in wing and shutter. (300)

Kabuki: Traditional Japanese theatre of great spectacle and powerful stories, often heroic and chivalric or military. (421)

Kathakali: Traditional Indian dance-drama form. (417)

Kuttambalam: Theatre type used by an Indian *Kuttiyattam* (which see): square, roofed stage with audience on three sides. (417)

Kuttiyattam: Indian theatrical form, derived from Sanskrit drama. (416)

Kyogen: Japanese theatre form: comic interludes between parts of a Noh performance. (420)

Latin Music Drama: Medieval dramas performed inside churches by clergy. The dramas unfolded in Latin rather than the vernacular and were sung rather than spoken, thus the name. Also called Liturgical Drama. (269)

Laughing Comedy: Specifically, comedy dating from the late eighteenth century and intended to restore the comic (laughing) spirit to the comedies of the age—in contrast to the then-popular sentimental or tearful comedies. (See entry.) (333)

Lazzi: Stock bits of business designed to provoke a particular response, usually laughter, from the audience. Associated particularly with the *commedia dell'arte* and the French farce of the seventeenth century. (303)

Lenaia: One of three major Athenian religious festivals devoted to the public worship of the god Dionysus at which drama was recorded. The home of comedy. See also *Festivals.* (237)

Light Plot: The lighting designer's graphic rendering of the arrangement of lights and their connections. (199)

Lines of Business: A range of roles in which an actor would specialize for the major part of his or her acting career. Particularly important during the seventeenth and eighteenth centuries. (314)

Little Theatre Movement: In the early twentieth-century United States, the appearance of noncommercial theatres throughout the country dedicated to art; many became community theatres. (359)

Liturgical: Associated with the liturgy of the church; in drama, the kinds of plays that were done inside churches as part of the religious services and thus were performed in Latin, by the clergy, and were usually chanted or sung rather than spoken. Liturgical drama is also called Latin Music Drama. (269)

Liturgy: The rites of worship, as in the medieval church. Thus, *liturgical drama* was a body of plays created to play within the worship service. (269)

Long Run: Uninterrupted sequence of performances of the same play, "long" by comparison with that of others like it: A dozen performances would have been a long run in the seventeenth century; on today's Broadway, a long run can last years.

Low Comedy: A kind of comedy that depends for its humor primarily on situation, visual gags, or obscenity. See also *Comedy.*

Ludi: 1. In Rome, festivals or *ludi* were given for public worship of a variety of gods and on various public occasions like military victories and the funerals of government officials. As drama was often included as a part of the festivals, they are important in a history of Roman theatre. 2. Early medieval term for plays. (244)

Machine Plays: Plays written especially to show off the special effects and movable scenery in a theatre. Especially popular during the Neoclassical period, when regular plays obeyed "unity of place" and so had few opportunities for elaborate scenic changes. (307)

Mansion: The particularized setting in the medieval theatre that, together with the *platea,* or generalized playing space, constituted the major staging elements of the theatre. Several mansions were placed around or adjacent to the *platea* at once—thus "simultaneous staging." See also *Platea.* (263)

Masque: Spectacular theatrical form, especially of the Renaissance and the Neoclassical periods, usually associated with *court theatres* (see entry) or special events. Emphasis was put on costumes and effects, with much music and dancing; amateur actors frequently performed. For example, Ben Jonson's many court masques. (285)

Master Artist: A term, coined by Richard Wagner, to identify the person responsible for the unification of a complex work of art like a music drama; someone who controls every aspect of a performance. (335)

Master Artwork: *Gesamtkunstwerk.* Both term and concept popularized by Richard Wagner, who argued that such a work would be the artistic fusion of all major artistic elements, including music, into a single work under the artistic supervision of a single master artist. (335)

Master of Secrets: That craftsman/artist of the medieval theatre charged with the execution of special effects in the dramas. (267)

Meaning: Intellectual content suggested or inspired by a play or a performance. All plays have meaning, however trivial, and most plays and performances have several meanings. Best thought of as "range of meaning" or "world of meaning." (50)

Mechane: Machine, or *machina.* In classical Greece, a crane by means of which actors and objects could be flown into the playing area. (232)

Medieval: That period of world history dating roughly from the fall of the Western Roman Empire (c. A.D. 550) to the fall of Constantinople and the beginning of the Renaissance (c. 1450). In drama, the period between 975, the first record of drama, and c. 1550, when religious drama was outlawed in many countries throughout Europe. (259)

Melodrama: Literally "music drama." A kind of drama associated with a simplified moral universe, a set of stock characters (hero, heroine, villain, comic relief), rapid turns in the dramatic action, and a dual-issue ending. Leading form of drama throughout the nineteenth century. (331)

Method: The American version of Stanislavski's "system" of actor training. (361)

Middle Ages: An early name for the period dating roughly from the fall of Rome to the Renaissance.

Middle Comedy: That transitional kind of Greek comedy dating from c. 404 B.C., the defeat of Athens by Sparta, to 336 B.C., the beginning of the Hellenistic Age. Less topical than Greek old comedy, middle comedy dealt more with domestic issues and everyday life of the Athenian middle class. (237)

Milk an Audience: When a performer tries to evoke responses from an audience beyond that which it seems inclined to give. (30)

Mime: 1. A kind of drama in which *unmasked* actors of both sexes portrayed often bawdy and obscene stories. In Rome, it became the most popular kind of drama after the first century A.D. 2. Form of silent modern theatre. (251)

Miracle Plays: Medieval plays treating the lives of saints. (270)

Modernism: Name for art of a period (roughly 1890–1950) identified by radical experimentation with form and nonrealism.

Monopoly: Legal control or exclusive domination of a theatrical locale; the courts of both France and England in the late seventeenth century, for example, granted licenses to a limited number of theatres that thus gained *monopolies.* (310)

Morality Plays: Allegorical medieval plays, like *Everyman,* that depict the eternal struggle between good and evil that transpires in this world, using characters like Vice, Virtue, Wisdom, and so on. (270)

Motivation: In Stanislavskian vocabulary, the internal springboard for an action or a set of behaviors onstage. (133)

Music: One of Aristotle's six parts of a play: the material for diction. Popularly, the kind of art form having harmony and rhythm. (53)

Musical: An American musical comedy, a form traceable to the mid-nineteenth century and now typified by a spoken text or *book* (see entry) with songs and (usually) dances and a singing-dancing chorus.

Mystery Plays: Usually drawn from Biblical stories, these medieval plays were often staged in cycles, treating events from the creation to the last judgment. Often staged in connection with Christian festivals, some mysteries were quite elaborate and took days or even weeks to perform. (270)

Myth: Story with a religious or magical base, featuring a myth hero who typifies important features of the culture, for example, the myth of Oedipus (ancient Greece) or the myth of Skunniwundi (Native American). In a less precise sense, some critics speak of the myth behind or imbedded in a work of narrative art and even of a dream, that is, the culturally important pattern that can be found there.

Naturalism: A style of theatre and drama most popular from c. 1880 to 1900 that dealt with the sordid problems of the middle and lower classes in settings remarkable for the number and accuracy of details. Practitioners included Émile Zola, André Antoine, and Maxim Gorky. See also *Determinism*. (342)

Natyasastra: Ancient Indian (Sanskrit) work on theatre aesthetics. (415)

Neoclassicism: A style of drama and theatre from the Italian Renaissance based loosely on interpretations of Aristotle and Horace. Major tenets were verisimilitude, decorum, purity of genres (see all of these entries), the five-act form, and the twofold purpose of drama: to teach and to please. (294)

Neoromanticism: Literally, "new Romanticism." A style of theatre and drama of the late nineteenth century that sought to recapture the idealism and exoticism of early nineteenth-century Romanticism. A reaction against the pessimism and sordidness of the Realists and the Naturalists.

New Comedy: That form of Greek comedy dating from the Hellenistic and Graeco-Roman periods and treating the domestic complications of the Athenian middle class. A major source for Roman comedy. (241)

Noble Savage: A manifestation of *primitivism* (see entry) that depicted a romanticized view of primitive people and led to an artistic presentation of Native Americans, African slaves, and so on as major figures in art. (323)

Obie: Awards given annually to performers, playwrights, designers, and productions that made significant contributions to the Off-Broadway theatre scene. Name comes from the first letters of Off-Broadway.

Objective: In Stanislavskian vocabulary, a character's goal within a beat or scene; the goal of a motivation. (134)

Obstacle: Barrier, difficulty; in acting, something preventing the reaching of an objective.

Off-Broadway: Popularly, those small, originally experimental but now often quite commercial theatres that are located outside the Times Square/Broadway area. Theatres with a seating capacity of fewer than three hundred that pay lower wages and fees than the larger Broadway houses. (88)

Off-Off-Broadway: Popularly, the very small nontraditional theatres located in churches, coffee houses, and so on that fall considerably out of the commercial mainstream. Theatres with highly limited seating capacities that may be granted exemptions from a wide variety of union regulations and scales. (89)

Old Comedy: That form of Greek comedy written during the Classical period (see entry) and featuring topical political and social commentary set in highly predictable structural and metrical patterns. (237)

Orchestra: 1. That area of the Greek and Roman theatre that lay between the audience area and the scene house. 2. Originally the circular space where actors and chorus danced and performed plays; later a half circle that was used as a seating space for important people and only occasionally as a performance area. 3. In modern times, the prized seating area on the ground level of a theatre and adjacent to the stage.

Organic: Suggesting growth from a definable beginning; developing naturally.

Orta Oyunu: Traditional Turkish comic theatre form. (413)

Pacing: Apparent rate of performance; partly a matter of speed with which the performance goes forward, but also related to intensity of action and complication and the artistic ways (actor's intensity, for example) that the action is realized. (172)

Pageant: In the medieval period, a movable stage, a wagon on which plays were mounted and performed in parts of England, Spain, and occasionally Continental Europe. By extension, the plays performed on such wagons. (264)

Pageant Wagon: See **Pageant.**

Pantomime: In the Roman theatre, a dance/story performed by a single actor with the accompaniment of a small group of musicians, particularly during the Christian era. In the eighteenth and nineteenth centuries, a "minor" form of entertainment marked by elaborate spectacle and often featuring *commedia* characters and a scene of magical transformation. (251)

Paratheatrical: Related to or parallel to the theatrical. Used to refer to activities tangential to theatre: circus, parades, and so on.

Patent: An official document that confers a right or privilege to the bearer. In several countries during the seventeenth and eighteenth centuries, only men who held patents from the king could open and operate theatres. (312)

Patio: Ground-level audience area in the Spanish *corrales* (which see). (288)

Performance: In life, the execution of an action (or the action executed) or a behavior taken in response to a stimulus. In art, the action of representing a character in a play, or, more generally, any public presentation. (5)

Performance Art: An avant-garde form that blends several arts (most often music, painting, dance, and theatre) into a visual, more than literary, expression of an often very personal truth. (395)

Performance Criticism: Analysis and explanation of performance (rather than of drama alone). (312)

Performance Studies: A branch of study that compares life and theatre in order to increase the understanding of each. (6)

Performance Theory: Systematic description of the nature of performance (rather than of written drama alone). (208)

Performing Arts: Those arts that depend on a live performer in the presence of a live audience, for example, theatre, dance, opera, musical concerts. (9)

Periaktoi: Stage machines in use by the Hellenistic period in Greece. An early method of scene changing that consisted of a triangle extended in space and mounted on a central pivot so that when the pivot was rotated, three different scenes could be shown to an audience. (247)

Period Movement: Actors' movements imitative or suggestive of the way people moved, or are thought to have moved, in another historical period. (129)

Perspective: Simulation of visual distance by the manipulation of size of objects. (298)

Phallus: Simulation of the male sex organ. In Greek old comedy and satyr plays, phalluses were enlarged and otherwise made prominent for purposes of comic effect. (233)

Phonetic: Relating to the human voice and human speech; symbolizing (in letters or pictures, for example) precise human sounds, as in the phonetic alphabet.

Physical Theatre: The theatre building: its architecture and decorations, including the audience, stage, and backstage areas.

Pictorialism: Directorial use of the proscenium stage's potential for creating pictures for both aesthetic and ideological ends.

Picturization: Directorial creation of stage groupings ("pictures") that show or symbolize relationships or meanings; storytelling through stage pictures. (167)

Pit: 1. Area of the audience on the ground floor and adjacent to the stage. Historically an inexpensive area because originally no seats were provided there and later only backless benches were used. By the end of the nineteenth century, a preferred seating area (now called the orchestra section). 2. Now refers often to the area reserved for members of the orchestra playing for opera, ballet, and musical comedy. (277)

Plague (as metaphor): For Antonin Artaud, theatre is like a plague in its ability to rid society of corruption. See *Theatre of Cruelty.* (377)

Platea: The unlocalized playing area in the medieval theatre. See also *Mansion.* (263)

Plot: 1. In Aristotle, one of the six parts of a play and the most important of the six; the formal cause of character; the soul of tragedy; the architectonic part of a play. 2. Popularly the story of a play, a novel, and so on. (45)

Point of Attack: The place in the story where a dramatic plot begins. Typically Greek plays, like *Oedipus Rex,* have a late point of attack, and medieval and Shakespearean plays, like *King Lear,* have an early point of attack. (45)

Political Theatre: The kind of theatre devoted to achieving political and social rather than artistic goals. (95)

Possession of Parts: During the seventeenth and especially the eighteenth centuries, the practice of leaving a role with an actor throughout a career. Under the system, a sixty-year-old woman playing Juliet in Shakespeare's tragedy was not unheard of. (314)

Postmodernism: A critical approach that doubts the possibility of objectivity and that favors, consequently, the open acknowledgement of socially constructed meanings and investigates the implications of those meanings. (211)

Presentational: Style of performance and design that lays emphasis on *presenting* a theatrical event to an audience. Contrasts with representational (see entry), which stresses the reproduction of life on stage for an audience that merely looks on.

Preview: Public performance given prior to the official opening of a play, often to test the audience's response. (178)

Primitivism: Interest in life and societies of primitive people; associated in particular with the Romantic movement of the late eighteenth and early nineteenth centuries.

Private Theatre: In Elizabethan and Stuart England, indoor theatres that were open to the public but were expensive because of their relatively limited seating capacity. Located on monastic lands, these theatres were outside the jurisdiction of the city of London. Initially they housed children's troupes, but later the regular adult troupes used them as a winter home. (279)

Probability: In drama, the internally closed system that allows each event in a play to seem likely and believable for that play (for example, the appearance of God in a medieval cycle play). (368)

Prologue: In Greek drama, that part of the play that precedes the entrance of the chorus. In other periods, a short introductory speech delivered by an actor, either in or out of character, to set the scene, warm up the audience, defend the play, or entertain.

Properties: Objects used on stage—furniture, cigarettes, dishware.

Proscenium (Arch, Theatre): Theatre building in which the audience area is set off from the acting area by a proscenium arch that frames the stage, protects the perspective, masks the backstage area, etc. The audience views the onstage action from one side only. (82)

Protagonist: In Greek theatre, the first (or major) actor, the one who competed for the prize in acting. Later, the leading character in any play (the "hero"). (234)

Psychological Realism: A kind of theatre that relies on a view of human behavior as defined by late nineteenth-century and twentieth-century psychology.

Public Relations: The business of causing the public to understand and esteem an event, institution, or cause. In theatre, it usually includes activities like advertising plays, developing essays for programs, designing posters, and inducing the public to have goodwill toward the theatrical organization before and after, as well as during, a specific production. (213)

Public Theatre: In Elizabethan and Stuart England, outdoor theatres like the Globe. Because larger than the indoor theatres, public theatres tended to be relatively inexpensive and so attract a general audience. (277)

Purity of Genres: Neoclassical tenet that elements of tragedy and those of comedy could not be mixed. The injunction was not merely against including funny scenes in tragedy but also against treating domestic issues or writing in prose, these elements being of the nature of comedy. (296)

Quem Quaeritis: A liturgical trope that opens, "Whom do you seek?" and that has early connection to drama, most especially in Ethelwold's *Regularis Concordia,* where the trope is accompanied by directions for staging. (261)

Raisonneur: In drama, a character who speaks for the author. (49)

Raked Stage: Stage slanted up from front to back to enhance the perspective. Stages began their rakes either at the front of the apron or at the proscenium line. (301)

Rasa: Important element of Sanskrit aesthetic theory—the inducing of an appropriate emotion in the audience. (415)

Realism: The style of drama and theatre dating from the late nineteenth and early twentieth centuries that strove to reproduce on stage the details of everyday life with a view to improving the human and social condition. (340)

Regional Theatre: Theatre outside New York City in the United States and Canada; term usually restricted to professional, nontouring companies. (90)

Register: A written, official version of a medieval cycle play. By seizing a register a person could prevent the production of a play. (273)

Rehearsal: The practicing of plays, either whole or in part, in order to improve their performance. (137)

Renaissance: Literally, "rebirth"; refers to a renewed interest in the learning and culture of ancient Greece and Rome. Beginning in Italy, the Renaissance spread throughout Western Europe from c. 1450 to c. 1650. (274)

Rendering: Theatrical designers' finished drawings or paintings intended to show how the item(s) will look when built and placed on the stage. (194)

Repertory: A set group of performance pieces done by a company. Also, the practice in such a company of alternating pieces so that they are done *in repertory.* Loosely, a resident professional theatre company in the United States, a *repertory theatre.*

Representational: A style of performance and design that lays emphasis on re-creating onstage aspects of daily life; the audience members are thought of as passive onlookers. Contrasts with *presentational* (see entry), a style that stresses *presenting* an event *for an audience.*

Restoration: The period of English history that dates from 1660, when King Charles II was restored to the throne. (312)

Reversal: According to Aristotle, a change in the direction of action or in the expectation of character. Reversals result in complex plots, preferred for tragedies over simple plots. (46)

Reviewer: A person who views an artistic event and then writes his or her descriptive evaluation of it for immediate publication. (215)

Revival: A new production of a play after its initial run.

Rhythm: Regular and measurable repetition. (172)

Rigging: The combination of ropes, lines, pulleys, pipes, and so on that permits the manipulation of scenic units backstage.

Ritual: Any oft-repeated act that has a specific goal. *Ritual theory:* a theory that asserts that drama derived from religious rituals (in Greece, for example, religious rituals devoted to the worship of the god Dionysus). (404)

Road: A complex of theatrical circuits for travelling and performing plays outside of New York City. (88) Road show: production for the road.

Roman: A period in theatre and drama dating from c. 364 B.C. to c. A.D. 550 and customarily subdivided into the Republican period (c. 364 B.C.–27 B.C.) and the Empire (c. 27 B.C.–c. A.D. 550).

Romanticism: A style of theatre and drama dating from c. 1790 to c. 1850 and marked by an interest in the exotic, the subjective, the emotional, and the individual. Began in part as a reaction against the strictures of Neoclassicism; grew out of the eighteenth century's sentimentalism (see entry). (323)

Royalties: Payments made to authors (and their representatives) for permission to reproduce, in text or in performance, their artistic products (plays, designs, etc.). (111)

Run-through: A kind of rehearsal in which the actors perform long sections of the play (or the whole play) without interruption, usually for the purpose of improving the sense of continuity, shaping the whole, and so on. (177)

Rural Dionysia: One of three Athenian festivals devoted to the public worship of the god Dionysus at which drama appeared. See also *Festivals.* (229)

Satyr Play: A short, rustic, and often obscene play included in the Dionysian festivals of Greece at the conclusion of the tragedies. (238)

Scaffold: In medieval staging in England, the localizing structure in or near the *platea.* See also *Mansion.* (263)

Scenario: In general, the prose description of a play's story. In the *commedia dell'arte,* the written outline of plot and characters from which the actors improvised the particular actions of performance. (302)

Scrim: Mesh used in scenery; becomes transparent when lighted from behind, opaque when lighted from the front; useful for transformations, misty effects, and so forth. (368)

Script: Play text. See also *Text* and *Book.*

Secular plays: Plays that treat matters of this world rather than the next. Often used in discussions of the Medieval period to distinguish between religious and worldly plays. (271)

Secularism: Belief in the validity and importance of life and things on earth. Often contrasted with spiritualism, other-worldliness, or religiosity. The Renaissance period was marked by a rising *secularism.* (274)

Semiotics: The study of signs, things that stand for other things. When applied to language, art, and criticism, semiotics focuses attention on the meanings that audiences create from the words or images of a playscript or a performance. (211)

Sense Memory: Recall of a sensory response—smell, taste, sound—with both its cause and the actor's reaction; important to the creation of a character's behavior in some theories of acting. (132)

Sententiae: Pithy, short statements about the human condition. Associated with the tragedies of Seneca and with those of his successors in the Renaissance. (249)

Sentimental Comedy: A kind of comedy particularly popular during the eighteenth century in which people's virtues rather than their foibles were stressed. The audience was expected to experience something "too exquisite for laughter." Virtuous characters expressed themselves in pious "sentiments." (316)

Sentimentalism: Prevalent during the eighteenth century, sentimentalism assumed the innate goodness of humanity and attributed evil to faulty instruction or bad example. A precursor of the Romanticism of the nineteenth century. (316)

Shareholder: Member of a sharing company who owned a part of the company's stocks of costumes, scenery, properties, and so on. Sharing companies were the usual organization of troupes from the Renaissance until the eighteenth century (and beyond), when some actors began to prefer fixed salaries to shares.

Shite: In Noh theatre, the protagonist. (419)

Shutter: Large flat, paired with another of the same kind, to close off the back of the scene in Italianate staging; an alternative to a backdrop; sometimes used for units at the sides. When pierced with a cutout, it became a "relieve" and showed a *diorama* (see entry). (300)

Sight Lines: Extreme limits of the audience's vision, drawn from the farthest and/or highest seat on each side through the proscenium arch or scenery obtruding farthest onstage. Anything beyond the sight lines cannot be seen by some members of the audience. (82)

Signature Music: Music associated with certain characters or certain types of characters, particularly in the melodramas of the nineteenth century. Stage directions indicate "Mary's music," "Jim's music," and so on. (332)

Silhouette: The outline of a body or costume—its mass.

Simultaneous Staging: The practice, particularly during the Middle Ages, of representing several locations on the stage at one time. In medieval staging, several *mansions* (see entry), representing particular places, were arranged around a *platea,* or generalized playing space. (262)

Single-Point Perspective: A technique for achieving a sense of depth by establishing a single vanishing point and painting or building all objects to diminish to it. (300)

Skene: The scene house in the Greek theatre. Its appearance can first be documented with the first performance of the *Oresteia* in 458 B.C. Its exact appearance from that time until the first stone theatre came into existence (probably in the late fourth century B.C.) is uncertain. (231)

Slice of Life: Critical notion closely associated with Naturalism and used to describe plays that avoided the trappings of Romanticism and the obvious contrivance of well-made plays in favor of a seemingly literal reproduction of daily life on the stage. (343)

Socialist Realism: The realism associated with the former Soviet Union, in which the problems of society were shown as solvable by application of socialist principles. (343)

Soliloquy: An intensely emotional passage, often lyric, delivered by a person onstage alone.

Spectacle: One of Aristotle's six parts of a play, the part of least interest to the poet but of most importance in differentiating the dramatic form from the narrative and the epic. In everyday parlance, all visual elements of production and, by extension, particular plays, scenes, or events in which visual elements predominate. (53)

Spine: In Stanislavskian vocabulary, the consistent line that connects all elements of a character through a play. See *Through line.* (135)

Spotlights: Stage lights with hard-edged focus intended to highlight a person or object in their beams. (199)

Stage Left: The left half of the stage as defined by someone standing onstage facing the audience. (168)

Stage Right: The right half of the stage as defined by someone standing onstage facing the audience. (168)

Standing Ovation: An audience stands and claps in order to show supreme approval of a performance. (30)

Star: Dominant actor whose name and presence draw an audience.

Star System: Company organization in which minor characters are played by actors for the season, while central roles are taken by stars (see entry) brought in for one production; still common in opera, sometimes seen in summer theatres. (329)

Stock Company: Theatre company in which actors play standardized roles and (originally) owned shares of stock in the company. (329)

Storm and Stress: *Sturm und Drang;* a theatrical movement in Germany during the 1770s and 1780s that was marked by its militant experimentation with dramatic form, theatrical style, and social statement. (331)

Story: Narrative; coherent sequence of incidents; "what happens." A general, nontechnical term that should not be confused with *plot.* (64)

Street Theatre: Theatre, often political, that takes place outside traditional theatre spaces and without traditional theatrical trappings. (387)

Striplights: Series of lights connected together and located overhead or in the wings; usually used to bathe the stage in light. (199)

Style: 1. Distinctive combination of elements. 2. In Aristotelian terms, the way in which the manner is joined to the means. 3. Particulars of surface, as distinguished from substance. 4. "The way a thing is done" in a time and place. (71)

Subtext: In Stanislavskian vocabulary, action "between the lines," implied but not stated in the text.

Suffering: According to Aristotle, an awareness. The material out of which discoveries are made. (46)

Superobjective: In Stanislavskian vocabulary, the "life goal" of the character. (134)

Surprise: An unexpected discovery or event. In dramatic surprise, the surprise, although unanticipated, must be seen in retrospect to be quite probable. (64)

Surrealism: A style popular immediately following World War I that rejected everyday logic in favor of a free expression of the subconscious (or dream) state.

Suspense: An increasing sense of expectation or dread, provoked by establishing strong anticipations and then delaying outcomes. (64)

Symbolism: A style of theatre and drama popular during the 1890s and the early twentieth century that stressed the importance of subjectivity and spirituality and sought its effects through the use of symbol, legend, myth, and mood. (369)

Take a Bow: To appear in front of the audience to acknowledge its applause, usually at the end of a play. Women customarily curtsy and men bow. (30)

Take an Encore: From the French *encore*, meaning *again*. A performer repeats a part of a performance or offers an additional piece in performance at the insistence of an audience, which claps until the encore is begun. (30)

Technical Director: The person charged with coordinating backstage activities preparatory to production, including the coordination required to transform the scenic designer's vision into finished settings. (195)

Technical Rehearsal: Rehearsal devoted to the practice and perfection of the various technical elements of the show (lighting, sound, flying, trapping, and so on). (178)

Tendencies: In Stanislavskian vocabulary, aspects of an actor's performance that digress from the *through line* (see entry). (135)

Text: The written record of a play, including dialogue and stage directions; a playscript.

Theatre of Cruelty: Phrase popularized by Antonin Artaud to describe a kind of theatre that touched the basic precivilized elements of people through disrupting normal "civilized" expectations about appearance, practice, sound, and so forth. (378)

Theatre for Development: Use of theatrical techniques for both community involvement and community instruction. (428)

Theatre History: Theatre's past. Also, a study of the theatre's traditions, including its plays, performers, designers, buildings, and methods of payments. Also, a field of scholarly endeavor devoted to such studies.

Theory: Any systematic attempt to explain a phenomenon. (209)

Three Unities: In Neoclassical (Western) dramatic theory, the unities of time, place, and action.

Through Line: In Stanislavskian vocabulary, a consistent element of character running through a scene or a play. (135)

Thrust Stage: Dominant kind of staging during Shakespeare's time in England that is being revived in many contemporary theatres. Also called *three-quarter round* because the audience surrounds the action on three sides as the stage juts into the audience area. (82)

Timing: Actor's sense of tempo and rhythm. (174)

Tiring House: The building from which the Elizabethan platform, or thrust, stage extended. A place where the actors attired themselves. (277)

Tony: Annual awards made by the directors of the American Theatre Wing in memory of Antoinette Perry to recognize outstanding contributions to the current New York theatrical season.

Tragedy: In popular parlance, any serious play, usually including an unhappy ending. According to Aristotle, "an imitation of a worthy or illustrious and perfect action, possessing magnitude, in pleasing language, using separately the several species of imitation in its parts, by men acting, and not through narration, through pity and fear effecting a catharsis of such passion." At this point in theatrical history, almost indefinable.

Transformation: 1. Technique popularized in the 1960s whereby an actor portrayed several characters without any changes in costume, makeup, or mask, relying instead on changing voice and body attitudes in full view of the audience. 2. In medieval and Renaissance theatre, seemingly magical changes of men into beasts, women into salt, and so on. 3. In English pantomime, magical changes made by Harlequin's wand.

Trap: Unit in stage floor for appearances and disappearances; varies from a simple door to complex machines for raising and lowering while moving forward, backward, and sideways.

Trope: An interpolation in a liturgical text. Some believe medieval drama to have been derived from medieval troping. (261)

Turkey: A play expected to fail, so called because of the earlier practice of opening such plays during Thanksgiving week.

Unified Art Work: A work in which all elements are brought together to form an artistic whole; associated with the theories of Richard Wagner. See *Master Artwork*. (335)

Union: An alliance of persons formed to secure material benefits and better working conditions. Major theatrical unions are USAA (United Scenic Artists of America, for designers); Equity (Actors Equity Association, for actors); IATSE (International Alliance of Theatrical Stage Employees, for theatre technicians). (86)

Unit Set: A single setting on which all scenes may be played.

Unity: Cohesion or consistency. When applied to a text, it refers to the method of organizing: unity of plot, unity of character, unity of action. When applied to design, it refers to how well all the visual elements fit together to achieve an artistic whole.

Upstage: The sections of the stage closest to the back wall. Comes from a time when stages were raked, or slanted, from the front to the back, so that upstage meant quite literally walking up the stage toward the back wall. (168)

Vaudeville: 1. In America in the nineteenth and twentieth centuries, vaudeville was popular family entertainment featuring a collection of variety acts, skits, short plays, and song-and-dance routines. 2. In France in the eighteenth and nineteenth centuries, *vaudeville* referred to *comédie-en-vaudeville,* short satiric pieces, often topical, that were interspersed with new lyrics set to familiar tunes and sprinkled with rhyming couplets (*vaudevilles*). The form in France is roughly equivalent to the *ballad opera* (see entry) in England.

Verisimilitude: Central concept in Neoclassical theory and criticism. Literal meaning is "truth-seemingness," but used historically, at a time when *truth* referred to the general, typical, categorical truth. Not to be confused with "realism." (295)

Villain: Character in melodrama who opposes the forces of good (represented by the hero and the heroine) and who, at the play's end, is punished for his evil ways. Typically the villain propels the action of a melodrama. (332)

Vocal Folds: Tissue in the throat over which air passes to make sound; incorrectly called *vocal cords.* (130)

Vomitory: Audience entrance (Roman audience) into middle of auditorium through passage under part of audience area.

Wagon: Wheeled platform that moves on and off a stage, particularly a proscenium stage; also, in medieval theatre, a movable scenic unit and playing area, or pageant (which see).

Waki: In Noh theatre, the second character, usually a confidant. (419)

Well-Made Play: A play written by or in the manner of Eugène Scribe and marked by careful preparation, seeming cause-and-effect organization of action, announced entrances and exits, and heavy reliance on external objects or characters to provide apparent connections among diverse lines of action. Now often used as a term of derision. (333)

Wing and Drop: An illusionistic arrangement, common from the Renaissance through the nineteenth century in Europe and the United States, of paired wings along the sides and a drop along the back of the stage. See *wings;* see *drop.*

Wings: 1. Scenic pieces (*flats*) placed parallel to the stage front, or nearly so, on each side of the stage; combined with overhead units for "wing-and-border" settings. 2. The offstage area beyond the side units of scenery—"in the wings." (From which is derived *wing space,* the amount of room offstage at the sides.)

Women's Theatre: A theatre whose repertories and practices are devoted to the advancement of women. Such theatres offer some combination of theatre by women, for women, and about women. (391)

Wright: "Maker," as in playwright.

Yard: Another name for the pit in the Shakespearean theatre; where patrons stood on the ground in front of the stage. (277)

Yoruba opera: Nigerian theatrical form. (410)

Zanni: In *commedia dell'arte,* the group of comic servants that includes Arlecchino, Trufaldino, etc. (303)

Index

Note: This is primarily an index of names, terms, and titles. Historical subjects within periods (e.g., Elizabethan acting) are not so indexed but can be located using the headings listed on page 221. Technical and historical terms are also listed in the glossary (which is not indexed). The color section is not indexed.